SECOND EDITION

Academic Universe:
Research and Writing at Oklahoma State University

Department of English
Oklahoma State University

Printed in the United States of America

10 9 8 7 6 5 4 3 2 1

ISBN 978-0-7380-4345-6

Hayden-McNeil Publishing
14903 Pilot Drive
Plymouth, MI 48170
www.hmpublishing.com

Frohock 4345-6 W12

Acknowledgments

From *The Year of the Flood*, by Margaret Atwood. Copyright © 2009 by O.W. Toad Ltd. Used by permission of Nan A. Talese/Doubleday, a division of Random House.

Julia Baird, "Mad Women, Not Mad Men," *Newsweek*, August 23, 2010, p. 26. Reprinted by permission of *Newsweek* via PARS International.

Barboza, David. "Chinese Factories, Flouting Labor Laws, Hire Children From Poor, Distant Villages." *The New York Times*. May 10, 2008. A5. Reprinted by permission of *The New York Times* via RightsLink.

Alexandra Beeden and Joost de Bruin, "The Office: Articulations of National Identity in Television Format Adaptation," *Television & New Media*, 2010, Vol. 11, No. 1, pp. 3–19. Reprinted with permission obtained via RightsLink.

Acknowledgments and copyrights are continued at the back of the book on pages 435–437, which constitute an extension of the copyright page.

Acknowledgments

Editors

Richard Frohock, Karen Sisk, Jessica Glover, Joshua Cross, James Brubaker, Jean Alger, Jessica Fokken, Kerry Jones, Kimberly Dyer-Fisher, and Ron Brooks

Contributors

Joe Myers, Lexi Brackett, Dannie Chalk, and Andrew Terhune

Table of Contents

Food Economics and Subcultures

Television and Cultural Studies

Literacy and Multiculturalism

Conservation and Consciousness

General Introduction

Welcome to Composition II (English 1213), the second course in the two part sequence offered by OSU's first-year writing program. Many of you recently will have completed Composition I (English 1113), a course that focuses on argument. In Composition I, students learn how to identify and analyze arguments in academic and popular texts, and they also acquire strategies and techniques for presenting their own persuasive points in writing assignments and formal essays. Composition II takes things a step further, building on what students learned about argumentation by adding independent, scholarly research to the equation. Composition II is not a literature class, then, but rather a class that covers research and writing techniques employed across the many colleges and disciplines that make up our university. It is a course that concentrates on methods for researching and generating data and building arguments that are informed not only by careful argumentation but by a thorough study of a broader public conversation about the subject. English 1213 is a course every bit as relevant for the engineering student as for students in the humanities, then, because we all participate in the common educational endeavor of acquiring and advancing the newest knowledge about academic problems and questions in our diverse disciplines.

Academic Universe: Research and Writing at Oklahoma State University (2nd Ed.) has been designed specifically for use in Composition II at Oklahoma State University by the instructors who teach the course. To make reading assignments and topics resonate with OSU students as much as possible, we have built five chapters around cutting edge academic topics and problems currently being researched by OSU faculty. The five chapters cover the following diverse subjects: "Apparel Merchandising and Social Responsibility"; "Literacy and Multiculturalism"; "Television and Cultural Studies"; "Food Economics and Subcultures"; and "Conservation and Consciousness."

Each chapter features an interview with an OSU faculty member who researches and publishes in the area and an OSU faculty publication. (In this edition, we have also included an appendix with seven interviews of faculty members from other disciplines.) Additional readings in each chapter range from complex treatments of the subject from refereed professional journals, to selections from newspapers, works of fiction, and popular magazines, to pop culture offerings for a general audience. The readings in each chapter represent a range of viewpoints and approaches to each issue, exemplifying the multiplicity of perspectives that always characterizes serious engagement with difficult and complex topics. This book invites you to enter into these academic discussions, listening carefully, evaluating with deliberation, and adding your own voice in the scholarly conversation.

Richard Frohock and Ron Brooks

Library Introduction

The Edmon Low Library, the main library on the OSU campus, holds over 2.5 million books and journal volumes. Built in 1953, the building is in the center of campus and is one of the academic symbols of the university. The Library subscribes to over 40 thousand online magazines, journals and newspapers which are available to you on- and off-campus. These publications can supply you with authoritative articles for research papers and save you time looking through the web for suitable material for your research paper. To search through these publications or periodicals, the Library provides access to several databases which allows searching for articles by your keywords or subject terms.

The Library's home page (*www.library.okstate.edu*) is the portal to these databases as well as the Library's book catalog. From the Library's home page click on *Databases* under the column *Find Articles*. The databases, in alphabetical order, are either multi-disciplinary, covering a broad range of subjects, or subject-specific, focusing on a single subject.

A popular multidisciplinary database is **ProQuest**. From the list of alphabetical databases scroll to the **P**'s and click on **ProQuest** link. Next, click on the Continue button. A set of boxes are provided to type in your keywords or subjects.

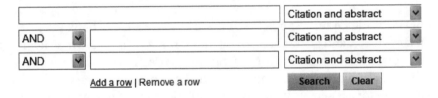

Use one keyword or subject term per line, and when you are finished click on the "search" button.

ProQuest will provide you with a list of citations containing your keywords or subject terms from over 3,000 periodicals. This particular database groups these citations into 4 groups:

1. Scholarly journals (articles are longer, more in-depth; author is usually an expert; usually has footnotes and/or bibliography; article normally reviewed by other experts or peers before published)

2. Magazines (articles are shorter, written for a broad audience; author may not be expert; usually includes no bibliography)

3. Trade publications (articles written for a specific audience with technical language)

4. Newspapers

Besides an abstract, you may notice that some citations have a PDF icon. These are links to the full image of the article, which would be a photocopy of the article as it appears in the publication. If the article is available in "full text," then all of the words from the article are available but not pictures or graphics. If the article is not available in "full text" or PDF, click on the button

Next, click on a pink colored button.

A program will attempt to locate this article for you in another database. If successful, there will be a link to the article. If not successful, you can click on the link "Request a copy of this article," fill out the form, and receive a free PDF copy of the article within a few days.

Searching for books is even easier. From the Library's home page type in your subject or keywords into the box labeled

BOSS, or Big Orange Search System, will produce a list of book titles, maps, videos, and DVD's containing the words you entered. These items are sorted by relevancy, so the more times your item has the words you entered, the higher its ranking. To locate the item in the library, ask a librarian for assistance. If you have trouble retrieving book or journal articles or just need a starting point, feel free to talk to a reference librarian located on the 1st floor of the Library.

Steve Locy

FOOD ECONOMICS AND SUBCULTURES

**Department of Psychology,
College of Arts and Sciences**

Introduction

Many academic disciplines focus on food. Fields as diverse as psychology, biology, engineering, agriculture, nutritional science, and the humanities have addressed the subject, so in this chapter we focus on the big questions: What should we eat? How should we eat? How should we produce the food we eat? What limits, if any, should be placed on food? Should the government be more involved with our food? Or less? How can we afford the best food for us? What is the best food for us? This unit seeks to show possible solutions to our food problems that different groups have embraced and the possible issues with those possible solutions: locavorism, vegetarianism, hunting, and freeganism. These solutions each comprise a food subculture whose members base their approaches to food on what they believe answer the food dilemmas which face us.

Karen Sisk

Interview with Dr. Jayson Lusk

Dr. Lusk is a professor and the Willard Sparks Endowed Chair in the department of Agriculture Economics at Oklahoma State University. He has published widely on the economics of food production. His article, "The Locavore's Dilemma: Why Pineapples Shouldn't Be Grown in North Dakota" is included in this chapter. Dr. Lusk agreed to give us insight into his interest in the locavore movement, the field of Agricultural Economics, and his writing.

How did you become interested in writing on the locavore movement?

About a year ago, I listened to the NPR podcast *Intelligence Squared.* The podcast is a series of Oxford-style debates, and the particular debate in question revolved around the merits of organic foods, but the discussion bled over to local foods, too. The debaters arguing in favor of the promotion of organic and local foods won the audience over in a landslide. But, I grew up around agriculture. My reading on the issue coupled with my economic training led me to believe the local food movement was largely "hype" and many of the reasons given to support the movement were fallacious when one looked at the economics. I was frustrated by the inability of the "other side" to articulate a cogent and persuasive argument against government promotion of local foods. Thus, I thought I would try my hand at it.

Could you tell us about some other topics in Agriculture or Agricultural Economics currently being researched at OSU?

1. Genetically modified food production

2. Using genetic markers to predict the profitability of beef cattle

3. Cost and benefits of animal welfare legislation

4. Consumer preferences for animal welfare

5. Consumer preferences for fairness and the distribution of outcomes within the farm sector and across the food supply chain

6. Development and refinement of non-market valuation methods used to value food safety, environmental amenities, food product attributes, etc.

7. Market impacts of cloned animals in the agricultural food supply chain

8. The effects of food prices on obesity

Our department's website, http://www.agecon.okstate.edu/faculty/research.asp, would probably better match what most people think of as "traditional" agricultural economics.

Expectations for writing often change from field to field. What elements of your writing do you think are most important when writing for publication in your field?

You have to make a persuasive case that what you're doing is important and clearly identify how the research advances the current state of knowledge. The best writing addresses an interesting topic with clear "real world" relevance using novel or innovative methods or theory.

"The Locavore's Dilemma: Why Pineapples Shouldn't Be Grown in North Dakota" seems to be aimed at a general audience. Are there any other types of documents that you frequently read or write for your work?

I constantly read academic journals and books. I probably spend no less than 2–3 hours a day just reading other scientific articles and books; this is what is required to stay abreast of developments in the field. I write approximately 10 articles a year for academic journals and write books aimed at an academic audience.

You worked with a co-author on your article. How did you decide to do this? How did your writing process differ from papers you have written alone?

Most of my work is co-authored. Although I have published several sole-authored articles, I find that my writing and analysis is improved when there is someone else to work through ideas and problems. In agricultural economics (but not the extent that it occurs in other disciplines), not all co-authors contribute to the actual writing of the final paper; some co-authors may have been responsible for the original idea behind the research, for the funding to carry out the research, or for the collection of the data.

Do students write often in your courses? What do you look for in student writing? Do you have any advice for student writers in your college?

I teach two graduate courses and both involve a great deal of writing. In one course, students write a research proposal, and in the other they must write a research paper. The advice to my students is the same as what I said previously about what elements are important in my field. Students need to motivate their work, make a persuasive case that what they're doing is important, and clearly identify how the research advances the current state of knowledge. This is difficult for students because they are often relying on the advisors to tell them why an issue is important or to tell them whether they have a unique view point or analysis that is not previously expressed by other writers. Even though most of my students' (and my own) writing is scientific and academic in nature, I encourage students to be "story tellers." We live in an information age, and people won't spend time reading your paper unless it is interesting and important.

By Phillip Heasley

Updated by Karen Sisk

Divided We Eat

Lisa Miller, Ian Yarett, Jesse Ellison

Lisa Miller is a senior editor at *Newsweek*. She oversees all of the magazine's religion coverage and writes the weekly "Belief Watch" column. Ian Yarett reports on science, the environment, and health for *Newsweek*. Jesse Ellison is an Articles Editor for *Newsweek*, where she covers education, culture, and women's issues.

For breakfast, I usually have a cappuccino—espresso made in an Alessi pot and mixed with organic milk, which has been gently heated and hand-fluffed by my husband. I eat two slices of imported cheese—Dutch Parrano, the label says, "the hippest cheese in New York" (no joke)—on homemade bread with butter. I am what you might call a food snob. My nutritionist neighbor drinks a protein shake while her 5-year-old son eats quinoa porridge sweetened with applesauce and laced with kale flakes. She is what you might call a health nut. On a recent morning, my neighbor's friend Alexandra Ferguson sipped politically correct Nicaraguan coffee in her comfy kitchen while her two young boys chose from among an assortment of organic cereals. As we sat, the six chickens Ferguson and her husband, Dave, keep for eggs in a backyard coop peered indoors from the stoop. The Fergusons are known as locavores.

Alexandra says she spends hours each day thinking about, shopping for, and preparing food. She is a disciple of Michael Pollan, whose 2006 book *The Omnivore's Dilemma* made the locavore movement a national phenomenon, and believes that eating organically and locally contributes not only to the health of her family but to the existential happiness of farm animals and farmers—and, indeed, to the survival of the planet. "Michael Pollan is my new hero, next to Jimmy Carter," she told me. In some neighborhoods, a lawyer who raises chickens in her backyard might be considered eccentric, but we live in Park Slope, Brooklyn, a community that accommodates and celebrates every kind of foodie. Whether you believe in eating for pleasure, for health, for justice, or for some idealized vision of family life, you will find neighbors who reflect your food values. In Park Slope, the contents of a child's lunchbox can be fodder for a 20-minute conversation.

Over coffee, I cautiously raise a subject that has concerned me of late: less than five miles away, some children don't have enough to eat; others exist almost exclusively on junk food. Alexandra concedes that her approach is probably out of reach for those people. Though they are not wealthy by Park Slope standards—Alexandra works part time and Dave is employed by the city—the Fergusons spend approximately 20 percent of their income, or $1,000 a month, on food. The average American spends 13 percent, including restaurants and takeout.

And so the conversation turns to the difficulty of sharing their interpretation of the Pollan doctrine with the uninitiated. When they visit Dave's family in Tennessee, tensions erupt over food choices. One time, Alexandra remembers, she irked her mother-in-law by purchasing a bag of organic apples, even though her mother-in-law had already bought the nonorganic kind at the grocery store. The old apples were perfectly good, her mother-in-law said. Why waste money—and apples?

The Fergusons recall Dave's mother saying something along these lines: "When we come to your place, we don't complain about your food. Why do you complain about ours? It's not like our food is poison."

"I can't convince my brother to spend another dime on food," adds Dave.

"This is our charity. This is my giving to the world," says Alexandra, finally, as she packs lunchboxes—organic peanut butter and jelly on grainy bread, a yogurt, and a clementine—for her two boys. "We contribute a lot."

According to data released last week by the U.S. Department of Agriculture, 17 percent of Americans—more than 50 million people—live in households that are "food insecure," a term that means a family sometimes runs out of money to buy food, or it sometimes runs out of food before it can get more money. Food insecurity is especially high in households headed by a single mother. It is most severe in the South, and in big cities. In New York City, 1.4 million people are food insecure, and 257,000 of them live near me, in Brooklyn. Food insecurity is linked, of course, to other economic measures like housing and employment, so it surprised no one that the biggest surge in food insecurity since the agency established the measure in 1995 occurred between 2007 and 2008, at the start of the economic downturn. (The 2009 numbers, released last week, showed little change.) The proportion of households that qualify as "hungry"—with what the USDA calls "very low food security"—is small, about 6 percent. Reflected against the obsessive concerns of the foodies in my circle, and the glare of attention given to the plight of the poor and hungry abroad, even a fraction of starving children in America seems too high.

Mine seems on some level like a naive complaint. There have always been rich people and poor people in America and, in a capitalist economy, the well-to-do have always had the freedom to indulge themselves as they please. In hard times, food has always marked a bright border between the haves and the have-nots. In the earliest days of the Depression, as the poor waited on bread lines, the middle and upper classes in America became devoted to fad diets. Followers of the Hollywood 18-Day Diet, writes Harvey Levenstein in his 1993 book *Paradox of Plenty,* "could live on fewer than six hundred calories a day by limiting each meal to half a grapefruit, melba toast, coffee without cream or sugar, and, at lunch and dinner, some raw vegetables."

But modern America is a place of extremes, and what you eat for dinner has become the definitive marker of social status; as the distance between rich and poor continues to grow, the freshest, most nutritious foods have become luxury goods that only some can afford. Among the lowest quintile of American families, mean household income has held relatively steady between $10,000 and $13,000 for the past two decades (in inflation-adjusted dollars); among the highest, income has jumped 20 percent to $170,800 over the same period, according to census data. What this means, in practical terms, is that the richest Americans can afford to buy berries out of season at Whole Foods—the upscale grocery chain that recently reported a 58 percent increase in its quarterly profits—while the food insecure often eat what they can: highly caloric, mass-produced foods like pizza and packaged cakes that fill them up quickly. The number of Americans on food stamps has surged by 58.5 percent over the last three years.

Corpulence used to signify the prosperity of a few but has now become a marker of poverty. Obesity has risen as the income gap has widened: more than a third of U.S. adults and 17 percent of children are obese, and the problem is acute among the poor. While obesity is a complex problem—genetics, environment, and activity level all play a role—a 2008 study by the USDA found that children and women on food stamps were likelier to be overweight than those who were not. According to studies led by British epidemiologist Kate Pickett, obesity rates are highest in developed countries with the greatest income disparities. America is among the most obese of nations; Japan, with its relatively low income inequality, is the thinnest.

Adam Drewnowski, an epidemiologist at the University of Washington, has spent his career showing that Americans' food choices correlate to social class. He argues that the most nutritious diet—lots of fruits and vegetables, lean meats, fish, and grains—is beyond the reach of the poorest Americans, and it is economic elitism for nutritionists to uphold it as an ideal without broadly addressing issues of affordability. Lower-income families don't subsist on junk food and fast food because they lack nutritional education, as some have argued. And though many poor neighborhoods are, indeed, food deserts—meaning that the people who live there don't have access to a well-stocked supermarket—many are not. Lower-income families choose sugary, fat, and processed foods because they're cheaper—and because they taste good. In a paper published last spring, Drewnowski showed how the prices of specific foods changed between 2004 and 2008 based on data from Seattle-area supermarkets. While food prices overall rose about 25 percent, the most nutritious foods (red peppers, raw oysters, spinach, mustard greens, romaine lettuce) rose 29 percent, while the least nutritious foods (white sugar, hard candy, jelly beans, and cola) rose just 16 percent.

"In America," Drewnowski wrote in an e-mail, "food has become the premier marker of social distinctions, that is to say—social class. It used to be clothing and fashion, but no longer, now that 'luxury' has become affordable and available to all." He points to an article in *The New York Times,* written by Pollan, which describes a meal element by element, including "a basket of morels and porcini gathered near Mount Shasta." "Pollan," writes Drewnowski, "is drawing a picture of class privilege that is as acute as anything written by Edith Wharton or Henry James."

I finish writing the previous paragraph and go downstairs. There, in the mail, I find the Christmas catalog from the luxury retail store Barneys. HAVE A FOODIE HOLIDAY, its cover reads. Inside, models are covered—literally—with food. A woman in a red $2,000 Lanvin trench has an enormous cabbage on her head. Another, holding a green Proenza Schouler clutch, wears a boiled crab in her bouffant. Most disconcerting is the Munnu diamond pendant ($80,500) worn by a model who seems to have traded her hair for an octopus. Its tentacles dangle past her shoulders, and the girl herself wears the expression of someone who's stayed too long at the party. Food is no longer trendy or fashionable. It is fashion.

Tiffiney Davis, a single mom, lives about four miles away from me, in subsidized housing, in a gentrifying neighborhood called Red Hook. Steps from her apartment, you can find ample evidence of foodie culture: Fairway, the supermarket where I buy my Dutch cheese, is right there, as is a chic bakery, and a newfangled lobster pound. Davis says she has sometimes worried about having enough food. She works in Manhattan, earning $13 an hour for a corporate catering company (which once had a contract with NEWSWEEK), and she receives food stamps. She spends $100 a week on food for herself and her two kids. Sometimes she stretches her budget by bringing food home from work.

Davis is sheepish about what her family eats for breakfast. Everybody rises at 6, and there's a mad rush to get the door, so often they eat bodega food. Her daughter, Malaezia, 10, will have egg and cheese on a roll; her son, 13-year-old Tashawn, a muffin and soda. She herself used to pop into at Dunkin' Donuts for two doughnuts and a latte, but when New York chain restaurants started posting calories on their menus, she stopped. "I try my best to lessen the chemicals and the fattening stuff," she says, "but it's hard."

Time is just part of the problem, Davis explains, as she prepares Sunday dinner in her cheerful kitchen. Tonight she's making fried chicken wings with bottled barbecue sauce; yellow rice from a box; black beans from a can; broccoli; and carrots, cooked in olive oil and honey. A home-cooked dinner doesn't happen every night. On weeknights, everyone gets home, exhausted—and then there's homework. Several nights a week, they get takeout: Chinese, or Domino's, or McDonald's. Davis doesn't buy fruits and vegetables mostly because they're too expensive, and in the markets where she usually shops, they're not fresh. "I buy bananas and bring them home and 10 minutes later they're no good…Whole Foods sells fresh, beautiful tomatoes," she says. "Here, they're packaged and full of chemicals anyway. So I mostly buy canned foods."

In recent weeks the news in New York City has been full with a controversial proposal to ban food-stamp recipients from using their government money to buy soda. Local public-health officials insist they need to be more proactive about slowing obesity; a recent study found that 40 percent of the children in New York City's kindergarten through eighth-grade classrooms were either overweight or obese. (Nationwide, 36 percent of 6- to 11-year-olds are overweight or obese.) Opponents of the proposal call it a "nanny state" measure, another instance of government interference, and worse—of the government telling poor people what to do, as if they can't make good decisions on their own. "I think it's really difficult," says Pickett, the British epidemiologist. "Everybody needs to be able to feel that they have control over what they spend. And everybody should be able to treat themselves now and again. Why shouldn't a poor child have a birthday party with cake and soda?"

But Davis enthusiastically supports the proposal. A 9-year-old boy in her building recently died of an asthma attack, right in front of his mother. He was obese, she says, but his mom kept feeding him junk. "If these people don't care at all about calorie counts, then the government should. People would live a lot longer," she says.

Claude Fischler, a French sociologist, believes that Americans can fight both obesity and food insecurity by being more, well, like the French. Americans take an approach to food and eating that is unlike any other people in history. For one thing, we regard food primarily as (good or bad) nutrition. When asked "What is eating well?" Americans generally answer in the language of daily allowances: they talk about calories and carbs, fats, and sugars. They don't see eating as a social activity, and they don't see food—as it has been seen for millennia—as a shared resource, like a loaf of bread passed around the table. When asked "What is eating well?" the French inevitably answer in terms of "conviviality": togetherness, intimacy, and good tastes unfolding in a predictable way.

Even more idiosyncratic than our obsession with nutrition, says Fischler, is that Americans see food choice as a matter of personal freedom, an inalienable right. Americans want to eat what they want: morels or Big Macs. They want to eat where they want, in the car or alfresco. And they want to eat when they want. With the exception of Thanksgiving, when most of us dine off the same turkey menu, we are food libertarians. In surveys, Fischler has found no single time of day (or night) when Americans predictably sit together and eat. By contrast, 54 percent of the French dine at 12:30 each day. Only 9.5 percent of the French are obese.

When I was a child I was commanded to "eat your eggs. There are starving children in Africa." And when I was old enough to think for myself, I could easily see that my own eaten or uneaten eggs would not do a single thing to help the children of Africa. This is the Brooklyn conundrum, playing out all over the country. Locally produced food is more delicious than the stuff you get in the supermarket; it's better for the small farmers and the farm animals; and, as a movement, it's better for the environment. It's easy—and probably healthy, if you can afford it—to make that choice as an individual or a family, says the New York University nutritionist Marion Nestle. Bridging the divide is much harder. "Choosing local or organic is something you can actually do. It's very difficult for people to get involved in policy."

Locavore activists in New York and other cities are doing what they can to help the poor with access to fresh food. Incentive programs give food-stamp recipients extra credit if they buy groceries at farmers' markets. Food co-ops and community-garden associations are doing better urban outreach. Municipalities are establishing bus routes between poor neighborhoods and those where well-stocked supermarkets exist.

Joel Berg, executive director of the New York City Coalition Against Hunger, says these programs are good, but they need to go much, much further. He believes, like Fischler, that the answer lies in seeing food more as a shared resource, like water, than as a consumer product, like shoes. "It's a nuanced conversation, but I think 'local' or 'organic' as the shorthand for all things good is way too simplistic," says Berg. "I think we need a broader conversation about scale, working conditions, and environmental impact. It's a little too much of people buying easy virtue."

Even the locavore hero Pollan agrees. "Essentially," he says, "we have a system where wealthy farmers feed the poor crap and poor farmers feed the wealthy high-quality food." He points to Walmart's recent announcement of a program that will put more locally grown food on its shelves as an indication that big retailers are looking to sell fresh produce in a scalable way. These fruits and vegetables might not be organic, but the goal, says Pollan, is not to be absolutist in one's food ideology. "I argue for being conscious," he says, "but perfectionism is an enemy of progress." Pollan sees a future where, in an effort to fight diabetes and obesity, health-insurance companies are advocates for small and medium-size farmers. He dreams of a broad food-policy conversation in Washington. "The food movement," he reminds me, "is still very young."

Berg believes that part of the answer lies in working with Big Food. The food industry hasn't been entirely bad: it developed the technology to bring apples to Wisconsin in the middle of winter, after all. It could surely make sustainably produced fruits and vegetables affordable and available. "We need to bring social justice to bigger agriculture as well," Berg says.

My last stop was at Jabir Suluki's house in Clinton Hill, about two miles from my home. Suluki has toast for breakfast, with a little cheese on top, melted in the toaster oven. He is not French—he was born and raised in Brooklyn—but he might as well be. Every day, between 5 and 7, he prepares dinner for his mother and himself—and any of his nieces and nephews who happen to drop by. He prepares food with the confidence of a person descended from a long line of home cooks—which he is.

Both Suluki and his mother are diabetic. For them, healthy, regular meals are a necessity—and so he does what he can on $75 a week. "To get good food, you really got to sacrifice a lot. It's expensive. But I take that sacrifice, because it's worth it." Suluki uses his food stamps at the farmers' market. He sorts through the rotten fruit at the local supermarket. He travels to Queens, when he can get a ride, and buys cheap meat in bulk. He is adamant that it is the responsibility of parents to feed their children good food in moderate portions, and that it's possible to do so on a fixed income.

For dinner he and his mother ate Salisbury steak made from ground turkey, with a little ground beef thrown in and melted cheese on top "because turkey doesn't have any taste"; roasted potatoes and green peppers; and frozen green beans, "heated quickly so they still have a crunch." For dessert, his mother ate two pieces of supermarket coffeecake.

Suluki thinks a lot about food, and the role it plays in the life of his neighbors. He doesn't have soda in his refrigerator, but he opposes the New York City soda proposal because, in light of the government's food and farm subsidies—and in light of all the other kinds of unhealthy cheap foods for sale in his supermarket—he sees it as hypocrisy. "You can't force junk on people and then criticize it at the same time." Suluki is a community organizer, and sees the web of problems before us—hunger, obesity, health—as something for the community to solve. "We can't just attack this problem as individuals," he tells me. "A healthy community produces healthy people." That's why, on the weekends, he makes a big pot of rice and beans, and brings it down to the food pantry near his house.

Discussion Questions

1. Annotate and summarize this article. First, go through and underline what you think to be the most important points Miller, Yarett, and Ellison make in "Divided We Eat." Then, use what you have underlined to write a summary of this article.

2. In "Divided We Eat," the authors bring up "food insecurity." What is it? Why is it an issue? How do the people living with food insecurity in this article deal with it?

3. Do you identify anyone you know with anyone in this article? Why or why not? Interview that person as if you were going to include him or her in this article. Using your interview, write about that person as if he or she were going to be included within this article.

4. Among the terms used in this article are "foodie" and "locavore." Look those terms up and define them. In searching for the definitions, did you encounter any other food culture terms? If so, what were they and what are their definitions?

5. This article mentions that New York has programs that allow the poor to use food stamps at farmers' markets. Go online and research if Oklahoma has any programs to help get local food to those who might not be able to afford it. If there are such programs, what are they? How do they help?

Introduction: Our National Eating Disorder

Michael Pollan

Michael Pollan writes books and articles about the places where nature and culture intersect: on our plates, in our farms and gardens, and in the built environment. He is the author of four *New York Times* bestsellers: *Food Rules: An Eater's Manual* (2010); *In Defense of Food: An Eater's Manifesto* (2008); *The Omnivore's Dilemma: A Natural History of Four Meals* (2006); and *The Botany of Desire: A Plant's-Eye View of the World* (2001). *The Omnivore's Dilemma* was named one of the ten best books of 2006 by both the *New York Times* and the *Washington Post*. It also won the California Book Award, the Northern California Book Award, the James Beard Award, and was a finalist for the National Book Critics Circle Award.

What should we have for dinner?

This book is a long and fairly involved answer to this seemingly simple question. Along the way, it also tries to figure out how such a simple question could ever have gotten so complicated. As a culture we seem to have arrived at a place where whatever native wisdom we may once have possessed about eating has been replaced by confusion and anxiety. Somehow this most elemental of activities—figuring out what to eat—has come to require a remarkable amount of expert help. How did we ever get to a point where we need investigative journalists to tell us where our food comes from and nutritionists to determine the dinner menu?

For me the absurdity of the situation became inescapable in the fall of 2002, when one of the most ancient and venerable staples of human life abruptly disappeared from the American dinner table. I'm talking of course about bread. Virtually overnight, Americans changed the way they eat. A collective spasm of what can only be described as carbophobia seized the country, supplanting an era of national lipophobia dating to the Carter administration. That was when, in 1977, a Senate committee had issued a set of "dietary goals" warning beef-loving Americans to lay off the red meat. And so we dutifully had done, until now.

What set off the sea change? It appears to have been a perfect media storm of diet books, scientific studies, and one timely magazine article. The new diet books, many of them inspired by the formerly discredited Dr. Robert C. Atkins, brought Americans the welcome news that they could eat more meat and lose weight just so long as they laid off the bread and pasta. These high-protein, low-carb diets found support in a handful of new epidemiological studies suggesting that the nutritional orthodoxy that had held sway in America since the 1970s might be wrong. It was not, as official opinion claimed, fat that made us fat, but the carbohydrates we'd been eating precisely in order to stay slim. So conditions were ripe for a swing of the dietary pendulum when, in the summer of 2002, the *New York Times Magazine* published a cover story on the new research entitled "What if Fat Doesn't Make You Fat?" Within months, supermarket shelves were restocked and restaurant menus re-written to reflect the new nutritional wisdom. The blamelessness of steak restored, two of the most wholesome and uncontroversial foods known to man—bread and pasta—acquired a moral stain that promptly bankrupted dozens of bakeries and noodle firms and ruined an untold number of perfectly good meals.

So violent a change in a culture's eating habits is surely the sign of a na-tional eating disorder. Certainly it would never have happened in a cul-ture in possession of deeply rooted traditions surrounding food and eat-ing. But then, such a culture would not feel the need for its most august legislative body to ever deliberate the nation's "dietary goals"—or, for that matter, to wage political battle every few years over the precise design of an official government graphic called the "food pyramid." A country with a stable culture of food would not shell out millions for the quackery (or common sense) of a new diet book every January. It would not be sus-ceptible to the pendulum swings of food scares or fads, to the apotheosis every few years of one newly discovered nutrient and the demonization of another. It would not be apt to confuse protein bars and food supple-ments with meals or breakfast cereals with medicines. It probably would not eat a fifth of its meals in cars or feed fully a third of its children at a fast-food outlet every day. And it surely would not be nearly so fat.

Nor would such a culture be shocked to discover that there are other countries, such as Italy and France, that decide their dinner questions on the basis of such quaint and unscientific criteria as pleasure and tradition, eat all manner of "unhealthy" foods, and, lo and behold, wind up actually healthier and happier in their eating than we are. We show our surprise at this by speaking of something called the "French paradox," for how could a people who eat such demonstrably toxic substances as foie gras and triple crème cheese actually be slimmer and healthier than we are? Yet I wonder if it doesn't make more sense to speak in terms of an American paradox—that is, a notably unhealthy people obsessed by the idea of eat-ing healthily.

To one degree or another, the question of what to have for dinner assails every omnivore, and always has. When you can eat just about anything nature has to offer, deciding what you *should* eat will inevitably stir anxiety, especially when some of the potential foods on offer are liable to sicken or kill you. This is the omnivore's dilemma, noted long ago by writers like Rousseau and Brillat-Savarin and first given that name thirty years ago by a University of Pennsylvania research psychologist named Paul Rozin. I've borrowed his phrase for the title of this book because the omnivore's dilemma turns out to be a particularly sharp tool for understanding our present predicaments surrounding food.

In a 1976 paper called "The Selection of Foods by Rats, Humans, and Other Animals" Rozin contrasted the omnivore's existential situation with that of the specialized eater, for whom the dinner question could not be simpler. The koala doesn't worry about what to eat: If it looks and smells and tastes like a eucalyptus leaf, it must be dinner. The koala's culinary preferences are hardwired in its genes. But for omnivores like us (and the rat) a vast amount of brain space and time must be devoted to figuring out which of all the many potential dishes nature lays on are safe to eat. We rely on our prodigious powers of recognition and memory to guide us away from poisons (*Isn't that the mushroom that made me sick last week?*) and toward nutritious plants (*The red berries are the juicier, sweeter ones*). Our taste buds help too, predisposing us toward sweetness, which signals carbohydrate energy in nature, and away from bitterness, which is how many of the toxic alkaloids produced by plants taste. Our inborn sense of disgust keeps us from ingesting things that might infect us, such as rotten meat. Many anthropologists believe that the reason we evolved such big and intricate brains was precisely to help us deal with the omnivore's dilemma.

Being a generalist is of course a great boon as well as a challenge; it is what allows humans to successfully inhabit virtually every terrestrial environment on the planet. Omnivory offers the pleasures of variety, too. But the surfeit of choice brings with it a lot of stress and leads to a kind of Manichaean view of food, a division of nature into The Good Things to Eat, and The Bad.

The rat must make this all-important distinction more or less on its own, each individual figuring out for itself—and then remembering—which things will nourish and which will poison. The human omnivore has, in addition to his senses and memory, the incalculable advantage of a culture, which stores the experience and accumulated wisdom of countless human tasters before him. I don't need to experiment with the mushroom now called, rather helpfully, the "death cap," and it is common knowledge that that first intrepid lobster eater was on to something very good. Our culture codifies the rules of wise eating in an elaborate structure of taboos, rituals, recipes, manners, and culinary traditions that keep us from having to reenact the omnivore's dilemma at every meal.

One way to think about America's national eating disorder is as the return, with an almost atavistic vengeance, of the omnivore's dilemma.

The cornucopia of the American supermarket has thrown us back on a bewildering food landscape where we once again have to worry that some of those tasty-looking morsels might kill us. (Perhaps not as quickly as a poisonous mushroom, but just as surely.) Certainly the extraordinary abundance of food in America complicates the whole problem of choice. At the same time, many of the tools with which people historically managed the omnivore's dilemma have lost their sharpness here—or simply failed. As a relatively new nation drawn from many different immigrant populations, each with its own culture of food, Americans have never had a single, strong, stable culinary tradition to guide us.

The lack of a steadying culture of food leaves us especially vulnerable to the blandishments of the food scientist and the marketer, for whom the omnivore's dilemma is not so much a dilemma as an opportunity. It is very much in the interest of the food industry to exacerbate our anxieties about what to eat, the better to then assuage them with new products. Our bewilderment in the supermarket is no accident; the return of the omnivore's dilemma has deep roots in the modern food industry, roots that, I found, reach all the way back to fields of corn growing in places like Iowa.

And so we find ourselves where we do, confronting in the supermarket or at the dinner table the dilemmas of omnivorousness, some of them ancient and others never before imagined. The organic apple or the conventional? And if the organic, the local one or the imported? The wild fish or the farmed? The trans fats or the butter or the "not butter"? Shall I be a carnivore or a vegetarian? And if a vegetarian, a lacto-vegetarian or a vegan? Like the hunter-gatherer picking a novel mushroom off the forest floor and consulting his sense memory to determine its edibility, we pick up the package in the supermarket and, no longer so confident of our senses, scrutinize the label, scratching our heads over the meaning of phrases like "heart healthy," "no trans fats," "cage-free," or "range-fed." What is "natural grill flavor" or TBHQ or xanthan gum? What is all this stuff, anyway, and where in the world did it come from?

My wager in writing *The Omnivore's Dilemma* was that the best way to answer the questions we face about what to eat was to go back to the very beginning, to follow the food chains that sustain us, all the way from the earth to the plate—to a small number of actual meals. I wanted to look at the getting and eating of food at its most fundamental, which is to say, as a transaction between species in nature, eaters and eaten. ("The whole of nature," wrote the English author William Ralph Inge, "is a conjugation of the verb to eat, in the active and passive.") What I try to do in this book is approach the dinner question as a naturalist might, using the long lenses of ecology and anthropology, as well as the shorter, more intimate lens of personal experience.

My premise is that like every other creature on earth, humans take part in a food chain, and our place in that food chain, or web, determines to a considerable extent what kind of creature we are. The fact of our om-nivorousness has done much to shape our nature, both body (we possess the omnicompetent teeth and jaws of the omnivore, equally well suited to tearing meat and grinding seeds) and soul. Our prodigious powers of observation and memory, as well as our curious and experimental stance toward the natural world, owe much to the biological fact of omnivorous-ness. So do the various adaptations we've evolved to defeat the defenses of other creatures so that we might eat them, including our skills at hunt-ing and cooking with fire. Some philosophers have argued that the very open-endedness of human appetite is responsible for both our savagery and civility, since a creature that could conceive of eating anything (in-cluding, notably, other humans) stands in particular need of ethical rules, manners, and rituals. We are not only what we eat, but how we eat, too.

Yet we are also different from most of nature's other eaters—markedly so. For one thing, we've acquired the ability to substantially modify the food chains we depend on, by means of such revolutionary technologies as cooking with fire, hunting with tools, farming, and food preservation. Cooking opened up whole new vistas of edibility by rendering various plants and animals more digestible, and overcoming many of the chemi-cal defenses other species deploy against being eaten. Agriculture allowed us to vastly multiply the populations of a few favored food species, and therefore in turn our own. And, most recently, industry has allowed us to reinvent the human food chain, from the synthetic fertility of the soil to the microwaveable can of soup designed to fit into a car's cup holder. The implications of this last revolution, for our health and the health of the natural world, we are still struggling to grasp.

The Omnivore's Dilemma is about the three principal food chains that sustain us today: the industrial, the organic, and the hunter-gatherer. Different as they are, all three food chains are systems for doing more or less the same thing: linking us, through what we eat, to the fertility of the earth and the energy of the sun. It might be hard to see how, but even a Twinkie does this—constitutes an engagement with the natural world. As ecology teaches, and this book tries to show, it's all connected, even the Twinkie.

Ecology also teaches that all life on earth can be viewed as a competition among species for the solar energy captured by green plants and stored in the form of complex carbon molecules. A food chain is a system for passing those calories on to species that lack the plant's unique ability to synthesize them from sunlight. One of the themes of this book is that the industrial revolution of the food chain, dating to the close of World War II, has actually changed the fundamental rules of this game. Industrial agriculture has supplanted a complete reliance on the sun for our calories with something new under the sun: a food chain that draws much of its energy from fossil fuels instead. (Of course, even that energy originally came from the sun, but unlike sunlight it is finite and irreplaceable.) The result of this innovation has been a vast increase in the amount of food energy available to our species; this has been a boon to humanity (allowing us to multiply our numbers), but not an unalloyed one. We've discovered that an abundance of food does not render the omnivore's dilemma obsolete. To the contrary, abundance seems only to deepen it, giving us all sorts of new problems and things to worry about.

Each of this book's three parts follows one of the principal human food chains from beginning to end: from a plant, or group of plants, photosynthesizing calories in the sun, all the way to a meal at the dinner end of that food chain. Reversing the chronological order, I start with the industrial food chain, since that is the one that today involves and concerns us the most. It is also by far the biggest and longest. Since monoculture is the hallmark of the industrial food chain, this section focuses on a single plant: *Zea mays,* the giant tropical grass we call corn, which has become the keystone species of the industrial food chain, and so in turn of the modern diet. This section follows a bushel of commodity corn from the field in Iowa where it grew on its long, strange journey to its ultimate destination in a fast-food meal, eaten in a moving car on a highway in Marin County, California.

The book's second part follows what I call—to distinguish it from the industrial—the pastoral food chain. This section explores some of the alternatives to industrial food and farming that have sprung up in recent years (variously called "organic," "local," "biological," and "beyond organic"), food chains that might appear to be preindustrial but in surprising ways turn out in fact to be postindustrial. I set out thinking I could follow one such food chain, from a radically innovative farm in Virginia that I worked on one recent summer to an extremely local meal prepared from animals raised on its pastures. But I promptly discovered that no single farm or meal could do justice to the complex, branching story of alternative agriculture right now, and that I needed also to reckon with the food chain I call, oxymoronically, the "industrial organic." So the book's pastoral section serves up the natural history of two very different "organic" meals: one whose ingredients came from my local Whole Foods supermarket (gathered there from as far away as Argentina), and the other tracing its origins to a single polyculture of grasses growing at Polyface Farm in Swoope, Virginia.

The last section, titled Personal, follows a kind of neo-Paleolithic food chain from the forests of Northern California to a meal I prepared (almost) exclusively from ingredients I hunted, gathered, and grew myself. Though we twenty-first-century eaters still eat a handful of hunted and gathered food (notably fish and wild mushrooms), my interest in this food chain was less practical than philosophical: I hoped to shed fresh light on the way we eat now by immersing myself in the way we ate then. In order to make this meal I had to learn how to do some unfamiliar things, including hunting game and foraging for wild mushrooms and urban tree fruit. In doing so I was forced to confront some of the most elemental questions—and dilemmas—faced by the human omnivore: What are the moral and psychological implications of killing, preparing, and eating a wild animal? How does one distinguish between the delicious and the deadly when foraging in the woods? How do the alchemies of the kitchen transform the raw stuffs of nature into some of the great delights of human culture?

The end result of this adventure was what I came to think of as the Perfect Meal, not because it turned out so well (though in my humble opinion it did), but because this labor- and thought-intensive dinner, enjoyed in the company of fellow foragers, gave me the opportunity, so rare in modern life, to eat in full consciousness of everything involved in feeding myself: For once, I was able to pay the full karmic price of a meal.

Yet as different as these three journeys (and four meals) turned out to be, a few themes kept cropping up. One is that there exists a fundamental tension between the logic of nature and the logic of human industry, at least as it is presently organized. Our ingenuity in feeding ourselves is prodigious, but at various points our technologies come into conflict with nature's ways of doing things, as when we seek to maximize efficiency by planting crops or raising animals in vast monocultures. This is something nature never does, always and for good reasons practicing diversity instead. A great many of the health and environmental problems created by our food system owe to our attempts to oversimplify nature's complexities, at both the growing and the eating ends of our food chain. At either end of any food chain you find a biological system—a patch of soil, a human body—and the health of one is connected—literally—to the health of the other. Many of the problems of health and nutrition we face today trace back to things that happen on the farm, and behind those things stand specific government policies few of us know anything about.

I don't mean to suggest that human food chains have only recently come into conflict with the logic of biology; early agriculture and, long before that, human hunting proved enormously destructive. Indeed, we might never have needed agriculture had earlier generations of hunters not eliminated the species they depended upon. Folly in the getting of our food is nothing new. And yet the new follies we are perpetrating in our industrial food chain today are of a different order. By replacing solar energy with fossil fuel, by raising millions of food animals in close confinement, by feeding those animals foods they never evolved to eat, and by feeding ourselves foods far more novel than we even realize, we are taking risks with our health and the health of the natural world that are unprecedented.

Another theme, or premise really, is that the way we eat represents our most profound engagement with the natural world. Daily, our eating turns nature into culture, transforming the body of the world into our bodies and minds. Agriculture has done more to reshape the natural world than anything else we humans do, both its landscapes and the composition of its flora and fauna. Our eating also constitutes a relationship with dozens of other species—plants, animals, and fungi—with which we have coevolved to the point where our fates are deeply entwined. Many of these species have evolved expressly to gratify our desires, in the intricate dance of domestication that has allowed us and them to prosper together as we could never have prospered apart. But our relationships with the wild species we eat—from the mushrooms we pick in the forest to the yeasts that leaven our bread—are no less compelling, and far more mysterious. Eating puts us in touch with all that we share with the other animals, and all that sets us apart. It defines us.

What is perhaps most troubling, and sad, about industrial eating is how thoroughly it obscures all these relationships and connections. To go from the chicken (*Gallus gallus*) to the Chicken McNugget is to leave this world in a journey of forgetting that could hardly be more costly, not only in terms of the animal's pain but in our pleasure, too. But forgetting, or not knowing in the first place, is what the industrial food chain is all about, the principal reason it is so opaque, for if we could see what lies on the far side of the increasingly high walls of our industrial agriculture, we would surely change the way we eat.

"Eating is an agricultural act," as Wendell Berry famously said. It is also an ecological act, and a political act, too. Though much has been done to obscure this simple fact, how and what we eat determines to a great extent the use we make of the world—and what is to become of it. To eat with a fuller consciousness of all that is at stake might sound like a burden, but in practice few things in life can afford quite as much satisfaction. By comparison, the pleasures of eating industrially, which is to say eating in ignorance, are fleeting. Many people today seem perfectly content eating at the end of an industrial food chain, without a thought in the world; this book is probably not for them. There are things in it that will ruin their appetites. But in the end this is a book about the pleasures of eating, the kinds of pleasure that are only deepened by knowing.

Discussion Questions

1. What question does Pollan claim that *The Omnivore's Dilemma* answers? Why does he find that question so complicated to answer?

2. How does Pollan define "the omnivore's dilemma"? What sort of relationship does he claim that Americans have with "the omnivore's dilemma"?

3. What food chains does Pollan claim that humans participate in? What do all three have in common? How does he define each?

4. Research several different ways particular animals relate to food chains. For example, Guinea pigs—herbivores that are domesticated animals—are a staple of many South American diets, where as in the United States they are kept as pets. How do they differ from the food chains that Pollan describes?

5. Research the critical response to *The Omnivore's Dilemma*. What do supporters of his book claim? What do the naysayers claim?

The Locavore's Dilemma: Why Pineapples Shouldn't Be Grown in North Dakota

Jayson L. Lusk, F. Bailey Norwood

Dr. Jayson Lusk is a professor and the Willard Sparks Endowed Chair in the department of Agriculture Economics at Oklahoma State University. He has published widely on the economics of food production. Dr. F. Bailey Norwood is an associate professor in the department of Agricultural Economics at Oklahoma State University and has also published a variety of work on the economics of food production.

> "Local food is generally more expensive than non-local food of the same quality. If that were not so, there would be no need to exhort people to 'buy local.'"

Oklahoma's government, like those of 45 other states, funds a farm-to-school program encouraging cafeterias to buy their food from local sources. U.S. Representative Chellie Pingree (D-Maine) wants to help; she recently introduced the *Eat Local Foods Act* (HR 5806) to assist schools in providing local foods in school lunches. From Michelle Obama's White House garden to grants from the U.S. Department of Agriculture's "Know Your Farmer, Know Your Food" initiative, an agenda has emerged to give local foods more prominence on our dinner plates. Interestingly, no agricultural economist has informed the public that a key claim of local-food advocates—that local-food purchases enhance the local economy—violates the core economic principles taught in every introductory economics class. Until now.

For more information, see "Comparative Advantage" and "Free Trade" in the *Concise Encyclopedia of Economics.*

A major flaw in the case for buying local is that it is at odds with the principle of comparative advantage. This principle, which economists have understood for almost 200 years, is one of the main reasons that the vast majority of economists believe in free trade. Free trade, whether across city, state, or national boundaries, causes people to produce the goods or services for which they have a comparative advantage and, thus, makes virtually everyone wealthier. Princeton University economist Paul Krugman, who won the Nobel Prize in economics for his contributions to the economics of international trade, called comparative advantage "Ricardo's Difficult Idea"[1] because so many non-economists deny it and are unwilling to understand it. But if people understood comparative advantage, much of the impetus for buying local foods would disappear.

When the tomatoes are ripe and the price is right, we, the two authors, enjoy local food. In fact, we grow vegetables in our own backyards. But, according to some bestselling authors, daytime talk show hosts, celebrity chefs, and the U.S. government, we aren't growing and buying enough. These groups have offered a host of economic arguments to promote the sale of local food—arguments that are fundamentally wrong.

The public is prone to chasing fad diets, so given the touted benefits of local foods and the limited information consumers possess, we are not surprised that the general public has jumped on the local-foods bandwagon. But we are surprised by the seemingly large numbers of agricultural economists who actively support the local-food movement or, at a minimum, don't oppose it. In fact, *Choices* (an agricultural economics magazine) devoted a whole issue[2] to the local-foods movement, neglecting to note its inconsistency with economic principles. A recent *Choices* article on local foods argued: *"An ideal regional food system describes a system in which as much food as possible to meet the population's food needs is produced, processed, distributed, and purchased at multiple levels and scales within the region."*[3] But the article fails to justify this position on economic grounds. One of our alma maters, via the N.C. Cooperative Extension Service, is actively encouraging local-food consumption, arguing that the money diverted from non-local to local food would *"be available in the state's economy."*[4]

To support local foods and deny comparative advantage and gains from trade, surely there must be offsetting benefits from the sale of local foods that would produce a positive cost-benefit calculation. The aforementioned issue of *Choices* outlined several such benefits. We are not convinced. We are not against consumers choosing to buy local food, and indeed, we both regularly stroll through our local farmers' market. What we find disturbing is the state or federal policy agenda on local foods and the almost complete silence of agricultural economists on its adverse consequences. Consider the main arguments for buying local.

Argument 1: Buying Local Foods Is Good for the Local Economy

Tom Vilsack, the current Secretary of Agriculture, stated, "In a perfect world, everything that was sold, everything that was purchased and consumed would be local, so the economy would receive the benefit of that."[5] Apparently Vilsack believes that we'd be richer if we made our own shoes, iPods, and corn. Adam Smith and David Ricardo must be rolling in their graves.

Local food is generally more expensive than non-local food of the same quality. If that were not so, there would be no need to exhort people to "buy local." However, we are told that spending a dollar for a locally produced tomato keeps the dollar circulating locally, stimulating the local economy. But, if local and non-local foods are of the same quality, but local goods are more expensive, then buying local food is like burning dollar bills—dollar bills that could have been put to more productive use. The community does not benefit when we pay more for a local tomato instead of an identical non-local tomato because the savings realized from buying non-local tomatoes could have been used to purchase other things. Asking us to purchase local food is asking us to give up things we otherwise could have enjoyed—the very definition of wealth destruction.

If we, as consumers, require that our food be grown locally, we cause the food not to be grown in the most productive, least-cost location. When the government encourages consumers to pay higher prices for a local product when a lower-cost non-local product of equal quality is readily available, it is asking the community to destroy its wealth because the local farmer cannot compete with non-local farms. If we really want to help local farmers, we'd be better off giving them a donation equal to our savings from buying non-local food. We would have redistributed our income, but at least we wouldn't have destroyed wealth.

See "The Buy-Locally-Owned Fallacy" by Karen Selick and the podcast Boudreaux on the Economics of "Buy Local" on EconTalk for more discussion about keeping dollars local.

The "keep the dollars local" argument fails to recognize that a dollar sent out of the local economy by buying a non-local food must, eventually, return to the local economy in terms of dollars spent on exports. Consider a concrete example. What if people in our city of Stillwater, Oklahoma kept spending dollars on "imports" from places other than Stillwater, and none of these dollars ended up being spent on Stillwater "exports"? Then, Stillwater would run low on money to buy even local goods and services. With less money chasing goods and services, prices in Stillwater would fall. This fall in prices would entice outsiders to buy Stillwater goods—and those sales to outsiders would be exports. Simultaneously, the extra dollars available outside Stillwater would cause outsiders to bid more for outside goods and services. Outside prices would rise, further discouraging people in Stillwater from "importing." In real life, it takes only a few pennies' difference in price to cause people to shop elsewhere. Economists call this arbitrage. Arbitrage opportunities would quickly cause the outsiders to start importing from Stillwater, causing Stillwater's imports and exports to balance. Of course, we use the words "imports" and "exports" broadly to include purchases or sales of bonds, land, etc. The balance-of-payments formula that applies to countries operating with different currencies is equally applicable to local economies trading in the same currency with their neighbors.

The balance-of-payments equation must hold: it is not a conjecture. If an economy is in what economists call a "steady-state equilibrium," local consumption must equal income from local sales and therefore, imports must, over the long run, equal exports:

Local Consumption + Consumption of Imports = Income from Local Sales + Income from Exports

Locavores seek to export goods without importing, which can happen only if the exports are given away for free—the equivalent of foreign aid. This cannot be the objective of the local-food movement, can it?

Consider an example. Suppose that local lettuce sells for $5 and non-local lettuce of equivalent quality sells for $3. Purchasing local lettuce creates $5 of income for local vendors. So far, so good. However, purchasing non-local lettuce and spending the $2 saved on local (or non-local goods) also creates $5 of income for local vendors—giving the consumer both the lettuce and whatever can be purchased with the extra $2. If $5 is spent only on local goods, then there is no offsetting export. If $3 is spent on non-local lettuce and $2 spent on local goods, the $3 in imports is eventually offset by $3 of exports, providing $5 of income to the local community. Finally, if the whole $5 is spent on non-local goods, the local economy will realize $5 in exports. Thus, purchasing local lettuce provides the same income to the local community (the accounting identity must hold), but it causes the individual to forgo the pleasure of what the $2 could have purchased—again, the definition of wealth destruction. Wealth is destroyed because the local-food movement convinced individuals to forgo the increase in wealth provided by comparative advantage.

Surely a critic would stop us here and argue that our logic breaks down because local and non-local foods are not of the same quality. That may be true (at least during certain seasons), but the oft-cited argument is that local food is *implicitly* better for the local economy *because it is local*. The "keep the dollars local" argument is not an argument about quality.

Argument 2: Buying Local Foods Is Good for the Environment

Even if local foods aren't a boon to the economy, we are told that the environment benefits from the purchase of local food.[6] Whether this is true is ultimately an empirical question. Local foods travel fewer miles, but an environmentalist must be concerned with more than the tailpipe emissions from farm to market. Consumers must also travel to buy their food, and the variety of foods offered in supermarkets minimizes the need to make multiple trips. An extra trip by a consumer to the farmers' market is likely to expend more energy than was saved by reducing the distance the food travels. Moreover, fresh local foods often require more at-home preparation, where energy use is less efficient relative to that of large-scale processing facilities.

The truth is that the energy expended transporting food is relatively unimportant. According to USDA-ERS data, consumers spent $880.7 billion on food in 2006. Only four percent of these expenditures can be attributed to post-farm transportation costs. One recent study indicated that over 80 percent of the global-warming impacts of food consumption occur at the farm, and only ten percent are due to transportation.[7] After an extensive literature review, other researchers have concluded that "it is currently impossible to state categorically whether or not local food systems emit fewer [greenhouse gasses] than non-local food systems."[8] Minimizing the use of natural resources entails producing food in the least-cost location, which will not typically be local.

But energy use is a red herring. The goal of most people is not to minimize the use of energy, but rather to enjoy life, given our wealth and the prices we face. As Harvard economist Robert Dorfman put it in a letter written to *Science* in 1977, "Energy is indeed a scarce and valuable resource, but it is only one of many, and there is a good deal more to life than British thermal units."[9]

The most common counter-critique to this argument is that cheap, non-local food is a mirage because the prices for energy and transportation are "too low." That is, according to this argument, the market price fails to reflect externalities in the production and transportation of "industrialized," non-local food. We have already pointed out that production of non-local food may consume less energy than local food production. Even if it doesn't, recall that gasoline is *already* taxed; federal and state taxes together average about $0.40/gallon.

Would locavores really be satisfied with the outcomes that would result even if prices perfectly accounted for externalities? It can be hard for concerned locavores to accept the idea that people's free choices in markets produce a wiser allocation of resources, but clear thinking requires a bit of humility.

Argument 3: Local Is Fresher and Tastier

But surely, say the locavores, local food is fresher—at least when it's available. Yes, it may be. But then people can—and do—make tradeoffs between the higher cost of buying local against the higher freshness. Moreover, freshness need not equate to localness. The best Midwestern seafood restaurants have fresh menu items flown in daily, and any of us can have a live Maine lobster delivered to our door tomorrow with the click of the mouse.

But shouldn't government subsidize local food out of a sense of social justice, so that poorer people can eat fresher foods, too? It is absurd to presume that poorer people's greatest need is the freshness of locally-grown food. If someone cares about the plight of the poor, as we do, shouldn't we want them to be able to stretch their food dollars as far as possible?

Argument 4: Local Food Is Healthier and Should be Served in School

Author Michael Pollan argues that the government should require that school lunches include a portion of food grown within 100 miles of the school. In an interview on Bill Moyers' television show on PBS,[10] Pollan stated:

> And let's require that a certain percentage of that school lunch fund in every school district has to be spent within 100 miles to revive local agriculture, to create more jobs on farms, to, you know, rural redevelopment. You will achieve a great many goals through doing that. You will have a healthier population of kids who will perform better in the afternoon after that lunch. You will have, you know, the shot in the arm to local economies through helping local agriculture. And you will, you know, teach this generation habits that will last a lifetime about eating.

So, at least we can be comforted by knowing that our children will eat healthier food at school. Or will they? If improving nutrition is the objective, why not seek more-nutritious food regardless of where it is grown? Requiring schools to provide better nutrition *and* local food is a double whammy. Given a fixed lunchroom budget, there is a tradeoff between providing a larger quantity of more-nutritious non-local foods and a smaller quantity of more-nutritious local foods. Because a "buy local" policy adds a constraint, such a policy can only decrease the level of nutrition obtainable for a fixed budget, particularly because it is simply impossible to grow numerous healthy foods at certain times of the year and in certain locations. If children in North Dakota are to eat pineapple, they must look south. And we don't mean South Dakota.

Conclusion

The decision to buy local foods is a *shopping* decision, not a *moral* one. If you can find tasty local food at a price you are willing to pay, then go for it. But it doesn't make sense to cajole others into making the same choice you do, and it especially doesn't make sense to *force* others to do so. There is a romanticism about buying local food, but the reality is that local-food policies destroy wealth and institutionalize prejudices for one human over another based on such arbitrary criteria as the location of their farm. Local-food advocates imagine the movement providing a host of non-economic benefits, promoting a sense of community and "belonging." But buying local food limits one's community to only those we can physically see and imparts trust to only those whom we personally know. However, a shopper involved in the global food chain is part of a much larger community—one that requires a great deal more trust than one is required to muster at the farmers' market. If we want to foster the civic virtues of trust, trustworthiness, and community, the local-food movement is a move in the wrong direction—it is little more than nativism.

The local-food movement enjoys broad, fervent support, and politicians have hopped on the bandwagon, but that only makes it all the more important to eschew political correctness and critically evaluate the consequences of local-food policies. Economists are a diverse bunch, but we have a few core principles, two of which are that there is a balance of payments and that there are gains from trade. These universal principles are as timeless as the law of gravity. If politicians and activists proposed to suspend belief in gravity, physicists would not cower. They would resolutely defend reality. So should we.

Footnotes

1. Paul Krugman, "Ricardo's Difficult Idea." Available at http://web.mit.edu/krugman/www/ricardo.htm, accessed on December 16, 2010.

2. King, Robert P. (Guest Editor). 2010. *Choices*. Special Issue on Local Foods. 25(1).

3. Clancy, K. and K. Ruhf. 2010. "Is Local Enough? Some Arguments For Regional Food Systems." *Choices*. 25(1).

4. Extension Online News. "N.C. Cooperative Extension Partners With 10% Campaign To Promote Local Foods." Accessed September 3, 2010 at http://chathamchatlist.com/highlights/2010/08/22/nc-cooperative-extension-partners-10-campaign-promote-local-foods/.

5. *The Washington Post*. February 11, 2009. "Tom Vilsack, The New Face Of Agriculture." Accessed September 3, 2010 at http://www.washingtonpost.com/wp-dyn/content/story/2009/02/10/ST2009021002624.html.

6. Specter, Michael. 2009. *Denialism*. The Penguin Press: New York, NY. Hylton, Susan. January 25, 2009. "Panel to discuss benefits of consuming local foods." *Tulsa World*. Section A, Page 16. *The Economist*. February 13, 2010. "Green Communities: Kicking Carbon." Page 61.

7. Engelhaupt, E. (2008). "Do Food Miles Matter?" *Environmental Science and Technology* 42:3482.

8. Edwards-Jones, G., L. Milà i Canals, N. Hounsome, M. Truninger, G. Koerber, B. Hounsome, P. Cross, E.H. York, A. Hospido, K. Plassmann, I.M. Harris, R.T. Edwards, G.A.S. Day, A.D. Tomos, S.J. Cowell and D.L. Jones (2008). "Testing the Assertion That 'Local Food is Best': The Challenges of an Evidence Based Approach." *Trends in Food Science and Technology.* 19:265-274.

9. Dorfman, R. 1977. "Social Cost." *Science.* 196:940.

10. Bill Moyers Journal. November 28, 2008. Interview with Michael Pollan. Accessed September 2, 2010 at http://www.pbs.org/moyers/journal/11282008/transcript1.html.

Discussion Questions

1. What expectations does the title "The Locavore's Dilemma: Why Pineapples Shouldn't Be Grown in North Dakota" give you as a reader? Does this article fulfill those expectations? Why or why not?

2. What are the different arguments for the locavore movement that Lusk and Norwood refute? What are each of their counter-arguments? What evidence do they use in each of those counterarguments?

3. Lusk and Norwood cite Pollan in this article. Besides the similarity in title, what connections do you find between "The Locavore's Dilemma: Why Pineapples Shouldn't Be Grown in North Dakota" and "Introduction: Our National Eating Disorder" from *The Ominvore's Dilemma*?

4. Lusk and Norwood claim that "The truth is that the energy expended transporting food is relatively unimportant." Many others have written about this particular issue. Use the Internet to track down some of those arguments. What did you find? What are the different stances you found? How do those stances support or refute Lusk and Norwood's claim?

5. Both "Divided We Eat" and "The Locavore's Dilemma: Why Pineapples Shouldn't Be Grown in North Dakota" address economic issues associated with the locavore movement. Find at least one other article that in some way addresses an economic issue associated with the locavore movement. Does that argument complement either "Divided We Eat" or "The Locavore's Dilemma: Why Pineapples Shouldn't Be Grown in North Dakota"? How?

Spotlight on OSU's Farmers' Market

Jessica Fokken

In 2009, Oklahoma State University Dining Services began incorporating Made in Oklahoma products into dining options on campus. As a part of the new program, University Dining Services (UDS) partnered with the Robert M. Kerr Food and Agricultural Products Center in 2010 to start the Farmers' Market. Held on the second and fourth Thursday of each month from June to October, the Farmers' Market offers yet another venue for Made in Oklahoma products to be available to the Stillwater community but, more importantly, readily accessible to the OSU student body.

Made in Oklahoma is partnered with Oklahoma Department of Agriculture, Food, and Forestry, Oklahoma Grown, and the Made in Oklahoma Coalition and "works with Oklahoma agribusinesses at local, regional, and national levels to promote retail, industrial, and gourmet sales" ("About Us"). Vendors used by UDS purchase produce and other products from Made in Oklahoma companies, but UDS sought a way to increase the visibility of the Made in Oklahoma products. The Farmers' Market allows OSU students to buy Made in Oklahoma and other local products directly from the farmers or producers. UDS hopes the Farmers' market will "promote the economic well being of local farmers and growers" while encouraging students to buy locally and consider sustainability ("Farmers' market"). As of July 2011, vendors will offer products ranging from produce, meat, cheese, eggs, soap, milk, lotion, jelly, canned items, jewelry and other handcrafted items.

The 2011 season will be the second year of the Farmers' market, and it continues to grow among the student body.

References
"Farmers' market." *Student Union at Oklahoma State University.* n.d. Oklahoma State University. Web.

"About Us." *Made in Oklahoma.* n.d. Made in Oklahoma. Web.

Vegetarianism and Eating-Disordered Thinking

Marjaana Lindeman, Katariina Stark, and Krista Latvala

Marjaana Lindeman is a lecturer in the psychology department at the University of Helsinki. Her research interests include everyday thinking, lay ontology, and the psychology of superstitions and magical thinking.

Two studies compared food choice motives and symptoms of eating disorders among vegetarians and nonvegetarians. The participants filled in a food choice questionnaire and completed an eating attitude test (EAT, Study 1) and eating disorder inventory (EDI, Study 2). The vegetarians scored higher on EAT and on the ineffectiveness, interpersonal distrust, and maturity fears subscales of EDI than the nonvegetarians. However, no difference was found in the reported importance of weight control among the two groups. The results indicate vegetarianism and eating disorders are not independent but rather are intertwined phenomena. The potential common links, for example the possibility that vegetarianism is being used as a smokescreen for more severe eating pathology, are discussed.

Everyday experience and research evidence delineate as individuals who avoid animal products because they are morally concerned about animal and environmental welfare, and who strive for a nonviolent and healthy lifestyle (Amato & Partridge, 1989; Beardsworth & Keil, 1992; Jabs, Devine, & Sobal, 1998; Kenyon & Barker, 1998: Santos & Booth, 1996; Worsley & Skrzypiec, 1998). Because vegetarians typically do not mention weight control as their food choice motive, the possibility that vegetarians are excessively preoccupied with their body weight and might even be a risk group for eating disorders has seldom been brought up.

Yet, there is some tentative evidence which suggests that meat avoidance and disturbed eating patterns may indeed be interlinked. First, the literature on eating disorders (e.g., Kadambari, Gowers, Crisp, 1986; Polivy & Herman, 1985a; Schupak-Neuberg & Nemeroff, 1993; Szmukler, Dare, & Treasure, 1995) and vegetarianism (e.g., Amato & Partridge, 1989; Beardsworth & Keil, 1992; Kenyon & Barker, 1998; Lindeman & Stark, 1999; Worsley & Skrzypiec, 1998) indicates that the manifestation of modern vegetarianism and anorexia nervosa is similar in many respects. Both anorexics and vegetarians are typically young Western women who have changed their diet in their teenage years. They have adopted food attitudes that are more extreme, ascetic, and dichotomic than those of other people, and by nonconsumption of specific foods they both seem to strive for a stronger sense of purification, control, and identity.

Second, although the literature is limited, there is some empirical evidence about the cooccurrence of vegetarianism and anorexic behavior. Kadambari et al. (1986) analyzed the proportion of vegetarians among anorectic patients and found that 45% of the anorectic population in their study were vegetarians (for similar results, see Bakan, Birmingham, Aeberhardt, & Goldner, 1993). In Worsley and Skrzypiec's study (1997), in turn, vegetarian women were more concerned with being slim and they tended to restrict their energy intake more than nonvegetarian women. Martins, Pliner, and O'Connor (1999) obtained similar results, although in their study vegetarianism was associated with a higher level of dietary restraint only among women who had high scores on the feminism scale.

In short, only a few studies have addressed the relationship between vegetarianism and eating disordered behavior. The two studies presented here thus seek to examine this relationship further. In addition, given the apparent inconsistency between the potential dietary restraint and vegetarians' lack of emphasis on weight control in their self-reports, food choice motives are also analyzed.

STUDY 1

Method

Participants and Procedure
One hundred and eighty-seven high school students originally participated in the study. Because only two of the boys were vegetarians, only girls (N = 118, mean age = 16.44, age range 16–18) were included in the present study. Fifteen (12.7%) of the girls were vegetarians (i.e., they avoided red and white meat and fish).

The participants were recruited from three senior high schools in the Helsinki area. The classroom teachers delivered the questionnaires, which were filled in at home and returned to the teacher within a week.

Measures
Symptoms of eating disorders were measured by the short form of the Eating Attitudes Test (EAT: Garner & Garfinkel, 1979; Garner, Olmsted, Bohr, & Garfinkel, 1982). EAT includes 26 six-point items (1 = Never, 6 = Always) that measure behaviors and attitudes related to bulimia, body dissatisfaction, and drive for thinness. The most extreme response (6) was scored as 3, while the adjacent alternatives (5 and 4) were weighted as 2 points and 1 point, respectively, as suggested by Garner and Garfinkel (1979).

Food choice motives were assessed by the Food Choice Questionnaire (FCQ, Steptoe, Pollard, & Wardle, 1995), which taps nine food choice motives, namely health, mood, convenience, sensory appeal, natural content, price, weight control, familiarity, and ethical concern. Because the FCQ does not include food choice motives that might be important to vegetarians, the Ethical Concern subscale (originally consisting of one item for environmental welfare, one for political values, and one for country of food origin) was here replaced with three new subscales, specifically, animal welfare (two items), environmental welfare (three items) and political values (three items). These new scales have proved to be valid and reliable measures (Cronbach's α's .83, .85, and .81, respectively) for ethical food choice reasons (Lindeman & Vaananen, in press). Thus, the participants were asked to rate a total of 41 statements with a similar opening ("It is important that the food I eat on a typical day...") and a varying ending (e.g., "...has been produced in a way that animals have not suffered," "... has been prepared in an environmentally friendly way," or "...comes from countries I approve of politically"). The items were rated on a four-point scale (1 = not at all important, 4 = very important). Scores for the 12 food choice motives were computed by averaging the rating for the individual items on the scale.

Results

First, the differences between the vegetarians' and nonvegetarians' food choice motives were tested. Animal welfare, health, and environment protection were the most important food choice motives for vegetarians in that they emphasized these more than the other motives and more than the nonvegetarians. All means are given in Table 1.

Next, symptoms of eating disorders were analyzed among vegetarian and nonvegetarian participants. Vegetarians had higher EAT scores than the nonvegetarians (Table 1). Moreover, 20% of the vegetarians scored higher than the cutoff point of 20 (Garner et al., 1982) in the EAT, whereas the corresponding percentage among the nonvegetarians was 3.9%.

STUDY 2

The vegetarians' high scores in the EAT in Study 1 indicate that the vegetarians had more symptoms of anorexia nervosa than the nonvegetarians. EAT has proven to be a useful test for identifying abnormal eating attitudes. However, the specificity of the scale is sometimes rather low in that many normal dieters may also score high in the EAT (Garner, Olmstead, & Polivy, 1983; Slade, 1995). Therefore, in Study 2, the more disturbed attitudes that have been postulated to be the core of the psychopathology of anorexia nervosa (Garner et al., 1983) were addressed. Moreover, given the young age of the participants in Study 1, it seemed necessary to confirm and complement the results with a second study. Based on growing evidence of the disordered eating patterns of vegetarians, it was hypothesized that vegetarians differ from nonvegetarians on the more fundamental aspects of the psychopathology of anorexia nervosa, that is, on ineffectiveness, perfectionism, interpersonal distrust, maturity fears, and interoceptive awareness.

Table 1. Means and Standard Deviations for EAT and Food Choice Scales Among the Two Eating Status Groups

Scale	Nonvegetarians		Vegetarians		$t(116)$
EAT	6.01	(6.28)	11.53	(13.17)	2.68**
Food choice motives					
Health	2.73	(.59)	3.06	(.53)	1.98*
Mood	2.48	(.59)	2.67	(.44)	1.25
Convenience	2.73	(.58)	2.29	(.63)	2.64**
Sensory appeal	2.73	(.63)	2.73	(.51)	.014
Natural content	2.22	(.69)	2.48	(.48)	1.33
Price	2.88	(.56)	2.71	(.50)	1.10
Weight control	2.53	(.82)	2.45	(1.04)	0.37
Familiarity	1.83	(.62)	1.73	(.58)	0.55
Animal welfare	2.18	(.78)	3.10	(.76)	5.86***
Environmental protection	2.48	(.66)	2.96	(.79)	2.57*
Political issues	1.61	(.54)	2.30	(.78)	1.34***
Religion	1.42	(.82)	1.23	(.56)	0.84

*$p < .05$, **$p < .01$, ***$p < .001$

Method

Participants and Procedure

One hundred and thirty-one individuals originally participated, but only females ($N = 124$, mean age 27.19, age range 17–72) were included in the present study. Forty-four percent of the participants were full-time university students from over 10 fields of study, 48% were working, and 4% were neither working nor studying (for six persons, this information was missing). Vegetarians comprised 11.3% of the sample.

The participants were recruited from three introductory psychology courses, two held in the Open University of Helsinki and one in the University of Helsinki. The participants were told that the study concerned personality and food choices, and they filled in the question-naire during their lecture time.

Measures

Symptoms of eating disorders were assessed by EAT as in Study 1 and with the Eating Disorder Inventory (EDI; Garner et al., 1983). EDI includes 63 six-point items (1 = never, 6 = always) forming eight subscales. Three of the scales (drive for thinness, body dissatisfaction, and bulimia) assess attitudes and behaviors that, while central to anorexia nervosa, may also exist in other groups of dieters. The remaining five scales (ineffectiveness, perfectionism, interpersonal distrust, interoceptive awareness, and maturity fears), in turn, measure the core psychopathology of anorexia nervosa (Garner et al., 1983). EAT and EDI were scored as EAT in Study 1.

Results

The results of one-failed t-tests showed that the vegetarians had higher total scores for both EAT and EDI. In addition, vegetarians scored higher than nonvegetarians on every EDI subscale, although the difference was significant only on the scales of ineffectiveness, interpersonal distrust, and maturity fears. The means are given in Table 2. Of the vegetarians, 14.3% had a score higher than 20 in EAT, whereas the corresponding percentage among the nonvegetarians was 8.3%.

General Discussion

The majority of previous studies on vegetarianism have explored the conscious motives that vegetarians give for their food choices (Amato & Partridge, 1989; Beardsworth & Keil, 1992; Jabs et al., 1998; Kenyon & Barker, 1998; Santos & Booth, 1996; Worsley & Skrzypiec, 1998). In line with this work, the vegetarians in this study regarded animal welfare, environmental protection, health, and political issues as more important food choice motives than the nonvegetarians. No difference in the importance attached to weight control was found between the vegetarians' and the nonvegetarians' responses in the Food Choice Questionnaire. Nevertheless, compared with the nonvegetarians, the vegetarians displayed significantly more symptoms of eating disorders. The differences were found not only in abnormal eating attitudes, manifested in high EAT scores, but also in maturity fears, ineffectiveness, and interpersonal distrust that, together with interoceptive awareness and perfectionism, have been identified as fundamental aspects of the psychopathology of anorexia nervosa (Garner et al., 1983).

Table 2. Means (and Standard Deviations) for the 8 EDI Subscales and EAT Among the Four Eating Status Groups

Scale	Nonvegetarians		Vegetarians		/(122)
EAT	7.03	(6.93)	11.29	(7.91)	2.12*
EDI	22.43	(17.89)	33.76	(28.75)	2.06*
Drive for thinness	3.25	(4.31)	4.64	(4.89)	1.11
Body dissatisfaction	7.52	(7.16)	9.79	(10.31)	1.06
Bulimia	0.76	(1.83)	1.21	(3.70)	0.75
Ineffectiveness	1.98	(3.23)	3.71	(5.18)	1.76*
Perfectionism	3.32	(3.27)	4.83	(4.19)	1.57
Interpersonal distrust	1.65	(2.58)	3.00	(4.84)	1.64*
Interoceptive awareness	1.66	(2.88)	2.79	(4.79)	1.26
Maturity fears	2.29	(2.75)	3.79	(3.28)	1.87*

*$p < .05$

So far, the increasing prevalence of eating disorders and vegetarianism, as well as their individual progress have been seen as independent phenomena. Whereas the increase in anorexia over recent decades has often been traced back to the increasing emphasis by the media on slimness (e.g., Heinberg & Thompson, 1995; Szmukler & Patton, 1995), the rise of contemporary vegetarianism has been explained by the new movements for physical health, environmental welfare, animal liberation, and social justice (for a review of this topic see Amato & Partidge, 1989; Beardsworth & Keil, 1992). Similarly, whereas those prone to eating disorders are characterized as individuals with serious psychological problems, those who turn to vegetarianism are described as socially conscious individuals who have critically scrutinized ethical values and traditional foodways (Beardsworth & Keil, 1992; Worsley & Skrzypiec, 1998).

Together with previous work (Bakan et al., 1993; Kadambari et al., 1986; Martins et al., 1999), the present two studies suggest that vegetarianism and eating disorders are not independent but are somehow intertwined phenomena. The common link can, however, only be speculated. First, it might be possible that vegetarians and individuals prone to eating disorders are different people at the beginning and endorsing a vegetarian diet may not, as such, be a risk factor for anomalous eating habits. Anorexics, however, may turn to vegetarianism as part of their symptomatology (cf., Bakan et al., 1993; Kadambari et al., 1986). This, in turn, may contaminate research results obtained from a sample that includes healthy vegetarians: "real" vegetarians become a disordered-seeming group because of the inclusion of anorexics adopting their lifestyle. Anorexic behavior is liable to change as time passes. The rigid self-starving regime turns into bulimic outburst of bingeing and purging as the anorexic control becomes harder to maintain. This is a rather common occurrence in the course of anorexia (Bakan et al., 1993; Kadambari et al., 1986). According to Garfinkel, Moldofsky and Garner (1980), turning from anorexics into bulimics or bulimarexics happens to 40% of anorexic patients. Vegetarianism could be another way of maintaining the food-centered lifestyle—a lifestyle that, however, is easier to defend than anorexia, bulimia, or a weight-loss diet. For example, Krizmanic (1992) proposes that a vegetarian diet simplifies the life of an eating-disordered individual by giving him or her valid reasons for avoiding social eating situations like meetings with friends for meals or traditional family dinners, providing structure for food choices—a clear set of dos and don'ts—and an acceptable way to eat only lighter and safer food like fruit and vegetables. Hence, it could be assumed that some vegetarians are in fact eating-disordered people who are hiding their anomalous eating habits behind the veneer of socially acceptable vegetarianism, as suggested by Martins et al. (1999).

Second, the factors contributing to eating disorders and vegetarianism may be similar. A possible common factor might be a tendency to solve problems related to identity formation by concrete lifestyle choices. Purity and cleanliness in food choices may come to present the sought-for simplicity in wider issues and create a sense of belongingness in a prestigious group, health-conscious, educated class in the case of vegetarians, and glamorously thin and ascetic in the case of the eating-disordered. Thus, it might be possible that, for some unknown reason, some individuals are able to canalize their psychological distress into vegetarianism while others, suffering from similar problems, go on to severe eating disorders. If this is the case, vegetarians, like bulimics (Campbell, 1995), might be regarded as spared anorexics.

There might also be continuum-like development from vegetarian food concerns to eating-disordered food concerns. The food-focus—connecting vegetarians with dieters—may also be a risk-inducing factor, turning a chosen diet from harmless occupation into obsession and disorder. Polivy and Herman propose in their restraint theory (1985b) that the harmful aspect of dieting is the fact that it turns normal hunger-motivated eating into a cognitively regular activity, thus decreasing the dieters' ability to recognize and respect their internal cues for hunger and satiety. If cognitively regulated eating is a risk for eating disorders, then vegetarianism looks like a risk factor—it restricts the food choices and develops good and bad categories in a manner similar to dieting.

The theoretical models have been more successful in explaining the maintenance than the development of eating disorders (Szmukler, Dare, & Treasure, 1995). In future studies, it might be useful to focus on the eating behavior and motivations of groups that are less pathological than anorexics and bulimics, for example by analyzing the sequence of development from vegetarianism to more restrictive and rigid focusing on food. Analyses of common and distinctive features of vegetarians and anorexics might add to our understanding of the factors that generate disturbed eating.

References

Amato, P. R., & Partridge, S. A. (1989). *The new vegetarians. Promoting health and protecting life.* New York: Plenum Press.

Bakan, R., Birmingham, C. L., Aeberhardt, L., & Goldner, E. M. (1993). Dietary zinc intake of vegetarian and nonvegetarian patients with anorexia nervosa. *International Journal of Eating Disorders, 13,* 229–233.

Beardsworth, A., & Keil, T. (1992). The vegetarians option: Varieties, conversions, motives and careers. *The Sociological Review 40,* 253–293.

Campbell, P. G. (1995). What would a causal explanation of the eating disorders look like? In G. I. Szmukler, C. Dare, & J. Treasure (Eds.), *Handbook of eating disorders* (pp. 19–64). Chichester: Wiley.

Garfinkel, P. E., Moldofsky, H., & Garner, O. M. (1980). The heterogeneity of anorexia nervosa: Bulimia as a distinct subgroup. *Archives of General Psychiatry, 37,* 1036–1040.

Garner, D. M., & Garfinkel, P. E. (1979). The eating attitudes test: An index of symptoms of anorexia nervosa. *Psychological Medicine, 9,* 273–279.

Garner, D. M., Olmsted, M. P., Bohr, Y., & Garfinkel, P. E. (1982). The eating attitude test: Psychometric features and clinical correlates. *Psychological Medicine, 12,* 871–878.

Garner, D. M., Olmsted, M. P., & Polivy, J. (1983). Development and validation of a multidimensional eating disorder inventory for anorexia and bulimia. *International Journal of Eating Disorders, 2,* 15–34.

Heinberg, L. J., & Thompson, J. K. (1995). Body image and televised images of thinness and attractiveness: A controlled laboratory investigation. *Journal of Social and Clinical Psychology, 14,* 325–338.

Jabs, J., Devine, C. M., & Sobal, J. (1998). Model of the process of adopting vegetarian diets: Health vegetarians and ethical vegetarians. *Journal of Nutrition Education, 30,* 196–202.

Kadambari, R., Gowers, S., & Crisp, A. (1986). Some correlates of vegetarianism in anorexia nervosa. *International Journal of Eating Disorders, 5,* 539–541.

Kenyon, P. M., & Barker, M. E. (1998). Attitudes towards meat-eating in vegetarian and non-vegetarian teenage girls in England—an ethnographic approach. *Appetite, 30,* 185–198.

Krizmanic, J. (1992). Perfection, obsession: Can vegetarianism cover up an eating disorder? *Vegetarian Times, 178,* 52–60.

Lindeman, M., & Stark, K. (1999). Pleasure, pursuit of health, or negotiation of identity? Personality correlates of food choice motives among young and middle-aged women. *Appetite, 33,* 141–161.

Lindeman, M., & Väänänen, M. (in press). Measurement of ethical food choice motives. *Appetite.*

Martins, V., Pliner, P., & O'Connor, R. (1999). Restrained eating among vegetarians: Does a vegetarian eating style mask concerns about weight? *Appetite, 32,* 145–154.

Polivy, J., & Herman, C. P. (1985a). Dieting and binging. *American Psychologist, 40,* 193–201.

Polivy, J., & Herman, C. P. (1985b). Dieting and bingeing: A causal analyses. *American Journal of Psychology, 40,* 193–201.

Santos, M. L. S., & Booth, D. A. (1996). Influences on meat avoidance among British students. *Appetite, 27,* 197–205.

Schupak-Neuberg, E., & Nemeroff, C. J. (1993). Disturbances in identity and self-regulation in bulimia nervosa: Implications for a metaphorical perspective of "body as self." *International Journal of Eating Disorders, 13,* 335–347.

Slade, P. (1995). Prospects for prevention. In G. I. Szmukler, C. Dare, & J. Treasure (Eds.), *Handbook of eating disorders* (pp. 385–398). Chichester: Wiley.

Steptoe, A., Pollard, T. M., & Wardle, J. (1995). Development of the motives underlying the selection of food: The food choice questionnaire. *Appetite, 25,* 267–284.

Szmukler, G. L., Dare, C., & Treasure, J. (Eds.). (1995). *Handbook of eating disorders.* Chichester: Wiley.

Szmukler, G. L., & Patton, C. (1995). Sociocultural models of eating disorders. In G. I. Szmukler, C. Dare, & J. Treasure (Eds.), *Handbook of eating disorders* (pp. 177–192). Chichester: Wiley.

Worsley, A., & Skrzypiec, G. (1997). Teenage vegetarianism: Beauty or the beast? *Nutritional Research, 17,* 391–404.

Worsley, A., & Skrzypiec, G. (1998). Teenage vegetarianism: Prevalence, social and cognitive contexts. *Appetite, 30,* 151–170.

Discussion Questions

1. What type(s) of research did Lindeman, Stark, and Latvala use in "Vegetarianism and Eating-Disordered Thinking"? Underline Lindeman, Stark, and Latvala's thesis. Explain how they support that thesis. What kinds of evidence do they use? What effect does that create?

2. Lindeman, Stark, and Latvala claim that "Both anorexics and vegetarians are typically young Western women who have changed their diet in their teenage years. They have adopted food attitudes which are more extreme, ascetic, and dichotomic than those of other people, and by the consumption of specific foods they both seem to strive for a stronger sense of purification, control, and identity." What assumptions about vegetarians are made in this statement? Research vegetarianism. Do these assumptions have a basis in what you found? Why or why not?

3. Lindeman, Stark, and Latvala cite four studies (Kadambari et al.; Bakan, Birmingham, Aeberhart, & Goldner; Worsley and Skrzypiec; and Martins, Pliner, and O'Connor) that previously addressed a possible "cooccurrence of vegetarianism and anorexic behavior." Find one of those studies. Which did you find? Does the study you found support the assumptions, findings, and/or conclusions of "Vegetarianism and Eating-Disordered Thinking"? Why or why not? Or locate something written after "Vegetarianism and Eating-Disordered Thinking" on the possible relationship between vegetarianism and eating disorders. Does this later piece support the assumptions, findings, and/or conclusions of Lindeman, Stark, and Latvala's article? Why or why not?

4. Locate an additional article from *Eating Disorders*. How is that article similar to this one? How does it differ? Considering both articles, what assumptions do you make about this journal? Why?

5. Find a vegetarian and interview him or her. Is this vegetarian's experience similar or different from the sorts of vegetarians discussed in this article? Why or why not?

What Would the World Be Like Without Animals for Food, Fiber, and Labor? Are We Morally Obligated To Do Without Them?

S. L. Davis

S. L. Davis is Professor Emeritus in Growth Biology at Oregon State University's Department of Animal Sciences. His main research interest is in bioethics on which he has published a great deal.

Abstract

Numerous animal rights and animal liberation theorists have concluded that nonhuman animals have moral standing and noninterference rights. Therefore, they say that humans are morally obligated to stop using animals for food, fiber, labor, and research. I disagree with that conclusion for at least 2 reasons. First, it has been suggested that food production models are possible using large herbivores that might actually cause less harm (kill) to animals than a vegan food production model. This is because intensive crop production used to produce food for a vegan diet kills (harms) far more animals of the field than extensive agriculture (pasture production). So, a combined food production system that includes crops and pasture harvested by large herbivores to be used for human food may kill fewer animals than would a vegan-crop model. Second, pragmatically, it is improbable that all peoples of the world could ever be convinced that they must give up animals. In fact, it may be unethical to try to do that, because in poor countries, these animals are essential to the survival of the human populations. But what about the richer nations? Maybe they will or should be convinced to do without animals because of the moral strength of the animal rights and animal liberation theories. However, I believe that there are far too many obstacles for that to happen. What then are we morally obligated to do about animals? I suggest that animals do have moral standing, and that we are morally obligated to recognize their unique species-specific natures and treat them accordingly. That would mean treating animals according to their physical and behavioral needs or telos. That, I believe, is the most likely outcome of the conversation about animal rights.

Key Words: animal rights • welfare • moral obligation

Introduction

In the past 40 years, increasing numbers of philosophers have examined the question of the moral status of nonhuman animals and our moral obligations to them. Perhaps the most notable of these philosophers are Regan (1983, 1996) and Singer (1975, 1996). In his 1975 book titled *Animal Liberation*, Singer (1975) used a utilitarian approach to examine our moral obligations to animals. This method of ethical analysis looks at the consequences of our actions and requires that we take those actions that have the best consequences (for the animals). In other words, we must do what results in maximizing the benefits and minimizing the harm to animals. He concluded that contemporary animal agriculture causes much pain and suffering to animals, and therefore, the animals should be liberated. Regan's (1983) book called *A Case for Animal Rights*, on the other hand, uses a rights-based approach to analyzing our moral obligations to animals. He reasoned that animals are subjects of a life, have inherent value that has nothing to do with their economic value, and they have interests that are as important to them as similar interests are to humans. He therefore concluded that animals have noninterference rights. That means that they should be liberated and be able to live their lives without human interference. So, even though Regan and Singer used different approaches, they came to similar conclusions and suggest that humans must become vegans or vegetarians. In fact, those humans who do decide to become vegans and vegetarians and become animal rights (AR) activists do so with good reason and strong moral convictions and deserve respect and support for their position. As Thompson (2004) puts it, "there are innumerable reasons why someone might choose to become an ethical vegetarian, and those reasons deserve respect." Therefore, this paper will not try to convince anyone why they should not choose to become an ethical vegetarian. Rather, it will examine some of the weaknesses of the AR-animal liberation conclusion and suggest that the most pragmatic (concerned with practical considerations or consequences; Merriam-Webster, 1997) course of action worldwide is not with the elimination of animals for food, fiber, and labor.

What Would the World Be Like Without Animals for Food, Fiber, and Labor?

The simplest answer to that question is hungry, cold, and tired! Of course, it could be argued that we need not be hungry, because we can eat grains, fruits, and vegetables; we need not be cold because of the availability of synthetics and plant-based fibers; and we need not be tired, because we have mechanical methods of plowing, planting, and harvesting our food. And this is true, at least for some people in some regions of the world. However, it is not true for hundreds of millions of humans who live in impoverished countries and will continue needing to use animals for these purposes (Bradford et al., 1999). Therefore, it may not be possible to apply a universal utopian moral theory about animal use worldwide.

So, the 2 competing visions of what the world would be like are, on the one hand, hungry, cold, and tired and, on the other hand, a world in which humans no longer cause animals pain and suffering and animals are able to live without human interference. As Regan and Francione (1996) stated: "The goal of the animal rights movement is nothing less than the total liberation of nonhuman animals from human tyranny." However, even if animals have rights, and most people are skeptical that they do, it is highly improbable that people of the world will ever be convinced to give up the use of animals for food, fiber, labor, research, etc.

Are We Morally Obligated to Do Without Them?

I argue that we are not, for at least 2 pragmatic reasons. The first of these reasons is that there are models of food production which include animals that might actually harm (kill) fewer animals than a strict vegan model of food production. The AR theory (Regan, 1996) predicts that, if animals were no longer produced as human food, fewer animals would be killed (harmed) in food production. A paper written by Davis (2003) challenges that conclusion and begins with the question, what is the morally relevant difference between the field mouse and the pig that makes it acceptable to kill 1 of them (the field mouse) so that we may eat but not the other (pig)? It is known that intensive agriculture to produce foods like corn, beans, peas, and other vegetables (vegan model) kill far more animals of the field than does extensive agriculture to produce crops like pasture that can be converted to human food by large herbivores. This latter model has been termed a burger vegan model (Lamey, 2007). Davis (2003) estimated that at least 15 field animals would be killed per hectare in the production of food in the vegan model. According to the USDA, there are currently 120 million hectares of cropland harvested each year. If all those acres were used to produce corn, grains, beans, etc., then 15 × 120 million or 1,800 million (1.8 billion) field animals would be killed to produce a vegan diet. On the other hand, it was estimated that only 7.5 field animals might be killed per hectare in the production of pasture grasses that could be harvested by large ruminants, resulting in only 1.35 billion animals killed in the burger vegan (Lamey, 2007) model. These estimates are not conclusive, but they do suggest that models of food production involving animals may exist that harm fewer animals than a vegan model.

The second reason I say no to the question is a matter of pragmatism. Wise (2004) has listed numerous obstacles to the application of ethical vegetarianism. Although Wise (2004) states that he believes that these obstacles can be overcome by proceeding "one step at a time," I believe that these obstacles are too great to be overcome, even taking them one step at a time. The obstacles include:

1. Physical obstacles. Over 30 billion animals are killed annually for food worldwide.

2. Economics. The animal industries from production to processing to marketing involve hundreds of billions of dollars.

3. Political. Because of the money and political power of the animal production and meat industries worldwide, it is unlikely that animals will ever be granted legal rights and be liberated.

4. Religion. According to the Bible, God gave humans dominion over the animals. "The old and new testaments, St. Paul, St. Augustine, and St. Thomas Aquinas stitched into the fabric of Judeo-Christian doctrine the idea that nonhuman animals had been created for humans." (Wise, 2004).

5. Historical. The notion that animals were created for human use has been pervasive in societies since ancient times.

6. Legal. "The legal problem is simple and stark...law divides the physical universe into persons and things" (Wise, 2004). So, if an animal is not a person, it is a thing.

7. Psychological. "Millions believe nonhumans lack every important mental ability; they are made for humans, and this is how the universe was designed" (Wise, 2004).

To this list of obstacles, I would add a cultural obstacle. It would be highly problematic, if not unethical, to try to convince some peoples of the world to give up the use of animals. As Thompson (2004) writes, "arguments that purport to establish vegetarianism as a universal moral norm face a tough hurdle. It just does not seem reasonable to claim that goat-herding peasants or pig-herding Maring of New Guinea (or for that matter, the countless American pioneers who kept a cow, a pig, and a few chickens) are doing something to their animals that is comparable to the practice of human slavery. What is more likely is that people, like ourselves, reasonably well off and living in an advanced industrial society, may have some duties of diet that we are neglecting. But if our goal is to improve the lot of animals, the most effective way to redress this neglect is to build a network of producers and consumers who are dedicated to that end."

Though their long-term objective is still total animal liberation, even some AR-animal liberation (AL) advocates are calling for a short-term pragmatic approach to AR theory. For example, Stallwood (1996) who was editor-in-chief of *The Animals' Agenda* says that "there are two fundamentally important challenges which we face...as an animal rights movement. The first challenge is learning how to balance our utopian vision of animal liberation with the pragmatic politics of animal advocacy." In addition, Ingrid Newkirk (1996) of People for the Ethical Treatment of Animals recognized that AR groups must be pragmatic and should endorse animal welfarism and that total animal liberation is "unrealistic."

Finally, although AR-AL theorists conclude that we are morally obligated to become vegetarian, I believe that it is unrealistic, perhaps even unethical, to force this conclusion on people of the world. Such an action, in my view, would be analogous to forcing Islam, Christianity, or Judaism on everyone in the world. In other words, just because I am Christian and believe totally that it is the 1 true religion doesn't give me the right to impose my beliefs on everyone else. The same is true for the AR-AL.

Conclusion

At a minimum, the AR-AL theories suggest that animals do count morally and that humans do have moral duties toward them. The pragmatist would say that, even in the United States and European Union, those duties include allowing animals the opportunity to live according to their specific species needs, allowing animals to express their telos (Rollin, 1995).

References

Bradford, E., R. L. Baldwin, H. Blackburn, K. G. Cassman, P. R. Crosson, C. L. Delgado, J. G. Fadel, H. A. Fitzhugh, M. Gill, J. W. Ottjen, M. W. Rosegrant, M. Vavra, and R. O. Wilson. 1999. Animal Agriculture and Global Food Supply. Council for Agricultural Science and Technology. Task Force Report no. 135. Counc. Agric. Sci. Technol., Ames, IA.

Davis, S. L. 2003. The least harm principle may require that humans consume a diet containing large herbivores, not a vegan diet. *J. Agric. Environ.* Ethics 16:387–394.[CrossRef][Web of Science]

Lamey, A. 2007. Food fight! Davis vs Regan on the ethics of eating beef. *J. Soc. Philos.* 38:331–338.[CrossRef]

Merriam-Webster. 1997. *Webster's College Dictionary.* Random House, New York, NY.

Newkirk, I. 1996. The animal rights movement must embrace animal welfarism. Pages 202–206 in *Animal Rights: Opposing Viewpoints.* D. Bender and B. Leone, ed. Greenhaven Press Inc., San Diego, CA.

Regan, T. 1983. *A Case for Animal Rights.* Univ. Calif. Press, Berkeley.

Regan, T. 1996. The case for strong animals rights. Pages 34–40 in *Animal Rights: Opposing Viewpoints.* D. Bender and B. Leone, ed. Greenhaven Press Inc., San Diego, CA.

Regan, T., and G. Francione. 1996. The animal rights movement must reject animal welfarism. Pages 194–201 in *Animal Rights: Opposing Viewpoints.* D. Bender and B. Leone, ed. Greenhaven Press Inc., San Diego, CA.

Rollin, B. E. 1995. *Farm Animal Welfare: Social, Bioethical and Research Issues.* Iowa State Univ. Press, Ames.

Singer, P. 1975. *Animal Liberation.* Random House, New York, NY.

Singer, P. 1996. All animals are equal. Pages 17–33 in *Animal Rights: Opposing Viewpoints.* D. Bender and B. Leone, ed. Greenhaven Press Inc., San Diego, CA.

Stallwood, K. 1996. The animal rights movement must be politically pragmatic. Pages 214–220 in *Animal Rights: Opposing Viewpoints.* D. Bender and B. Leone, ed. Greenhaven Press Inc., San Diego, CA.

Thompson, P. B. 2004. Getting pragmatic on farm animal welfare. Pages 140–159 in *Animal Pragmatism: Rethinking Human-Nonhuman Relationships.* E. McKenna and A. Light, ed. Indiana Univ. Press, Bloomington.

Wise, S. M. 2004. Animal rights one step at a time. Pages 19–50 in *Animal Rights: Current Debates and New Directions.* C. R. Sunstein and M. C. Nussbaum, ed. Oxford Univ. Press, New York, NY.

Discussion Questions

1. What is Davis's thesis statement in "What Would the World Be Like Without Animals for Food, Fiber, and Labor? Are We Morally Obligated to Live Without Them?"? What points does Davis make to support his thesis? Are they effective? Why or why not?

2. What claims does Davis make about food chains within which humans are involved? How are his claims similar to and/or different from Pollan's introduction to *The Omnivore's Dilemma*?

3. Davis claims that one of the obstacles "to the application of ethical vegetarianism" is "Political. Because of the money and political power of the animal production and meat industries worldwide, it is unlikely that animals will ever be granted legal rights and be liberated." Research animal rights legislation. Did your findings support Davis's claim? Why or why not?

4. Davis uses the terms "animal liberation," "animal rights activists," and "ethical vegetarianism." Look up these terms. What definitions did you find for each? Are those definitions similar to the way in which Davis uses those words? Why or why not?

A View to a Kill

Jenny Rose Ryan

Jenny Rose Ryan is a professional writer and editor with more than 12 years of experience in a spectrum of styles: newsletters and employee communications, grant writing and award proposals, television and radio scripts, marketing copy, outdoor adverts and magazine and newspaper features.

More than just a pastime for rifle-toting mountain men, northern Wisconsin's annual white-tailed-deer hunt also attracts a surprising number of women. And whether it's for food, for friendship, or just for fun, these gals all have their own reasons for pulling the trigger.

EVERY NOVEMBER, SHOTS ring out in the Wisconsin wilderness. That's the month when thousands of people descend on the state's forests and fields in search of camaraderie, relaxation, and yes, animals to kill. They're there to hunt white-tailed deer; it's as much a part of the regional culture as riding snowmobiles and cutting wood for winter warmth. This hunt is what hunting-ethics groups call a "fair chase"—watching and waiting, tracking and following animals in an open, wild area. And it's not just a bunch of dudes wearing blaze-orange jackets.

While it's often touted as an activity for manly-man gun nuts, hunting duties have been shared by the women of Wisconsin since before the first European settlers arrived in the 1800s. Women of the Native American Ho-Chunk tribe joined in yearly expeditions to the prairie to hunt bison. Ojibwe women hunted in the winter, complementing their other methods of living off the land. And as settlers arrived and cleared the forest to create farms and tend livestock, both men and women also hunted for food and clothing. This practice created a local women's hunting culture that has only become stronger over the centuries.

While men's participation in gun hunting in Wisconsin has declined in recent years, the number of women under 30 who are taking it up continues to rise. According to the University of Wisconsin and the Wisconsin Department of Natural Resources, in the year 2000, 48,022 girls and women in the state purchased licenses to hunt deer, accounting for 7.4 percent of all gun-hunting licenses sold that year. In 2007 that number rose to 8.4 percent. Today in northern Wisconsin, girls regularly take gun-safety classes alongside boys and skip just as many days of school to attend family turkey or pheasant hunts. And they hunt for the same reasons men do: they want to be outside in nature; they want to spend time with the people they love; and they want to live self-sufficiently by killing and processing their own food. "It's a great tradition to keep for the rest of your life," says Kelly Wondra, 21, a student and lifelong hunter from Frederic, WI. "And I'll be able to share it with my own kids someday."

Wondra hunts white-tailed deer for their meat—something she recognizes is sometimes difficult for people outside Wisconsin to understand. "I grew up in a small town, and [hunting] wasn't that big of a deal because everyone here pretty much does it," she says. "But if you come from a bigger city, it might seem a little weird. Some people might think that it's cruel to the animals. But we don't just shoot them for the heck of it; we actually will use all of the meat."

Jolleen Jensen, 32, of Fall Creek, WI, also hunts with the aim of harvesting meat to eat. She's been bow-hunting white-tailed deer for more than six years, since she picked up archery from her boyfriend, who is also a hunter. Yes, Jensen hunts with a bow and arrow—a skill that takes patience and practice. "It could take days, weeks, or even years to harvest something that you are looking for," she says. For Jensen, any deer she shoots is a prize. "For someone new to hunting, whether it's big or small, it will always be a trophy to you. Whether you find the game you are looking for or not, it's still fun just to go out and see the wildlife." She says hunting is about the experience—the watching and waiting and being in the native environment of the animal she's looking to harvest.

One of the biggest challenges Jensen says women hunters face that their male counterparts do not is maintaining the patience it takes to wait for the right animal in nature when nature calls. After all, going to the bathroom when you're out in the woods all day in a tree is a challenge. "I started out with a one-piece suit, then went to bibs [overalls] but still had to take off the jacket to take the bibs off the shoulders," she explains of her complicated hunting attire. "Now I have insulated pants, so that has been a little easier, especially if you're up 20 feet in a tree."

For women like Jensen who learn to hunt as adults, Wisconsin has a growing number of resources to get them up to speed. Becoming an Outdoors Woman (BOW) is a wilderness-skills program that began in 1991 as a way for women interested in hunting to gain the knowledge they need to confidently participate. Peggy Farrell, BOW's director says that while historically women have attended BOW workshops for various reasons, in the past 5 to 10 years she has seen an increase in the number interested specifically in self-sufficiency. This mirrors her own interest in hunting animals for food. "I think we need to think long and hard about how we treat animals harvested for meat," she says. To hunters like Farrell, this means teaching a new generation of female hunters how to make a clean shot to minimize the animal's suffering. "A lot of people ask me, 'If you love [an animal], why shoot it?'" she says. "One answer I would give is that a lot of animals wouldn't do as well as they do if we didn't have management [practices] that included hunting."

The blood and gore of killing for food is not something that generally fazes women like Farrell. Since it's a part of the culture and practices of the region, it's a given—a necessary step in the process. Yet, it's not taken for granted. Killing the animal is just one aspect of hunting; there's also preparing, waiting, failing, waiting some more, finally killing something, then processing, butchering, storing, and sharing the meat. "When you choose to harvest an animal (or choose not to because the timing or situation isn't right), you understand the animal—its behavior, how it lives and thinks," says Farrell. "When you take it home and prepare it in a way that does it justice, you have the whole story, and you enjoy every minute of the food you prepared. You don't earn this same connection when you're not hunting."

For some women, however, just the act of spending time with the hunting community out in nature and enjoying the meals that come from someone else's successful kill make the annual snowy trek worthwhile. One such enthusiast is Katie Blake Cook, 33, a land surveyor from Frederic, WI. When Cook was four, she began joining her parents as they hunted from a platform built in a tree, known as a deer stand. Being in the woods early in the morning taught her to appreciate nature and inspired her to work to protect it. And to this day, joining others on the annual deer hunt helps inform her work and inspires her to remain committed to resource protection. "This year opening day was pretty successful," she says of the hunt. "I got to my stand well before daylight, and in the darkness, I could hear leaves crunching around me through the woods. I could hear the crunching close to my stand but couldn't see what was making the sound. Later, the ice on all the tree branches began to melt in the sun, and it rained down as the thawing trees snapped and popped." Cook also recalls that last year was a success, because a large gray owl perched on a branch at eye level. "It was eerie to be captured in the gaze of such a huge, graceful, night hunter," she says. "I felt like a mouse."

Despite the decades she's spent hunting, Cook has killed only three or four animals. And after the first one, when she was 12, she cried. Today, she says, the experience is more about enjoying the Mardi Gras-like atmosphere of the northern Wisconsin white-tailed deer season. It's about connecting with her roots and appreciating where her food comes from when others in her hunting party share what they shoot. And primarily it's about understanding wild places and the wild things humans affect every day in ways both big and small. "It's not *easy* to kill an animal, psychologically," says Cook. "The process of watching the wild animal move through its natural environment, deciding to end its life, pulling the trigger, processing the animal into food…it's taxing. It's much easier to remain removed from the gruesome parts of creating food from animals. However, I feel like killing an animal for food myself has allowed me a better opportunity to be respectful of life and its sacrifice than I would have if I only ever wandered through the meat department in a grocery store."

Whether they do it for food, camaraderie, or to be out in nature, the women who hunt in Wisconsin's wilderness share a deep respect for the tradition and for the woods where the animals live. In rural counties with tons of deer, young women routinely join their dads and brothers for long, cold days of tracking (and watching and waiting) in November. Many, like their dads and brothers, return home with grandiose stories about "the one that got away." And sharing these community stories is just as important as the hunt itself.

Meghan Grindell, 33, a medical assistant from Frederic, WI, knows all about that. Her quintessential hunting story involves the day she had a 12-point white-tailed buck in her sight when she was 12 years old. As she crouched just a few feet away in a spot high in the trees, the buck looked around, nose twitching. Behind her, Grindell's dad whispered, "Easy… easy…wait," as she put her finger on the trigger. The deer paused. "Now fire!" her dad urged in her ear. She squeezed the trigger. Click. Nothing. The buck paused, sniffed, and bounded away as they watched. "I heard a whole bunch of not-typical language fly out of my dad's mouth as he hopped up with his gun to fire at the buck," says Grindell, seeming to enjoy the memory of bonding with her dad much more than she seems to regret missing out on that handsome rack of antlers. "Ever since then, I've been hooked."

Grindell went on to participate in many successful family hunts as a teenager, and now, as a busy parent of four, she's hoping to see her kids (including her daughters) follow in her footsteps. "I would never force my girls to hunt—they can choose to take part in any activity they're interested in," she says. But Grindell also concedes she has a deep desire to initiate her girls into the world of the traditional family hunt. "I would love to share what I know with them," she says. "I have wonderful memories of hunting with my dad, and I really think it's good bonding for a father and a daughter or a mother and a daughter. Hopefully my girls' memories will be as fond as mine."

Discussion Questions

1. What assumptions about hunting and gender would prompt Ryan to write "A View to a Kill"? Does your knowledge of and/or experience with hunting confirm or disprove these assumptions?

2. How does the hunting culture described by Ryan relate to Pollan's food chains in "Our National Eating Disorder"? Why?

3. What is the argument in "A View to a Kill"? How is that argument constructed? How is it different or similar to previous articles in this chapter?

4. Go online and find groups, like BOW, for women and/or girls interested in hunting. How do these groups present themselves? What do they say about the women and/or girls interested in hunting?

5. Go to the *Bust* website. What do you think the audience for this magazine is based on that website? What other magazines do you think are geared at this audience? Why?

Gleaning from Gluttony: An Australian Youth Subculture Confronts the Ethics of Waste

Ferne Edwards, David Mercer

Ferne Edwards works extensively within the fields of environmental anthropology, food politics and social movements. Her academic experience includes research on the *Anti-consumerism in the Contemporary West* project, RMIT University, and as Technical Assistant evaluating the Sustainability Street project, Victoria University. In ACSIS (Australian Centre for Science, Innovation and Society), Edwards is the Sustainable Cities Research Officer and part of the Victorian Eco-Innovation Lab project. David Mercer has served on the editorial boards of several journals, including the *Australian Journal of Natural Resources and Policy*, the *Open Environmental Journal* and the *Annals of Leisure Research*. He is an associate professor in RMIT University's Department of International Urban and Environmental Management. Since 2005 he has been an official assessor for the EIANZ's Certified Environmental Practitioner Scheme.

Abstract

As part of the global 'rights to the city' movement and mounting concern over food waste, results are presented here of an ethnographic study of young people in Australia who choose to glean food from supermarket 'dumpster bins' and open markets primarily for political reasons. These youth form part of an international 'freegan' subculture: the belief in 'minimising impact on the environment by consuming food that has literally been thrown away' (*Macmillan English Dictionary Online* 2002). The study explores the emergence of two related subcultures: 'Dumpster Diving' (the act of procuring food from a supermarket dumpster bin for individual consumption) and 'Food Not Bombs' (a global-spanning group who collect left-over food from markets to cook and serve to people on the street). The analysis focuses on the ethics embedded within their alternative consumption diets. These findings are analysed in terms of the creation of their alternative identities performed on temporal–spatial terrains, exemplifying the role of the contemporary activist's use of space, place and culture in relation to social issues.

Introduction

> And when ye reap the harvest of your land, thou shalt not make clean riddance of the corners of thy field when thou reapest, neither shalt thou gather any gleaning of thy harvest: thou shalt leave them unto the poor, and to the stranger.
>
> Leviticus 23: 22

Recent years in the more affluent countries have witnessed an explosion of interest—both in academic circles and more widely—in the ethics of food consumption and production, in differential access to quality food in retail outlets, and in the analysis of different food economies (Norberg-Hodge et al. 2002; Wrigley 2002; Singer & Mason 2006). Geographers have played a leading role in this resurgence. In part, research interest has accelerated because of various 'food scares' that have shaken public confidence in agricultural production and distribution systems in the UK, in particular (Lyons et al. 2004; Scrinis 2007). In part, it is also a response to concerns over escalating greenhouse gas emissions associated with expanded 'food miles' as well as growing recognition of the enormous global divide separating the majority, who are undernourished, and those in the affluent world who often exhibit obesity and attendant health problems associated with overeating. In many cases, too, as the 'food deserts' research has highlighted, there are often pockets of serious disadvantage in affluent countries where there is only limited access to healthy and nutritious food (Whelan et al. 2002). The most recent of the regular, population health surveys conducted in Victoria, for example, revealed the disturbing finding that 1 in 20 of those surveyed ran out of food in the previous year. Moreover, almost 25 per cent reported that this happened on a regular basis (Department of Human Services 2005).[1] At the other extreme, farmers' markets are becoming increasingly popular with more affluent consumers willing to pay higher prices for good-quality, fresh farm produce.

The issue of food security is becoming increasingly important at both the national and local scales in all countries. Adapted from California's Community Food Security Coalition (www.foodsecurity.org), this has been defined in Australia by VicHealth (2005, p. 2) as:

> …the state in which all persons obtain nutritionally adequate, culturally acceptable, safe foods regularly through local non-emergency sources. Food security broadens the traditional conception of hunger, embracing a systemic view of the causes of hunger and poor nutrition within a community while identifying the changes necessary to prevent their occurrence. Food security programs confront hunger and poverty.

In Victoria, the State government agency, VicHealth, has taken a lead role in promoting research into identifying those groups most vulnerable to food insecurity and—through its Food For All program—encouraging action at the grassroots level. Certain local municipalities, especially in inner-city Melbourne, have been active in addressing the food insecurity question. With the highest level of public housing rental tenancy in Victoria, the City of Yarra has been particularly proactive.

Another related issue that has captured both public and academic attention—and is the main focus of this paper—is that of waste (Chappell & Shove 1999; Bulkeley et al. 2005). Waste in general, and food waste in particular, challenge our environmental integrity and the recklessness of overproduction and the attendant over-consumptive lifestyles. It also raises issues of value and social inequality (Thompson 1979; Hawkins & Muecke 2002; Scanlan 2005; Hawkins 2006). It has been estimated, for example, that Australians waste nearly 3.3 million tonnes of food each year (Smith 2005), and a more recent study in the UK has found that around 33 per cent of all food purchased by households is thrown away (or 15 pence for every pound spent) (Waste and Resources Action Programme 2007). This excess garbage places undue pressure on landfill sites, contributing to environmental degradation and greenhouse gas emissions. Food waste occurs at all stages along the food chain from field to market to landfill, with Australian research finding that the most wasteful consumers are young people aged between 18 and 24 years (Hamilton & Mail 2003a). Interestingly, this Australian 'demographic' also reflects the largest decline in environmental concern over the years, falling from 57 per cent in 2001 to 49 per cent in 2004 (ABS 2004; Bentley et al. 2004).

However, notwithstanding this disturbing trend, two international youth subcultures have emerged to confront the scandal of food waste produced within over-consuming capitalist societies. Individuals within the subcultures of 'Dumpster Divers' (DD)[2] and 'Food Not Bombs' (FNB)[3] live their environmental and social justice beliefs by practising alternative consumption choices. These lifestyle choices go beyond 'sustainable consumption' options, such as green or ethical consumption, to participate in 'anti-consumerist' activities, choosing to reduce their consumption by transforming their housing, transport, work practices and social values, rather than simply purchasing 'environmentally friendly' products. These 'anti-consumerist' lifestyles are often coupled with political and environmental activism that can span the globe through the actions of what have been termed highly mobile flaneur activists (Leontidou 2006).

Consisting mainly of young people, individuals who DD and participate in FNB procure their food in accordance with the philosophy of 'freeganism'. This is a term first coined around the year 2000, but the concept has much in common with the earlier 'voluntary simplicity' movement (Elgin 1981). It is defined as the belief in 'minimising impact on the environment by consuming food that has literally been thrown away' (*Macmillan English Dictionary Online* 2002).[4] DD and FNB represent freegan subcultures as DD procure food from supermarket dumpster bins for individual consumption, while FNB possesses the characteristics of an urban social movement comprised of a globally spanning group who redistribute organic food donated by markets and shops to feed the urban poor at no cost. FNB, for example, have been particularly active in New Orleans in the aftermath of Hurricane Katrina. Another Australian equivalent charity organisation is SecondBite. Each Sunday, after trading has ceased at one of Melbourne's largest fruit and vegetable markets, the South Melbourne Market, some 500 kg of unsold produce is sorted by 85 volunteers and distributed to the needy (Port Phillip Leader 2007). Little academic research has been conducted into these forms of political gleaning (Lack 1995; Clark 2004; Rush 2006), though as the quotation from the Bible at the start of this article clearly demonstrates, the principle of gleaning has a very long heritage. In more recent times (in 2000) the practice was publicised in Agnes Varda's French documentary film *The Gleaners and I.*

The research presented in this paper bridges the divide between the broad research areas of food production consumption (Holloway et al. 2007) and urban social movements demanding a right to the city (Lefebvre 1968; Pickvance 2003; Massey 2005). It also links in strongly with Gibson-Graham's (2006) important project on post-capitalist politics and provides an important alternative interpretation of Australian youths' consumption patterns, documenting how subcultures use anticonsumption practices to ascribe alternative identities to oppose mainstream Western societal norms, while negotiating inequalities within a neoliberal framework.

Based on ethnographic research, we document and analyse how young people in Australian cities are drawn to these subcultures and the ethics embedded within their alternative consumption diets. These findings are analysed in terms of the creation of their alternative identities performed on temporal-spatial terrains to exemplify the role of the contemporary activist's use of space, place and culture in relation to social issues.

Background to DD and FNB

DD (or 'dumpstering', 'dumping', 'binning', 'bin scaben', 'trashing', 'scabbing' or 'skip-dipping') has existed for as long as there have been dumpsters and excessive waste. The practice of DD also extends to 'diving' for non-food items and scavenging materials. In the USA the term 'dumpster diving' is also used in relation to identity theft, the stealing of sensitive information from rubbish bins. DD and FNB often have a strong political connotation, with members of these subcultures gleaning food as a symbolic, political act against capitalist overproduction and waste. This 'political gleaning' contrasts with the foraging of wild foods (such as is a legal entitlement in Scandinavia), the scavenging of recyclable materials, or food scavenging as practised by the homeless. For this study, we focus on people who choose to glean food for a blend of economic, political and environmental reasons within these subcultures.

Food Not Bomb's history is documented from its political origins in the USA in 1980 when a group of friends were protesting against the Seabrook nuclear power station project in Cambridge, Massachusetts. FNB originally formed as the Cambridge Collective, evolving through the Affinity Group and the National Organising Period stages to number over 214 autonomous Chapters in the present international era (Butler & McHenry 2000; Food Not Bombs Seattle 2004). These groups share a common praxis endorsed by shared experiences and ideas gained from working together at servings, through participation at fundraising events, and from representation on international websites, and from participation at annual international FNB convergences (Food Not Bombs 2005; Food Not Bombs News 2005).

Methodology

The main source of information for this study was provided by interviews with 30 participants who were involved in freegan activities mainly within Australia, although some had also participated in freegan activities in the USA, the UK and Mexico. The interviews were qualitative and semi-structured, and predominantly conducted individually. In addition, we undertook ethnographic research of associated freegan activities such as FNB food collection, preparation, serving and fundraising, 'dumpster dinners', warehouse parties, gleaning co-operatives, and activist events such as Critical Mass and Reclaim the Streets, both of which seek to reclaim the streets from cars.

Respondents were selected from attendance at such events or recommended by participating friends. The sample consisted of 20 men and 10 women, ranging in age from 18 to 58 years, with the majority in their early 20s. Two Australian capital cities served as the research bases for the study, allowing site comparisons. This sample provided a useful overview of contemporary political gleaners as it represented people who: (i) practised either DD or FNB, (ii) practised both activities, and (iii) one person who exclusively collected 'wasted' food put aside by supermarket and bakery staff in separate boxes and bags. While most of the people interviewed moved within similar subcultures, the sample also included people who practised gleaning activities outside of these subgroups. Also, seven people interviewed no longer participated in either DD or FNB, providing insights as to why participants discontinue these activities.

Who participates, and why?

The people drawn to Dumpster Divers and Food Not Bombs are predominantly male, in their mid-20s, and from well-educated middle-class backgrounds. They have strong ideological beliefs, basing their lifestyle choices, such as diet and career choices, on ethical bases. For instance, freegans consider where and how their food is produced in terms of environmental and humanitarian concerns and many respondents devoted much of their time to activism. As also found in Fincham's (2007) recent study of the bicycle courier subculture in the UK, 'fun' and 'socialising' are two, additional, major motivators for people who dumpster dive and participate in FNB alike. The sociality of gleaned food is evident in the way people first became aware of food 'waste', methods of appropriation of food, and its incorporation within associated activities and activist subcultures. For example, people often became aware of DD and FNB through friends, eating at FNB servings, and through participation in the vegan network or participating in street protests. Associated activities included dumpster dinners, the establishment of dumpster households and the redistribution of DD food to DD-friendly households. People often dumpster dive with their friends, while some FNB members will travel over an hour on public transport to attend a FNB preparation and serving.

Although DD food is generally shared with only DD-friendly people, FNB extends this reach to redistribute gleaned food within the public domain, often drawing together 'punk' subcultures, the disadvantaged, the mentally ill and Indigenous and war veteran communities. These people do not all participate for purely social reasons, but all end up socialising just the same. An FNB participant describes this communion:

> …and the socialising that happens on the street with everyone, all the different people who are brought together for it. Like you've got all your crusties who go and eat there or who cook there, and are into activism and that and come there because it's FNB and its ethical and cool. Then you've got all the people in the commission flats who love it because it's the best and healthiest meal you can get for free on the streets…It's really, really good and you know it—people say it all the time, the regulars who come…(Mas FNB/DD5)[5]

FNB contributes not only to the individual's personal gratification but also the wider community, extending its public outreach to provide regular food drop-offs to various community groups and by feeding people who attend environmental, social and Indigenous justice events.

Associated freegan activities

The freegan philosophy to minimise the impact on the environment by using fewer resources also extends to other anti-consumerist activities. These activities can be defined as the DIY-punk (or 'do-it-yourself' punk) movement. This movement correlates with freegan philosophy, activities and politics by advocating for people to live outside the capitalist system and hence not support environmental exploitation or social injustices embedded within capitalist power structures. Associated DIY-punk activities include squatting, scavenging, living in community warehouses, cycling, second-hand clothes' shopping, fare evasion, 'zine' (magazine) production and making one's own clothes or music. It also complements more conventional ideas of sustainable gardening and housing design—yet materials used to make these gardens ideally would be scavenged rather than purchased (Hoffman 1993). As one FNB participant explains:

> Yep, that's basically really what anarchists do, and it's what FNB started on really. 'X' is a perfect example of that—it's a warehouse set up by people who are within the scene, open to people who want to go to that scene. People can practice there, they have their own recording rooms, they printed their own cds, t-shirts and everything. It was like, you know, no involvement of corporations whatsoever, that's what it really is—an avoidance of corporations…Yep definitely. Capitalism is the opposite of punk. (Fem FNB2)

As another FNB participant elaborates:

> DIY is taking something into your own hands and out of other peoples' hands…With dumpster diving you're taking that back in your own hands, your own life back in your own hands. That's your DIY—if I do it myself and spend less, essentially the more of my life I'm able to spend doing what I'd love to do…Stuff that's beneficial to myself and to the community…It could be about putting out a record that's not a label…I would really like to try and get my own sustainable veggie garden. I make my own clothes; I listen to mainly DIY music. (Mas FNB/ DD6)

Aside from dumpster diving, squatting—the occupation of privately owned buildings that are not being used (Labourlawtalk n.d.)—is another key example of a DIY-punk activity.[6] A dumpster diver comments:

> Yep, [there's] definitely a correlation between dumpster diving and squatting—they've basically let the house become a bin…Thrown it away…We used to have a joke that the house was just a big dumpster…We had all these appliances we DD as well, like sandwich grills, grinders, juicers and stuff. We used to joke that we'd get this garbage and spread it with this garbage, put some garbage in it, stick

in the hot garbage…All the ingredients in the toasted sandwich were dumpstered including the appliance. (Mas FNB/DD5)

This freegan form of 'DIY-punk' demonstrates the acceptance of an 'informal economy' within an alternative economic space, allowing freegans to decrease their dependence on the capitalist economy whilst proving that alternative lifestyles are possible. However, as acknowledged on the CrimethInc. Workers' Collective website, 'being a one-person economy is extremely difficult' (D.B. n.d.). To counter alienation, they advocate for the creation of a DIY-punk community with people who share similar values and practices working together for mutual support (D.B. n.d.).

Activist subcultures

In addition to the overarching DIY-punk theme, there exist overlapping activist subcultures. Each of these has slightly different discourses and practices, yet are involved in Dumpster Divers or Food Not Bombs to different degrees. Members can be identified loosely according to dress, their lifestyle politics and whom they socialise with, yet much overlap and socialisation occurs between the groups. For this reason, and given that people are hesitant to be 'boxed' into static identities, most people are reticent to identify with a particular subgroup. However, according to a dumpster diver (Mas DD5), activist subgroups can be roughly delineated along the following lines:[7]

1. Purist (university) food co-op hippies. The diver elucidates: So they'll all do lots of work at [an environmental park] and plant big beautiful gardens [and] wear really flowing pretty dresses…Most of them won't DD largely because they'll be more into organic food and being healthy and good to your body, but there's edges of that community that will also be into squatting and DD. (Mas DD5)

2. The anarcho-punk community (also known as 'pc-punks'). The anarcho-punks are generally politically aware and 'intellectual'. They are heavily involved in FNB and moderately involved in DD (Mas DD5).

3. The autonomistas represent a smaller activist subculture that arose in Australia out of protests such as at the World Economic Forum in Melbourne on 11 September 2000, and at the Woomera detention centre in South Australia in 2002. Autonomistas are generally well-educated and '…they're all into being really intellectual about their politics and they're autonomist socialists and all…' (Mas DD5). Autonomistas are also often involved in independent media projects.

4. The forest ferals. They are described as sporting 'a shaved head with crusty hair out the back, kinda anti-intellectual' (Mas DD5) who originated in the Jabiluka protests against the mining of uranium in Kakadu National Park since 1998. According to the dumpster diver (who identifies as an autonomista), ferals are central to DD, yet it would be rare to see a feral doing FNB, although they may come to eat at FNB.

Our research found that gleaned food predominates in anarcho-punk and forest feral subcultures, with FNB generally favoured by anarcho-punks and DD by forest ferals. However, these affiliations change over time, with one FNB site which was originally dominated by 'hippies' having since been appropriated by 'punk-ravers',[8] then to become run almost exclusively by 'anarcho-punks' (Fem FNB/DD1; Fem FNB/DD4; Mas FNB/DD8). Furthermore, from the ethnographic research, associated activities such as Reclaim the Streets (a street protest to reclaim street space for pedestrians rather than cars) tended to be dominated by 'crusty-' and 'anarcho-punks', whereas the Students for Sustainability Conference, a national conference held since 1991 for students pursuing environmental and social justice causes, traditionally had a majority of forest ferals in attendance.

The ethics of eating 'garbage'

The selection of gleaned food by participants of DD and FNB depends upon factors such as the potential health risks, personal preference and the source. General foods collected by DD (in declining order of popularity) include vegetables and fruit, damaged packaged goods (such as rice and canned food), bread, eggs and cheese. The range of food available from DD is best explained by a diver:

> Basically, when it comes to food, anything you can think of that the supermarket stocks, you can get it in the bin from organic macadamia nuts to apples to laundry detergent to fertiliser to jars of olives to fetta cheese…(Mas FNB/DD5)

The main FNB site in the study collected fruit and vegetables directly from an organic market. This produce—generally highly priced—is donated by stallholders at the end of the day when no market is to be held on the following day. Food donors in New South Wales and Victoria[9] are protected from liability by the Good Samaritan Law (see Victorian Government 2002), which allows edible, safe food to be given away.

Potential health risks

Although they consume 'garbage', every participant in the study claimed that they had never been aware of falling ill from food either dumpstered or prepared by FNB, except for a single person who ate dumpstered mushrooms wrapped in plastic found in a warm climate (Fem FNB/DD4). These health standards are upheld while keeping within an environmental ethos, by boiling the cutlery frequently and following standard food safety precautions. For dumpstered food, the negotiation of health is ensured through the wide selection of food available, a vegan or vegetarian diet and food preparation knowledge. The condition of the gleaned food is explained by a previous FNB participant:

> There's no high risk food [because there's no meat or dairy] and the food's at its point where it's at its height in ripeness and it's the most nutritionally good when the shops would throw it away…It's because of its shelf life—you can't have something there that would be rotten by the end of the next day…(Fem FNB2)

The Food Not Bombs soup kitchen menu considers the nutritional content of the food, the physical state of its clients (nothing too spicy and providing a variety of dishes for anyone with allergies), and their established food tastes (for example, baked potatoes are offered as a healthy alternative to hot chips). Excess organic produce is also given away at the serving, so people attending can cook their own food during the week.

Personal food preferences

The study revealed that all participants were aware of the ethics of food consumption and related their consumption practices to their beliefs and identity. These dietary preferences reflected predominant environmental and vegan discourses, with participants' diets including alternative forms of freegan diets such as the vegetarian 'dumpsterian' or 'frego' diets, and diets such as 'raw foodism' (a diet consisting of fruit, vegetables, nuts and sprouts), 'veganic' (vegan organic foods), and the consumption of roadkill.

Participants' motivations for dietary preferences include not contributing to demand for products that are ethically unacceptable, such as industrial agriculture which promotes 'chemical, pesticide, industrial waste-ridden food' (Mas FNB/DD3) and animal cruelty. Meat consumption was sometimes considered acceptable to some if farmed sustainably or if found in a dumpster bin or killed by cars. In the latter example, roadkill would be consumed 'to show [animals] the dignity they deserve' (Mas FNB/DD6) by placing value on meat that would otherwise go wasted.

The ethical implications of food consumption were taken to the extreme by one FNB participant who supported the dietary preference of vegan 'raw foodism', defined as 'you don't eat anything that is cooked or manufactured' (Mas FNB1), due to a combination of animal rights ethics, waste and nutrition. Furthermore, many participants raised the issue of fossil fuels and food consumption, favouring locally-based diets as they used '…less transport, energy, refrigeration, packaging' (Mas FNB1). These beliefs in supporting local, sustainable food production were further endorsed by some participants who complemented dumpstered food by purchasing organic food from local independent stores.

This ethical consideration of diet was upheld by the practice of FNB which served either vegan, vegetarian or often organic food. The denomination of the FNB menu emerged from the preference and physical environment of each local chapter, illustrating FNB's capacity to adjust to different circumstances and promote its message and function throughout the world.

However, the central issues of the redistribution of waste and the issue of maintaining strict vegan food came into conflict in 2005 at a second FNB site. As one FNB participant explains:

> This one time we cooked up this incredible meal but then we put in some breadcrumbs. And this guy found that the breadcrumbs had very small traces of an additive that was made from fish oil. And this guy was adamant that we couldn't serve this food and there was tons of it and it was really good. (Fem FNB/DD1)

She continues to explain that—as they had to respect everyone's opinion because of FNB's consensus decision-making process—they chose not to serve the food. Instead, FNB participants who were not strict vegans took the food home.

Freegan food sources

Ethical factors for choosing Dumpster Diver locations often take priority over other considerations such as the quality and quantity of food, proximity to food collection locations and the degree of ease. These ethical factors consider issues such as the company's history, labour conditions, the environmental and social background of the products they sell, and the sheer volume of waste they generate that contributes towards environmental degradation. Although people can DD from almost any source, big supermarket chains are favoured over smaller independent stores because they generally support large-scale industrial farming, often importing foods from overseas to the detriment of local farmers, while endorsing the unequal distribution of wealth between the poor and affluent worlds.[10] Multinational chains are also chosen on account of their impersonal nature and their use of micromanagement techniques within the stores to induce citizens to consume more (Mas FNB/DD3). The latter was a particular point of criticism in the recent UK study mentioned above (Waste and Resources Action Programme (WRAP) 2007). The WRAP report was strongly critical of supermarket chains for packaging up too many items in pre-packaged packs of fruit, vegetables and meat.

By targeting these large corporations, dumpster divers may be perceived as modern day 'Robin Hoods', redistributing wealth to people who need it, choosing to spend their money and time on products and activities that endorse their politics. A dumpster diver recalls a fine example of this style of behaviour:

> When we found thirty frypans in the dumpster…[we felt] that the public should have those frypans…We put them all in a trolley and took them all down to the Brotherhood [a local charity store]. (Mas DD9)

People also dumpster dive from small stores but for different reasons. These stores' bins often provide gourmet- or health-related produce, highly valued by those who dive. Given the shops' smaller size, they are often more resourceful with their stock than larger stores, producing less waste overall and investing more time in shop details. As one participant explains the difference in practice:

> The bigger the stores, the less likely they are to have these policies—like smaller organic bakeries will give food…Whereas bigger ones will say it's too much of an effort and chuck it out. (Mas DD9)

Hence, through their alternative consumption, freegans consider and act upon the long-term social and environmental ethics embedded within the food chains of their diets. This freegan consumption often takes place within a social setting, ascribing a sense of collective identity. Thus, the individual and collective identity of freegans and their opposition to mainstream capitalist economy are physically and symbolically ascribed. The next section discusses how freegans choose to construct themselves as 'other'.

Freegans as 'other'

Freegans' ability to construct their identity in order to oppose mainstream Western societal norms through the consumption of food 'waste' occurs in terms of their anarchist discourse, practice and structure, and through their performance of these alternative identities on temporal–spatial terrains. These opposite characteristics are listed in Table 1.

Table 1. Characteristics of gleaners vs 'mainstream' capitalist culture

Gleaning culture	Mainstream capitalist culture
Informal economy	Capitalist economy
Free food	Commodified food
No hierarchy nor organised structure	Hierarchy/organised structure
Chaos/anarchy—order relies on internal control	External control exercised by government and corporations
Food found dumped in bin	Food found stacked neatly on supermarket shelves
Eat 'raw' or 'rotten' foods	Eat 'cooked' foods
'Dirty'	'Hygienically clean'
No label—rely on senses to determine food safety	Rely on label to dictate food state
Slow food/lifestyle	Fast food/lifestyle
Eat food on footpath	Eat food within contained, regulated and often commodified spaces
Social collection, distribution and consumption of food	Greater individualization of food collection, i.e. less social interaction in supermarkets

Freegans' anarchistic discourse and practice

Freegans' political discourse of anarchism rejects capitalism in terms of anticonsumerism, anti-corporatism and anti-bureaucracy. As one respondent describes:

> It's set up so that if you don't consume, you're identity-less and you don't exist, so you find yourself consuming just to feel like you're still here. And especially when travelling, you find yourself quite lonely sometimes and you'll just go to a cafe and drink a coffee just so you're doing something legitimate and that's how people validate their existence on mass scales...(Mas DD9)

This 'othering' has been described by theorists Douglas (1970) and Clark (2004). Douglas (1970) explores the issue of cultural demarcation using the categories of purity and danger. Applying Douglas's theory to the consumption of 'wasted' food, it would be considered 'repulsive and disgusting' by mainstream society as it transcends societal norms by reappropriating food that has been set aside as 'untouchable'. Clark (2004) further examines 'othering' by applying Levi-Strauss's categories of the raw, cooked and rotten to the related topic of punk subculture's ideologies and identities with relation to DD cuisine. He finds that punks generally identify industrially processed (or 'cooked') food as corporate-capitalist 'junk food' which supports cash cropping, causing cancer and leading to the objectification of nature. Punks wishing to break free from the fetishism of products choose to eat 'raw' (unprocessed) or 'rotten' meals (such as stolen natural foods from health shops or groceries from dumpster bins) rather than 'cooked' foods. Clark (2004) explains that by appropriating their provisions outside of the marketplace, punks maintain their anti-consumerist identity by symbolically returning blemished 'cooked' food to a 'raw' status, rendering it acceptable for anarcho-punk consumption. The freegan appropriation of waste can also be viewed as transforming tainted products (including meat) into 'pure' acceptable raw foods, as it places value on products that have been socially devalued as 'waste'.

Freegans' appropriation of 'wasted' food from a bin also sets them apart as an 'other' contrasted to modern consumer culture's preoccupation with domestic cleanliness. The issue of gleaning healthy food from 'garbage' confronts the modern Western concept of cleanliness and hygiene. Notions of cleanliness have altered throughout history and are closely associated with changing concepts of the body. Historically we can identify three distinctive health discourses: humours, miasmas and germs. The former refers to the infiltration of disease through the porous human body by heat or water, while miasmas associate disease with decay and smell. The modern discourse of disease is germ based, which calls for responsible individual behaviour to ensure self-protection (Vigarello 1998; Shove 2003). All three discourses are challenged by the behaviour of gleaners, and especially dumpster divers, who experience the physical proximity of mixed rubbish, strong odours and invisible germs. This changing cultural perception of hygiene illustrates the importance of the socio-political context in defining garbage (see also Hawkins 2006).

The germ-based theory is countered by the 'Hygiene Hypothesis'—the hypothesis that living in an overly clean environment makes us sick. Using this hypothesis, epidemiologist David Strachan attempted to explain how the 'allergy epidemic' rose dramatically in industrialised countries due to cleaner living standards and smaller family sizes over the last 30 years. As a consequence, individuals received less exposure to infection during childhood, thus weakening their immune systems (see Stanwell-Smith & Bloomfield 2004). The sentiments of this hypothesis are often raised by freegans. As expressed by one respondent:

> I've done some travelling…And I really know that we have a super-high standard of food, and we don't expect to eat things that have a blemish on them or little weevils in them. Does that really affect your health? I don't believe it does…[I recently read an] article

about diabetes and the high level of cleanliness—that the immune system hasn't got enough to deal with so it's attacking itself…I think you can maintain a reasonable standard and still be a gleaner…(Fem Gleaner)

And a joking remark that also attacks the mainstream understanding of hygiene:

'Yes, definitely…me and my friend used to have this joke: for a healthier immune system, lick the walls of a dumpster…' (Mas FNB/DD5).

Another participant further questions this notion of cleanliness in relation to the generally accepted practice of chemical 'hygiene':

Modern health inspectors are so fastidious about germs that they don't stop to consider chemicals…How many industrial chemicals are used in cleaning stuff that are not beneficial to your health? (Mas FNB/DD2)

Rather than relying on use-by dates to tell them what food is edible and safe, freegans use their innate senses of touch, taste and smell. This attitude marks a conscious shift away from corporate control enabling the diver to reclaim a connection to their senses and to the natural world.

Freegan anarchist structure

The discourse of anarchy among the subcultures is also apparent as a lack of organised or formalised structure. For example, FNB has no hierarchy or single person in control. Delight in anarchy is also symbolised by the jumbled collection of food from the bin found among the squashed, rotten and discarded. Gleaning as an informal economy also challenges the Western assumption that neoliberalism is the only viable global economic option. Ironmonger (1996, cited in Gibson-Graham 2003, p. 55) acknowledges that 30–50 per cent of the total economic output of the developed and developing worlds takes place within the non-commodity sector. The act of gleaning, and thus DIY-punk, reaffirms freegans' identities as 'citizens' rather than 'consumers', illustrating that (albeit partial) alternative economies do exist and are viable. Gibson-Graham (1996, pp. x–xi) claims that the diversity of 'non-capitalist ones had been relatively "invisible" because the concepts and discourses that could make them "visible" have themselves been marginalised and suppressed'. A more recent text (Gibson-Graham 2006) provides many concrete examples of 'community economies' and challenges the hegemony of an undifferentiated capitalist economy. In addition, Clode (2007) has provided a useful guide to the rich diversity of alternative economies that now exist and are expanding rapidly in the UK.

Performing difference through the use of time

Increased time is required to collect and prepare gleaned meals in con-trast to corporate fast food consumption, as many dumpster divers (after the initial thrill) choose to take fruit and vegetables home to wash and cook, rather than consuming processed foods. This anti-consumerist stance is further endorsed by the freegans' choice to work as little as pos-sible in low-paying, low-skilled employment, preferring to spend their time on activities that they personally value, such as activist campaigns, creative projects or social occasions. This chosen time allocation paral-lels a preference for a 'slow' lifestyle, reconstructing temporality to their personal values rather than endorsing capitalist values of modernisation and speed (see Parkins 2004). The alternative 'work ethic' perspective is expressed online by CrimethInc. Workers' Collective, which unites un-happiness with low-skilled work, as it is repetitive, there is little choice in activities and because it often does not directly benefit humanity. Happiness, instead, is associated with creativity, working actively on proj-ects that people value (CrimethInc. Workers' Collective n.d.). This work trend is reflected in freegans' career choices, often choosing studies that will lead to social justice causes rather than money-based careers (for ex-ample, one participant changed their course from neurosurgeon to social worker). In a sense, this freegan lifestyle pattern represents an extension of Hamilton and Mail's (2003b, p. 8) concept of 'downshifting': 'people who make a voluntary longterm lifestyle change that involves accepting significantly less income and consuming less'. Downshifting is often used to describe an older and wealthier demographic, while the freegan case study broadens this term by representing a younger population who have the opportunities to earn money, but choose instead to live out their so-cial beliefs.

Performing difference through the use of space

The freegans' consumption of food on the public footpath also feeds into the anarchistic 'other' in the public presentation of an alternative economic space. While many respondents would like to present DD as a public political statement to highlight the waste and inequalities present within the capitalist system, they felt that it should remain a private (or hidden) activity due to the threat of heightened security and potential loss of food supply.

The private behaviour of Dumpster Divers contrasts sharply with the public nature of Food Not Bombs. FNB is seen as a public vehicle to educate people about the extent of food waste resulting from Western over-consumption of resources and to visualise and partially address social inequalities existing within the heart of the city. FNB serving locations often reflect the permaculture concept of the 'edge' (Crabtree 1999) located at the interface or overlap between two ecosystems, on street corners shouldering poor and affluent communities. These fringe territories convey the activists' identity and message to a range of social 'bodies' within this communicative zone. From the FNB sites in the study, a broad spectrum of people ranging from business commuters, people going out to dinner or art exhibitions, to university students and travellers witnessed FNB feeding a blend of punks, 'ferals' and the homeless and hungry. Hetherington (2004, p. 170) expresses the public reappearance of 'unfinished disposal' as 'haunting': where the act of second burial, such as disposal at the end of the market day, has failed (see also Gordon 1997). According to Hetherington (2004), 'haunting' represents an unacknowl-edged lingering of guilt, such as the wasting of food while people are hun-gry. The reappropriation of food by members of FNB conveys the public message of capitalist impotence, with its mismanagement of resources and inability to protect its citizens from hunger. As such, the urban streetscape represents a key 'haunting' site to contest the capitalist erosion of the realms of common provision, the commodification of resources and rights, and social inequalities (Burgmann 2003).

However, the occupation of this public space sometimes needs to be negotiated with other communities that are often 'invisible' to the gen-eral public. Some friction has occurred at FNB serving sites where the predominance of punk youth attending the serving encroached on an Indigenous place, intimidating the homeless and disrespecting the site. This conflict raises the issue of the exclusivity of punk members and ferals who adopt distinct dress codes and behaviours. This community's 'other-ing' makes them unapproachable to some, compromising their ability to project their message to the general public. As one participant explained:

> Yeah—I just don't think the people who do it have a public per-sona that would let a broad demographic of people understand the issues…I think the general public are kind of scared…whereas the homeless people are just jolly people who are happy that they're get-ting fed. (Fem FNB2)

This use of space as an opposition to mainstream behaviours is also il-lustrated by the activities of Food Not Bombs and its relationship to other soup kitchens. One key difference between FNB and other soup vans is that after serving, FNB participants serve themselves and sit down on the street kerb to eat their dinner with whoever attended. This action dis-solves any symbolic and physical boundaries that normally exist between those who serve and those who are served by people at other soup kitch-ens. As one FNB participant explains:

The other thing that amazed me is that they [the people at other soup vans] never ate the food…And we'd offer them food…and the guy would say that he'd try not to eat on these days so I can identify with the cause, and we're like, the hunger cause? I find it really patronising for these people to come and serve people food and not eat it themselves, as if it's not good enough for them…Whereas FNB is completely different because you've got all these students and activists and just bums…And we sit down and have a meal together and it's this big social occasion where everyone is on the same level and there's no 'I'm the server, I'm the pious server'. (Mas FNB/DD5)

Food Not Bombs also provides an alternative 'ideological space' to the environment of many religious-based soup kitchens. Studies by Sager and Stephens (2005, p. 297) identify that people eating at proselytising soup kitchens find them 'coercive, hypocritical, condescending, and conflicting with their beliefs'. One post-FNB member outlines the differences between her father's church soup van and FNB:

[My dad]…does free brekkies like FNB but they preach to homeless people…How it's not free at all as it comes with a price of Christianity, like preaching, which is what's so beautiful about FNB because in an anarchistic way there's no political view that's being forced onto people like religion or dogma. (Fem FNB/DD3)

Conclusion

In this study, we have described and analysed a subculture that defies and provides an alternative to Western mainstream culture's consumption practices. The people drawn to this Australian freegan subculture are primarily young, male, well-educated, politically motivated, from the middle-class and are involved in activism. Through their shared consumption of food 'waste' they construct themselves as a social 'other', working alongside other activist groups to contribute towards greater environmental and social justice.

In a period dominated by a succession of Australian governments espousing a neoliberal ethic, these groups strive to bridge the gap between the rich and those the welfare system fails. Freegans, and more specifically participants of FNB, do this through the creation of a communitarian 'third space' between the public and private sectors. Through their alternative consumption practices, participants within freegan subcultures challenge Western mainstream societal norms by contesting conventional notions of hygiene, the use of public space, and temporality in the form of downshifting. Ultimately, they represent anti-consumerist subcultures that broaden the ethics of responsibility from the individual to consider the longterm and far-reaching consequences of conventional industrial agricultural practices both within the West and developing worlds. This ethnographic study provides a fuller understanding of contemporary Australian youth's attitudes towards consumer culture, whilst contributing to social theory in the fields of youth identity construction and anti-consumerism. It also adds an additional 'food economy' category to the classificatory scheme recently produced by Holloway et al. (2007).

This study has raised many more questions than could be addressed within this article. Further research could be conducted into other forms of freegan practices such as squatting, links to international anti-consumerist movements and the effectiveness of government vs. grassroots charity. The future of freeganism could also be explored with the international increase of Food Not Bombs Chapters and freegan web- and blog-sites. One interesting recent development has been heightened media interest in Dumpster Divers, in particular. What until recently was an activity known to relatively few has now become much more widely discussed in the print and electronic media, leading some supermarkets (perhaps fearful of legal action) to constrain this activity by locking dumpster bins and/or donating 'waste' food to central collection agencies such as VicRelief for later distribution to charity outlets.

Freegans are more than 'kids playing in bins for fun'. Freeganism has emerged within a rapidly changing world bombarded with growing incidences of terrorism, global warming-related disasters and recently introduced work casualisation and anti-terrorism laws, which together threaten free speech, the physical environment and social equality. The freegan counter-community shows that a commitment towards finding alternatives for greater social equality and environmental sustainability persists among youth in Australian society. Eating 'garbage' may not be the answer for all, but it is actively seeking change whilst symbolically illustrating the excesses of the West.

Acknowledgements

In addition to one anonymous referee especially, the authors would like to thank the following for their comments on an earlier draft of this paper: Dr. Anitra Nelson, RMIT University, Melbourne, and Professor Lily Kong, National University of Singapore. The authors would also like to thank all who participated in the interviews as well as Dr. Ruth Lane and Pam Morgan, RMIT University, for ongoing debate and information sharing around issues of waste and food security in contemporary urban Australia.

Notes

1. By contrast, a recent survey of low-income diets and nutrition in the UK (the LIDNS study) came up with the perhaps surprising finding that there is little difference in the nutritional value of the diets of the poorest 15 per cent of the population than the average for that country (see Nelson et al. 2007).

2. See www.dumpsterdiving.net

3. See www.foodnotbombs.net

4. See www.freegan.info

5. The respondents are coded to protect their identities. 'Mas' is male respondent, 'Fem' is female respondent, 'FNB' is participates in FNB, 'DD' is participates in DD, and 'FNB/DD' is participates in both FNB and DD activities.

6. The perception and legalities of 'squatting' vary according to where it is practised. For example, squatting is sanctioned by the state in the Netherlands.

7. Please note that these observations are based on the respondent's opinions and do not serve as an authoritative definition of each of these subcultures.

8. Punk-raver scene: this scene refers to a youth culture that participates in outdoor parties, which are often arranged outside mainstream societal procedures and are often associated with party drugs (Fem FNB/DD4).

9. Also present in national legislation in the USA.

10. One DD participant noted this discrepancy of wealth and its consequences for the developing world when she established a FNB at Cancun, Mexico, in defiance of the World Trade Organisation's conference (Fem FNB/DD3).

References

AUSTRALIAN BUREAU OF STATISTICS (ABS) (2004) Environmental issues: people's views and practices, ABS, Canberra.

BENTLEY, M., FIEN, J.&NEIL, C. (2004) Sustainable consumption: young Australians as agents of change, report, National Youth Affairs Research Scheme, Canberra.

BULKELEY, H., WATSON, M., HUDSON, R. & WEAVER, P. (2005) 'Governing municipal waste: towards a new analytical framework', Journal of Environmental Policy & Planning 7, pp. 1–23.

BURGMANN, V. (2003) Power, profit and protest: Australian social movements and globalisation, Allen & Unwin, Sydney.

BUTLER, C. & MCKENRY, K. (2000) Food Not Bombs, Sharp Press, Tucson.

CHAPPELL, H. & SHOVE, E. (1999) 'The dustbin: a study of domestic waste, household practices and utility services', International Planning Studies 4, pp. 267–80.

CLARK, D. (2004) 'The raw and the rotten: punk cuisine', Ethnology 43, pp. 19–31.

CLODE, R. (2007) 'Another life is possible', The Ecologist 37, pp. 38–9.

CRABTREE, L. (1999) 'Sustainability as seen from a vegetable garden', unpublished Honours thesis, Department of Human Geography, Macquarie University, Sydney.

CRIMETHINC. WORKERS' COLLECTIVE (n.d.) 'How ethical is the work "ethic"? Reconsidering work and "leisure time"', available at: www.crimethinc.com/library/english/howethic. html (accessed 29 March 2007).

D.B. (n.d.) 'How I spent my permanent vacation', CrimethInc. Workers' Collective website, available at: www.crimethinc.com/library/english/vacation.html (accessed 29 March 2007).

DEPARTMENT OF HUMAN SERVICES (2005) Victorian population health survey, DHS, Melbourne.

DOUGLAS, M. (1970) Purity and danger: an analysis of concepts of pollution and taboo, Routledge & Kegan Paul, London.

ELGIN, D. (1981) Voluntary simplicity, Morrow, New York.

FINCHAM, B. (2007) "Generally speaking people are in it for the cycling and the beer": bicycle couriers, subculture and enjoyment', Sociological Review 55, pp. 189–202.

FOOD NOT BOMBS (2005) Food Not Bombs website, available at: www. foodnotbombs.net (accessed 29 March 2007).

FOOD NOT BOMBS NEWS (2005) Food Not Bombs News website, available at: www. fnbnews.org (accessed 29 March 2007).

FOOD NOT BOMBS SEATTLE (2004) Seattle Food Not Bombs website, available at: www. scn.org/activism/foodnotbombs (accessed 29 March 2007).

GIBSON-GRAHAM, J.K. (1996) The end of capitalism (as we knew it): a feminist critique of political economy, Blackwell, Oxford.

GIBSON-GRAHAM, J.K. (2003) An ethics of the local, Rethinking Marxism 15, pp. 49–74.

GIBSON-GRAHAM, J.K. (2006) Post-capitalist politics, University of Minnesota Press, Minneapolis.

GORDON, A. (1997) Ghostly matters, University of Minnesota Press, Minneapolis.

HAMILTON, C. & MAIL, E. (2003a) Overconsumption in Australia: a seachange in pursuit of happiness, Australia Institute, Canberra.

HAMILTON, C. & MAIL, E. (2003b) Downshifting in Australia, Australia Institute, Canberra.

HAWKINS, G. (2006) The ethics of waste, University of New South Wales Press, Sydney.

HAWKINS, G. & MUECKE, S. (eds) (2002) Culture and waste: the creation and destruction of value, Rowman & Littlefield, Lanham, MD.

HETHERINGTON, K. (2004) 'Secondhandedness: consumption, disposal, and absent presence', Environment and Planning D: Society and Space 22, pp. 157–73.

HOFFMAN, J. (1993) The art and science of dumpster diving, Loompanics Unlimited, Washington, DC.

HOLLOWAY, L., KNEAFSEY, M., VENN, L., COX, R., DOWLER, E. & TUOMAINEN, H. (2007) 'Possible food economies: a methodological framework for exploring food production–consumption relationships', Sociologia Ruralis 47, pp. 1–19.

LABOURLAWTALK (n.d.) Labour Law Talk Dictionary webpage, available at: http://encyclopedia.laborlawtalk.com/Squatter (accessed 29 March 2007).

LACK, T. (1995) 'Consumer society and authenticity: the (il)logic of punk practices', Undercurrent 3, available at: www.uoregon.edu/uc3/3-lack.html (accessed 29 March 2007).

LEFEBVRE, H. (1968) Le droit a la ville, Anthropos, Paris.

LEONTIDOU, L. (2006) 'Urban social movements: from the "right to the city" to transnational spatialities and flaneur activists', City 10, pp. 259–68.

LYONS, K., BURCH, D., LAWRENCE, G. & LOCKIE, S. (2004) 'Contrasting paths of corporate greening in antipodean agriculture: organics and green production', in Jansen, K. & Vellema, A. (eds) Agribusiness and society: corporate responses to environmentalism, market opportunities and public regulation, Zed Books, London, pp. 91–113.

MACMILLAN ENGLISH DICTIONARY ONLINE (2002) 'Freegan', available at: www.macmillandictionary.com/New-Words/040213-freegan. htm (accessed 29 March 2007).

MASSEY, D. (2005) For space, Sage, London.

NELSON, M., ERENS, B., BATES, B., CHURCH, S. & BOSHIER, T. (2007) Low income diet and nutrition survey, Food Standards Agency, London.

NORBERG-HODGE, H., MERRIFIELD, T. & GORELICK, S. (2002) Bringing the food economy home: local alternatives to global agribusiness, Zed Books, London.

PARKINS, W. (2004) 'Out of time: fast subjects and slow living', Time & Society 13, pp. 363–82.

PICKVANCE, C. (2003) 'From urban social movements to urban movements: a review and introduction to a symposium on urban movements', International Journal of Urban and Regional Research 27, pp. 102–9.

PORT PHILLIP LEADER (2007) 'Appetite for good deeds sways market', 3 July.

RUSH, E. (2006) Skip dipping in Australia, Australia Institute, Canberra.

SAGER, R. & STEPHENS, L. (2005) 'Serving up sermons: clients' reactions to religious elements at congregation-run feeding establishments', Nonprofit and Voluntary Sector Quarterly 34, pp. 297–310.

SCANLAN, J. (2005) On garbage, Reaktion Books, London.

SCRINIS, G. (2007) 'From techno-corporate food to alternative agri-food movements', Local–Global: Studies in Community Sustainability 4, pp. 112–40.

SHOVE, E. (2003) Comfort, cleanliness and convenience: the social organization of normality, Berg, Oxford and New York.

SINGER, P. & MASON, J. (2006) The way we eat: why our food choices matter, Rodale, Emmaus, PA.

SMITH, B. (2005) 'Australia wastes three million tonnes of food', The Age (Melbourne) 6 May.

STANWELL-SMITH, R. & BLOOMFIELD, S. (2004) The hygiene hypothesis and implications for home hygiene, report commissioned by the International Scientific Forum on Home Hygiene, Nexthealth SRC, Milan.

THOMPSON, M. (1979) Rubbish theory: the creation and destruction of value, Oxford University Press, Oxford.

VICHEALTH (2005) Healthy eating—food security investment plan 2005–2010, Melbourne.

VICTORIAN GOVERNMENT (2002) Wrongs and other acts (Public Liability Insurance Reform) Act 2002.

VIGARELLO, G. (1998) Concepts of cleanliness: changing attitudes in France since the middle ages, Cambridge University Press, Cambridge.

WASTE AND RESOURCES ACTION PROGRAMME (WRAP) (2007) Packaging innovation to reduce food waste, WRAP, London.

WHELAN, A., WRIGLEY, N., WARM, D. & CANNINGS, E. (2002) 'Life in a "food desert"', Urban Studies 39, pp. 2083–100.

WRIGLEY, N. (2002) '"Food deserts" in British cities: policy context and research priorities', Urban Studies 39, pp. 2029–40.

Discussion Questions

1. How do you react to dumpster diving and dining culture as explained in "Gleaning from Gluttony: An Australian Youth Subculture Confronts the Ethics of Waste"? What causes your reaction?

2. "Gleaning from Gluttony" is an ethnographic study—a study in which a group of people that form a culture or subculture are studied. Based on reading this article, what sort of research is done in an ethnographic study? What is the rhetorical effect of that research?

3. What are the different groups involved in dumpster diving and dining? How are they different?

4. Research the freegan movement in the United States. How is it similar to the Australian movement described in this article? How is it different?

5. Look at an encyclopedia entry on gleaning. How does that entry define gleaning? What historic tradition does gleaning have? How are the authors of "Gleaning from Gluttony" using that tradition?

6. "Gleaning from Gluttony: An Australian Youth Subculture Confronts the Ethics of Waste" mentions several subcultures. Choose one of those subcultures and research it. How would you define this subculture? Why do they exist? Do you know of anything similar in Oklahoma? How is it similar? If not, can you find anything similar? Why or why not?

The Year of the Flood

Margaret Atwood

Margaret Atwood is a Canadian poet, novelist, literary critic, essayist, and environmental activist. She is among the most-honored authors; she has won the Arthur C.
Clarke Award and the Prince of Asturias award for Literature, has been shortlisted for
the Booker Prize five times, winning once, and has been a finalist for the Governor
General's Award seven times, winning twice. *Oryx and Crake* and *The Year of the Flood*
are Atwood's two concurrent dystopian novels. They take place in a future in which
corporations have taken over all government institutions. Practices like genetic engineering run completely amok without institutions to regulate the corporations. In *The
Year of the Flood*, Atwood focuses on an environmental religious cult, the Gardeners,
who resist the corporate world in which they live through removal from the greater
society, vegetarianism, and sustainable living. The novel has two speakers, both former members of the cult, Toby and Ren. This excerpt focuses on Ren and her description of living as a Gardener as a child.

Chapter 12

When Lucerne and Zeb first took me away from the Exfernal World to
live among the Gardeners, I didn't like it at all. They smiled a lot, but they
scared me: they were so interested in doom, and enemies, and God. And
they talked so much about Death. The Gardeners were strict about not
killing life, but on the other hand they said Death was a natural process,
which was sort of a contradiction, now that I think about it. They had the
idea that turning into compost would be just fine. Not everyone might
think that having your body become part of a vulture was a terrific future
to look forward to, but the Gardeners did. And when they'd start talking
about the Waterless Flood that was going to kill everybody on Earth, except maybe them — that gave me nightmares.

None of it scared the real Gardener kids. They were used to it. They'd
even make fun of it, or the older boys would—Shackie and Croze and
their pals. "We're all gonna diiiie," they'd say, making dead-person faces.
"Hey, Ren. Want to do your bit for the Cycle of Life? Lie down in that
dumpster, you can be the compost." "Hey, Ren. Want to be a maggot? Lick
my cut!"

"Shut up," Bernice would say. "Or you're going into that dumpster yourself because I'm shoving you in!" Bernice was mean, and she stood her
ground, and most kids would back off. Even the boys would. But then I'd
owe Bernice, and I'd have to do what she said.

Shackie and Croze would tease me, though, when Bernice wasn't around
to push back at them. They were slug-squeezers, they were beetle-eaters.

They tried to gross you out. They were trouble — that's what Toby called them. I'd hear her saying to Rebecca, "Here comes trouble."

Shackie was the oldest; he was tall and skinny, and he had a spider tattoo on the inside of his arm that he'd punched in himself with a needle and some candle soot. Croze was a stumpier shape, with a round head and a missing side tooth, which he claimed had been knocked out in a street battle. The had a little brother whose name was Oates. They didn't have any parents; they'd had some once, but their father had gone off with Zeb on some special Adam trip and had never come back, and then their mother had left, telling Adam One she'd send for them when she'd got herself established. But she never had.

The Gardener school was in a different building from the Rooftop. It was called the Wellness Clinic because that's what used to be in there. It still had some leftover boxes full of gauze bandages, which the Gardeners were gleaning for crafts projects. It smelled of vinegar: across the hallway from the schoolrooms was the room the Gardeners used for their vinegar making.

The benches at the Wellness Clinic were hard; we sat in rows. We wrote on slates, and they had to be wiped off at the end of each day because the Gardeners said you couldn't leave words lying around where our enemies might find them. Anyway, paper was sinful because it was made from the flesh of trees.

We spent a lot of time memorizing things and chanting them out loud. The Gardener history, for instance — it went like this:

> *Year One, Garden just begun; Year Two, still new; Year*
> *Three, Pilar started bees; Year Four, Burt came in the door;*
> *Year Five, Toby snatched alive; Year Six, Katuro in the mix;*
> *Year Seven, Zeb came to our heaven.*

Year Seven should have said that I came too, and my mother, Lucerne, and anyway it wasn't heaven, but the Gardeners liked their chants to rhyme.

> *Year Eight, Nuala found her fate; Year Nine, Philo began to shine.*

I wanted Year Ten to have Ren in it, but I didn't think it would.

The other things we had to memorize were harder. Mathematical and science things were the worst. We also had to memorize every saint's day, and every single day had at least one saint and sometimes more, or maybe a feast, which meant over four hundred of those. Plus what the saints had done to get to be saints. Some of them were easy. Saint Yossi Leshem of

Barn Owls—well, it was obvious what the answer was. And Saint Dian Fossey, because the story was so sad, and Saint Shackleton, because it was heroic. But some of them were really hard. Who could remember Saint Bashir Alouse, or Saint Crick, or Podocarp Day? I always got Podocarp Day wrong because what was a Podocarp? It was an ancient kind of tree, but it sounded like a fish.

Our teachers were Nuala for the little kids and the Buds and Blooms Choir and Fabric Recycling, and Rebecca for Culinary Arts, which meant cooking, and Surya for Sewing, and Mugi for Mental Arithmetic, and Pilar for Bees and Mycology, and Toby for Holistic Healing with Plant Remedies, and Burt for Wild and Garden Botanicals, and Philo for Meditation, and Zeb for Predator-Prey Relationships and Animal Camouflage. There were some other teachers — when we were thirteen, we'd get Katuro for Emergency Medical and Marushka Midwife for the Reproductive System, whereas all we'd had so far was Frog Ovaries—but those were the main ones.

The Gardener kids had nicknames for all of the teachers. Pilar was the fungus, Zeb was the Mad Adam, Stuart was the Screw because he built the furniture. Mugi was the Muscle, Marushka was the Mucous, Rebecca was the Salt and Peppler, Burt was the Knob because he was bald. Toby was the Dry Witch. Witch because she was always mixing things up and pouring them into bottles and Dry because she was so hard, and to tell her apart from Nuala, who was the Wet Witch because of her damp mouth and her wobbly bum, and because you could make her cry so easily.

In addition to the learning chants, the Gardener kids had rude ones they made up themselves. They'd chant softly — Shackleton and Crozier and the older boys would start, but then we'd all join in:

> Wet Witch, Wet Witch,
>
> Big fat slobbery bitch,
>
> Sell her to the butcher, make yourself rich,
>
> Eat her in a sausage, Wet Wet Witch!

It was especially bad about the butcher and the sausage, because meat of any kind was obscene as far as the Gardeners were concerned. "Stop that," Nuala would say, but then she'd sniffle, and the older boys would give each other a thumbs-up.

We could never make Dry Witch Toby cry. The boys said she was a hard-ass—she and Rebecca were the two hardest asses. Rebecca was jolly on the outside, but you did not push her buttons. As for Toby, she was leathery inside and out. "Don't try it, Shackleton," she would say, even though her back was turned. Nuala was too kind to us, but Toby held us to account, and we trusted Toby more: you'd trust a rock more than a cake.

Chapter 13

I lived with Lucerne and Zeb in a building about five blocks from the Garden. It was called the Cheese Factory because that's what it used to be, and it still had a faint cheesy smell to it. After the cheese it was used for artists' lofts, but there weren't any artists left, and nobody seemed to know who owned it. Meanwhile the Gardeners had taken it over. They liked living in places where they didn't have to pay rent.

Our space was a big room, with some cubicles curtained off—one for me, one for Lucerne and Zeb, one for the violet biolet, one for the shower. The cubicle curtains were woven of plastic-bag strips and duct tape, and they weren't in any way soundproof. This wasn't great, especially when it came to the violet biolet. The Gardeners said digestion was holy and there was nothing funny or terrible about the smells and noises that were part of the end product of the nutritional process, but at our place those end products were hard to ignore.

We ate our meals in the main room, on a table made out of a door. All of our dishes and pots and pans were salvaged—gleaned, as the Gardeners said—except for some of the thicker plates and mugs. Those had been made by the Gardeners back in their Ceramics period, before they'd decided that kilns used up too much energy.

I slept on a futon stuffed with husks and straw. It had a quilt sewed out of blue jeans and used bathmats, and every morning I had to make the bed first thing, because the Gardeners liked neatly made beds, though they weren't squeamish about what they were made of. Then I'd take my clothes down from the nail on the wall and put them on. I got clean ones every seventh day: the Gardeners didn't believe in wasting water and soap on too much washing. My clothes were always dank, because of the humidity and because the Gardeners didn't believe in dryers. "God made the sun for a reason," Nuala used to say, and according to her that reason was for drying our clothes.

Lucerne would still be in bed, it being her favourite place. Back when we'd lived at HelthWyzer with my real father she'd hardly ever stayed inside our house, but here she almost never went out of it, except to go over to the Rooftop or the Wellness Clinic and help the other Gardener women peel burdock roots or make those lumpy quilts or weave those plastic-bag curtains or something.

Zeb would be in the shower: *No daily showers* was one of the many Gardener rules Zeb ignored. Our shower water came down a garden hose out of a rain barrel and was gravity-fed, so no energy was used. That was Zeb's reason for making an exception for himself. He'd be singing:

Nobody gives a hoot,

Nobody gives a hoot,

And that is why we're down the chute,

Cause nobody gives a hoot!

All his shower songs were negative in this way, though he sang them cheerfully, in his big Russian-bear voice.

I had mixed feelings about Zeb. He could be frightening, but also it was reassuring to have someone so important in my family. Zeb was an Adam—a leading Adam. You could tell by the way the others looked up to him. He was large and solid, with a biker's beard and long hair—brown with a little grey in it—and a leathery face, and eyebrows like a barbed-wire fence. He looked as if he ought to have a silver tooth and a tattoo, but he didn't. He was strong as a bouncer, and he had the same menacing but genial expression, as if he'd break your neck if necessary, but not for fun.

Sometimes he'd play dominoes with me. The Gardeners were skimpy on toys—*Nature is our playground*—and the only toys they approved of were sewed out of leftover fabric or knitted with saved-up string, or they'd be wrinkly old-person figures with heads fashioned from dried crabapples. But they allowed dominoes, because they carved the sets themselves. When I won, Zeb would laugh and say, "Atta girl," and then I'd get a warm feeling, like nasturtiums.

Lucerne was always telling me to be nice to him, because although he wasn't my real father he was *like* my real father, and it hurt his feelings if I was rude to him. But then she didn't like it much when Zeb was nice to me. So it was hard to know how to act.

While Zeb was singing in the shower I'd get myself something to eat—dry soybits or maybe a vegetable patty left over from dinner. Lucerne was a fairly terrible cook. Then I'd go off to school. I was usually still hungry, but I could count on a school lunch. It wouldn't be great, but it would be food. As Adam One used to say, Hunger is the best sauce.

I couldn't remember ever being hungry at the HelthWyzer Compound. I really wanted to go back there. I wanted my real father, who must still love me: if he'd known where I was, he'd surely have come to take me back. I wanted my real house, with my own room and the bed with pink bed curtains and the closet full of different clothes in it. But most of all I wanted my mother to be the way she used to be, when she'd take me shopping, or go to the Club to play golf, or off to the AnooYoo Spa to get improvements done to herself, and then she'd come back smelling nice. But if I mentioned anything about our old life, she'd say all was in the past.

She had a lot of reasons for running off with Zeb to join the Gardeners. She'd say their way was best for humankind, and for all the other creatures on Earth as well, and she'd acted out of love, not only for Zeb but for me, because she wanted the world to be healed so life wouldn't die out completely, and didn't it make me happy to know that?

She herself didn't seem all that happy. She'd sit at the table brushing her hair, staring at herself in our one small mirror with an expression that was glum, or critical, or maybe tragic. She had long hair like all the Gardener women, and the brushing and the braiding and the pinning up was a big job. On bad days she'd go through the whole thing four or five times.

On the days when Zeb was away, she'd barely talk to me. Or she'd act as if I'd hidden him. "When did you last see him?" she'd say. "Was he at school?" It was like she wanted me to spy on him. Then she'd be apologetic and say, "How are you feeling?" as if she'd done something wrong to me.

When I'd answer, she wouldn't be listening. Instead she'd be listening for Zeb. She'd get more and more anxious, even angry; she'd pace around and look out our window, talking to herself about how badly he treated her; but when he'd finally turn up, she'd fall all over him. Then she'd start nagging—where had he been, who had he been with, why hadn't he come back sooner? He'd just shrug and say, "It's okay, babe, I'm here now. You worry too much."

Then the two of them would disappear behind their plastic-strip and duct-tape curtain, and my mother would make pained and abject noises I found mortifying. I hated her then, because she had no pride and no restraint. It was like she was running down the middle of the mallway with no clothes on. Why did she worship Zeb so much?

Now I can see how that can happen. You can fall in love with anybody—a fool, a criminal, a nothing. There are no good rules.

The other thing I disliked so much at the Gardeners was the clothes. The Gardeners themselves were all colours, but their clothes weren't. If Nature was beautiful, as the Adams and the Eves claimed—if the lilies of the field were our models—why couldn't we look more like butterflies and less like parking lots? We were so flat, so plain, so scrubbed, so dark.

The street kids—the pleebrats—were hardly rich, but they were glittery. I envied the shiny things, the shimmering things, like the TV camera phones, pink and purple and silver, that flashed in and out of their hands like magician's cards, or the Sea/H/Ear Candies they stuck into their ears to hear music. I wanted their gaudy freedom.

We were forbidden to make friends with the pleebrats, and on their part they treated us like pariahs, holding their noses and yelling, or throwing things at us. The Adams and the Eves said we were being persecuted for our faith, but it was most likely for our wardrobes: the pleebrats were very fashion-conscious and wore the best clothes they could trade or steal. So we couldn't mingle with them, but we could eavesdrop. We got their knowledge that way—we caught it like germs. We gazed at that forbidden worldly life as if through a chain-link fence.

Once I found a beautiful camera phone, lying on the sidewalk. It was muddy and the signal was dead, but I took it home anyway, and the Eves caught me with it. "Don't you know any better?" they said. "Such a thing can hurt you! It can burn your brain! Don't even look at it: if you can see it, it can see you."

Chapter 14

I first met Amanda in Year Ten, when I was ten: I was always the same age as the Year, so it's easy to remember when it was.

That day was Saint Farley of Wolves — a Young Bioneer scavenging day when we had to tie sucky green bandanas around our necks and go out gleaning for the Gardeners' recycled-materials crafts. Sometimes we collected soap ends, carrying wicker baskets and making the rounds of the good hotels and restaurants because they threw out soap by the shovelful. The best hotels were in the rich pleebs—Fernside, Golfgreens, and the richest of all, SolarSpace—and we'd hitch rides to them, even though it was forbidden. The Gardeners were like that: they'd tell you to do something and then prohibit the easiest way to do it.

Rose-scented soap was the best. Bernice and me would take some home, and I'd keep mine in my pillowcase, to drown out the mildew smell of my damp quilt. We'd take the rest to the Gardeners, to be simmered into a jelly in the black-box solarcookers on the Rooftop, then cooled and cut up into slabs. The Gardeners used a lot of soap, because they were so worried about microbes, but some of the cut-up soaps would be set aside. They'd be rolled up in leaves and have strands of twisted grass tied around them, to be sold to tourists and gawkers at the Gardeners' Tree of Life Natural Materials Exchange, along with the bags of worms and the organic turnips and zucchinis and the other vegetables the Gardeners hadn't used up themselves.

That day wasn't a soap day, it was a vinegar day. We'd go to the back entrances of the bars and nightclubs and strip joints and pick through their dump boxes, and find any leftover wine, and pour it into our Young Bioneer enamel pails. Then we'd lug it off to the Wellness Clinic building, where it would be poured into the huge barrels in the Vinegar Room and fermented into vinegar, which the Gardeners used for household cleaning. The extra was decanted into the small bottles we'd gather up during our gleaning, which would have Gardeners labels glued onto them. Then they'd be offered for sale at the Tree of Life, along with the soap.

Our Young Bioneer work was supposed to teach us some useful lessons. For instance: Nothing should be carelessly thrown away, not even wine from sinful places. There was no such thing as garbage, trash, or dirt, only matter that hadn't been put to a proper use. And, most importantly, everyone, including children, had to contribute to the life of the community.

Shackie and Croze and the older boys sometimes drank their wine instead of saving it. If they drank too much, they'd fall down or throw up, or they'd get into fights with the pleebrats and throw stones at the winos. In revenge, the winos would pee into empty wine bottles to see if they could trick us. I never drank any piss myself: all you had to do was smell the opening of the bottle. But some kids had deadened their noses by smoking the butt ends of cigarettes or cigars, or even skunkweed if they could get it, and they'd upend the bottle, then spit and swear. Though maybe those kids drank from the peed-in bottles on purpose, to give themselves an excuse for the swearing, which was forbidden by the Gardeners.

As soon as they were out of sight of the Garden, Shackie and Croze and those boys would take off their Young Bioneer bandanas and tie them around their heads, like the Asian Fusions. They wanted to be a street gang too—they even had a password. "Gang!" they'd say, and the other person was supposed to say "Grene." So, gangrene. The "gang" part was because they were a gang, and the "grene" stood for "green," like their head scarves. It was supposed to be a secret thing just for their gang members, but we all knew about it anyway. Bernice said it was a really good password for them, because gangrene was flesh rot and they were totally rotten.

"Big joke, Bernice," said Crozier. "P.S., you're ugly."

We were supposed to glean in groups, so we could defend ourselves against the pleebrat street gangs or the winos who might grab our pails and drink the wine, or the child-snatchers who might sell us on the chicken-sex market. But instead we'd break up in twos or threes because that way we could cover the territory faster.

On this particular day I started out with Bernice, but then we had a fight. We squabbled constantly, which I took as a sign of our friendship because no matter how viciously we fought we'd always make up afterwards. Some bond held us together: not hard like bone, but slippery, like cartilage. Most likely we both felt insecure among the Gardener kids; we were each afraid to be left without an ally.

This time our fight was over a beaded change purse with a starfish on it that we'd picked out of a trash pile. We coveted finds like that and were always looking for them. The pleeblanders threw a lot of stuff away, because—said the Adams and Eves—they had short attention spans and no morals.

"I saw it first," I said.

"You saw it first last time," said Bernice.

"So what? I still saw it first!"

"Your mother's a skank," said Bernice. That was unfair because I thought so myself and Bernice knew it.

"Yours is a vegetable!" I said. "Vegetable" shouldn't have been an insult among the Gardeners, but it was. "Veena the Vegetable!" I added.

"Meat-breath!" said Bernice. She had the purse, and she was keeping it.

"Fine!" I said. I turned and walked away, I loitered, but I didn't look around, and Bernice didn't hurry after me.

This happened at the mallway, which was called Apple Corners. This was the official name of our pleeb, though everyone called it the Sinkhole because people vanished into it without a trace. We Gardener kids walked through the mallway whenever we could, just looking.

Like everything else in our plebe, this mallway had once been classier. There was a broken fountain full of empty beer cans, there were built-in planters with a lot of Zizzy Froot cans and cigarette butts and used condoms covered (said Nuala) in festering germs. There was a holospinner booth that must once have spun out suns and moons, and rare animals, and your own image if you put money in, but it had been trashed some time ago and now stood empty-eyed. Sometimes we went inside it and pulled the tattered star-sprinkled curtain across, and read the messages left on the walls by the pleebrats. *Monica sucks. So does Darf only betr. UR $? 4 U free, baBc8s! Brad UR ded.* Those pleebrats were so daring, they'd write anywhere or anything. They didn't care who saw it.

The Sinkhole pleebrats went into the holospinner to smoke dope—the booth reeked of it—and they had sex in there: we could tell because of the condoms and sometimes the panties they'd leave behind. Gardener kids weren't supposed to do either one of those things—hallucinogenics were for religious purposes, and sex was for those who'd exchanged green leaves and jumped the bonfire—but the older Gardener kids said they'd done them anyway.

The shops that weren't boarded up were twenty-dollar stores called Tinsel's and Wild Side and Bong's—names like that. They sold feather hats, and crayons for drawing on your body, and T-shirts with dragons and skulls and mean slogans. Also Joltbars, and chewing gum that made your tongue glow in the dark, and red-lipped ashtrays that said, Let Me Blow It For You, and In-Your-Skin Etcha-Tattoos the Eves said would burn your skin down to the veins. You could find expensive stuff at bargain prices that Shackie said were boosted from the SolarSpace boutiques.

Tawdry rubbish, all of it, the Eves would say. If you're going to sell your soul, at least demand a higher price! Bernice and I paid no attention to that. Our souls didn't interest us. We'd peer in the windows, giddy with wanting. *What would you get? We'd say. The LED-light wand? That's baby! The Blood and Roses video? Gross, that's for boys! The Real Woman Stick-on Bimplants, with responsive nipples? Ren, you suck!*

After Bernice had left that day, I wasn't sure what to do. I thought maybe I should just go back, because I didn't feel too safe, alone. Then I saw Amanda, standing on the other side of the mallway with a group of Tex-Mexican pleeb girls. I knew that group by sight, and Amanda had never been with them before.

Those girls were wearing the sort of clothes they usually wore: miniskirts and spangled tops, candyfloss boas around their necks, silver gloves, plasticized butterflies clipped into their hair. They had their Sea/H/Ear Candies and their burning-bright phones and their jellyfish bracelets, and they were showing off. They were playing the same tune on their Sea/H/Ear Candies and they were dancing to it, swiveling their bums, sticking our their chests. They looked as if they already owned everything from every single store and were bored with it. I envied that look so much. I just stood there, envying.

Amanda was dancing too, except she was better. After a while she stopped and stood a little apart, texting on her purple phone. Then she stared straight at me and smiled, and waved her silver fingers. That meant *Come here.*

I checked that no one was looking. Then I crossed the mallway.

Discussion Questions

1. Even though Atwood wrote a piece of fiction, she is making an argument. What is her argument? How is she making it?

2. Go through this excerpt from *The Year of the Flood* and underline where Atwood includes references to recycling, gleaning, and locally produced food. How many references did you find? List them.

3. How does the excerpt from *The Year of the Flood* relate to "Gleaning from Gluttony: An Australian Youth Subculture Confronts the Ethics of Waste"?

4. Based on this excerpt, what do you think the rest of the novel is about? Why?

5. Locate several book reviews of *The Year of the Flood*. What has been the response to the novel? What do you think caused that response?

6. Atwood has written a few dystopias, including *The Year of the Flood*. Look up dystopia. What is the definition? How do you think this form of writing works with the argument you think that Atwood is making in this novel? Why?

FOOD ECONOMICS AND SUBCULTURES

Library Resources

As you have seen from the articles in this section, food culture can be approached from many different angles. Some databases that will help you with further research on the topics presented in this section are **AGRICOLA**, **Global Health**, **PsycINFO**, and **Science Direct**.

AGRICOLA is produced by the National Agricultural Library (NAL). **AGRICOLA** covers subjects related to agriculture such as from animal and veterinary sciences, plant sciences and forestry, agricultural economics, farming and farming systems, food and human nutrition, and earth and environmental sciences. Some of the sources you will find include articles from peer reviewed journals, conference papers, and books. Its coverage extends from 1970–present.

CAB Abstracts is considered the authority on agricultural topics. Like **AGRICOLA**, it covers all aspects of agriculture with a more international approach. There are citations from over 50 languages and 140 countries available in this database, and its coverage extends from 1910–present. Also, **CAB Abstracts** contains **Global Health**, an international public health database.

Science Direct contains full text of over 1,000 journals in the life, physical, medical, technical, and social sciences as well as indexing for journals from co-operating publishers.

If you are uncertain of what you would like to write about, beginning in a more general database such as **Academic Search Premier** or **ProQuest** and typing in search phrases such as "local food" "food and mental health" or "food and economy" may help you find some articles that help you decide where your food culture interests are.

If you already have an idea for a topic, select the database that most appropriately relates to your topic. When you click on **AGRICOLA** within the alphabetical list of databases, you will be taken to EBSCO to conduct your search. Type in phrases related to your topic, such as "food and economy" or "local food" or "genetically modified food." These phrases may call up several results, so you can narrow your results by adding other words or phrases.

Follow a similar strategy with **CAB Abstracts** or **Science Direct**. Though the search platform looks different, keyword searches function in the same way. Type in words related to your topic, such as "health and nutrition" and narrow or broaden your search parameters as needed.

Medline and **PsycINFO** may also be useful databases, as Medline focuses on aspects of health and will be particularly useful for nutrition information, and PsycINFO gathers abstracts related to psychology and human behavior, which would be particularly useful if you wanted to research the relationship between food and mental health.

Remember to use the "Find Articles" button, or request articles through Interlibrary Loan if they are not available in full text online.

Further Readings

D'Silva, Joyce and John Webster. *The Meat Crisis: Developing More Sustainable Production and Consumption.* London: Earthscan, 2010.

Homepage. Temple Grandin. Web. 31 July 2011. <www.grandin.com>

Marcus, Erik. *Vegan: The New Ethics of Eating.* Ithaca: McBooks, 1998.

Merino, Noël. *Agricultural Subsidies.* Detroit: Greenhaven, 2020.

Pollan, Michael. *In Defense of Food.* New York: Penguin, 2008.

Pringle, Peter. *Food, Inc.: Mendel to Monsanto—The Promises and Perils of the Biotech Harvest.* New York: Simon, 2003.

Reichmann, James B. *Evolution, Animal "Rights" and the Environment.* Washington: The Catholic U of America P, 2000.

Roleff, Tamara L. *The Rights of Animals.* San Diego: Greenhaven, 1999.

Steinfeld, Henning et al. *Livestock's Long Shadow: Environmental Issues and Options.* Rome: Food and Agricultural Organization of the United Nations, 2006.

APPAREL MERCHANDISING AND SOCIAL RESPONSIBILITY

College of Human Environmental Sciences

Introduction

Housed in the College of Human Environmental Sciences, OSU's Apparel Design and Merchandising degree is one of several offered by the Department of Design, Housing, and Merchandising. No longer just about designing, displaying, and selling trendy clothes, today's Apparel Design and Merchandising students explore complex problems in the manufacturing, marketing, and selling of apparel to consumers. In the past, Fashion Merchandising degrees prepared students to design, construct, and purchase clothing lines for retail outlets, but today students must also be savvy in the business world; as the ADM Web site puts it, their mission is to offer programs "focusing on the development of solutions to contemporary and emerging problems within a framework of ethical and social responsibility."

Increasingly, today's consumers want textiles and clothing made without sweatshop labor, without unnecessarily harming the environment, and with "fair-trade" policies that benefit both American and international corporations. As you'll see from the articles that follow, none of these social problems is easily resolved.

In this chapter, you will read articles that focus on both the business aspects and the more human side of Apparel Design and Merchandising. We begin with an article that explores the complex issue of "sweatshop" labor. The article written by award-winning journalist Nicholas Kristof argues that there is potentially an upside to low-wage jobs. Next come two newspaper articles on the recruiting of young children to leave home and work in apparel factories in China for long hours and little pay. The authors of these three articles make it clear that the issue is complicated and the potential solutions are not always clear.

One proposed solution to the problem of the unethical treatment of workers in factories is for consumers to be willing to pay higher prices to help ensure that the workers who make the merchandise can work in safe environments and make living wages. Nadia Mustafa shows how one company has discovered how to cater to those consumers willing to pay a slightly higher price for "fair trade" apparel. "Shopping With a Social Conscience: Consumer Attitudes Toward Sweatshop Labor" provides an opportunity to explore the same issue as presented in an academic journal article and accompanied by the author's research.

We finish the section with a portion of the research conducted by Dr. Jane Swinney of OSU and Dr. Rodney Runyan of the University of Tennessee on Native American entrepreneurs in the state of Oklahoma.

As you'll see from these six articles, apparel merchandising is an exciting and challenging field, one that appeals to clothing designers, business professionals, social scientists, engineers, and entrepreneurs.

Jacqueline Megow

Interview with Dr. Jane Swinney

Jacqueline Megow and Laura Dumin interviewed Dr. Jane Swinney, Assistant Professor of Merchandising and Coordinator of the Merchandising Program in OSU's Department of Design, Housing, and Merchandising, to learn more about the field from an academic perspective. What follows are excerpts from that interview.

Apparel Merchandising appears to be about much more than clothes and window displays today. Could you explain a little about the field?

That's right. Some of the topics that our department is concerned with include e-commerce, international retailing, tourism retailing, retail store performance, and the social responsibilities of retailers. It's about trying to make money and cater to the American consumer's desire for new things.

Could you explain a little bit more about social responsibility?

Social responsibility is something that has been around in corporate America for a long time. Businesses want to do good things so that customers will patronize their businesses. Oil companies might talk about cleaning up the environment. Large retailers might publicize how they help a local community. Wal-Mart doesn't want clothes made by sweatshop labor.

What are some specific issues your undergraduate students might research or discuss related to social responsibility?

We discuss global trade issues; we'll talk about NAFTA (the North American Free Trade Agreement), CAFTA (which covers the Caribbean Basin Area), ASEAN (the Association of Southeast Asian Nations), and other trade associations. I'll tell them Wrangler had a plant in Colgate, Oklahoma—a good plant, but they couldn't find enough employees to work. They paid well, but people didn't want to sit at a sewing machine and make Wrangler jeans for a living, so the factory went to Mexico. So we might have a debate about a topic like this in class—it's tragic that people in Colgate lost their jobs, but the company couldn't sustain itself there because of the lack of a work force.

Another interesting topic is the debate over labeling laws, which are very strict in the United States. If the fabric for a garment was woven at a textile mill in South Carolina, then the fabric is American. But the fabric might be sent to El Salvador to be cut, then those cut pieces bundled and sent to Mexico to be sewn, then back to Texas to be inspected, bagged, and shipped. Where did the product come from? Is it "Made in America"?

Tell us a little more about your specific area of research.

My retail interest is in the small store in the rural community, which is something important to the economy of Oklahoma. I study the activities of the small businesses in their community in terms of social capital, meaning the people-to-people networking that exists in small towns like Stillwater. I specifically look at micro-businesses, defined as businesses that employ less than ten people, and I've found that they are a huge contributor to the national economy. If those small businesses really are the drivers of our economy, we ought to study them and find out what will help them succeed.

For example, Idabell, a town in southeastern Oklahoma, had a Wal-Mart come into town and negatively affect the downtown retail core. So I'm interested in finding what we can do to help those independent retailers survive. We have begun to investigate how the downtown Chamber of Commerce or other business development folks can positively impact local micro businesses. They can come up with an image for their community, or develop a festival to draw people in.

What kinds of writing are done in your field?

For an academic research article, I often start with a survey of downtown business people and visit with them if they'll let me. I write up my research and publish it in journals such as the *Journal of Small Business Management*, the *Journal of Developmental Entrepreneurship*, and the *Journal of Retailing*. Also, articles about upcoming trends are published in popular journals such as *Women's Wear Daily* and *Stores Magazine*. Some of the country's top newspapers, such as *The Wall Street Journal*, have fashion writers on staff. Lastly, several Web sites are important in our field—including www.style.com and www.dwr.com.

How has the field changed over the years?

If you go back thirty years, merchandising was under the umbrella of Home Economics. We taught students to sew; we also made sure every student had classes in foods, in child development, and so forth. Today, a student can come and study Design and Merchandising and never take a sewing class or a foods class. It's shifted dramatically to the business side. It's not about the homemaker anymore.

Besides what we've discussed here, what are some issues in your field that would be interesting to a first-year student?

The first one would be eco-friendly products: green products, organic cotton, natural dyes, leathers dyed with vegetable matter and not chemicals, etc. The second would be performance fabrics or textiles: things like wicking materials, safety fabrics, and other innovative textiles—such as the white peaks at the Denver airport and retractable domes over football fields—which are made out of textiles.

Thank you so much for your time.

Let Them Sweat

Nicholas D. Kristof

Mr. Kristof, a Pulitzer Prize-winning author and op-ed columnist for the *New York Times*, has written extensively on human rights abuses in Africa and Asia, which is why his criticism of the anti-sweatshop movement surprises some. In this article, Kristof calls on G-8 ("Group of 8," an international forum of the governments of Canada, France, Germany, Italy, Japan, Russia, the United Kingdom, and the United States), as well as anti-sweatshop activists, to consider beginning a "pro-sweatshop campaign." Keep in mind that his stated objective is to help the people who are most negatively affected by sweatshop labor.

When the G-8 leaders meet this week, cowering in a Canadian mountain resort beyond the reach of organized anarchists, here's a way for them to bolster terror-infested third world countries like Pakistan.

They should start an international campaign to promote imports from sweatshops, perhaps with bold labels depicting an unrecognizable flag and the words "Proudly Made in a Third World Sweatshop!"

The Gentle Reader will think I've been smoking Pakistani opium. But the fact is that sweatshops are the only hope of kids like Ahmed Zia, a 14-year-old boy here in Attock, a gritty center for carpet weaving.

Ahmed, who dropped out of school in the second grade, earns $2 a day hunched over the loom, laboring over a rug that will adorn some American's living room. It is a pittance, but the American campaign against sweatshops could make his life much more wretched by inadvertently encouraging mechanization that could cost him his job.

"Carpet-making is much better than farm work," Ahmed said, mulling alternatives if he loses his job as hundreds of others have over the last year. "This makes much more money and is more comfortable."

Indeed, talk to third world factory workers and the whole idea of "sweatshops" seems a misnomer. It is farmers and brick-makers who really sweat under the broiling sun, while sweatshop workers merely glow.

The third world is already battered by heartless conservatives in the West who peddle arms and cigarettes or who (like the Bushies) block $34 million desperately needed for maternal and infant health by the United Nations Population Fund. So it's catastrophic for muddle-minded liberals to join in and cudgel impoverished workers for whom a sweatshop job is the first step on life's escalator.

By this point, I've offended every possible reader. But before you spurn a shirt made by someone like 8-year-old Kamis Saboor, an Afghan refugee whose father is dead and who is the sole breadwinner in the family, answer this question: How does shunning sweatshop products help Kamis? All the alternatives for him are worse.

"I dream of a job in a factory," said Noroz Khan, who lives on a garbage dump and spends his days searching for metal that he can sell to recyclers. He earns about $1.40 a day, and children earn just 30 cents a day for scrounging barefoot in the filth—a few feet away from us, birds were pecking at the bloated carcass of a cow, its feet in the air.

Of course, Western anti-sweatshop activists mean well and aim only for improved conditions and a "living wage." But the reality is that the bad publicity becomes one more headache for companies considering operating in international hellholes (where the only lure is wages so low that it would be embarrassing if journalists started asking questions about them), and so manufacturers opt to mechanize their operations and operate in somewhat more developed countries.

For example, Nike has 35 contract factories in Taiwan, 49 in South Korea, only 3 in Pakistan and none at all in Afghanistan—if it did, critics would immediately fulminate about low wages, glue vapors, the mistreatment of women.

But the losers are the Afghans, and especially Afghan women. The country is full of starving widows who can find no jobs. If Nike hired them at 10 cents an hour to fill all-female sweatshops, they and their country would be hugely better off.

Nike used to have two contract factories in impoverished Cambodia, among the neediest countries in the world. Then there was an outcry after BBC reported that three girls in one factory were under 15 years old. So Nike fled controversy by ceasing production in Cambodia.

The result was that some of the 2,000 Cambodians (90 percent of them young women) who worked in those factories faced layoffs. Some who lost their jobs probably were ensnared in Cambodia's huge sex slave industry—which leaves many girls dead of AIDS by the end of their teenage years.

The G-8 leaders will never dare, of course, begin a pro-sweatshop campaign. But at a summit that will discuss how to bring stability and economic growth to some of the world's poorest nations, it would be a start if Westerners who denounce sweatshops would think less of feel-good measures for themselves and more about how any of this helps people like Ahmed and Kamis.

Discussion Questions

1. Do some internet research about Nicholas Kristof. Based on his experience and education, do you find him a credible source to discuss the plight of children and adults who work in so-called sweatshops?

2. Why does Kristof claim that the G-8 leaders can "bolster terror-infested third world countries" by promoting imports from sweatshops?

3. Who do you suppose Kristof is really addressing in his argument? Be as specific as you can.

4. Thomas Friedman is another columnist for the *New York Times* who writes frequently about globalization and low-wage jobs in developing countries. Find at least two of his editorials that address this issue. Write a short compare/contrast paper on the similarities and differences between the positions of Friedman and Kristof.

Chinese Factories, Flouting Laws, Hire Children From Poor, Distant Villages

David Barboza

David Barboza, a *New York Times* reporter based in China, explores the direct impact of child labor on factories, families, and entire communities. As he implies, child labor is a complicated issue, one with no easy answers.

The mud and brick schoolhouses in the lush mountain villages of this remote part of southwestern China are dark and barebones in the best of times. These days, they also lack students.

Residents say children as young as 12 have been recruited by child labor rings, equipped with fake identification cards, and transported hundreds of miles across the country to booming coastal cities, where they work 12-hour shifts to produce much of the world's toys, clothes and electronics.

"Last year I had 30 students. This year there are only 14. All the others went outside to find work," said Ji Ke Xiaoming, 35, a primary school teacher whose students in Erwu Village are mostly ages 12 to 14. "You know, we are very poor. Some families can't even afford a bag of salt."

China is now investigating whether hundreds, perhaps thousands, of poor children of the Yi ethnic minority group in Liangshan were lured or even kidnapped to work in factories that are increasingly desperate for the kind of cheap labor that powered China to prosperity over the past two decades.

Labor recruiters—government investigators and some local residents portray them as con men—have connected two radically different parts of China's turbulent society. They have brought together ethnic minorities untouched by economic development in their mountainous isolation, and factory owners in the prime export manufacturing zones of southern Guangdong Province, near Hong Kong.

Exporters have struggled to adjust to soaring inflation, a fast-rising currency and, with some irony, stricter enforcement of labor laws that make it harder to hire regular workers on a seasonal basis. Using child workers from a remote region, many of whom cannot even speak Mandarin, the country's main national dialect, have provided a temporary, albeit illegal, solution.

A scandal involving Liangshan's children first came to light late last month, when Southern Metropolis, a state-run newspaper, reported that as many as 1,000 school-age workers from the area were employed in manufacturing zones near Hong Kong.

The report was deeply embarrassing for Beijing, which is preparing to host the Olympics and coping with international criticism of its handling of riots in Tibet. Last week, the authorities in Liangshan said they had detained several people for recruiting children and illegally ferrying them off to factories.

And officials in Dongguan, one of the manufacturing zones where the children worked, said that they had "rescued" more than 160 young people from factories. The legal minimum working age in China is 16.

Now, officials have begun to play down the scandal, saying there is little evidence of widespread violations of child labor laws. A two-day government sweep involving more than 3,000 factories around Dongguan, which was conducted after the initial raids, turned up only 6 to 10 children, officials said.

But residents of Liangshan say abject poverty, drug abuse and a lack of jobs have forced many children to head for factories. Sometimes it is with their parents' permission. Other times, children disappear, on their own or with job recruiters, and then call home from a factory dormitory, hundreds of miles away.

"When our daughter left, we were quite worried," said 42-year-old Qi Si Gu Xi, whose 14-year-old daughter left last February. "We didn't know where to find her. Then she called us and told us she's a migrant worker in Guangdong."

Such stories are not unusual. In more than two dozen interviews this week, children who had returned home from factories told of hardship and abuse. Parents living in squalor acknowledged that their children had been lured into traveling to factories. And other residents said conditions in these mountain villages were so appallingly poor that young people felt they had no choice but to leave home.

On Wednesday, more than 10 families interviewed in the span of five hours in Zhaojue County, part of Liangshan, said they had children working in factories, often earning less than $90 a month for 12-hour days, seven days a week. Even if the children were of working age, the pay, equivalent to about 25 cents an hour, and the working conditions would violate China's labor laws. In the prime manufacturing zones, the official minimum wage is at least 65 cents an hour, and employers are required to pay significantly more for overtime.

Ji Ke Ri Sha said he had spent more than a year working in factories in several provinces, including Shandong and Shanxi. His family could not survive on farming alone, he said, and so he took a chance on the world outside. He hopped from factory to factory, holding four jobs before his 15th birthday.

"My father worried about me going away, but we had no money," he said quietly, squatting on the mud floor of a farmhouse. "I had to go outside, but the work turned out to be too difficult." An employment agent persuaded his parents that he could find their son a factory job. But the boy says the agent ended up making a secret deal with a factory, and pocketing half the boy's pay as a finder's fee.

Liangshan, formally known as the Liangshan Yi Autonomous Prefecture, may have become a target of child labor rings precisely because it is a place of desperation. The villages, populated almost exclusively by Yi, are reached by traveling for hours along winding roads through the thickly forested part of Sichuan Province. Most people survive on subsistence rice farming. Others fall prey to the drug trade. One of the main heroin trafficking routes passes through these parts on the way from northern Myanmar to Chengdu, the largest city in the region.

The area is plagued by drug abuse and AIDS. Many people have no formal education and cannot converse in Mandarin, making it difficult to seek employment in cities on their own.

Luo Gu A He, 69, said his 14-year-old granddaughter left Keqie Village for Beijing in March, after the death of her father, who had been addicted to drugs. She now earns about $4 a day working seven days a week at a construction site, he said.

"She is too young," the grandfather said. "I worry about her being alone in Beijing. But if she stays with me she couldn't live either; she'd starve to death."

A woman spoke of a daughter who left home at 15 to work in a brick factory in Shandong Province but returned recently. "My daughter was taken by a foreman," said the woman, Pa Cha Ri Gu, 62. "I was concerned, but we are poor. You see the small house we live in."

Residents say they have heard of children being kidnapped and forced to work in factories. Other villagers say that desperate parents, some addicted to drugs, resort to selling their children to child traffickers.

As the supply has grown, so has the demand. Over the past few years, coastal factories have complained of labor shortages and said many migrant workers were reluctant to work for low pay on factory campuses in the country's coastal provinces.

Factories find themselves caught in a squeeze between foreign buyers, who are addicted to lower prices for manufactured goods from China, and surging food and energy costs. Profit margins, never very fat, have shrunk, and Beijing has passed new labor laws that restrict the use of temporary workers.

Employment agents have come to the rescue, providing the factories with pliable children who carry falsified documents attesting that they have reached the legal working age, state news media and local parents said. They take half the child's wages, but people in Liangshan are hungry for any cash income.

During an interview with a group of residents in Keqie Village, a man in a leather jacket initially spoke up and identified himself as an employment agent, but then declined to give many details, saying only, "I help them find a way out."

Discussion Questions

1. China has adopted measures to correct past problems with child labor in factories, but as the recent problem discussed here indicates, some factories still engage in exploitive practices. What is the best way to solve this problem? International pressure on the Chinese government? An American boycott of Chinese imports? Campaigning for international monitoring of Chinese factories? Or some other solution? What would Kristof say?

2. Find one article from a European newspaper, one from Asia, and one from the U.S. (not *New York Times*) that reports on the problems in Liangshan. Are there differences in the writers' perspectives? Which specific problems are highlighted in each article? Who does each author seem to blame for the problem—corrupt governments? Indifferent consumers? Other social forces at work?

3. Discuss some of the differences you see in this article and the earlier ones. How is the writing different? The tone? The intended audience and purpose?

Freed Child Slaves Refuse To Go Home

Fiona Tam

The *South China Morning Post* is an English-language newspaper in Hong Kong with a large readership there and also in China and the U.S. The child labor scandal discussed in Tam's article was widely reported around the world, and China reacted quickly to the problem in order to prevent the type of heavy criticism for its labor policies that it has faced in the past.

Hundreds of freed child labourers illegally sold by overseers from Sichuan to factories in Dongguan, Guangdong province, have refused to leave the plants despite the brutal conditions, according to mainland media.

"I don't want to go home. My parents have already sold me to the overseers," a tearful teenage girl named Luo Siqi was quoted as telling a police officer in a report in the Southern Metropolis News yesterday.

About 40 children resold to another electronics manufacturer in Dongguan to evade a police crackdown said they were looking forward to working in new "profitable jobs" that paid 3 yuan (HK$3.34) an hour with mandatory overtime.

The report said thousands of children from remote Liangshan county in Sichuan province had been sold to Guangdong factories during the past five years. The children were abused and forced to work under slave-like conditions for 12 hours a day, almost every day. Most children were from ethnic minorities and aged between nine and 15.

A dealer in child labourers was quoted as saying that children who were abducted or bought in Sichuan were sold in cities in Guangdong, including Dongguan, Shenzhen, Guangzhou, Huizhou and Jiangmen.

"In Dongguan, there's a great demand for our child labourers …who never complain about the excessive workload. They can return children to us anytime when they get sick or suffer industrial injuries. We deal with it," the dealer said.

An unnamed child worker said overseers and their hired thugs used knives to threaten the children not to try to escape.

Another said: "My monthly salary was taken by the overseers, who claimed they sent it back to my parents. They gave me 10 yuan a day to rent a bed and buy food during the low season. That amount meant we could only afford steamed buns—pickled vegetables were an extravagance."

Some girls were raped by their overseers or even resold to brothels.

Critics said child labour had been a daily fact of life in Guangdong for years and something to which the government turned a blind eye.

Hou Yuangao, a researcher at the Central University for Nationalities in Beijing, said dire poverty in the country's ethnic minority regions was the main reason for the trade. "You may think it's untenable for children to work 13 to 14 hours a day, but about 300 yuan sent by the overseers to their parents can save the entire family from starvation," Mr Hou was quoted by the Southern Metropolis News as saying.

In Liangshan, the mother of one abducted child said she was pleased to know that her son was working in an electronics factory in Dongguan.

"My son was kidnapped in December last year...I'm glad to know he can eat cooked rice every two to three days," the malnourished mother was quoted as saying.

Discussion Questions

1. After reading this article, what are your feelings about the issue
    of child labor and the products you buy? Are you more or less
    likely to think twice about buying products made in China?

2. Kristof would likely have a strong reaction to this article. Write
    a paragraph or two on how he would respond. For an addition-
    al challenge, research the author Naomi Klein online, and write
    a paragraph on how she would respond.

3. The *South China Morning Post* has had recent troubles with its
    (now fired) editor. Do some research online to find out what
    happened. After reading what others have written about the
    issue, check the *Post*'s Web site (scmp.com) to see if they pub-
    lished anything on the issue. You might also check the satirical
    Web site ntscmp.com ("*The NOT South China Morning Post*")
    that was started as a result of this scandal (and to address other
    criticisms of the paper). Look specifically at ntscmp.com's mis-
    sion statement. Why does the Web site claim that the *Post*'s for-
    mer publishers are "two self-censored, Peking-aligned money
    making machines"?

Fair-Trade Fashion

Nadia Mustafa

Mustafa, an apparel and fashion reporter, discusses the recent efforts of the apparel company Fair Indigo to work with only those factories that employ fair labor practices. From Brazil to Nepal to Costa Rica, workers at factories associated with Fair Indigo receive a "fair wage," occasional bonuses, and other incentives. Also discussed are efforts to develop an official fair-trade certification for apparel, similar to the fair-trade certification currently used by coffee companies.

Start-up apparel company Fair Indigo pays each of its factory workers a living wage, not just the minimum one.

Just a few years ago, most Americans had never heard the phrase "fair trade." Today corporations as mainstream as McDonald's and Wal-Mart are using coffee beans harvested by growers in developing countries who are paid a living wage rather than the minimum one. And now the movement is coming into fashion…literally.

A company called Fair Indigo: Style With a Conscience hopes to do for apparel workers what fair-trade coffee has done for farmers. Launched last September with a catalog (made from postconsumer recycled paper, of course) and a Web site, Fair Indigo is one of the first mainstream fair-trade apparel brands in the U.S., on the heels of several recent European start-ups, most notably Britain's People Tree and Gossypium.

According to a survey solicited by the company, 86% of consumers care about whether their clothing is made by workers who are paid fairly and treated with respect. But what exactly is fair? There's no universal measuring stick, but it's generally accepted that it's a wage enabling workers to live relatively comfortably in their home region—i.e., enough money for housing, a generous amount of food, health care, education for their children and some disposable income.

This concept seemed like a no-brainer to Fair Indigo CEO Bill Bass, a former Army paratrooper raised in Knoxville, Tenn., who worked for the U.S. Department of Education before entering the business sector. "It's hard for me to feel right about not paying people fairly," he says. "But most apparel companies are focused on cutting the cost of production and see the people in their factories as commodities and replaceable parts." In 2005, Bass and three other executives from Lands' End, where he had been working as e-commerce chief, decided to leave the company and see if they could change that. "We wanted to start a smaller company that focused not only on the customer but also on the people making the products," he says. "We knew we could do the clothing, the catalog, the

Web site, the stores. We'd done all these things. The biggest question was if we could find factories that were willing to pay their employees fairly."

Over the next year, Bass and his partners scoured the globe for factories that met not only their standards for clothing but also their standards for wages. In what Bass, 44, describes as a "long, arduous process," they interviewed employees, audited payrolls and spoke with owners. "Oh, yeah, it was hard," he says. "Because nobody does that. There was an initial disbelief we had to overcome in some of these factories."

Bass and his colleagues eventually chose about 20 sites, most of which are family-owned and -managed and offer above-average wages and generous benefits. With their own capital, they assembled a staff of 30 (25 of whom used to work at Lands' End), but to this day, the founders still personally visit each factory on a regular basis. They also hand over 5% of the company's profits to the Fair Indigo Foundation, a not-for-profit organization dedicated to improving educational opportunities in the countries where the company's factories and co-ops are located.

Last November, Fair Indigo opened its first store, a 1,600-sq.-ft. eco-friendly space in Madison, Wis. The floors and shelves are made of sustainable bamboo, the walls are covered in wood pulp, and the clothes are draped on bamboo hangers. Customers can scan the bar code of any item at an Internet kiosk at the center of the store to read detailed information about the factory in which it was produced. Bass hopes to open four stores a year nationwide starting in 2008.

"Bill understands production and supply-chain issues," says Patti Freeman Evans, senior analyst for the retail industry at Jupiter-Research. "He is well able to evaluate not only the sales potential but also the financial ramifications of potentially lowering his margins in order to be price competitive."

Whereas fair-trade coffee is pricier than the conventional stuff; Bass insists that Fair Indigo clothing is just as stylish as other brands and its quality is just as high—only minus the markup for the do-good aspect. This is possible, he says, because he has eliminated the middle man. Bass relies heavily on worker-owned cooperatives, which slashes layers of overhead, and works directly with the owners of non-co-op factories. Moreover, unlike many clothing brands, Fair Indigo has a minimal advertising budget, counting instead on word of mouth, and it sells directly to consumers instead of through a retailer.

The brand's debut collection consisted of about 100 styles, but Bass says this fall's line will offer closer to 300, with a wider range of products, a broader color palette and more accessories. Each pair of jeans, he adds enthusiastically, will be made out of organic denim. The Fair Indigo aesthetic, which falls somewhere between J. Jill and J. Crew, is casual but fashionable, aimed at the 30-to-50-year-old set. (Think silk jackets, alpaca scarves and cashmere sweaters.)

It's not just the clothes that are socially conscious. Its line of Inara spa products is produced by women's cooperatives in the remote state of Maranhão in northeastern Brazil, and its amethyst-and-garnet geometric drop earrings are made at a Nepalese technical school in a community consisting largely of underprivileged families from the lower castes. The workers at one of the company's small Costa Rican cooperatives—where each sewer and cutter of the brand's twill pants and chinos helps make financial decisions—turned an exceptional profit last year and were able to give themselves a bonus of three months' pay.

There isn't yet an official fair-trade certification for apparel in the U.S., but Bass is consulting with TransFair USA, an independent third-party certifier of fair-trade goods, in hopes that Fair Indigo will be the impetus for a certification process. "The fair-trade movement is still in its infancy, but people in general are more socially conscious, and I think that's going to start filtering down into the apparel industry," says Bass. "Our goal is to start a movement that changes how the apparel industry works. The measure of its success will be how quickly other companies adopt it."

There's a long road ahead, says Freeman Evans, but it's a good lead to follow. "It doesn't mean that you need consumer demand for fair-trade products. It just means you need good products that are made with fair-trade practices."

Discussion Questions

1. Find online information about TransFair USA through a Google search. Then find two articles through ProQuest that discuss the organization. Write a one-to-two page mini-rhetorical analysis on the differences between the web-based and journal-based information about TransFair USA.

2. As Mustafa reports, Starbucks (and other coffee companies) have used the "fair-trade" certification for a while. Find out more about this certification; is it granted by an official business or agency? Who decides whether something can be called "fair-trade" or not? How does the designation affect a company's sales? Type up a short report on your findings. Don't forget to include a works cited list (you should have at least three sources, possibly including a personal interview with a local business that uses fair-trade coffee or an OSU professor who is knowledgeable about the subject).

3. This article seems to have much in common with "Shopping with a Social Conscience" by Fredrica Rudell. Would Rudell approve of Fair Indigo's business practices? Why or why not?

4. How conscious are you about social issues when you purchase clothing? Would you be willing to pay more for fair trade or fair labor practices? What can companies do to get young adults to purchase "fair trade" products?

5. Nadia Mustafa states, "There isn't yet an official fair-trade certification for apparel in the U.S." However, since the publication of "Fair-Trade Fashion" in 2007, Fair Trade USA has launched a fair trade certification for apparel that enables consumers to vote with their dollars. Visit the following website and read the detailed article by Sarah Kuck: http://dowser.org/fair-trade-certification-expands-to-the-apparel-industry/. Compare the two articles. Write a one page response about how the fair trade apparel industry has changed from 2007 to 2010. What challenges are still being faced? What improvements, if any, do you foresee for the future of this industry?

Shopping With a Social Conscience: Consumer Attitudes Toward Sweatshop Labor

Fredrica Rudell

In this excerpt of a larger article, Fredrica Rudell, Professor and Department Chair of Marketing and International Business at Iona College, brings a slightly different perspective to the field of apparel merchandising since her expertise and teaching experience is within the School of Business. In this article, Rudell explores how willing consumers are to shop with a social conscience to avoid exploited labor, even if it means paying higher prices.

The Global Sweatshop Issue

The increasing globalization of business and expansion of international trade has accelerated the geographic, economic, and cultural separation of producers and consumers. More and more goods purchased by Americans are imported, making outsourcing and "off-shoring" topics of heated social and political debate. The apparel industry has been particularly aggressive in its use of international sourcing, resulting in U.S. imports from more than 150 countries, many of them underdeveloped (Emmelhainz & Adams, 1999).

While U.S. apparel manufacturers have historically relocated production in search of cheap labor, first from the unionized Northeast to the low-wage, nonunionized South, Bonacich and Appelbaum (2000) traced the beginnings of offshore sourcing to the 1950s. The shift to imports accelerated in the 1980s and continued to increase as U.S. retailers (producing their own private-label lines) joined manufacturers in the "race to the bottom" to find the cheapest labor. Import share of domestic apparel consumption increased from about 2% in the 1960s, to 15% in 1980, 26% in 1988, and 31% in 1993 (Murray, 1995). By 2001, about two thirds of apparel worn by Americans was produced outside the United States (D'Innocenzio, 2001), and more recent estimates of U.S. apparel import penetration place it at about 75% by wholesale dollar value and 96% by number of garments (American Apparel & Footwear Association [AAFA], 2002).

Practices associated with sweatshops, including violation of wage, child labor, safety or health laws, and labor abuses including forced overtime and sexual and physical harassment have a long history and can be found in domestic and foreign factories (Firoz & Ammaturo, 2002; Ross, 2004; Smithsonian Institution, 1998). Cheek and Moore (2003) attributed the reemergence of apparel production sweatshops in an era of technological advances and prosperity to several interrelated market factors. These include the fragmented structure and operations of the apparel industry, economic globalization, the rise of multinationals and retail conglomerates, and the growing trend toward private labeling.

Fueled by consumer demand for low-priced fashion apparel, marketers and retailers put pressure on contractors and subcontractors, often located in developing countries, to keep manufacturing costs down. Newly industrializing countries welcome garment production, which is labor-intensive, requires little start-up capital, and boosts exports. Competitive bids can most easily be achieved through starvation wages and substandard working conditions, especially where government regulations are absent, weak, or not enforced. Workers, who may be desperately poor, uneducated, and/or undocumented, are in no position to bargain for better treatment.

Although not all apparel manufacturers can benefit from the practice—because of differences in size, type of market, need for access to domestic designers, and turnaround times—overseas contract manufacturing has long been an accepted method of reducing costs. For a labor-intensive industry such as apparel manufacturing, even allowing for differences in productivity, firms can reduce costs by paying $1.70 in Mexico, 86 cents in China, or 23 cents in Pakistan, compared with $12.17 per hour for U.S. workers (Sweatshopwatch.org, 2004; U.S. Bureau of Labor Statistics, 2004). "Official" hourly compensation rates for less developed countries may tell only part of the story, as actual wages that factor in forced overtime, fines on workers, and other costs to the worker may be much lower. Thus, a garment worker from Bangladesh can toil 14 hours a day, 7 days a week to earn about 14 cents an hour, or approximately 5 cents for sewing a Disney garment that retails for $17.99 in U.S. malls (Greenhouse, 2002).

It should be noted that sweatshops are not universally condemned. Low-wage plants making apparel and shoes for export are hailed by some as a sign of industrial progress, a necessary first step toward prosperity in developing countries, and far preferable to unemployment or alternative work, for example, prostitution (Kristof & WuDunn, 2000; Myerson, 1997). But critics maintain that "there should be a floor beneath which no one has to live" (Hayden & Kernaghan, 2002). Bonacich and Appelbaum (2000) pointed out that the less workers make, the less they can buy, which applies to both foreign workers and the U.S. workers they displace. "By continually trying to push labor costs ever lower, the apparel industry kills the goose that lays its golden egg" (p. 79).

Whereas many actors and forces in the marketing channel and environment serve to keep goods made by exploited labor on the market, others attempt to reduce the problem. The media play an important role in shining the "spotlight" on sweatshops and child labor (e.g., Schanberg, 1996), motivating some firms to take steps to curb abuses (Miller, 1997; Spar, 1998). Key players have shown a willingness to work together on solutions to the sweatshop problem. In 1996, a White House Task Force (the Apparel Industry Partnership) composed of industry, labor, and consumer and human rights groups was formed to create a code of conduct on wages and working conditions (Emmelhainz & Adams, 1999; Greathead, 2002; Greenhouse, 1997). The resulting Fair Labor Association (FLA) has won industry, nonprofit, and university support for its factory inspection and certification program (Pereira, 2001). A few companies, including Adidas, Levi Strauss, and Liz Claiborne, have taken the next step and posted their factory labor audits on the FLA Web site (Bernstein, 2003).

As Cheek and Moore (2003) concluded, apparel sweatshops will continue to exist as long as the industry expands and globalizes, making it more difficult to determine how and where apparel is produced; unethical retailers and manufacturers overlook labor regulations; ethical retailers and manufacturers find it difficult to monitor factories; and consumers demand low-priced apparel without considering their source. We now turn to those consumers.

Role of the Consumer

Karpatkin (1999) proposed that a "fair and just marketplace" be accomplished through the activities of a triangle of government, citizens, and business, with separate and overlapping roles and responsibilities. While the government must regulate and legislate to ensure a level playing field, companies must be more responsive to public concerns and take responsibility for their own actions. Citizens can work through organizations and community groups, as investors who influence business behavior, through litigation, and as informed consumers. In introducing expanded coverage of labor issues in her own publication, *Consumer Reports*, Karpatkin (1998) wrote, "Consumer pressure can force companies to adhere to regulations, and it can stimulate better codes, inspections and labeling. When consumers exercise the right to choose, they become the ultimate arbiters of human decency in the marketplace" (p. 7).

Some evidence exists of consumers' power to persuade companies to "do the right thing." Assisted by organized interest groups, consumers have increased corporate attention to the environment (recycled products, less packaging, sustainably-grown coffee), health (organic and low-fat foods), and concern for animals (product testing, dolphin-safe tuna). For example, boycotts were an important form of consumer activism for environmental protection and animal rights (Friedman, 1995). With respect to worker exploitation, consumers have expressed their concern at previous times in history, for example, via boycotts of grapes and lettuce in the 1960s. More recently, pressure from German consumers resulted in the industry's adoption of "Rugmark" labeling of Indian-made carpets, certifying those made without child labor (McCarthy, 1996). Various grassroots efforts are under way to ban products made in sweatshops from college stores or entire municipalities (e.g., United Students Against Sweatshops; Bangor, Maine "Clean Clothes Campaign").

Others have pointed out the importance of the consumer's role in ensuring an ethical marketplace. Human Rights Watch attributed growing global support for human rights to U.S., Canadian, and European consumers' desire to avoid complicity in repression through their consumption of goods manufactured under abusive labor conditions (Senser, 1997). Zadek (1997) observed the arrival of the "ethical consumer" in the United Kingdom, citing surveys suggesting that 86% of British consumers "were more likely to buy products positively associated with a social or environmental issue," and 66% would be willing to boycott products because of ethical concerns. It is estimated that about one third of the U.S. adult population could qualify as lifestyles of health and sustainability (LOHAS) consumers, "the kind of people who take environmental and social issues into account when they make purchases" (Cortese, 2003). Members of such a segment would be willing to pay a premium for products and services made in a way that minimizes harm to the environment and society.

Davidson (1998a) suggested that sellers' and manufacturers' ethical behavior should be considered an important attribute in consumers' purchase decisions, akin to price and quality. Elliot Schrage, Columbia Business School professor and adviser to companies on how to improve factory conditions, is quoted as saying that "the principle that the conditions under which products are made is a legitimate concern for consumers is now well established" (Greenhouse, 2000).

Shopping with a Social Conscience

How can apparel consumers act on their desire to shop with a social conscience? They are advised to seek information, to purchase from approved lists of socially responsible companies (e.g., Department of Labor *Trendsetters*, Co-op America *Greenpages*), and to request information about retailers' sourcing policies and companies' codes of conduct (Brown, 1994; Halbfinger, 1997; Holstein, 1996; "Shame of Sweatshops," 1999). But information is only as useful as it is accurate, because sweatshops leave no evidence of labor exploitation on the goods themselves. Although some have proposed that achievement of certain labor standards be a prerequisite for participation in trade agreements, for the most part, trade and labor standards are not linked (Burnett & Mahon, 2001). Moreover, "Made in USA" labels may not ensure that the product was made under fair working conditions, because sweatshops exist domestically and in U.S. territories such as Saipan. In some industries, especially apparel, domestic products may be hard to find, and union labels even more scarce, making it difficult for consumers to exercise their preferences.

At the extreme, shopping with a social conscience may call for boycotts, especially of repressive regimes (e.g., Burma/Myanmar). However, like many other "good deeds," ethical shopping may have unintended negative consequences, and most organized groups recognize the need to preserve jobs in the developing world. Attempts to end child labor in impoverished countries where children may be a family's only economic "asset" must be carefully considered by activists because of potential backlash effects. Closing factories might force children into other, more dangerous occupations, including prostitution. Alternative solutions such as controlled hours, providing education, meals, and health care have been proposed ("Consciences and Consequences," 1995; Fairclough, 1996; McCarthy, 1996).

Consumer Attitudes—Survey Evidence

Are consumers concerned enough to alter their shopping practices? Some recent polls and surveys have measured consumers' willingness to use their purchasing power to shop with a social conscience. Although a social desirability bias (to give the "acceptable" answer) surely affects the responses, the data are fairly consistent and reveal some trends.

Willingness to Pay More, Shop Elsewhere

In 1996, *U.S. News and World Report* reported the results of its own sweatshop poll: 89.3% of respondents said they were willing to pay a few more cents for "peace of mind" when buying, and 70.2% were willing to pay a few more dollars (Holstein, 1996). In a survey connected with his stakeholder analysis of the California strawberry industry, Davidson (1998b) found that 85% of respondents would be willing to pay more for strawberries to ensure improvement of working conditions.

A national poll on attitudes toward sweatshops was conducted for the Center for Ethical Concerns, Marymount University in 1995, 1996, and 1999 (Marymount University, Center for Ethical Concerns, 1999). In 1995 and 1996, the survey focused on domestic garment production, whereas the 1999 poll broadened the scope to global production. In 1995 and 1996, approximately 83% of shoppers were willing to pay $1 extra on a $20 item if it were guaranteed to be made in a legitimate shop. About

4 out of 5 respondents both years said they would avoid shopping at a retailer that sold garments made in sweatshops. When the study was repeated in 1999, the percentage of consumers willing to pay $1 extra on a $20 garment had increased slightly to 86%, but only 75% of respondents would avoid retailers who sold garments made in sweatshops.

A poll conducted for the National Consumers League in April and May of 1999 explored consumer attitudes and perceptions with respect to a variety of marketplace issues (Harris, 1999). The top source of concern for respondents was the use of sweatshops or child labor in the production of goods—61% said it worried them a great deal. If there was a label on some products to indicate that they were made without the use of child labor, more than three quarters (77%) of respondents said they would be very or somewhat likely to look for it, and 55% would be willing to pay more for products with such a label.

Perceived Responsibility for Labor Conditions

In 1995 and 1996, in the wake of publicity about undocumented alien workers smuggled into the country, respondents to the Marymount poll were asked to allocate responsibility for preventing sweatshops in the United States. The 1999 survey broadened the question to sweatshops in general, without reference to location. From the resulting responses (see Table 1), it appears that respondents credit manufacturers with the dominant responsibility for sweatshop conditions. However, there is a definite shift over time from manufacturers to retailers, or both.

Table 1. Responsibility for Preventing Sweatshops

Which of the following should have responsibility for preventing sweatshops?	1995	1996	1999
Manufacturers	76%	70%	65%
Retailers	7%	10%	11%
Both	10%	15%	19%
Neither	3%	1%	2%
Don't know/refused	4%	4%	3%

Source. Marymount University, Center for Ethical Concerns (1999).

Table 2. Usefulness of Information Types

What would help you to avoid buying clothes made in sweatshops?	
A label that says the garment was made under fair labor conditions	56%
A published list of stores and companies that have been identified as using or tolerating sweatshop labor	33%
Both would help	4%
Neither would help	3%
Don't know/refused	4%

Source. Marymount University, Center for Ethical Concerns (1999).

When asked about responsibility for monitoring labor conditions under which products are made, respondents to the National Consumers League survey (Harris, 1999) answered as follows: government (36%), companies (31%), independent watch groups (28%), no need (3%). When government was removed from the list, respondents favored self-monitoring by companies (55%) over independent watch groups (42%). This finding is contrary to current demands of activist groups such as the Workers Rights Consortium, which favors independent monitoring (and surprise inspections) but may reflect perceived responsibility for, rather than faith in, corporate self-monitoring.

Consumer Information Needs

The 1999 Marymount survey also included a new question regarding consumers' ability to shop with a social conscience: "What would most help you to avoid buying clothes that were made in sweatshops?" As shown in Table 2, the responses indicate a definite preference for labels (56%) over lists of stores and companies (33%).

In her study of 219 female apparel consumers, Dickson (1999) found that respondents felt more concerned than knowledgeable about issues affecting apparel industry workers. Responses given when asked about possible solutions are presented in Table 3.

As in the Marymount study, a label was perceived to be more useful than a list in assisting consumers with purchase decisions, suggesting the importance of a "No Sweat" or "Child Labor-Free" type of label. Support for government regulation is consistent with the perceived responsibility for monitoring labor conditions noted in the previous section.

Summary of Survey Findings

Keeping in mind the social desirability bias that might inflate percentages, it is clear from the surveys cited that many consumers are aware of, concerned about, and willing to address the sweatshop and child labor issue through their purchases, including paying more for "peace of mind." Although consumers perceive manufacturers as having primary responsibility for preventing sweatshops, retailers are beginning to share more of the burden as production is globalized, and consumers are willing to shop accordingly. Government is expected to play a role, by regulating and monitoring labor conditions and banning sale of products made by child labor. With respect to information, consumers consider labels more useful than lists of companies and stores in guiding them toward more socially conscious purchases.

Table 3. Solutions for Apparel Industry Issues

Issue	Mean (7-point Likert-type scale)	% Agree or Strongly Agree
Sale of products made by child labor should be banned.	5.9	73.6
I wish that there was a label on jeans telling consumers if they were made by socially responsible manufacturers.	5.7	63.6
There should be more governmental regulations protecting workers in the clothing manufacturing industry.	5.4	55.4
I would boycott buying clothing from businesses that do not act responsibly toward their employees.	5.0	41.5

Source. Adapted from Dickson (1999, Table 4, p. 50).

Discussion Questions

1. Rudell says that "by 2001, about two thirds of apparel worn by Americans was produced outside the United States" (131). This fact concerns many Americans because it eliminates jobs in the U.S. and sometimes leads to poor working conditions for employees overseas. But is Rudell correct? Research what "Made in America" really means. If clothing is ultimately made in the U.S., where are the raw materials assembled? Where are the pattern pieces cut? Where are company labels sewn on the garments?

2. Find the name of three companies that have made an effort to produce "socially responsible goods" by adopting a "no child labor" policy, "green" manufacturing, or other moves to address consumers' concerns about unfair business practices. What, specifically, have they done? How have their actions impacted their sales and profit levels? Be sure to properly cite the sources you use.

3. What can you, as a consumer, do to help promote fair business practices? Rudell gives several suggestions, as do other articles in this section. You might start with one of these suggestions and explain why and how you could follow it, or why you wouldn't be willing to follow it.

Native American Entrepreneurs and Strategic Choice

Jane Swinney, Rodney Runyan

We finish this chapter with an article co-written by OSU's Jane Swinney and Rodney Runyan, from the University of Tennessee. In their study of 149 entrepreneurs, Swinney and Runyan analyze the similarities and differences between Native American and non-native entrepreneurs so that community business leaders will know how best to help this important part of small-town economies. Professors Swinney and Runyan are among many academics and professionals who are concerned about the declines in the economies of rural communities, such as the ones they survey in Oklahoma, as the global economy drives production overseas and encourages the spread of large retailers such as Wal-Mart. Both have published extensively on this subject. You can read more about Dr. Swinney's research interests in the interview at the beginning of this chapter.

1. Introduction

For the past two decades, many rural states have seen their economies stagnate or decline (Miller, 1998). For rural areas with a declining agricultural sector and little other major industry the consequences have included increasing out-migration and a reduction in services and retail activity. Leistritz and Sell (2001) noted that rural states have attempted to counter this decline through economic diversity by capitalizing on local assets, entrepreneurs and small businesses. There is a tremendous desire and will to create and support entrepreneurship in rural communities ("Do entrepreneurs make a difference in rural communities?" 2005). Rural business owners have traditionally accounted for up to 80 percent of the U.S. economic growth (U.S. Chamber of Commerce, 1994; Woods *et al.* 1999).

The current research was conducted to explore entrepreneurship amongst Native American business owners. Specifically, we looked at small business owners operating in rural communities and compare Native American entrepreneurs with majority entrepreneurs using previously developed and tested scales. These scales were designed to measure strategic choice as manifested in the entrepreneurial and/or small business orientation of the small business owner. The uniqueness of the study is that it applies data collected exclusively in communities that are home to a significant proportion of indigenous (Native American) residents. The extant entrepreneurship literature has focused on non-indigenous entrepreneurs though some research has been conducted on culture-related entrepreneurship (Garsombke and Garsombke, 1998; Lindsay, 2005). Oklahoma, with the second largest state Native American population (more than 300,000) behind only California, provides the opportunity to examine strategic choice by ethnicity in communities that are populated by a significant percentage of Native Americans. This is an exploratory study to attempt to discern if there are statistically significant differences in strategic orientation choice between Native American and majority small business owners.

In the 2000 United States census, less than 1 percent of the population identified themselves as Native American. Oklahoma and California are home to more than 25 percent of those classifying themselves at Native Americans. With a large number of residents classified as Native Americans, Oklahoma may be home to a correspondingly large number of Native American entrepreneurs.

In the literature review we first present the magnitude of the Native American population in both the country and in Oklahoma to establish the importance of this group within the U.S. The concept of community is then discussed as a means of establishing a cultural context for the study with a particular focus to Native American communities. We then briefly present the study's theoretical framework from the strategic orientation literature. Following this, we propose and test our hypotheses, and then present and discuss the findings. We conclude with possible avenues for future research.

3. Entrepreneurial Orientation

Definitions of entrepreneurship are disparate, ranging from one who is an innovator, demonstrating initiative (Schumpeter, 1934), risk taking behaviors and proactive behaviors. Other definitions include characteristics including individuals with a personal value orientation (Gasse, 1982); one who is innovative and growth-oriented (Carland *et al.* 1984); one who displays competitive aggressiveness (Covin and Slevin, 1989); one who undertakes a "new entry" (Lumpkin and Dess, 1996); or one who simply owns and actively manages a small business (Stewart and Roth, 2001). Entrepreneurial characteristics are viewed as resources to both the entrepreneur as well as the firm (Alvarez and Busenitz, 2001). For the purposes of this study, an entrepreneur is an "individual who assumes risk" in a venture, and "provides management for the firm" (Kilby, 1977). Most very small businesses (such as the ones in the current study) have owners who also manage the business, thus fitting Kilby's (1977) definition.

The concept of entrepreneurial orientation (EO) refers to the processes, practices and decision activities leading to new entry or opportunity for an individual/firm (Covin and Slevin, 1989). Some of the constructs of EO were suggested by earlier authors in the strategy domain. For example, Miller and Friesen (1978) identified risk taking and innovation as effective management strategies. Fredrickson (1986) suggested proactiveness, risk taking and assertiveness. In the entrepreneurship domain, the construct of entrepreneurial orientation was operationalized by Miller (1983) and Covin and Slevin (1989). Their construct consisted of three dimensions: innovativeness, risk taking and proactiveness.

3.1. Innovativeness

Based on Schumpeter's (1934) early work, the concept of entrepreneurs as innovators is accepted in the literature. Innovativeness is an indicator of a firm's tendency to engage in and support new ideas, processes and creative methods. This type of activity may result in new processes, services or technologies (Lumpkin and Dess, 1996). Though the bulk of the extant innovation literature has focused on technology, innovation can occur in many areas. This includes management processes, promotion, human resources, visual merchandising and other aspects of running a small business. These are all areas where a firm or small business owner could employ innovative techniques to improve the performance of his/her business. Innovation is an important aspect of EO as it reflects the means by which firms might pursue new opportunities (Lumpkin and Dess, 1996).

3.2. Risk taking

One of the earliest characteristics ascribed to entrepreneurs was that of risk taking (Lumpkin and Dess, 1996). The very idea of working for "oneself" implies the risk of not only lost capital, but the opportunity cost of having earned wages in the employ of another firm.

The term risk has various meanings depending on the context of the application. Three types of strategic risk were identified by Baird and Thomas (1985) as: (a) venturing into the unknown; (b) investing a large portion of assets; and (c) heavy borrowing. The first of these types applies to small business owners in the sense that it implies a sense of uncertainty, as is discussed in the entrepreneurship literature in terms of social, personal or psychological risk (Gasse, 1982). Small business owners who adopt new ways of doing business or try a new product line are taking on risk to some degree.

Most studies of entrepreneurship have focused on the individual rather than the firm (Lumpkin and Dess, 1996). That fact is germane to this study, as the entrepreneurship component is measured at the individual rather than the business level. EO has been used by Miller (1983) and Covin and Slevin (1989) to investigate risk taking by individuals within firms. As is the case in most measures of behavior, there seems to be a range of risk taking (Lumpkin and Dess, 1996). Business owners range from risk averse to risk prone. Female and male small business owners have been found to have similar levels of risk-taking propensities as well as innovativeness (Sonfield *et al.* 2001). No studies have been found that examined risk-taking behaviors between Native Americans and majority business owners.

3.3. Proactiveness

Proactiveness is the act of anticipating problems or opportunities prior to their occurrence in order to be prepared for the problems and take advantage of the opportunities. Miller (1983) suggests that entrepreneurial firms are ones that are "first" to develop proactive innovations. This seems self-evident, as an innovation is a new way of doing something and thus, by definition, proactive. Although it is related to innovation, proactiveness is focused more on the pursuit of opportunities and initiating activities (Covin and Slevin, 1989).

Proactive firms seek new operations that may or may not be related to their present business, eliminate operations in declining stages of the life cycle and bring in new products ahead of the competition (Venkataraman and Ramanujam, 1989). They are willing to grab onto new market opportunities as leaders even if they are not the first (Lumpkin and Dess, 1996). Lumpkin and Dess also characterize the opposite of proactiveness as being "passive" rather than "reactive." This too is an important distinction, as a small business owner with little foresight (i.e., not proactive), who nonetheless reacts to a market change or opportunity is likely to be in better shape long-term than the one who is passive and does nothing. Covin and Slevin (1989) describe one of the attributes of proactiveness as being competitively aggressive. Competitive aggressiveness describes the manner in which firms or business owners relate or respond to competitors. More specifically, it refers to a firm's inclination to directly challenge its competition with intensity (Lumpkin and Dess, 1996) or even unconventional tactics (Cooper *et al.* 1986). Employing unconventional methods to compete with others in the marketplace may be particularly important for small business owners (Cooper and Dunkelberg, 1986; Stone, 1995).

Small retailers that succeed over the long term must adapt to change in a positive way and are proactive in the face of an ever-changing economy. The characteristics of innovativeness and proactiveness should describe the characteristics of all successful small business owners.

A continuum of business owners, from high to low on the entrepreneurial orientation scale, is likely to exist in any downtown. This is supported by Vesper (1980). Downtowns should have a mix of business owners that falls along the continuum. As with any organization, the largest number of businesses will probably fall in the middle, meaning they have some entrepreneurial tendencies, but are neither high on the EO continuum nor low. They are the small business owners who spend the majority of their time and energy on their business. These businesses lend stability to the downtown by exhibiting steady, measured growth.

7. Discussion

The non-metropolitan counties in Oklahoma are home to small business in communities seeking to remain viable and survive in an environment fraught with uncertainty and ups and downs of the oil and gas industries. It may be useful for economic development policy makers to know if strategies should be different for Native American small business owners or whether the same economic development policies can be used in all Oklahoma communities regardless of the proportion of the population that is classified as Native American.

The place of business operation is important in economic development planning. Communities with a heavily indigenous population could be anticipated to influence the entrepreneurial values of the business owners operating in those communities. Cultural values of indigenous peoples have been reported as different from the values of other ethnic groups. Indigenous entrepreneurial values are more holistic; success of the venture is measured in terms of various economic and non-economic dimensions (Dumont, 1993; Foley, 2003). Communities of indigenous peoples are more likely to emphasize quality of life (Redpath and Nielsen, 1997). These previous studies indicated that indigenous peoples are perhaps more collective in their community relationships than majority people. Anderson *et al.* (2006) argue that it is merely myth that indigenous people are more collective in their economic development than majority people. It was not known whether differences existed between the business owners operating businesses in small rural communities with a significant proportion of indigenous peoples living in the community. This research was conducted to advance the field of entrepreneurship study among indigenous peoples. Gathering data from business owners in communities with a significant indigenous population was intentional and the first known to focus on indigenous entrepreneurs operating in non-tribal, publicly incorporated communities. With the average community in Oklahoma reporting 7.9 percent of the population as Native American in our study, nearly 15 percent of the entrepreneurs reported themselves as Native American. Of these Native American entrepreneurs, 45 percent were female. Nationally, female-owned businesses account for 28 percent of all privately owned businesses (http://www.score.org/m_pr_20.html). The two business orientations: entrepreneurial and small business, while not dichotomous variables but discrete, do shed light on possible business strategies among different entrepreneurial orientations. The U.S. frame for entrepreneurial activity is set in a culture that values independent action, taking personal chances and self-reliance (McGrath *et al.* 1992). McGrath *et al.* (1992) suggest that programs designed to foster entrepreneurship that assume economic behavior to be guided by the values of individualistic cultures may run a serious risk of failure. The contribution of this research is to examine the indigenous culture embedded within the U.S. in heavily indigenous communities and its influence on entrepreneurial strategies of small business owners.

7.1. Entrepreneurial outcomes

Business owners with an entrepreneurial orientation are highly concerned with profits and growth. Hagen (1962) was the first to suggest that feelings of marginalization or deprivation could become the source of entrepreneurial energy. In this sense entrepreneurship can provide social recognition. Brenner (1987) noted that entrepreneurship is often a mechanism for combating adverse circumstances as a means of social integration when other paths are blocked. Dana (1995) suggests that opportunity identification is culture-bound. Lindsay (2005) proposed that indigenous entrepreneurial values reflect indigenous cultural values. Lindsay (2005) reported that entrepreneurial attitude of indigenous peoples demonstrate low levels of innovation. Our study followed a direction of research suggested by Lindsay (2005) in that it examines current entrepreneurial attitudes of indigenous and non-indigenous business owners to determine how models of entrepreneurial growth might be modified for indigenous entrepreneurs. These findings also address the need to understand more about indigenous entrepreneurship and how it diverges from non-indigenous entrepreneurship. A better understanding can lead to appropriate, culturally sensitive entrepreneurship development programming to help rural communities with a high proportion of Native Americans. Anderson *et al.* (2006) found entrepreneurial strategies that originate in the community are sought by indigenous peoples. The majority business owners reported a mean score of 4.13 to entrepreneurial orientation (proactivness, risk taking and innovativeness) while the indigenous entrepreneurs' mean score was 3.79. This difference was not statistically significant for our sample.

The majority entrepreneurs reported a mean score of 4.98 on the small business orientation scale (emotionally attached to the business and purposes and goals for the business). The indigenous entrepreneurs' mean score was lower at 4.94. Although the research literature points to a collective mindset (a concern with lifestyle and family among indigenous peoples), our study found no statistical support for strong Native American cultural influence operating for the Native American business owners in the participating small rural communities. However, what is of importance is that Hypothesis 2 was supported; the difference in reported entrepreneurial orientation scores and small business orientation scores was larger among indigenous entrepreneurs than among majority entrepreneurs. This suggests that perhaps for indigenous business owners the strength of the owner's stated purposes and goals as well as the owner's emotional attachment to the business is more clearly evidenced for indigenous entrepreneurs than for majority owners. In Table 2, the difference in scores for the indigenous business owners is 1.15 and only 0.85 for the majority owners. This finding is useful for community development officials as plans are formulated to strengthen the business environment of the downtowns in rural communities. If the place of family and business goals can be shown, and if funding sources recognize the strength of the emotional connection of indigenous peoples to their personal businesses, then efforts can be directed to attracting more indigenous peoples to become entrepreneurs.

None of the three components of entrepreneurial orientation (innovativeness, proactiveness and risk taking) are significantly different between Native American and majority business owners. This is in contrast to earlier research by Lindsay (2005) who proposed that innovativeness was lower for indigenous business owners. Thus, according to our study's findings, the strategic choice of entrepreneurial orientation is similar for Native American and majority entrepreneurs. Therefore, if differences in strategic choice do exist, they may exist in other areas. Recognition and understanding that a small business orientation is focused on the purposes and goals as well as the emotional attachment of the owner to their business can provide a starting point for discussions with indigenous people's efforts to become business owners. Thus, community development officials may promote the lifestyle advantages of entrepreneurship when addressing Native Americans and encouraging downtown entrepreneurship. It appears that communities clearly supporting local entrepreneurs results in few differences between the indigenous and the majority business owners in terms of their strategic orientations.

Forty-five percent of the Native American entrepreneurs and 48 percent of the majority entrepreneurs were female in this study. Nationally, 28 percent of small business owners are female. The higher proportion of Native American females as business owners in the small community points to support for Hagen's (1962) suggestions that feelings of marginalization or deprivation could become the source of entrepreneurial energy. In this sense, entrepreneurship could provide social recognition. Brenner (1987) noted that entrepreneurship is often a mechanism for combating adverse circumstances as a means of social integration when other paths are blocked. Perhaps these Native American females feel that owning their business provides them a mechanism to overcome feelings of marginalization and a means to combat adverse circumstances. This concept needs further investigation. Majority female business owners (48 percent of the majority owners) may be addressing some of the same issues in the small community.

7.2 Limitations and follow-up

More research needs to be done with Native American entrepreneurs both in heavily indigenous communities and communities not heavily populated by Native Americans. Due to the paucity of literature on Native American entrepreneurs, we sought to focus on this group of entrepreneurs. Despite being conducted in communities with up to 20 times more Native Americans than in the U.S. population as a whole, our study found a very small number of such small business owners. The reasons these numbers were so small are unclear. We attempted to increase the number of Native Americans in our sample by contacting local economic officials as well as some small business owners in two communities. We encountered resistance from both officials and small business owners. Therefore, it was not clear whether there were a larger number of Native American small business owners whom we missed in our sampling or if the actual number is indeed small. It seemed that we did find that self-identifying as Native American was unpopular.

In an effort to uncover the true situation, (i.e., few Native American entrepreneurs or reluctance to self-identify), we contacted members of one indigenous Native American Tribe. We were able to interview a chief and two members who were small business owners. From our discussions with each of them, we found that the answer though complicated, is that both situations exist. The tribal chief stated that many Native Americans do not like to self-identify as such when presented with surveys and inquiries from outside the tribe. Both entrepreneurs noted that there are few Native Americans who take advantage of resources available to start businesses as well as many who are simply not aware of public and private resources. This suppresses the number of entrepreneurs in Native American communities. Therefore, it is likely that the sample in this study is an under-representation of the actual number of Native American entrepreneurs as a result of identification problems. But it also supports the need for research such as this to bring the situation to the forefront. The results likely cannot be generalized to the greater population but it is a step in the right direction.

7.3. Directions for future research

Strategic orientation has been the focus of much of the work being done to cultivate entrepreneurship and to create an environment for growing entrepreneurial ventures. This exploratory study investigated strategy choices of majority and indigenous entrepreneurs operating businesses in heavily indigenous rural communities. Results provide insight and indicate that strategy choices are not significantly different between majority and indigenous entrepreneurs. These findings will be beneficial to rural community development and revitalization specialists. The need is great for further investigations of entrepreneurial strategy choices among cultural groups.

We also see a great need for learning more about how to derive a representative sample from a population that does not want to be identified. It is very likely that more qualitative methods will be needed rather than quantitative. This lowers the external validity of the study but greatly increases a study's internal validity.

References

Alvarez, S and L Busenitz (2001). The entrepreneurship of resource-based theory. *Journal of Management*, *27*(6), 755–775.

Anderson, T, B Benson and T Flanagan (eds.) (2006). *Self-Determination: The Other Path for Native Americans*. Stanford, CA: Stanford University Press.

Baird, I and H Thomas (1985). Toward a contingency model of strategic risk taking. *Academy of Management Review*, *10*(2), 230–243.

Baskerville, RF (2003). Hofstede never studied culture. *Accounting, Organization and Society*, *28*(1), 1–14.

Bonacich, E and J Modell (1980). *The Economic Basis of Ethnic Solidarity: Small Business in the Japanese American Community*. Berkeley, CA: University of California Press.

Brenner, R (1987). National policy and entrepreneurship: The statesman's dilemma. *Journal of Business Venturing*, *2*(2), 95–101.

Brenner, R and I Toulouse (1990). Business creation among the Chinese immigrants in Montreal. *Journal of Small Business and Entrepreneurship*, *7*(4), 38–44.

Busenitz, L and C Lau (1996). A cross-cultural cognitive model of new venture creation. *Entrepreneurship Theory and Practice*, *2*(4), 25–39.

Carland, JW, F Hoy, WR Boulton and JC Carland (1984). Differentiating entrepreneurs from small business owners: A conceptualization. *Academy of Management Review*, *9*(2), 354–359.

Chaganti, R and P Greene (2002). Who are the ethnic entrepreneurs? A study of ethnic entrepreneurs' ethnic involvement and business characteristics. *Journal of Small Business Management, 40*(2), 126–143.

Churchill, GA and D Iacobucci (2002). *Marketing Research: Methodological Foundations.* Mason, OH: South-Western Publishing.

Cooper, AC and W Dunkleberg (1986). Entrepreneurship and paths to business ownership. *Strategic Management Journal, 7,* 53–68.

Cooper, AC, GE Willard and CY Woo (1986). Strategies of high-performing new and small firms: A reexamination of the niche concept. *Journal of Business Venturing, 1*(3), 247–260.

Covin, JG and DP Slevin (1989). Strategic management of small firms in hostile and benign environments. *Strategic Management Journal, 10*(1), 57–75.

Dana, L (1995). Entrepreneurship in a remote sub-arctic community. *Entrepreneurship Theory & Practice, 20*(1), 57–72.

Davidsson, P. (1989). Entrepreneurship and after? A study of growth willingness in small firms. *Journal of Business Venturing, 4*(3), 211–226.

Dillman, D (2000). *Mail and Telephone Surveys: The Tailored Design Method* (2nd edition). New York, NY: John Wiley and Sons.

Do entrepreneurs make a difference in rural communities? (2005). *Small Community Quarterly*, Fall, 2–4.

Dumont, J (1993). Justice and Aboriginal People. In *Aboriginal Peoples and the Justice System: Report of the National Roundtable on Aboriginal Justice Issues by the Royal Commission on Aboriginal Peoples.* Ottawa, ON, Canada Communication Group, 42–85.

Foley, D (2003). An examination of indigenous Australian entrepreneurs. *Journal of Developmental Entrepreneurship, 8*(2), 133–151.

Fredrickson, JW (1986). The strategic decision process and organizational structure. *The Academy of Management Review, 11*(2), 280–298.

Garsombke, D and T Garsombke (1998). Non-traditional versus traditional entrepreneurs: Emergence of a Native American comparative profile of characteristics and barriers. Paper presented at the meeting of the United States Association for Small Business and Entrepreneurship, Clearwater, FL, January.

Gasse, Y (1982). Elaborations on the Psychology of the Entrepreneur, *Encyclopedia of Entrepreneurship.* CA Kent, D Sexton and KH Vesper (eds.). Englewood Cliffs, NJ: Prentice Hall, 209–223.

Gilder, G (1971). *The Spirit of Enterprise.* New York: Simon & Schuster.

Hagen, EE (1962). *On the Theory of Social Change: How Economic Growth Begins*. Homewood, IL: Dorsey Press.

Hindle, R, R Anderson, R Giberson and B Kayseas (2005). Relating practice to theory in indigenous entrepreneurship. *American Indian Quarterly*, 29(1/2), 1–23.

Hofstede, G (1980). *Culture's Consequences: International Differences in Work-Related Values*. Beverly Hills, CA: Sage Publications.

Kanter, RM (1988). Supporting innovation and venture development in established companies. *Journal of Business Venturing*, 1, 47–60.

Kilby, P (1977). *Entrepreneurship and Economic Development*, New York, NY: Free Press.

Leistritz, FL and RS Sell (2001). Socioeconomic impacts of agricultural processing plants. *Journal of the Community Development Society*, 32(1), 130–159.

Light, I (1984). Immigrant and ethnic enterprise in North America. *Ethnic and Racial Studies*, 7(2), 195–216.

Lindsay, N (2005). Toward a cultural model of indigenous entrepreneurial attitude. *Academy of Marketing Science Review*, 2005(5), 1–18.

Litz, R and A Stewart (2000). Charity begins at home: Family firms and patterns of community involvement. *Nonprofit and Voluntary Sector Quarterly*, 29(1), 131–148.

Lumpkin, GT and GT Dess (1996). Enriching the Entrepreneurial Orientation Construct—A reply to "Entrepreneurial Orientation or Pioneer Advantage." *Academy of Management Review*, 21(3), 605–607.

McGrath, R, I Macmillan, E Yang and W Tsai (1992). Does culture endure, or is it malleable? Issues for entrepreneurial economic development. *Journal of Business Venturing*, 7, 441–458.

Miller, D (1983). The correlates of entrepreneurship in three types of firms. *Management Science*, 29, 770–791.

Miller, D and P Friesen (1978). Archetypes of strategy formulation. *Management Science*, 24, 921–933.

Miller, N (1998). Local consumer spending: A reflection of rural community social and economic exchange. *Journal of the Community Development Society*, 29(2), 166–185.

Min, PG (1984). From white-collar occupation to small business: Korean immigrants' occupational adjustment. *Sociological Quarterly*, 25(3), 333–352.

Min, J and C Jaret (1985). Ethnic business success: The case of Korean small business in Atlanta. *Sociology and Social Research*, 69(3), 412–435.

Morrison, A (2000). Entrepreneurship: What triggers it? *International Journal of Entrepreneurial Behaviour & Research*, 6(2), 59–69.

North, DC (1990). *Institutions, Institutional Change, and Economic Performance*. New York: Norton.

Ports, A and RC Bach (1985). *Latin Journey*. Berkeley: University of California Press.

Redpath, L and MO Nielsen (1997). A comparison of native culture, non-native culture and new management ideology. *Canadian Journal of Administrative Sciences*, 14(3), 327–339.

Runyan, RC (2005). *Predicting Downtown and Small Business Success: A Resource-Based View*. Unpublished doctoral dissertation, East Lansing, Michigan: Michigan State University.

Runyan, R, C Droge and J Swinney (In Press). Entrepreneurial orientation versus small business orientation: What are their relationships to firm performance? *Journal of Small Business Management*.

Schumpeter, J (1934). The Theory of Economic Development, *Public Opinion Quarterly*, 58, 358–480.

Shane, S (1994). The effect of national culture on the choice between licensing and direct foreign investment. *Strategic Management Journal*, 15, 627–642.

Shapero, A (1984). The entrepreneurial event. In *The Environment for Entrepreneurship*, CA Kent (ed.), pp. 21–40, Lexington, MA: D.C. Heath.

Sonfield, M, R Lussier, J Corman and M McKinney (2001). Gender comparison in strategic decision-making: An empirical analysis of the entrepreneurial strategy matrix. *Journal of Small Business Management*, 39(2), 165–173.

Stewart, WH and PL Roth (2001). Risk propensity differences between entrepreneurs and managers: A meta-analytic review. *Journal of Applied Psychology*, 86(1), 145–153.

Stewart, WH, JC Carland, WE Watson and R Sweo (2003). Entrepreneurial dispositions and goal orientations: A comparative exploration of United States and Russian Entrepreneurs. *Journal of Small Business Management*, 41(1), 27–46.

Stone, KE (1995). *Competing with the Retail Giants: How to Survive in the New Retail Environment*. New York, NY: John Wiley & Sons.

U.S. Chamber of Commerce (1994). *Studies in Organizational Management*. Washington, DC: Industrial Development Institute Department.

Venkatraman, N and V Ramanujam (1989). Strategic orientation of business enterprises: The construct, dimensionality and measurement. *Management Science*, 35, 942–962.

Vesper, KH (1980). *New Venture Strategies*. Englewood Cliffs, NJ.: Prentice-Hall.

Woo, CY, AC Cooper and WC Dunkelberg (1991). The development and interpretation of entrepreneurial typologies. *Journal of Business Venturing*, 6(2), 93–115.

Woods, MD, VJ Frye and SR Ralstin (1999). *Blueprints for Your Community's Future: Creating a Strategic Plan for Economic Development* (Fact Sheet # WF-916). Stillwater, OK: Oklahoma Cooperative Extension Service.

Zacharaki, A (2001). Study cites tribal council interference as obstacle, *Navajo Times*, 40(7), A10.

Discussion Questions

1. Swinney and Runyan found that three qualities typify entrepreneurs: innovativeness, risk-taking, and proactiveness. Reread Section 3 (pp. 142–145), and then research one company, small or large, that was started and still exists in Oklahoma. Review that company's website, company literature, and/or what others have said about it, and write a 1–2 page paper on how and/or if these three qualities apply to the company's founders. Does one quality stand out more than the others? Be sure to properly cite your sources.

2. This article contains a long Works Cited list at the end. How many of these works are available through the OSU library? If the library doesn't have a book or article on hand, how can you get a copy? Finally, pick 10 sources (5 books and 5 journal articles) and convert them to MLA citations.

3. Swinney and Runyan hypothesized that "entrepreneurs in indigenous communities…report higher levels of small business orientation than entrepreneurial orientation." Did their findings support their original hypotheses? What reasons do Swinney and Runyan give for their conclusions? Do you suppose the findings are similar for the factory owners in China that other articles in this section address?

4. How do you anticipate measuring success in your life after college? Is it financial security? Having a job that you find fulfilling? The chance to be creative? A predictable schedule and income? Time with your family? Or something else? Reread section 7 – "Discussion" (pp. 145–149). Do your values correspond with those of the survey participants?

APPAREL MERCHANDISING AND SOCIAL RESPONSIBILITY

Library Resources

You may find a sufficient number of journal and magazine articles in **ProQuest** when using keywords such as "marketing" and "textiles." To find additional research articles use **Business Source Elite**. This database can be found in the alphabetical list of databases under the column *Find Articles*, as was done for the database **ProQuest**.

Business Source Elite provides full text coverage for nearly 1,100 business publications and economics journals, including nearly 500 peer-reviewed publications, from 1985 to the present. It also indexes core titles for fashion including *Women's Wear Daily* and *Apparel*. When you click on **Business Source Elite** a screen appears next in which you can select different business databases. Click on **EconLIT** and **Regional Business News** in addition to **Business Source Elite** and click on the Continue button.

The next screen allows you to type in your keywords or subject terms:

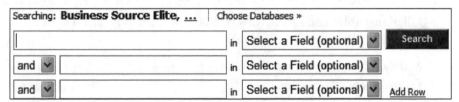

Type the term "textiles" on the first line and "marketing" on the second line and click the blue Search button. Results for journal, magazine and newspaper articles are displayed with the newest articles displayed first. Since this topic is quite broad, you could type other keyword terms like "green marketing" and "textiles" OR "china" and "textiles" and "marketing." If the pdf or full text of the article is not available follow the pink colored button for a full text or full image version of the article.

If a link is not working properly or a full text/pdf version of the article can't be located please ask a reference librarian for assistance.

Further Readings

Agins, Teri. *The End of Fashion: How Marketing Changed the Clothing Business Forever*. New York: William Morrow, 1999. Print.

Collins, Jane Lou. *Threads: Gender, Labor, and Power in the Global Apparel Industry*. Chicago: U of Chicago P, 2003. Print.

Dickerson, Kitty G. *Inside the Fashion Business*. 7th ed. Upper Saddle River, NJ: Prentice Hall, 2002. Print.

Jackson, Tim, and David Shaw, eds. *Mastering Fashion Marketing*. New York: Palgrave Macmillan, 2008. Print.

Kawamura, Yuniya. *Fashion-ology: An Introduction to Fashion Studies*. Oxford: Berg, 2005. Print.

Kremer, Roberta S., ed. *Broken Threads: The Destruction of the Jewish Fashion Industry in Germany and Austria*. Oxford: Berg, 2007. Print.

LaFeber, Walter. *Michael Jordan and the New Global Capitalism*. New York: Norton, 2000. Print.

Lillethun, Abby, and Linda Welters, eds. *The Fashion Reader*. Oxford: Berg, 2007. Print.

Malefyt, Timothy deWaal, and Brian Moeran, eds. *Advertising Cultures*. Oxford: Berg, 2003. Print.

Moor, Liz. *The Rise of Brands*. Oxford: Berg, 2007. Print.

Palmer, Alexandra, and Hazel Clark, eds. *Old Clothes, New Looks: Second-Hand Fashion*. Oxford: Berg, 2004. Print.

Ribeiro, Aileen. *Dress and Morality*. Oxford: Berg, 2003. Print.

Rivoli, Pietra. *The Travels of a T-Shirt in the Global Economy: An Economist Examines the Markets, Power, and Politics of World Trade*. Hoboken: John Wiley & Sons, 2005. Print.

Scott, Linda M. *Fresh Lipstick: Redressing Fashion and Feminism*. New York: Palgrave Macmillan, 2004. Print.

Woodward, Sophie. *Why Women Wear What They Wear*. Oxford: Berg, 2008. Print.

TELEVISION AND CULTURAL STUDIES

American Studies Program, College of Arts and Sciences

Introduction

Entirely interdisciplinary in nature, the American Studies program seeks to unite scholars across different fields. Students who are interested in literature, television, cultural studies, history, economics, religion, technology, and writing may find a home here, as the program offers a "systematic theoretical and practical exposure to understanding American society and culture through multidisciplinary study."

Students in American Studies engage questions about culture through a variety of academic lenses and, far from being a passive recipient of information, will be invited to think critically about historical and cultural arguments and to consider the broader implications of those arguments as they relate to our increasingly global economy.

This particular unit introduces students to the fields of Television Studies and Cultural Studies, and more specifically how the two fields intersect. These seven essays and articles clearly demonstrate Dr. Takacs' argument that Television Studies is "actually a Cultural Studies approach to the study of television." The authors examine a diverse sample of television programming—from the news coverage of Jessica Lynch to the offbeat comedy of *The Office*, from the contemporary portrayal of the 1960s in *Mad Men* to our current obsession with reality television—in order to illustrate what these programs reveal about the cultures that produce them and consume them.

These readings of television texts raise complex issues about class, race, gender, sexuality, and national identity. While these essays and articles provide only brief examinations of these topics, students should continue to explore the ways these issues play out in our daily television programming and the ways they shape our perceptions as viewers. As you read, consider, as Dr. Takacs phrases it, "the ways television both shapes the way we interact with the world and constitutes a site over which people struggle to represent themselves in some ways politically."

Ronald Brooks and Joshua Cross

Interview with Dr. Stacy Takacs

Stacy Takacs is assistant professor of American studies at Oklahoma State University. Her research interests include media and globalization, and the interrelationship between US television and US imperial politics in the contemporary era. She has published on these topics in the journals *Cultural Critique, Feminist Media Studies, American Studies, Science Fiction Studies, International Journal of Iraqi Studies,* and *Journal of Popular Culture.* Dr. Takacs kindly agreed to sit down with Joshua Cross to discuss the fields of Television Studies and Cultural Studies as well as her own research and writing.

Can you explain a little about the fields of Television Studies and Cultural Studies?

The two of those can't be separated. What makes Television Studies is actually a Cultural Studies approach to the study of television. This is in contrast to the way television had been studied previously, which was associated with mass communication. Now we treat television as a site of social struggle for power and position within society and we tend to analyze texts and audience responses more than we do industrial politics, though we do talk about political economy. This differs from mass communication approaches because those were developed to train new practitioners and to provide industry data. The result was that it tended to be really reductive of what the audience was, to treat people as interchangeable monads, and not to think about the ways in which people engage with the complexities of television narratives.

In the Television Studies approach, we actually go out and interview people in a more ethnographic way rather than a data collection way. It's more qualitative than quantitative. We use open-ended questions to get at the complexities and some of the differences also, so you see that men respond to the messages in different ways than women do. There's a lot of variety in what appears to be a singular message. So Television Studies is geared more toward these qualitative issues to think about the ways television both shapes the way we interact with the world and constitutes a site over which people struggle to represent themselves in some ways politically.

How did you get involved with these fields? What led to your interest in this subject?

In graduate school I took a number of courses with people working in Cultural Studies. I took classes with people like Michael Curtin and Barbara Klinger, and they took qualitative approaches to the analysis. I had been taking courses in postcolonial theory and studies, and I wanted to think about questions of empire, and if you want to talk about that in contemporary terms, you really have to talk about media, television in particular. The way in which we understand our relationship to others is constructed in large part through our access to images of them and through a kind of an extension of our electronic arm into their countries. Communication is essential to the perpetuation of imperial relations. I was looking at empire in a contemporary context, and that necessitated a look at television.

Can you tell us a bit about your research area and the kinds of questions you investigate?

My current book project is on the war on terrorism, so I'm looking at the way in which television has mediated and constructed our understanding of the war on terrorism, specifically in a domestic context. I'm interested in how the war was sold, how television partnered with the White House to win the hearts and minds of the domestic populace to this exploit. I'm looking at things like reality programs that the Department of Defense helped produce. There's a program called *Profiles from the Front Line* that Donald Rumsfeld signed off on personally. This program followed a number of units who were dispatched in the invasion of Afghanistan. The thing about it that's important is that these reality TV producers—it's a Jerry Bruckheimer produced series—they were given access to the front lines that was denied to journalists. So what kinds of reports are you going to get? You're going to get these puff pieces about intrepid American soldiers doing their duty to help rebuild Afghanistan. You won't see what we did before that. You won't see the consequences of US bombs.

I also look at *24* and the reemergence of the thriller genre at this particular historical moment. I look at a series of Iraq War dramas that have emerged recently that are more critical of the war. I'm looking at both the moments of clear collaboration that are going on between political and commercial entitles working together to effectively disseminate propaganda, but I'm also looking at ways in which television as a commercial medium changes with public opinion. If public opinion shifts, the kind of show we see shifts as well.

What are some of the prominent research questions in the field of Television Studies?

We like to look at how things like race, class, gender, and sexuality influence both the production of television programs and their circulation, and they do circulate globally. So if we have a racially inclusive program, like *LOST*, sometimes it's a strategic decision—not because we want to show diversity—but because it will sell better overseas. Questions of power and resistance and how people interpret the messages that are being sent to them in ways that are not passive at all but quite active.

Some TV scholars look at fan production and fan discourse. Right now a hot topic in fan studies is a lot of fan production is being co-opted by Hollywood entities. Fans are now doing labor for free for corporations. This is a qualitative shift. It used to be nobody cared about fan production; there was no money to be made doing it. Now it's big business. Is this really fandom anymore?

In general, what kinds of writing and publication are common in your research field?

It's a lot like literature studies. We have our own specialized journals. You're expected to write a book and have articles in peer-reviewed journals.

My students are asked to do a lot of writing. In part that's because we don't really have an active production program in Screen Studies. There is an active program over in Journalism and Broadcasting, so if I get those students, I sometimes write assignments with flexibility so if the students want to produce a video, they can do that. But even then I ask them to turn in the script. They're asked to analyze films and television programs, they're asked to go online and participate in fan forums and then analyze the discourse. In some ways it's very similar to what students taking literature courses are doing. Let's analyze the message, but let's also think, why this text, why now, what does it mean to receive it now as opposed to then, those sorts of questions.

How common is co-authorship?

In TV Studies it's not that common, and I'm not sure why that is. We're doing qualitative studies, and it involves a person sitting in a room watching every episode of *Buffy the Vampire Slayer* and getting on the online forums and analyzing the discourse. The result is usually a single-author essay.

In Cultural Studies there is some collaborative work in part because the politics of cultural studies support that. The notion that it is an interdisciplinary program also lends itself to that. It depends on what field you're looking at.

How has the field changed over the years?

There is definitely a shift from quantitative to qualitative methodologies, which is not to say that quantitative has disappeared. TV Studies is trying to establish itself the way Film Studies did in the 1970s, as a separate entity. We're trying to establish TV as an important cultural object of study, which has been an uphill battle.

What are some of the writing skills that you value in student work?

I value the ability to make a clear statement about your purpose. I value the ability to organize your thoughts, not necessarily in a linear fashion but in a cumulative one so that where we end up is different from where we started, so it's not circular: thesis, evidence, restatement of thesis, but rather a thinking through. The same set of analytical skills most people in an English Department require: the ability to do a close reading and make an argument about the importance of a text in a particular social situation.

Can you suggest some texts that would be useful to students working in the discipline?

Because Cultural Studies is interdisciplinary, there tend to be a lot of anthologies. *Media and Cultural Studies: KeyWorks* by Meenakshi Gigi Durham and Douglas M. Kellner is a good one. Any of them are good—they give you an idea of the diversity in the field, and what kinds of questions unify the different approaches.

In my Intro to TV Studies, I like to use Jason Mittell's *Television and American Culture*. It provides a broad overview to the entire industry from economics to reception and fan production. It's also fairly new, which, for TV, matters because it's undergone such a change in the last five years.

Dr. Takacs, thank you very much for your time.

Jessica Lynch and the Regeneration of American Identity and Power Post-9/11

Stacy Takacs

As she discussed in the preceeding interview, Dr. Takacs' work currently focuses on the war on terrorism and how "television has mediated and constructed our understanding...specifically in a domestic context." This article discusses the multiple documentaries about the rescue of Private Jessica Lynch and the gendered language employed by the media when discussing foreign and domestic policy in the wake of September 11.

Introduction

On April 1, 2003, the broken body of Pfc. Jessica Lynch was recovered by the US military from a hospital in Nasariyah, Iraq, where she lay suffering from injuries incurred in a combat-related Humvee crash. The rescue quickly took on larger-than-life proportions, however, as the vested interests of the military and commercial media coalesced around the need for a good story to clarify the moral stakes of the war in Iraq (John Kampfner 2003; Steve Ritea 2003; Peter Sussman 2003). Within days, the tale of the 507th Maintenance Unit's blunder into enemy lines had been framed as an "ambush," and Lynch's rescue had become a parable of American innocence lost and regained through the intervention of military might (Susan Schmidt & Vernon Loeb 2003). Thus sensationalized, the tale was embraced by the American public because it offered, through analogy, a reassuring resolution to the traumatic experience of September 11, 2001.

This essay will examine the Lynch rescue in relation to the on-going processes of national regeneration necessitated by 9/11. As Julie Drew (2004) has argued, "prevailing narratives of who and what we are, as Americans, took a hit" on September 11. The process of reconstructing national identity began almost immediately in public discourse following the attacks. Media scholars have shown how breaking news coverage (Amy Reynolds & Brooke Barnett 2003), newspaper editorials (Jack Lule 2002), and even advertisements (Christopher Campbell 2003) strategically framed the events in ways that made the US seem an innocent victim of a senseless act. Political elites, likewise, decontextualized terrorism, describing it as a "cowardly" act born of "hatred," "jealousy," and "evil," rather than politics (Drew 2004). Such rhetoric made "a unified military response" appear "the only real alternative to combat future devastation and terror" (Reynolds & Barnett 2003). In the process, it also tied national identity and security to notions of masculinity, rather than femininity.

"Characteristics, actions, and reactions deemed feminine—such as diplomacy, negotiation, and compromise" have been systematically devalued in public discourse since 9/11 in favor of "masculine characteristics of physical strength, punitive response, and violent aggression" (Drew 2004). The Lynch rescue dramatically illustrates this process of social reprioritization and provides an occasion for thinking through the consequences of this gendering for US foreign and domestic policy.

By examining documentary and docu-dramatic representations of the Lynch rescue, including *Saving Private Lynch* (A&E; 2003), *Saving POW Lynch* (Discovery; 2003) *Primetime*'s interview special "Pfc. Jessica Lynch: An American Story" (ABC; 2003), and the NBC made-for-TV-movie *Saving Jessica Lynch* (2003), this essay seeks to illustrate how militarism, masculinity, and national security have become conflated in public discourse post-9/11 and how this has cohered with and helped to naturalize the Bush administration's aggressive foreign policy agenda. President Bush has long conceived of the nation as a patriarchal family whose security depends upon military aggression, but it took 9/11 to convince him that national security could best be pursued through the militarized extension of US hegemony. The goal of this essay is to illustrate and, hopefully, disrupt the processes of consensus formation sustaining this counter-intuitive security policy, for the use of war to achieve peace only spreads insecurity and guarantees the political marginalization of those who fail to embody the ideals of masculinity authorized by security discourse.

Gender and National Security in the (Neo-)Conservative Mind

Historically, ideas about masculinity have encouraged political elites in the US to associate security with military strength and to avoid thinking about the physical and emotional consequences of war (Cynthia Enloe 2004, p. 126). This has not happened by accident; rather, it is a function of the gendered symbolic system adopted to interpret the US's relations to others in the world. As feminist scholar Carol Cohn has shown, national security discourse depends upon a gendered hierarchy of values, which privileges "masculine" traits like rationality, competition, and aggression over "feminine" ones like emotionality, cooperation, and conciliation (Cohn 1993, p. 229). As with most binaries, the value of the first term is dependent upon the devaluation of the second. The defense analysts Cohn studied, for example, used sexual imagery to police group identity, describing nuclear war as a "pissing contest" ([1987] 2003, p. 60) and labeling those who questioned the necessity or effects of war as "pussies," "fags" or "women" (1993, pp. 235–236). Such derogatory invocations of femininity and homosexuality permit the disavowal of vulnerability, which is necessary to make the work of calculating human destruction psychologically bearable (Cohn [1987] 2003, p. 57). However, it also associates militarism with omnipotence and makes war seem like a guarantee of security rather than a threat to it.

This specialized discourse of security has filtered out "to the military, politicians, and the public, and increasingly shapes how we talk and think about war" (Cohn 1993, p. 228). Conservatives, in particular (though not exclusively), have favored this view of militarism as the route to security because their value system already conceives of the nation as a patriarchal family requiring masculine protection (George Lakoff 2002). When the end of the Cold War deprived the US of a clear rationale for an activist foreign policy, conservatives did not abandon their priorities; rather, they searched for a new rationale to legitimate such activism. As early as 1992, Paul Wolfowitz, then Undersecretary of Defense for Policy, drafted a Defense Planning Guidance memo advocating the militarized extension of US hegemony as a means of guaranteeing global security. The best defense, he argued, was a good offense (Andrew Bacevich 2002, pp. 43–44). He and other prominent neoconservatives, including William Kristol, Robert Kagan, Elliott Abrams, Richard Perle, and Donald Rumsfeld, formed a think tank called the Project for the New American Century to press this agenda. They invoked the gendered language of national security to naturalize their positions. For example, they warned that President Clinton's multilateral containment strategy for Iraq left the US "weak," "helpless," and "dependent" on the good will of European allies (Robert Kagan 1998; Project for the New American Century 1998). They described the US as a "cowering superpower" and announced that "only violence... may recoup the damage that the [British] Labour Party, Bill Clinton, and the Near East Bureau of the State Department have done to America's standing" in the Middle East (Reuel Marc Gerecht 2001, p. 29). Weakness, helplessness, dependence, and fear are characteristics associated in US culture with femininity; hence militarized masculinity (violence) is viewed as the only possible antidote to the nation's "feminization." George W. Bush has not only incorporated a number of these individuals into his administration, he has embraced a number of their ideas.

Even before 9/11, President Bush viewed national identity and security in terms of competing definitions of masculinity. In his first major foreign policy speech, he (1999) described the Clinton administration's security strategy as promiscuous and, therefore, insufficiently masculine. By "multiplying missions" without regard to the nation's "vital interests," the Clinton administration "squander[ed] American will and drain[ed] American energy" (Bush 1999). Like sexual potency, Bush implied, military potency is undermined by overuse. Clinton's preference for diplomacy, moreover, made the US appear "soft." "There are limits to the smiles and scowls of diplomacy," Bush (1999) warned, "Armies and missiles are not stopped by stiff notes of condemnation. They are held in check by strength and purpose and the promise of swift punishment." Bush offered voters a vision of renewed national vigor guaranteed through Victorian restraint. The US would "[encourage] stability from a position of strength" but, like a good patriarch, would be "modest" and "humble" about its use of force to conserve that strength (Bush 1999). Clearly, Bush had not fully embraced the neo-conservatives' hegemonic agenda prior to 9/11, but he did share their view of security as defined by militarized masculinity. This made the transition to an offensive security strategy relatively easy to achieve once the terrorist attacks exposed the alleged dangers of national "feminization."

Remasculinization as a Public Necessity Post-9/11

The 9/11 terrorist attacks were depicted in gendered terms within public discourse in ways that reinforced and extended the Bush administration's extant assumptions about national identity and security. Breaking news coverage of the events set the tone by describing the attacks as "acts of war" directed at an innocent "America," rather than a geopolitically entangled United States. Reporters proclaimed Americans "united" behind the idea that the only "just" response would be violent retribution (Reynolds & Barnett 2003). Later news reports and eyewitness accounts described the attacks in terms of a "violation" and emphasized the generalized nature of feelings of fear, vulnerability, and helplessness. Images of men, even soldiers at the Pentagon, screaming, running, and crying were particularly evocative of this sense of violation, for they also violated cultural perceptions of stoic masculinity. This "discursive construction of the polis as far more pervasively feminine than was previously understood" (Drew 2004) implicitly corroborated the neo-conservative assumption that "weakness is provocative" (Secretary of State Donald Rumsfeld cited in Bacevich 2002, p. 84). Like the word "violated," this statement links the terrorist attacks to rape (Drew 2004) and implies that the US got what it deserved on 9/11 because it dressed improperly; its power was not sufficiently manifest.

The construction of the nation as overly feminized not only encouraged the Bush administration to embrace a military response in this instance; it facilitated the administration's adoption of the neo-conservative strategy for US hegemony. The 2002 National Security Strategy, a virtual replica of the 1992 Wolfowitz memo (Bacevich 2002, p. 45), left no doubt that the nation's security would be vested in the military, and that this remilitarization would also entail a remasculinization of national identity. The document is also exceedingly candid about what this implies for others since the key to securing the homeland is to create military "forces strong enough to dissuade potential adversaries from pursuing a military build-up in hopes of surpassing, or equaling, the power of the United States" ("National Security Strategy" 2002). In other words, to ensure that US potency cannot be challenged, every other nation must be effectively castrated.

Orientalism and the War on Terrorism

The War on Terrorism has provided the ideological framework necessary to depict US hegemonic aspirations as a form of altruistic self-sacrifice undertaken in the name of high ideals: the spread of "freedom, democracy, and free enterprise" and the rescue of "civilization" ("National Security Strategy" 2002). Orientalist assumptions about race and gender structure the opposition between civilization and barbarity in this discourse in ways that preclude the possibility of Arabs and Arab societies acting on their own behalf to secure these freedoms. Instead, action is reserved for the US military, which must save Arab societies from themselves.

Edward Said (1979) defines Orientalism as a "style of thought" predicated upon the distinction between the West (the Occident) and the East (the Orient). The Orient is both a material space and an imaginary construct whose purpose is to give coherence to the image of the West by serving as "its contrasting image, idea, personality, experience" (Said 1979, p. 2). Specifically, Orientalism seeks to identify the West with civilization by coding the East as barbaric. Again, gender assumptions structure the dichotomy (Jasbir Puar & Amit Rai 2002; Leti Volpp 2003). Orientalism "collaps[es] non-Europeans and women into an undifferentiated field" and understands "The East... as the site of passivity and irrationality, awaiting the conquest by the masculine and rational West" (Volpp 2003, p. 154). Western colonization of the Orient has been justified historically through the invocation of "women in need of uplift." Indeed, the project of European empire was virtually defined by "white men saving brown women from brown men" (Gayatri Spivak 1988, p. 297).

Taking a page from this imperial playbook, the Bush administration has characterized the invasions of Afghanistan and Iraq as rescue missions. Barely a month after the September 11 attacks, for example, First Lady Laura Bush prepared the ground for a US invasion of Afghanistan by delivering a Presidential Radio Address elaborating the plight of Afghan women under the Taliban. She proclaimed "the fight against terrorism" to be "a fight for the rights and dignity of women" and implied that the pending invasion was a moral duty that the US should undertake in the name of "civilized people throughout the world" (Laura Bush 2003, p. 250). A similar rhetorical strategy was adopted to legitimate Operation Iraqi Freedom. Though Iraqi men received the bulk of the state's violent correction under Saddam Hussein, President Bush has focused insistently on the rape of women, implying it was common, indiscriminate, and somehow more tragic than the torture of men. In public speeches regarding the invasion, he often invokes torture as a specifically female experience: "every *woman* in Iraq is better off because the rape rooms and torture chambers of Saddam Hussein are forever closed" (Bush 2004; emphasis mine). This emphasis on women facilitates the Orientalist confusion of the War in Iraq with the War on Terrorism, casting Hussein as a terrorist merely for having oppressed and persecuted women.

The manly application of retributive violence will not only rescue Arab women, however. It will rescue whole Arab societies, which have been feminized by their leaders. Military dictatorships and theocratic tyrants have left individuals in the Middle East "victims and subjects" rather than "citizens," Bush claims (2003b). Therefore, it is the moral duty of the United States, as the leader of the civilized world, to rescue these victims. In the case of Iraq, the whole society was depicted as cowed into passivity and in need of salvation, which is perhaps why US military planners assumed the troops would be greeted as liberators. The gendered discourse of national security, abetted by Orientalist thinking, thus legitimated the invasion as a vital rescue mission undertaken in the name of civilization.

Domesticating Foreign Policy: The Lynch Documentaries

The discursive conflation of militarism, masculinity, and security post-9/11 reached its apotheosis in media depictions of the rescue of Pfc. Jessica Lynch. Documentaries about the rescue fetishized Lynch's femininity and vulnerability in order to remasculinize a coed military and militarize the identities of civilian men and women in ways that would perpetuate the project of hegemony. Using melodramatic techniques reminiscent of captivity narratives from the colonial era, these documentaries personalized the political and made Lynch's recovery seem a matter of family honor. As in most captivity narratives, gender, race, sex, and class assumptions were invoked to police the boundaries of communal identity, excluding those deemed other and justifying the use of violence by coding it as defensive (Melani McAlister 2003; Emily Rosenberg 2003). The documentaries transform Lynch from a soldier at war to a symbol of the American family under attack in order to authorize the US mission in Iraq and elicit popular consent for the perpetuation of the project of US hegemony.

As a small, young, blond, white, female from rural America, whose visibly broken body renders her completely dependent on the kindness of strangers, Jessica Lynch fits the role of damsel in distress to a tee (Deepa Kumar 2004, p. 300). A&E's documentary, *Saving Private Lynch* (2003), acknowledges as much in its opening monologue: "[her dramatic story] has all the ingredients of a Hollywood movie with its heroes, suspense, the rescue of a young woman in captivity and a bittersweet ending." Rushed to production just eighteen days after the rescue, this documentary follows the paths of the three female soldiers of 507th Maintenance Unit as they encounter different "fates," but focuses most intently on Lynch, who is repeatedly referred to as "the blond 19 year old from Palestine, West Virginia." As this description makes clear, Lynch is selected for media stardom over the other candidates, Lori Piestewa, a Hopi Indian from Arizona, and Shoshana Johnson, an African-American from Texas, because her race, age, and background identify her with the American heartland and connote the maximum vulnerability.

Both the Lynch biography and the television depictions of her story invoke her roots in Palestine to fix a particular image of the American homeland in the viewers' minds. Absent Lynch herself, her hometown becomes the center of media attention, and the values it embodies are "traditional family values." These values equate national identity with notions of blood and soil and privilege filiation over affiliation in defining citizenship. Lynch's biographer, Rick Bragg, tells us, for example, that Lynch's "kin believe she is alive, in part, because she comes from this place [West Virginia], because she has the right blood in her... Even though she is small and a little prissy, she carries the blood of the mountains—the blood of people who fought and worked and loved here" (Bragg 2003, p. 15). If Lynch is a pioneering American spirit, this passage implies, her defining qualities are inherited not learned. A perception of Palestine as uniquely, timelessly, and exclusively American also pervades the documentaries. For example, *Primetime's* "Pfc. Jessica Lynch: An American Story" (2003) uses frequent aerial shots of the hillsides of Wirt County to connote the "tightknit" quality of the community there. It also obsessively focuses on the symbols of patriotism displayed in the county—American flags, yellow ribbons, prayer vigils, and support rallies that culminate in the playing of Lee Greenwood's "Proud to Be an American." This exclusive yet reassuring image of national identity conforms to the Bush administration's own conception of the homeland as a vulnerable community in need of militarized protection. Such images domesticate foreign policy and turn the home into a key site for the ideological reproduction of consent for the project of American hegemony.

The documentary representations of the ambush and rescue facilitate the conflation of militarism, masculinity, and security in a variety of ways. First, the documentaries fetishize her femininity and vulnerability so as to reassert traditional gender norms challenged by the presence of women in the military (John Howard & Laura Prividera 2004; Deepa Kumar 2004). As Bill Kurtis (*Saving Private Lynch* 2003) acknowledges: "The reality of a volunteer army where women are equal partners hits Americans hard." Lynch's hyper-femininity allays popular anxieties about such gender in-subordination. The television documentaries all refer to Lynch by her hair color, eye color, stature, and youth because these make her clearly and safely a "girl." Lynch is also "'rhetorically stripped' of her military identity" (Howard & Prividera 2004) by announcers who refer to her as "Jessica" and feature photos of her in civilian, rather than military, cloth-ing: her senior class portrait, a picture of her posing by a tree outside the family home, and, most importantly, shots of her as a be-gowned Miss Congeniality at the Wirt County Fair. The narratives also take care to explain that Lynch only joined the Army to help pay for college, not as a feminist statement. Her dreams for her life are modest and stereotypically feminine: she wants to settle in Wirt County and become a housewife and kindergarten teacher.

In addition to being "small" and "prissy" (Bragg 2003, p. 15), Lynch is ut-terly incapacitated by her injuries. She cannot help herself and so must be helped by others. This extreme passivity activates cultural assumptions that portray women as weak and vulnerable while men are strong and protective. The rescue footage provided by the Department of Defense and incorporated into the documentaries reinforces these assumptions by literalizing the classic Hollywood mandate: "men act, women appear" (Laura Mulvey [1975] 1993). While the camera focuses obsessively on Lynch's face during the evacuation, the shot obscures all but the moving arms and legs of her male rescuers. Her immobility is thus contrasted with their hypermobility. Like a Hollywood starlet, Lynch facilitates the movement of the masculine narrative of war through her passivity. Her need for rescue provides the US military with the excuse to exercise its manly might.

Because Lynch embodies the homeland and its values, her personal vul-nerability evokes the nation's vulnerability and makes remilitarization appear the only viable means to achieve security. The documentaries implicitly link the ambush in Nasariyah to the terrorist attacks of 9/11, both of which are imagined as unmotivated crimes perpetrated against innocents. The non-combat status of Lynch's military unit is vital to this construction, as is her status as an all-American girl next door (Kumar 2004). *Primetime* ("Pfc. Jessica Lynch" 2003) makes the implicit explicit by opening the segment about her captivity with bucolic shots of her family home and the voiceover narration: "West Virginia, terror strikes the Lynch family at home!" Recalling the discursive framing of 9/11, this invocation of a vulnerable domestic sphere incites spectators to identify with the need for a militarized security solution. Lynch's status as all-American girl deepens this commitment, for if she is imagined as "'everyone's sister or daughter'... her enemies [become] ours. In the process of identifying with a soldier, the public [is] invited to consent to the US's goals" in the Middle East and elsewhere (Kumar 2004, p. 304).

Finally, the documentaries aid in the process of consensus formation by exaggerating Lynch's personal vulnerability. They do this in two ways: by speculating about the nature of her experience in captivity and by casting her as a fish out of water in Iraq. The documentaries virtually obsess about the danger to women posed by combat duty. Speaking of the videos of the five POWs from the 507th Maintenance Unit aired on Al-Jezeerah, Bill Kurtis (*Saving Private Lynch* 2003) contends, "the sight of women being held is startling to Americans. What seems to worry people most are the accounts of the torture of POWs who were held by Iraqis during the first Persian Gulf War." This is followed almost immediately by references to Col. Rhonda Cornham, who was molested by an Iraqi soldier during the Gulf War after her helicopter crashed in the desert. Each of the documentaries contains a similar sequence, and all of them mention Cornham's story. None of them mentions the story of Specialist Melissa Rathbun-Nealy, who was also captured during that war but who did not suffer sexual abuse (Howard & Prividera 2004).

This illustrates how assumptions about female vulnerability are constructed, rather than reflected, by the media. Lacking access to information about Lynch's injuries, the documentaries simply assume that she was violated in captivity. For example, the Discovery channel's *Saving POW Lynch* (2003) claims, "it is unclear whether she sustained her injuries while she desperately fought for her life during the ambush or during her captivity." We now know her injuries were the result of a Humvee crash, but the suggestion that she was violated lingers nevertheless. Even Diane Sawyer's *Primetime* interview with Lynch, which occurred seven months after the rescue, contains such speculation: "In addition to the wounds that we know about," Sawyer says, "There may have been another wound, so brutal that there's nothing that can reach into her memory and make it real." Sawyer notes that Lynch's Army medical file shows she "may" have been sodomized. Though the language of the report is hesitant and contradicted by Lynch's Iraqi doctors, *Primetime* sanctions the rape scenario by ending on Rick Bragg's firm assertion of support for the military version. Such innuendo constructs Lynch as vulnerable and transforms her from American soldier to ordinary woman. It relocates American identity in the private sphere and depicts that sphere as constitutively susceptible to attack, the better to legitimate the perceived need for militarized masculinity.

The documentaries also construct Lynch's vulnerability by depicting her as alienated and alone in Iraq, a stranger in a strange land. As a narrative frame, this motif clarifies for the audience the difference between the foreign and the domestic, "them" and "us," and effectively justifies "our" anxieties about "them." The Iraqi landscape is always depicted, for example, as not just unfamiliar but otherworldly. *Primetime* ("Pfc. Jessica Lynch" 2003) begins its discussion of the ambush by having Lynch read portions of the following passage from her biography:

> It was flat, dull and yellow-brown, except where the water had turned the dust to reddish paste. She got excited when she saw a tree. Trees made sense. She had grown up in the woods, where the solid walls of hardwood had sunk roots deep in the hillsides and kept the ground pulled tight, as it should be, to the planet. All this empty space and loose, shifting sand unsettled her mind and made her feel lost, long before she found out it was true. (Bragg 2003, p. 8)

The American homeland, the passage implies, is fixed, familiar, and solid, like a planet "should be," while Iraq is empty, irregular, and inscrutable. Because the treeless, red dust landscape seems more like Mars than Earth, the Iraqis are implicitly likened to aliens. The contrast is heightened by the strategy of intercutting that juxtaposes West Virginia to Iraq in order to emphasize Lynch's representative American-ness. For instance, *Saving POW Lynch* (2003) and *Saving Private Lynch* (2003) both juxtapose file footage of random, chaotic combat scenes in Iraq with placid pictures of Lynch in civilian clothes. Not only does this distance Lynch from her military identity and heighten the illusion of her victimization, it implies that chaos is the norm in Iraq. The conspicuous absence of shots of Iraqi civilians performing the ordinary tasks of everyday life enhances the impression that violence is endemic to Iraq. In contrast, lavish attention is paid to Lynch's private life and family, their routines, and especially their personal faith.

Melodramatic techniques used to heighten the identification with Lynch further distance the audience from the Iraqis. For example, *Primetime* ("Pfc. Jessica Lynch" 2003) repeatedly blurs focus in order to invoke the "fog of war," suturing the audience into the "ambush" scene and inviting them to interpret it as a terrorist attack. The depiction of the assault on the convoy deliberately disorients the viewer so as to convey the chaotic experience of war: fragmented combat sounds and syncopated martial music punctuate a dizzying montage of trucks sticking in sand, Humvees whizzing by, and explosions ripping through the air. The sentence fragments in Diane Sawyer's voice-over enhance the perception of urgency by suggesting a paucity of both words and time to describe the barbarism of the Iraqis: "her brutal injuries, the missing hours, what doctors say about a sexual assault." The other documentaries adopt similar strategies, using random combat footage to convey the meaning of "ambush" and addressing the audience directly to facilitate an identification with the experience: "Imagine if your daughter or son were over in Iraq, and you got word that they were taken prisoner of war" (*Saving POW Lynch* 2003). These melodramatic techniques accomplish an astounding reversal of fortune, as the US becomes the victim of a war it initiated. Moreover, the ambush is coded as an attack, not just on the 507th Maintenance Unit, but on the entirety of the domestic US population and specifically an invasion of the family home from which only a strong military can protect us.

If Lynch's vulnerability cries out for a heroic rescue, her status as a passive spectator at the event mirrors the status of the television viewer watching the war from the safety of home. The analogy positions the audience to embrace a military identity as a means of preempting their own anxieties about increased globalization and the terrorism it facilitates. All of the documentaries foreground the first exchange between Lynch and her rescuers and read her willingness to identify with a military identity as a sign of her courage. When the US commandos first burst into Lynch's hospital room, they reportedly said: "Jessica Lynch, we are United States soldiers come to take you home." Lynch responded, "I'm an American soldier, too." *Saving Private Lynch* (2003) consults several experts in military psychology who all agree that such affirmation "means that she viewed herself, even in her vulnerable state, still as a warrior." In fact, Lynch perceives herself as a survivor, not a hero or a soldier ("Pfc. Jessica Lynch" 2003). In the post-9/11 context, however, survival has become its own form of heroism (Isabelle Freda 2004). Ordinary Americans, particularly the wives and children of the victims of 9/11, have been lauded in popular culture merely for carrying on with their lives. President Bush ([2001] 2003a, p. 242) has argued that the best way to defeat terrorism is to "live your lives and hug your children," to go shopping and visit Disney World. The real value of the Lynch rescue for US foreign policy thus lies in its conflation of mundanity and heroism, domestic identity and military identity. Her rescue brings the war home and codes everyone as a potential hero in the fight against terrorism. These documentaries ensure that, like Lynch herself, no one will be left behind in the War on Terrorism and the project of global hegemony it facilitates.

US Hegemony as Civilizing Mission: NBC's Saving Jessica Lynch

The patriarchal assumptions that prepared the US populace to embrace the Lynch rescue as an homage to militarism and masculinity also reproduce the Orientalist assumptions used to legitimate US aggression as a defense of civilization against a barbaric Arab other. The NBC made-for-TV-movie version of Lynch's rescue, *Saving Jessica Lynch*, provides the most elaborate example of this process of othering, for the construction of Lynch's identity is always relative to the construction of an Iraqi menace. Kumar has argued that the movie at least attempts to distinguish between "good" and "bad" Iraqis by incorporating images of Iraqi heroism (2004, p. 309). I would argue, however, that whatever "goodness" is imputed to Iraqis is defined through identification with things American, and, therefore, the presence of good brown characters does not seriously challenge the Orientalist dichotomy of the film or the mission it legitimates. Despite being based on the account of the rescue provided by Mohammed Al Rehaief, the Iraqi lawyer who reported Lynch's whereabouts to the Marines, the film is a paradigmatic study in the demonization of Arab peoples. Its agenda is to affirm a consensual American identity by offering the public a clear and undifferentiated enemy image. Both narratively and visually, the film manipulates extant race and gender codes to transform individual Iraqis into an alien mass recognizable as barbaric so that "we" may appear civilized and justified in our pretensions to rule.

Like the documentaries, the film presents Lynch as an American innocent abroad, lost and alone in a strange environment. The opening credit sequence establishes Lynch's dislocation by fetishizing her race and size. The titles roll over images of the US convoy in inexorable motion with a tiny Lynch (Laura Regan) driving an out-sized truck into an endless horizon. These shots convey a sense that Lynch is already out of place—her social place—before a sandstorm halts the convoy and literally disorients the unit. A conversation between Lynch and her comrades, Lori Piestewa (Chrystle Lightening) and Shoshana Johnson (Denise Lee), during the brief rest reinforces this perception by contrasting the self-evidently American Lynch to Piestewa, a Hopi Indian from Tuba City, Arizona. Lynch looks around at the landscape and sees nothing familiar. Piestewa looks and says, "you know I grew up on land like this. Joined the Army just to get away from it." Lynch insists, "You can't get any further from Arizona than this," but Piestewa replies, "I don't know." While this might be viewed as a sly critique of US race relations, which have made Indians like Piestewa feel alienated from their native land, the exchange also, and more importantly, affirms Lynch's innocence about those relations as representatively American. Shortly after this exchange, we see Lynch staring curiously at a group of nomads and camels silhouetted against the desert sky. Intercutting is again used to emphasize the distance between the home Lynch knows and the desert she finds herself in, as the camels fade into shots of verdant West Virginia scenery. A brief montage depicts Lynch's farewell to Palestine and concludes with her father's voice telling her to "remember where you came from" and ordering her to "come home." Home is presented as a place with clear boundaries and stable content. Iraq, on the other hand, is represented as inscrutable: its sand covered roads and invisible berms entrap the military vehicles, and its combatants are indistinguishable from its civilians.

The depiction of Lynch as a naïve traveller is further developed by the choice to present the ambush from Lynch's perspective using a subjective camera. Lynch becomes the eyes of the audience, and her gaze organizes the sequence into a pseudo-narrative whereby the Iraqis fuse into a single menacing entity. As the convoy enters Nasariyah, we see a series of Iraqi civilians lining the road and staring back at us as if at Lynch. They talk among themselves but only in Arabic, which Lynch cannot understand. Since she does not know what they are saying, she assumes it is negative: "So much for the celebrating," she remarks. The Iraqis are generally denied the benefit of a return shot, which means they are objects to be looked at, not subjects capable of returning the gaze. A shot of a mother and her child watching the convoy, for example, slides off the screen before we return to see Lynch watching the scenery.

One exception is the man who organizes the ambush. Lynch first sees him riding in the backseat of a passing car. At the point when the vehicles cross, the sequence goes into slow motion, and the two characters lock eyes. A shot-reverse-shot sequence depicts him as powerful enough to return her gaze. Lynch's imperial perspective is effectively undone by his look, and, from that point on, Lynch and her compatriots become victims rather than conquerors. When the ambush begins, the man assumes narrative control, striding down the street with an AK-47 on his hip as if challenging the trucks to a duel. Lynch, on the other hand, becomes utterly disoriented. She does not fire her weapon or even attempt to; instead, she looks around frantically trying to find something to fix her gaze on. Her commander even enjoins her to "stay focused," but her eyes register nothing but panic (indeed, Lynch's sole function in this scene is to manifest terror). Her loss of subjectivity is confirmed by her lack of dialogue; during the last hour of the film she has only six brief lines. Thus, she literally becomes "an object about which stories [are] told" (Kumar 2004, p. 310).

The subjective camera work portrays the Americans as victims of a brutal and unwarranted Iraqi assault and invites viewers to empathize with their situation. Swish pans and special effects incorporate the audience into the chaos by mimicking the exchange of gunfire. We also witness the Humvee crash from the inside as if we are one of the occupants. The Iraqi assailants, meanwhile, are depicted as inhuman zealots. At one point, for example, we see a gleeful Iraqi firing into the cab of an overturned truck, shouting "Allah, Allah" and waving his gun in the air in triumph (the celebration is captured in slow motion to emphasize its inhumanity). The unnamed Fedayeen Colonel (Navid Negahban) who takes charge of the prisoners after the ambush is presented as the ultimate embodiment of Iraqi cruelty, however. His power over the Americans is affirmed by the extreme camera angles used to depict the surrender of Sergeant James Riley (Dak Rashetta). Riley kneels shaking in the dirt and begins to announce his name, rank, and serial number, according to Geneva conventions. As he does this, the camera looks over his shoulder and up at the Fedayeen Colonel, enhancing the Colonel's stature. Riley is then literally knocked down. The Colonel is also shot from a low angle as he crouches over Lynch's broken body and says, somewhat sarcastically, "Welcome to my country." Lynch immediately blacks out, and a disembodied scream provides the bridge into the next scene. The implication is that the Colonel has done something to harm Lynch. Because the Colonel and the leader of the ambush are the only Iraqis to achieve individuation at this point, they come to represent all Iraqis. The civilian dress of the ambush leader even implies that ordinary Iraqis are really Fedayeen in disguise. Thus, the entire society is demonized for the brutality of Saddam Hussein's specially trained military units. The attempt to convey Lynch's sense of disorientation subjectively, by, for example, blacking out when she does and filtering the screen to indicate a drugged state, makes even the doctors and nurses who care for her appear menacing and evil.

The depiction of Mohammed Al Rehaief (Nicholas Guilak) reaffirms, rather than challenges, the Orientalist portrayal of the Iraqi people as an undifferentiated, menacing mass. This is because Al Rehaief is distinguished from other Iraqis through his association with American popular culture and American family values. His identification with a paternal, militarized masculinity effectively de-racializes him, enabling he and his family to be folded into the realm of civilization. From his first appearance, Al Rehaief is explicitly contrasted with the Fedayeen and the barbaric values they represent. When told by a nurse not to go down a particular hallway because the Fedayeen "are interrogating an American prisoner of war," Al Rehaief replies, "Do you know what I just saw. I saw them drag my neighbor... through the streets. Do you know what her crime was? She waved, waved, at a US Army helicopter, so I know who the Fedayeens are." His disgust and lack of fear separate him from the mass of Iraqis implicitly identified with the Fedayeen. When Al Rehaief does venture down the hallway, he allegedly witnesses Lynch being slapped by one of the interrogators (Lynch and her doctors both claim this never occurred). His reaction is paternal: "She's just a girl, a child." This paternalism identifies him with the Americans, who have imagined their incursion into Iraq as a benevolent mission of salvation, and, like the Americans, he vows to help the helpless Lynch. That this reaction is not "Iraqi" is illustrated by his wife's disapproval: "There are millions of her [Lynch's] countrymen marching on our country right now... the Americans have made this into a new crusade. They are ruining our country." In response to her political perspective on the war, Al Rehaief invokes the abstract values of kinship: "When I look at that girl, I see our daughter."

Later, his wife will blame Al Rehaief's mother for having "poisoned your mind with all of those John Wayne movies." Al Rehaief's association with American popular culture, and the militarized masculinity of Wayne, in particular, prepares the audience to accept him as the "star" of the rescue narrative. His alienation from his Iraqi identity is completed when he goes to find the Marines and gets lost in his own land. This disorientation makes him structurally analogous to Lynch, which also makes him worthy of salvation. The film concludes, appropriately enough, with the double rescue of Lynch from Saddam General Hospital and of Al Rehaief and family from Iraq. The redemption of Lynch thus facilitates the redemption of Al Rehaief, which, in turn, redeems the US mission in Iraq. By filtering its narrative through an Orientalist prism, the film characterizes the invasion as a benevolent civilizing mission designed to save barbarous others from themselves.

Conclusion

The invocation of patriarchal race and gender norms in the video recreations of the rescue of Jessica Lynch enables both the remasculinization of the military (Howard & Prividera 2004; Kumar 2004) and the remilitarization of foreign policy (Enloe 2004). By foregrounding Lynch's femininity, passivity, and vulnerability, the videos invite Americans to embrace militarized masculinity as the only logical antidote to national insecurity. The videos illustrate how public discourse post-9/11 has reconstructed national identity in ways that naturalize and extend a conservative view of the nation and of national security. By popularizing the conception of the nation as a patriarchal family in need of masculine providence and protection, such discourse has also made palatable the neo-conservative philosophy of security, which views war as the means to achieve peace.

It is important to understand how gender assumptions frame notions of security because discursive constructions have material consequences. The Bush administration has used public enthusiasm for its conservative foreign policy to push through conservative domestic policies, as well.

As Drew (2004) notes, the administration's "budget priorities and legislative initiatives…disproportionately target women, children, the poor and citizens of color." Tax cuts, for example, have been enacted at the expense of social welfare programs; federal aid for community assistance has been redirected to "faith-based initiatives," and reproductive rights have been significantly curtailed on Bush's watch. The situation is even worse for those women "liberated" by the US military in Afghanistan and Iraq. Not only have they been virtually excluded from the reconstruction processes, they have been targeted by fundamentalist groups struggling with each other and with weaker secular forces for power in both nations. In both cases, initial political and social gains have given way to chronic personal insecurity and political marginalization.[1]

In Iraq, for example, feminist politicians and political organizations have been excluded from the political process in favor of conservative women's groups willing to subordinate women's rights to national security or Islamic identity. Women have been subject to kidnappings, rapes, and assaults and confined to their homes or forced to assume the veil to escape being targeted (Haifa Zangana 2004). Basic necessities, like food, water, electricity, and health care, are scarce, and education has been disrupted. The situation has become so bad, that some Iraqi women now warn their children to behave by shouting: "Quiet, or I'll call democracy" (Zangana 2004). This is the real danger of continuing to value masculinized toughness and militarized hegemony as a means to regenerate national identity and achieve national security. Democracy will become a bogeyman to be feared rather than a political ideal to be pursued, and spreading freedom will come to look an awful lot like spreading terror, particularly to women whose subjectivities and priorities are routinely subordinated within the masculinized discourse of national security.

Acknowledgements

I wish to thank Dafna Lemish and the anonymous reviewers of *Feminist Media Studies* for their extremely thorough and helpful comments for revision. I hope the final product adequately reflects their insights.

Note

1. For information on the status of both Afghan and Iraqi women's rights post-invasion, see the website for the international human rights organization MADRE: An International Women's Human Rights Organization. Available at http://www.madre.org/ (Dec. 2004).

References

BACEVICH, ANDREW (2002) *American Empire: The Realities and Consequences of US Diplomacy*, Harvard University Press, Cambridge.

BRAGG, RICK (2003) *I Am a Soldier, Too: The Jessica Lynch Story,* Alfred A. Knopf, New York.

BUSH, GEORGE W. (1999) "A distinctly American internationalism", *FreeRepublic.Com* [Online] Available at: http://www.freerepublic.com/forum/a395503e07c50.htm (Dec. 2004).

BUSH, GEORGE W. [2001] (2003a) "Address to a joint session of congress and the American people (September 20, 2001)," in *History and September 11*, ed. Joanne Meyerowitz, Temple University Press, Philadelphia, pp. 241–243.

BUSH, GEORGE W. (2003b) "President Bush discusses freedom in Iraq and Middle East: Remarks by the President at the twentieth anniversary of the national endowment for democracy," *The White House* [Online] Available at: http://www.whitehouse.gov/news/releases/2003/11//20031106-2.html (Dec. 2004).

BUSH, GEORGE W. (2004) "Bush's opening statement: President opens third primetime news conference with 16-minute statement on Iraq conflict," *MSNBC*, 13 April [Online] Available at: http://msnbc.msn.com/id/4734018/ (Dec. 2004).

BUSH, LAURA (2003) "Radio address on women in Afghanistan (November 17, 2001)," in *History and September 11*, ed. Joanne Meyerowitz, Temple University Press, Philadelphia, pp. 249–250.

CAMPBELL, CHRISTOPHER (2003) "Commodifying September 11: Advertising, myth, and hegemony," in *Media Representations of September 11*, eds Steven Chermak, Frankie Y. Bailey & Michelle Brown, Praeger, Westport, CT, pp. 47–66.

COHN, CAROL (1993) "War, wimps, and women: Talking gender and thinking war," in *Gendering War Talk*, eds. Miriam Cooke & Angela Woollacott, Princeton University Press, Princeton, pp. 227–246.

COHN, CAROL [1987] (2003) "Sex and death in the rational world of defense intellectuals," in *Women on War: An International Anthology of Women's Writings From Antiquity to the Present*, ed. Daniela Gioseffi, The Feminist Press at the City University of New York, New York, pp. 56–68.

DREW, JULIE (2004) "Identity crisis: Gender, public discourse and 9/11," *Women & Language*, vol. 27, no. 2 [Online] Available at: OCLC FirstSearch (June 2005).

ENLOE, CYNTHIA (2004) *The Curious Feminist: Searching For Women in a New Age of Empire*, University of California Press, Berkeley.

FREDA, ISABELLE (2004) "Survivors in *The West Wing*: 9/11 and the United States of emergency," in *Film and Television After 9/11*, ed. Wheeler Winston Dixon, Southern Illinois University, Carbondale, pp. 226–246.

GERECHT, REUEL MARC (2001) "A cowering superpower," *Weekly Standard*, 30 July pp. 26–29.

HOWARD, JOHN & PRIVIDERA, LAURA (2004) "Rescuing patriarchy or saving 'Jessica Lynch': The rhetorical construction of the American woman solider," *Women & Language*, vol. 27, no. 2 [Online] Available at: OCLC FirstSearch (June 2005).

KAGAN, ROBERT (1998) "Saddam's impending victory," *The Weekly Standard*, 2 Feb., pp. 22–25.

KAMPFNER, JOHN (2003) "The truth about the saving of Private Jessica Lynch," *The Guardian*, 16 May [Online] Available at: http://www.guardian.co.uk (Dec. 2004).

KUMAR, DEEPA (2004) "War propaganda and the (ab)uses of women: Media constructions of the Jessica Lynch story," *Feminist Media Studies*, vol. 4, no. 3, pp. 297–313.

LAKEOFF, GEORGE (2002) *Moral Politics: How Liberals and Conservatives Think*, University of Chicago Press, Chicago.

LULE, JACK (2002) "Myth and terror on the editorial page: *The New York Times* responds to September 11, 2001," *Journal of Mass Communication Quarterly*, vol. 79, no. 2, pp. 275–293.

MADRE (n.d.) [Online] Available at: http://www.madre.org/.

MCALISTER, MELANI (2003) "A cultural history of the war without end," in *History and September 11*, ed. Joanne Meyerowitz, Temple University Press, Philadelphia, pp. 94–116.

MULVEY, LAURA [1975] (1993) "Visual pleasure and narrative cinema," in *Feminisms: An Anthology of Literary Theory and Criticism*, eds. Robyn R. Warhol & Diane Price Herndl, Rutgers University Press, New Brunswick, NJ, pp. 432–442.

NATIONAL SECURITY STRATEGY (2002) *The White House* [Online] Available at: http://www.whitehouse.gov/nsc/nssall.html (Dec. 2004).

"PFC. JESSICA LYNCH: AN AMERICAN STORY" (Videorecording) (2003) *Primetime*, ABC, Nov. 11.

PROJECT FOR THE NEW AMERICAN CENTURY (1998) "Speaking of Iraq," *The New York Times*, 27 Jan., p. A21.

PUAR, JASBIR K. & RAI, AMIT S. (2002) "Monster, terrorist, fag: The war on terrorism and the production of docile patriots," *Social Text*, vol. 20, no. 3, pp. 117–148.

REYNOLDS, AMY & BARNETT, BROOKE (2003) "'America under attack': CNN's verbal and visual framing of September 11," in *Media Representations of September 11*, eds. Steven Chermak, Frankie Y. Bailey & Michelle Brown, Praeger, Westport, CT, pp. 85–102.

RITEA, STEVE (2003) "Jessica Lynch's story: A little too perfect?," *American Journalism Review*, August/September [Online] Available at: Academic Expanded ASAP Plus (March 2005).

ROSENBERG, EMILY (2003) "Rescuing women and children," in *History and September 11*, ed. Joanne Meyerowitz, Temple University Press, Philadelphia, pp. 81–93.

SAID, EDWARD (1979) *Orientalism*, Vintage Books, New York.

SAVING JESSICA LYNCH (Videorecording) (2003) "NBC," 9 Nov.

SAVING POW LYNCH (Videorecording) (2003) "Discovery," 12 Nov.

SAVING PRIVATE LYNCH (Videorecording) (2003) "A&E," 18 April.

SCHMIDT, SUSAN & LOEB, VERNON (2003) "She was fighting to the death," *Washington Post*, 3 April p. A1.

SPIVAK, GAYATRI CHAKRAVORTY (1988) "Can the subaltern speak?," in *Marxism and the Interpretation of Culture*, eds. Cary Nelson & Lawrence Grossberg, University of Illinois Press, Chicago, pp. 271–313.

SUSSMAN, PETER (2003) "Rescuing Private Lynch—and rescuing journalism: The pressure for a compelling story can eclipse the actual news," *The Quill*, November [Online] Available at: Expanded Academic ASAP Plus (March 2005).

VOLPP, LETI (2003) "The citizen and the terrorist," in *September 11 in History: A Watershed Moment?*, ed. Mary L. Dudziak, Duke University Press, Durham, pp. 147–162.

ZANGANA, HAIFA (2004) "Quiet, or I'll call democracy," *Guardian Unlimited*, 22 Dec. [Online] Available at: http://www.guardian.co.uk/comment/story/0,3604,1378411,00.html (Dec. 2004).

Discussion Questions

1. Where were you on September 11, 2001? What do you remember about the media coverage of the attacks?

2. Takacs says the goal of her essay "is to illustrate and, hopefully, disrupt the processes of consensus formation sustaining [President George W. Bush's] counter-intuitive security policy." What does she mean by "consensus formation," and how does her essay develop this idea? Mark specific places in the essay she does so.

3. Takacs discusses the gendering of a "symbolic system" and "hierarchy of values." In what ways is this discourse gendered? What other evidence of gendering do you see in the article? In the media?

4. In what ways does Takacs link Lynch and America? How does this help (or hinder) her argument?

5. Do you think 9/11 shaped or does it continue to shape our media coverage? Why or why not? Find a news clip to support your answer.

6. Can you find other sources on 9/11 as national identity formation? Use Google Scholar or a similar search engine to find further research on this topic.

Mad Women, Not Mad Men: On TV, the Seeds of a Revolution

Julia Baird

Julia Baird's article discusses the women of *Mad Men*, their sufferings, and the beginnings of second wave feminism. Though the article is brief, Baird connects the trials of the women of *Mad Men* to today's feminism. As you read, pay attention to the way Baird uses secondary sources to support her argument.

In October 1959, the golden-haired poet Sylvia Plath dreamed that Marilyn Monroe appeared to her, like a "fairy godmother," and gave her a manicure, hairdressing advice, and an invitation to visit at Christmas. Four years later, both women were dead. Others followed. Monroe's death, according to *Time*'s obituary, was "the trigger of suicides in half a dozen cities."

The years that preceded the onset of the second-wave women's movement were marked by a strange kind of private violence and turmoil. While suicides were still rare, between 1960 and 1970 the number of American women who took their own lives increased by 32 percent. More commonly, there was a deep frustration, restlessness, and resentment many women tried to articulate to spouses, doctors, and therapists—as Betty Friedan put it, a "problem that had no name." This problem was often treated with drugs, alcohol, psychotherapy, and, at its extreme, electroconvulsive therapy. Psychologists argued about why more women were considered mentally ill than men, why more were drugged and institutionalized. In her bestselling book *Women and Madness,* Phyllis Chesler argued that women's anger, or rebellion, was frequently misdiagnosed as sickness.

Which is why I often wonder, as we watch another gripping season of *Mad Men,* now set in 1965, why it isn't called *Mad Women.* In the early 1960s, men's rebellious or indulgent behavior may have been destructive and odd, but it was seen as normal, or at least explicable, while women's was stigmatized or pathologized. And these women are getting mad. We can see the beginnings of the women's movement in the flashes in the eyes of the female workers, lovers, and spouses—the hurt look on Don's secretary's face when he gives her an envelope of cash for her Christmas bonus the morning after he slept with her. We see it when Joan throws a box of roses at a boss she thought had professed his love for her, crying, "I am not your darling." She hates, she says, being made to feel like "a helpless, stupid little girl." And we see it in Peggy's regret and loneliness as she lies in bed with a man who thinks he "took" her virginity (ignoring again her gynecologist's warning not to become a "strumpet"). Men slept around with little consequence. If women like Peggy did, it was scandalous and scarring.

And we see what Friedan called a "strange stirring," especially in the beautiful, bored housewife Betty Draper and her dull anxiety, buried fury, halfhearted attempts to conform, and brittle, harsh mothering. She drinks in the daytime, sleeps with a stranger, and seems unable to fathom her own unhappiness. When the series began, her hands shook inexplicably; she saw a therapist, who reported back to her husband.

The anger of the women of *Mad Men* has simmered throughout the series; yet while today we can pick up their cues and wince at their slights, or abuse, at the time they would have been dismissed as suffering from neuroses or bad temper. As Lisa Appignanesi wrote in *Mad, Bad and Sad: A History of Women and the Mind Doctors,* by the end of the 1950s "defiance, unruliness, disobedience were characteristics [therapists] translated all too readily into the language of illness." *Mad Men* is set on the cusp of a time when anger becomes rage. When women realized they weren't insane, or hysterical—they were mad. And that they weren't alone in being belittled, fondled, cheated on, abused, and, in Joan's case, raped. (In 1963 it was still legal to rape your wife.) In 1960, nine out of every 1,000 women had divorced; by 1980, 22 had, and 60 percent of married women worked.

All this is worth remembering because in so many abstract, judgmental debates about women today, we forget the madness and acute frustration of generations past—as well as what remains the same. Sure, the show's sexism can be funny—when it's clearly retro, witty, and overt. Roger says, "When God closes a door, he opens a dress," and we laugh. But when Don says, "I won't let a woman talk to me this way," it's more revealing than funny, because it still rings true. When *Mad Men*'s women hear Monroe has died, they grieve. Joan tells Roger: "This world destroyed her." In a way, her death in '62 marked the end of a time of mute, tragic victims and the beginning of an era when women began to speak, loudly, and refused to be the strumpets and "stupid little girls" too easily dismissed, or destroyed, by the world. Today feminism is scapegoated for many ills and depicted as anti-mother. We forget how much, in fact, it helped keep our own mothers—all of us—sane.

Discussion Questions

1. At the end of the article, Baird writes, "In so many abstract, judgmental debates about women today, we forget the madness and acute frustration of generations past—as well as what remains the same." What does remain the same for women between the 1960s and today? Why do you think this is?

2. Later, Baird says, "Today feminism is scapegoated for many ills and depicted as anti-mother. We forget how much, in fact, it helped keep our own mothers—all of us—sane." What sorts of things do we blame feminism for today? Do you see any correlation between what we blame it for today, and what it was blamed for in the 1960s?

3. How does the outside information (quotes, statistics, etc.) function with the discussion of the women of *Mad Men*? What does Baird gain or lose by including this information?

4. Baird claims that Marilyn Monroe's death in 1962 "marked the end of a time of mute, tragic victims and the beginning of an era when women began to speak, loudly, and refused to be the strumpets and 'stupid little girls' too easily dismissed, or destroyed, by the world." How does Takacs' discussion of the media treatment of Jessica Lynch complicate this argument?

5. Research "Second-wave feminism." How did this movement start? What were its main aims? Its weaknesses? How would you define feminism today? If you don't know, research feminism also. How has feminism evolved, and why do you think it evolved?

No Fun: Debunking the 1960s in *Mad Men* and *A Serious Man*

J.M. Tyree

As J.M. Tyree notes in this article, the Baby Boomer generation views the 1960s as a decade of happy, wishful thinking. However, Tyree argues *Mad Men* and *A Serious Man* are indicative of the true nature of the decade. As you read, take note of the way Tyree constructs his argument and his discussion of masculinity.

"Living in the past is my future," laments Charley (Julianne Moore) in Tom Ford's film *A Single Man*, an adaptation from Christopher Isherwood set in 1962 Los Angeles. Charley is nostalgic for remembrances of things past with her gay best friend George (Colin Firth). But her remarks could be made to reflect on a major television series (*Mad Men*) and a crop of 2009 films (*A Single Man*, *An Education*, and *A Serious Man*) set in the 1960s. As a demographic group, many of the filmmakers, writers, and producers of these works can be included in the tail end of the Baby Boom. But they all experienced the decade as children, not politically awakening university students—it appears significant that all of these productions have pre-'68 settings. Joel Coen (b. 1954) and Ethan Coen (b. 1957) set *A Serious Man* in 1967 in a suburban Minnesotan Jewish enclave seemingly insulated from social turmoil. The screenplay by Nick Hornby (b. 1957) for *An Education*, set in 1961, frames the sexual coming-of-age of its female protagonist as a dubious lark. Ford (b. 1961) juxtaposes private grief with the unfolding Cuban missile crisis. *Mad Men*'s executive producer, Matthew Weiner (b. 1965), views the decade through the cynical lens of advertising. These productions are remarkable for their skepticism about the liberating potential of social change. About the lure of sexual revolution, they are downright uneasy.

"We're selling America," claims an executive from the Lucky Strike cigarette corporation during the very first episode of *Mad Men*. Don Draper (Jon Hamm), marketing guru at the New York firm of Sterling Cooper, counters that "advertising is based on one thing—happiness." It's "freedom from fear…a billboard on the side of the road that screams, with reassurance, that whatever you're doing is okay. You are okay." Don is likeable because of this cutting cultural intelligence, and also because he is a loner, an outsider drawn to other outsiders with secret lives. In the show's opening episode, he becomes attracted to a Jewish department store owner, Rachel Mencken (Maggie Siff), who "knows what it feels like to be out of place" as both an ethnic minority and a businesswoman. The introduction of Don's wife, Betty (January Jones), is held in reserve as a final shock at the end of the episode, positioning his perfect suburban family life as a perfect lie. As the season continues, flashbacks gradually reveal a secret past: a dustbowl childhood and a mystery subplot in which he assumed the identity of Don Draper from a comrade killed in the Korean War. Don is not even Don. He's Dick Whitman, whose long climb out of desperate poverty has produced a literally "self-made" man.

Yet because Don is out of joint with his times, he's also a refreshing antidote to the stifling conformity of the early 1960s world. His sexual politics, although accurately appalling—"I won't have a woman speak to me that way," he initially says of Rachel in a meeting—are put in the shade by even worse men at work. There appears to be another side to Don's character, first revealed when he sticks up for his new secretary, Peggy Olson (Elisabeth Moss). When she gets pregnant by the sleazy mid-level executive Peter Campbell (Vincent Kartheiser) after her very first day at work, Don becomes a kind of mentor. He encourages her to dump the baby and move on with her career, and the historical, ethical, political, and psychological complexities of this act are not shirked in *Mad Men*. In season 3, Don appears similarly helpful to Salvatore Romano (Bryan Batt) about the latter's own secret life as a closeted gay man attempting to survive the fraternal order of corporate culture. Which is not to go so far as to suggest that Don is a saint: he turns on Salvatore ("You people!") when he refuses to give on-the-job sexual favors to the scion of Lucky Strike. The culture's underlying nastiness about other people's desires is most apparent in the show's harsh depictions of brutality toward women. The sexual revolution has no corollary in feminism. When the show's most lively and wise character, Joan Holloway (Christina Hendricks), is sexually assaulted at work by her fiancé, she continues the relationship. For Peggy, the pleasures promised by the Pill offer no real liberation—a doctor pours moralizing contempt on her, then prescribes the medication without explaining how it works. (*An Education* is set in the year Minister of Health Enoch Powell approved the two-shilling price for the contraceptive pill, and shares *Mad Men*'s cautionary, even conservative concern with the downside of a new sexual freedom.)

Don's decency toward minorities at work—gathering them into what at times appears to be an alternative family unit—sits uneasily with an impersonal, all-business attitude that verges on the sociopathic. He therefore becomes a cultural metonym for the inherent tolerance embedded in American capitalism but also its cruel utilitarianism—all are welcome to consume and be exploited, to be self-made and self-unmade. And there's a quasi-Fordist, mechanized aspect to Don's assembly line of extramarital affairs, as though his lovers are interchangeable parts or throwaway consumer products like the ones he's helping to sell. Yet unlike his picture-perfect blond wife, his serious mistresses are almost always dark-haired, as if selected from a lifestyle marketing catalogue of feisty intellectual brunettes. "What you call love," he tells Rachel in season 1 with an air of suave confidence, "was invented by guys like me, to sell nylons."

One of Don's bosses, Bert Cooper—played by Robert Morse, who four decades earlier had been the youthfully aspirant lead in *How to Succeed in Business Without Really Trying* (1967)—gives him a copy of Ayn Rand's *Atlas Shrugged* in season 1. Yet while Don often appears to others as a self-reliant businessman–artist who wouldn't be out of place in King Vidor's 1949 production of *The Fountainhead*, he's actually more like a living critique of Rand's ideas. Gary Cooper's Howard Roark in Vidor's film is incorruptible and heroically alone throughout much of the story, whereas Don finds his solitude far less comfortable. He looks for solace in the soft-limbed chimera of what today probably would be called a sex addiction. And while Roark's singular architectural genius is relentlessly emphasized as being the result of his refusal to "give in" to pleasing the masses, in season 3 Don becomes embroiled in a campaign to militate public opinion in favor of demolishing a gem of a building, New York's Penn Station. Mad Men takes pains to show the campaigns of Sterling Cooper as rather mediocre affairs combined from a bodge of market research and second-run sex appeal. Rand would not have approved. This is still a world of graft, compromise, and sheer old-fashioned unhappiness. As a post on a Rand forum (4aynrandfans.com) put it rather concisely about *Mad Men*, "These characters, almost all of them, are miserable!"

This isn't, however, a one-note show. There's room for more optimistic storylines and, in particular, Peggy's gradual steps toward empowerment in the wake of her childbirth, costly and hard-won, feel like genuine progress. During a lighter moment, Peggy gets high with her office mates during the creative phase of a "Daiquiri Beach" ad campaign for Barcardi—asserting her newfound status and self-image by saying, "I'm Peggy Olson and I want to smoke some marijuana." She's not experiencing false consciousness. But *Mad Men* boils down depressingly. As historical fiction, it limns similar territory as the 2002 Adam Curtis documentary *The Century of the Self*, which argues that the rise of marketing and public relations gave impetus to an increasingly "isolated, vulnerable, greedy self." Curtis notes that the inventor of the focus group, Ernest Dichter, believed that advertising and mass consumerism would reinforce civic values and make both citizens and society more stable. *Mad Men* depicts a more troubling scenario in which the concept of the family—whether Don's abandoned marriage or Peggy's abandoned child—is by 1960 already pulverized beyond recognition. Success in this world entails not only the constant violation of the categorical imperative, but also a debilitating form of loneliness. (Many shots in *Mad Men* discover characters isolated in urban spaces—offices, bars, diners, even stairwells—evocative of the lonely-looking paintings of Edward Hopper.) An American paradox is that the much-vaunted Emersonian characteristic of self-reliance dovetails rather nicely with the goals of big business to create a nation of isolated, vulnerable, and greedy selves who can be persuaded that buying products is a form of self-expression. If Curtis is right in arguing that "satisfaction of individual desires is our highest priority" as a culture, then Don Draper and Peggy Olson are emblematic figures in the rise of a funny kind of freedom.

———

Some puzzlement attends the curious Yiddish prologue of *A Serious Man*, which is set in a completely different era and setting from the 1967 world of its main story. The parable of the visitor, Reb Groshkover (Fyvush Finkel), who gets stabbed because he may or may not be a dybbuk, frames the rest of the film as a story about religious Jews living in a world without God. Assuming that the appearance of blood on Groshkover's shirt is a sign that he's not, in fact, a demon—and therefore that the universe of *A Serious Man* has no supernatural dimension, so no interventionist deity controlling it (the point is not trivial to the film's meaning)—his laughter over his own injury is cosmic. In the spirit of Kafka, the Coens want to position their film in a space where one can appreciate the humor of things that are not at all funny, to make us laugh at the literal and figurative stabbings we are all destined to receive at one time or another. At the end of *The Trial*, Kafka's protagonist Josef K. also gets stabbed in the heart. Like Larry Gopnik (Michael Stulbarg), the film's earnest protagonist, Josef K. is the victim of a mysterious smear campaign. Larry is wounded in many ways throughout the film, although unlike Groshkover, he doesn't get the joke.

In another Kafka work, a short parable, a lost man races around an unfamiliar town trying to find the train station, only to encounter a laughing policeman who advises him to "Give It Up!" Many viewers of *A Serious Man* will surely have had a similar thought while watching Larry vainly try to survive a series of personal disasters that befall him in suburban Minnesota. His marriage is hijacked by a relentlessly cheerful adversary, Sy Ableman (Fred Melamed), who brings Larry wine and hugs him while stealing Judith (Sari Wagner Lennick). Though he utters friendly public platitudes—"Let's have a good talk!" and "We're going to be fine"—Sy writes poison-pen letters to the tenure committee at the small technical college where Larry teaches physics. Sy's a bit like a refugee from the Human Potential Movement who has studied the art of transpersonal psychology but seems interested in using it purely for his own selfish agenda. Meanwhile, a junior rabbi, Scott Ginzler (Simon Helberg), uses vague and worthless New Age mumbo-jumbo concepts to console Larry about his crumbling life. Encouraging Larry to examine the parking lot outside, he suggests that "with the right perspective" all his problems will simply vanish. Larry seeks another opinion. The second clergyman, Rabbi Nachtner (George Wyner), tells him a weirdly delightful but ultimately meaningless story about a Jewish dentist who finds a message etched in Hebrew letters on a patient's teeth: "Help me, save me." (As the dentist's story unfolds on-screen, Jimi Hendrix's 1969 "Machine Gun" plays anachronistically but powerfully on the soundtrack, unsettling the images of smalltown establishments, from dental office to Red Owl supermarket.) Yet the cabbalistic story of the goy's teeth, as it turns out, is an old Nachtner standby designed to lead listeners into unquestioning acceptance of God's mystery. "Why does God make us feel the question if he's not going to give us answers?" Larry asks Nachtner. "What does it mean?" "He hasn't told me," says the rabbi, as if dispensing wisdom. With Sy, Rabbi Scott, and Rabbi Nachtner, the 1960s vocabulary of universal brotherhood, the power of good vibes, and the parable-making of religious gurus amount to gibberish that is actively unhelpful. It's all a dodge, if not a con, like the slogans dreamed up in the offices of Sterling Cooper.

"Receive with simplicity everything that happens to you," suggests the Jewish sage Rashi in the film's epigraph. By the end of the film, these "Eastern," hippie-ish words encouraging passivity take on a pointedly ironic, even mocking tone. "Accept the mystery," suggests a father (Steve Park) attempting to bribe Larry on behalf of his son, who has failed the midterm. But doing so doesn't seem like a very good idea. The philosophy of Larry's brother Arthur (Richard Kind)—"It's all shit, Larry, it's all fucking shit!"—seems in better accord with the world we're shown. In *A Serious Man*, the fundamental state of things is perhaps best revealed, in a scene that could have been written by Kafka, when a lawyer who has found "a nifty way out" of Larry's property dispute with his anti-Semitic neighbor drops dead of a heart attack just as he's about to disclose his secret solution. In a dream sequence with similar import, Larry helps Arthur escape to Canada after Arthur's arrest for solicitation and sodomy in North Dakota, but just as Arthur waves goodbye he's shot in the back of the head with a bullet from a hunting rifle fired by the same anti-Semitic neighbors. It's not going to work out—that's the theme. Efforts to decipher the scheme of things are futile. Uncle Arthur's private obsession is a hand-scrawled scientific treatise of some kind called "The Mentaculus," which is described at one point as "a probability map of the universe" but in fact turns out to be page after page of incoherent designs and meaningless signs. *A Serious Man* presents much of life as a series of symbols and languages that cannot be interpreted in any definitive way. Larry's compassion for others flies in the face of all the evidence mounting in his world against the existence of any meaningful order. He takes on a Job-like mantle of virtuous patience simply by staying nice—but unlike in the case of his biblical predecessor, in the end God fails to return the favor. In a very poignant moment, Larry hugs his brother at the side of the empty pool of the Jolly Roger motel where they've both been exiled from the family home. The Coens depict Larry as quasi-heroic by virtue of sheer decency in the face of suffering and humiliation.

Larry is a sort of anti-Don Draper. Faced with the reappearance of his own half-brother, Adam (Jay Paulson), from his secret past in season 1 of *Mad Men*, Don views him as a threat to his new life. He tries to buy him off with $5,000 in exchange for leaving New York forever, but Adam hangs himself instead. Larry, by contrast, feels obliged to be his brother's keeper even following his arrest. In the opening episode of season 3 of *Mad Men*, Don cavorts with a stewardess on a business trip in a luxury hotel; Larry sleeps next to his disgraced brother in the bleak motel by the highway. Don maintains a steely calm, while Larry bares his searching soul to useless spiritual and legal counselors. Larry weeps in his lawyer's office and fields calls from his son about the TV antenna during billable hours; Don has constructed a wall around his place of work so as to be unreachable. While both Don and Larry are juggling to keep up the facade of family life in the face of social upheaval, Don's selfishness belongs to the realm of pathology, while Larry's selflessness makes him a bit of a saint and a bit of a dupe. Don confuses masculinity with a lack of vulnerability. Larry remains an open book whose pulsing need to care for others is both oddly touching and pathetic. Of all the characters in *A Serious Man*, it's Judith, not Larry or Sy Ableman, who most resembles the hardheaded, unemotional, and self-sufficient Don Draper.

As in *Mad Men*, widespread use of marijuana in the square community is one element of the 1960s that appears as unadulterated fun here. The sequence in *A Serious Man* in which Larry's son Danny (Aaron Wolf) gets his bar mitzvah while stoned and then meets with the venerable Rabbi Marshak (Alan Mandell) is the closest the film comes to an affirmation of the peace-and-love philosophy. For a moment, the wise old traditional sage and the baked young fan of The Jefferson Airplane share a similar goofy bleariness about the eyes with Peggy Olson, the rising career woman attempting to generate ideas on an equal footing with her male colleagues. There's an interesting verbal link too. Peggy's team stays on after hours to concoct cheery slogans for rum, a job where, as the season 1 tagline has it, "The truth lies." Marshak and Danny, by contrast, bond over the explicitly countercultural lyrics to "Somebody to Love," namely, "When the truth is found to be lies…" In their different ways, these characters improvise ad hoc narratives, cultural or countercultural, to replace broken traditional 1950s ways of life. Marshak lights on the bleakest phrases in the Airplane song as his gambit for connecting with Danny, without delving into the chorus, an anthemic precursor to the Summer of Love. Yet the song's affectionate sentiment provides the humane notion that mitigates the Coens' film. In plot terms, *A Serious Man* is terribly fatalistic, apparently confirming the assessment that life really is "all shit" and "lies." But Larry's goodness and fortitude are all the more touching, and perhaps even all the more credible, precisely because they would seem to be utterly ineffectual. For surely we presume that Danny will perish in the tornado moving implacably towards his school in the final shot of *A Serious Man*, and that if the twister doesn't get Larry then his newly diagnosed cancer will.

"Come together," The Beatles sang in 1969, but that same year The Stooges, sending a message from Detroit, had started calling the bluff of the passing decade: "No fun to hang around…No fun to be alone." This alternative take on the feel-good decade fits *Mad Men* and *A Serious Man*, revisionist fictions that present distinct but overlapping counter-mythologies of the 1960s, rueful and scornful ripostes to Baby Boomer self-congratulation.

In *Mad Men*, historical events appear as direct and relevant forces. Characters witness and respond to the key events unfolding on television: Kennedy's election and assassination, Martin Luther King Jr.'s Freedom Walk, self-immolating Vietnamese monks. Special features on the season 3 DVD release include documentaries about murdered civil rights activist Medgar Evers and the history of cigarette advertising. (Don Draper is said to be based in part on Draper Daniels, who created the Marlboro Man campaign.) In the 1967 world depicted in *A Serious Man*, by contrast, we see the satirical television war comedy *F Troop*, but the escalating war in Vietnam gets no air time. This absence of history itself could be read not so much as a flaw than as a gap that forms an acid comment about the dreamlike detachment of Middle America from any consciousness of what's happening in the wider world. The counterculture, meanwhile, in the form of sex (a naked sunbathing neighbor), drugs (whether taken by adults or children), and rock'n'roll (as prepackaged by the Columbia Record Club), seeps through suburban life entirely disconnected from any political meaning.

These dramas debunk a rosy view of pre-'68 Americana, excavating a bedrock of depression and insincerity beneath the rhetoric of change and freedom. *Mad Men* is perhaps more thrilled with the era's frolicsome guilty pleasures, yet finally both works are fundamentally aligned with the scorn of a commentator like Joan Didion, to whom 1960s dreams of transformation seemed fatuous and dangerous. "That huge generation that believed it had the power to do anything," she bitingly remarked of the Boomers in television journalist Tom Brokaw's 2007 book *Boom! Personal Reflections on the '60s and Today* (Random House). If *Mad Men* predicts the channeling of such generational esprit de corps into the narcissism of consumer culture, *A Serious Man* invites a more cosmic rebuke about the nature of individual helplessness *tout court*. As Didion wrote in her blistering final note to "On the Morning After the Sixties" (1970), collected in *The White Album* (Simon and Schuster, 1979), "it would be less than honest to say that I expect to happen upon...a happy ending." In their 1970 protest song, "Chicago," Crosby, Stills, Nash and Young summoned up hope for a happy ending even in the face of violent unrest and political injustice. But the song's refrain—"we can change the world"—contains a notion that *Mad Men* and *A Serious Man*, fictions for a less hopeful time, resolutely refuse.

Discussion Questions

1. How does Tyree build his argument? What is his main claim?

2. Tyree writes, "An American paradox is that the much-vaunted Emersonian characteristic of self-reliance dovetails rather nicely with the goals of big business to create a nation of isolated, vulnerable, and greedy selves who can be persuaded that buying products is a form of self-expression" (35). How are self-reliance and the goals of big business, as expressed by Tyree, related?

3. What comes to mind when you think about the 1960s? How do *Mad Men* and *A Serious Man* confirm or contradict those ideas?

4. How would you define masculinity? With a classmate, develop a list of characteristics that make someone masculine. Now try to find clips of *Mad Men* and *A Serious Man*. Which of the two main characters, Don Draper or Larry Gopnik, best fit your definition? How might the ideas of masculinity have changed between the 1960s and today?

5. Baird discusses the idea of "mad women" in *Mad Men*. Look again at question 4. How might Don Draper's idea of masculinity (not to mention the other characters') influence the idea of mad women? How do these ideas of masculinity in turn define our ideas of femininity?

6. Research the field of masculinity studies. When did it emerge? Why?

The Office: Articulations of National Identity in Television Format Adaptation

Alexandra Beeden, Joost de Bruin

In this article, Alexandra Beeden and Joost de Bruin analyze the first seasons of the British and American versions of *The Office*. They argue that these adaptations articulate ideas of national identity and cultural belonging for their respective audiences. As you read, pay attention to the ways the authors develop and support their argument.

This article analyses the first series of both the original British and American remake of the sitcom *The Office*. We discuss how television format adaptations work through articulations of national identity, and suggest that the success of an adaptation may be linked to its ability to reflect and interpret its new context. Despite the global success of the sitcom genre there are clear differences in the situations, characters and humor used by British and American sitcoms which must be addressed by an adaptation. The way in which *The Office* has adapted to the institutional context, culture and humor of the United States, after its success as a British sitcom, illustrates that national identity is a vital part of the global television format trade. While it may appear that the growth of format adaptations reflects the increasingly globalized contemporary world, in fact, format adaptations encourage articulations of national identity and cultural belonging.

"Americans just don't get it!" cried fans and critics alike when it was first announced that NBC would be producing an American remake of the British sitcom *The Office*.[1] Producer Greg Daniels, co-creator of the animated sitcom *The Simpsons* (Fox: 1989–), was told that the program was "a suicide mission,"[2] and disgusted fans of the original series recalled disappointing predecessors of the trans-Atlantic remake, such as the American versions of *Cracker* (ABC: 1997–1998), *Coupling* (NBC: 2003), and *Men Behaving Badly* (NBC: 1996–1997). There was further outrage as rumors flew of Brad Pitt taking the lead role of the office boss, immortalized by Ricky Gervais in the British original. When the British series first screened on BBC America, the *Los Angeles Times* asked readers to

> imagine a television series about mid-level workers stuck in dead-end jobs. Now imagine producing it without big stars, laugh tracks, tidy endings or glamour…It sounds, well, un-American, doesn't it?[3]

Why was there such concern about an American version of the comedy? At the heart of this outrage and disgust was the belief that *The Office* was a quintessentially British sitcom. As one fan announced, "Ricky Gervais

IS *The Office*";[4] and a remake of the same quality and with the same resonance as in its home country was believed to be impossible. There was a strong belief that the originality and success of the sitcom was grounded in its "Britishness" and therefore could not be reproduced in the United States.

The Office, written by Ricky Gervais and Stephen Merchant, follows the tedious daily lives of employees at a paper company, focusing on the embarrassing actions of their socially incompetent and offensive regional manager. The sitcom is filmed as if by an unseen camera crew, making use of documentary characteristics such as jerky shots and individual interviews, rather than the traditional sitcom "studio," which positions the audience as a "fourth wall," and the use of canned laughter. The first series of *The Office* follows the characters as they learn of possible redundancies at the office and as romance blossoms between the receptionist and sales representative. It first aired in July 2001 on BBC2, with very low ratings (an audience share of between 6 and 10 percent over the six episodes[5]), although it was generally well received by critics. *The Office* won Best New Comedy at the British Comedy Awards in December 2001, and a repeat screening of the first series in January 2002 increased its ratings and was followed by BAFTAs for Best Sitcom and Best Comedy Performance for Ricky Gervais in April 2002. The second series gained better ratings, with the concluding episode attracting a 22 percent audience share. The 2003 Christmas specials on BBC1 also achieved high ratings: a 30 and 25 percent audience share for the first and second episode, respectively.

The British series *The Office* has been exported to more than sixty countries[6] and has been officially adapted for American, French, and Canadian audiences, as well as unofficially in Germany.[7] It screened in the United States in January 2003 on BBC America, where it performed well on the minority channel. Within a year of the beginning of its American screening, the sitcom was the unexpected and relatively unknown winner of two Golden Globe awards for Best Comedy Series and Best Comedy Actor for Gervais. *The Office* was the first British show to ever be nominated for the award and was only eligible because of BBC America's nominal contribution to the budget of the second series.[8]

In August 2003, Daniels confirmed that his company Reveille was developing an American adaptation of the British series, titled *The Office: An American Workplace*. Within a week of the Golden Globe wins, an American cast was announced, and pre-production started on a pilot to be screened on the NBC network. Such television format adaptations have become increasingly common in the current media landscape, particularly in the reality television genre. Amongst the many programs that have been remade for a different national audience, there have been distinct successes as well as abysmal failures. A key part of the success of a format adaptation appears to be the ability to adapt to and incorporate the context of the new country—to interpret rather than copy the original program. It was this method that the American *The Office* adopted, and after a slow start it has become a successful and award-winning show, with Steve Carell (who took the role of the American boss) collecting a Golden Globe for Best Comedy Performance at the 2006 Awards. Most recently, the sitcom won 2008 Screen Actors Guild Awards for Outstanding Performance by an Ensemble in a Comedy Series and Outstanding Performance by a Male Actor in a Comedy Series (Steve Carell). After the initial first series of six episodes, the program fell into the usual American pattern of much longer seasons, with twenty-two and twenty-three episodes in the second and third series, respectively. By the end of the 2007–2008 season, it had averaged an 11 percent audience share.[9] The American sitcom has now been renewed for a sixth season in 2009–2010, is screening internationally, and will become available for syndication in late 2009 with TBS and Fox acquiring rights.[10] In contrast, Gervais and Merchant ensured that the British series concluded after the second Christmas special (a total of fourteen episodes).

This article analyzes the first series of both the original British and American remake of *The Office*. We will demonstrate how format adaptations work through articulations of national identity and suggest that the success of an adaptation may be linked to its ability to reflect and interpret its new context. Despite the global success of the sitcom genre, there are clear differences in the situations, characters, and humor of British and American sitcoms that must be addressed by an adaptation. The way in which *The Office* has effectively adapted to suit the institutional context, culture, and humor of the United States, after its success as a British sitcom, illustrates that national identity is a vital part of the global format trade. While it may appear that the growth of international format adaptations reflects the increasingly globalized contemporary world, in fact, television format adaptations encourage articulations of national identity and cultural belonging.

National Identity and Format Adaptation

The concept of "national identity" suggests that inhabitants feel a sense of unity based on their residence in a shared national space, even in the face of social and cultural differences within their nation.[11] Benedict Anderson has suggested that the nation is an "imagined community" because the members of a nation "will never know most of their fellow-members, meet them, or even hear of them" and nonetheless a sense of communion exists between them.[12] This emphasis on imagined links between people shows that national identity is a cultural process rather than purely biological or physical and is something that is (consciously or subconsciously) learned.[13] The role of media, in particular television, therefore becomes increasingly significant, as they are important in the construction of a shared sense of national belonging.

The practice of selling television program formats to overseas markets, and adapting them to appeal to national sensibilities, has seen a marked increase in recent years. Albert Moran attributes this increase to a number of factors, including changes in national television systems due to deregulation, privatization, and the advent of new distribution technologies that have multiplied the number of television channels available within national boundaries.[14] Television formats are flexible and allow for modifications to the original program to "nationalize" it; the format "serves as a general framework or guide,"[15] rather than a fixed design. The ability to adapt to the environment of the new country is a vital part of producing a successful format adaptation, and the original format may need to be varied to fit production resources, channel image, buyer preference, and other broadcast regulations, as well as the culture of the new country.[16] The global format trade thus allows for the creation of new and original texts that encourage articulations of national identity.

In relation to the comedy genre, it is important to acknowledge that, despite the spread of American television sitcoms around the world, humor remains a locally based phenomenon. This can have significant implications for the international trade of comedy as programs may be understood in different ways by other cultures.[17] This was illustrated by offense taken by Chinese audiences to the attitudes displayed toward the elderly in the Australian sitcom *Mother and Son* (ABC: 1983-1998) when it screened in China.[18] The "nationalization" of comedy television forms such as the sitcom is therefore particularly necessary for success in a new country. Many British sitcoms that have been remade for the American market have had great difficulty with success, for example (as noted in the introduction), *Coupling* (which was cancelled after four episodes) and *Men Behaving Badly*. These sitcoms all adhered closely to the British originals rather than interpreting the format to fit the American audience, and this is perhaps one of the contributing factors to their failure.

Echoing such findings of local preference is Joseph D. Straubhaar's theory of "cultural proximity," in which he states that "audiences seem to prefer television programs that are as close to them as possible in language, ethnic appearance, dress, style, humour, historical reference, and shared topical knowledge."[19] With the aim of achieving a sense of cultural belonging for audiences, television format adaptations, according to Silvio Waisbord, "organise experiences of the national."[20] Because formats are relatively open texts, there is room for the incorporation of local stories, characters, and events. In his book *Copycat TV*, Albert Moran analyzes the ways in which format adaptations acquire cultural proximity through references to objects, practices, and beliefs of a particular nation. Writing about Dutch format adaptations *Vrouwenvleugel* (RTL4: 1993–1995, from the Australian *Prisoner*) and *Goede Tijden, Slechte Tijden* (RTL4: 1990–, from the Australian *The Restless Years*), he describes how images and sounds of the programs provide a vocabulary of elements "from which an imaginary harmony that is the Dutch nation can in turn be assembled."[21]

The trade of television formats, whilst international in structure, thus enables the creation of national belonging and identity within "national-ized" programs. Media play an important role in establishing a sense of national identity, and it is the genre of sitcom that has long-standing links both with the articulation of social and cultural issues as well as creating a feeling of belonging to a national community.

The Sitcom Genre

Although traditionally the sitcom genre has been associated with a set of stable and easily recognizable characteristics, several more recent programs have attempted to create new forms of the sitcom and escape any conservative connotations that have come from such stability. These "new sitcoms" (including *The Office*) have sought to avoid the visual and stylistic characteristics of the genre. Sitcoms that have used documentary codes and conventions have been termed "comedy verite" by Brett Mills. He describes this as a style in which "the visual characteristics of [cinema] verite have been adopted by sitcom for comedic purposes."[22] Such con-temporary developments suggest that the sitcom genre is moving beyond its conservative origins and is capable of being a vital part of innovative television. These new forms of sitcom can be seen in both Britain and the United States as a larger reaction to developments within the media (such as the rise of reality television) and institutionally (including the need to attract the increasingly fragmented audience with innovative new programming).

The central situation of a sitcom revolves around a group of characters trapped within a continuous cycle of disrupted equilibrium, conflict, and return to the status quo. The perceived conservatism of the traditional sitcom is often related to its association with the domestic or family sit-com, a form that presents "the bourgeois nuclear family as a model of stability, of 'normality.'"[23] In the 1970s, this nuclear family was replaced by "a family of coworkers" in sitcoms such as *The Mary Tyler Moore Show* (CBS: 1970–1977), *M*A*S*H* (CBS: 1972–1983), *Taxi* (ABC: 1978–1983), and *Cheers* (NBC: 1982–1993).[24] Both types of sitcoms place the central characters within a situation from which they cannot escape, either as a domestic family or within the workplace. This sense of entrapment is vital to the continuing narrative of the series, as it ensures a return to the original equilibrium despite the conflicts that occur.

These conflicts and disruptions within the central situation are often caused by socially derived problems[25], and the sitcom is a genre that is able to discuss current social and ideological issues, such as race, class, gender, and sexuality. For the purposes of analyzing differences between the British and American versions of *The Office*, the issues of class and race seem most relevant. The British class system is an integral and fundamental aspect of the country's psyche and is a theme that has been greatly explored by the sitcom. Phil Wickham notes, "There are few cultural forms that have offered a better analysis of the changing British class system, and the conflicts and prejudices it produces."[26] Issues of class can be seen in sitcoms such as *Absolutely Fabulous* (BBC1: 1992–2005) and *You Rang M'Lord* (BBC1: 1988–1993), with their clear upper- and middle-class distinctions.[27] The class system is often the source of humor, particularly when characters attempt to move up from their "rightful" status. The familiar character of the "loser" in British sitcom, with his failed attempts at ambition, can be perceived in terms of class aspirations. Similarly, the issue of race informs a number of American sitcoms, the most famous one being *The Cosby Show* (NBC: 1984–1992). Herman Gray has provided a detailed discussion of the history of representation of black Americans on television and has highlighted the sensitive position that race holds in American society. Gray describes the way in which "conflict, rage, and suspicion based on race and class are central elements of contemporary America,"[28] due to the country's history of slavery and civil rights conflicts, and it is because of this that the issue of race is a complex and difficult subject for humor in American sitcom.

Differences between the British and the American sitcom have been apparent since the 1950s, and many of these have remained in contemporary programs. According to Mills, up until the 1950s the sitcoms produced in the two countries were remarkably similar in terms of shooting style, form, and content. It was not until the development of the British sitcom *Hancock's Half-Hour* (BBC Light Programme: 1954–1959; BBC1: 1956–1960) that dissimilarities became apparent, with tone and style unlike anything seen before in American sitcom.[29] One of the most apparent variations between British and American sitcom is based around character, and there are obvious distinctions between the common character types in each. Casey et al., in their analysis of the British sitcom *Hancock's Half-Hour*, describe Tony Hancock as "self-obsessed, pretentious, stubborn, a loser…unlike the witty, intelligent heroes of American sitcom."[30]

According to Mills,

> British sitcom repeatedly focuses on characters who are incapable
> of communicating and for whom relationships and family are prob-
> lematic and stifling...All these programmes deal with groups who
> the audience is intended to find funny because of their inability to
> understand one another...While American sitcom often invites us
> to laugh *with* its characters, Britcom instead offers pleasure in us
> laughing *at* them.[31]

Mills suggests that although the source of comedy in American sitcoms is
also based on characters dealing with life's problems, they are presented in
two different ways from the British sitcom. First, although friends, family, and colleagues are often the cause of the narrative's conflicts, they also
"constitute a significant support network," and therefore there is more of a
sense of community within the sitcom; and second, the characters tend to
have "a degree of self-awareness about their own predicaments" that their
British counterparts commonly lack.[32]

However, the development of reality television formats such as the docusoap have influenced some of the more recent British sitcoms to allow
characters a greater sense of self-awareness. The docusoap focuses on a
"traditional" documentary subject but prioritizes entertainment and personal stories through the use of fast-paced editing and the interweaving
of short sequences.[33] It is a format that showcases conscious performances
and a desire for celebrity amongst those filmed, and these conventions
can now be seen in several sitcoms. In *The Office*, Frances Gray notes,
embarrassment plays a key role, and the characters have an awareness
of their "status as comedified selves," just as in the docusoap.[34] However,
whilst reality television has affected the self-awareness of sitcom characters, the distinct personality traits of previous British and American characters can still be seen in many contemporary sitcoms.

It is often noted that existing studies of television sitcom fail to acknowledge the element of humor and instead focus on the genre's social role,
representation, and narrative structure.[35] However, humor is obviously
a vital part of the sitcom and has an important sociocultural function,
both generally and within the sitcom. As Joseph Boskin notes, a comic
situation is often determined by "the recognition of a familiar form." He
goes on to explain that "the introduction of non-recognisable or strange
comedy often produces puzzlement, as, for example, when an American
attempts to fathom an English joke. The comic is invariably involved
with repetitive play."[36] Boskin believes that one must be familiar with the
"cultural code" of a society to understand the comedy and jokes of that
nation.[37] Differences between British and American sitcom, therefore, can

be seen through the forms and subjects used to create humor for that national audience.

Humor can also function to establish power structures within the sitcom. The telling of a joke creates a bond between those involved and a relationship of power over those excluded from such bonds. The sitcom can be seen as extending this "bonding activity" and as an "institutionalising of the pleasures and processes involved in such joke-telling."[38] This sense of community created by humor is reiterated by Ronald de Sousa's belief that "I cannot really laugh with you, unless I have the right to laugh; and I only have the right to laugh at you if there is a clear possibility of identification with you."[39] The "us" and "them" differentiation made in a joke forms a sense of belonging to "us" and directing humor toward "them."[40] It is clear that the humor in sitcoms therefore has an important socio-cultural function and is vital to the genre's creation of a sense of national identity and inclusion in the "community" of the joke, the sitcom, and ultimately the nation.

The Office

This analysis will focus on the first series of the British and American versions of *The Office*, with specific interest in six "parallel" episodes: the pilots (I.i), the British "staff training" (I.iv) and American "Diversity Day" (I.ii) episodes, and the British "pub quiz" (I.iii) and American "basketball game" (I.v) episodes.[41] Institutional differences between the two countries meant that the American episodes were only approximately twenty minutes long due to the inclusion of commercials,[42] rather than the approximately twenty-nine minute running time of the British.[43] Commercial imperatives also affected the arrangement of scenes within American episodes to allow for "peaks" in the narrative before advertisement breaks. Despite these modifications, the comedy verite style and the structure of individual episodes remained very similar, particularly the downbeat conclusion of each, in contrast to the traditional sitcom's return to the positive and community-affirming equilibrium. More pronounced differences between the two versions are apparent in articulations of national identity within situations, characters, and types of humor in the sitcom. We will see how, along the lines of these three categories, the original British version and the American adaptation of *The Office* can be read as "British" and "American."

Situations

The situations used by each of the two versions of *The Office* have been constructed to reflect culturally specific British and American signifiers. The central situation around which the sitcom is constructed is that of the office workplace, continuing the tradition of "coworker" sitcoms. *The Office* takes place in a paper distribution office: Wernham-Hogg in Slough in the British series and Dundler-Miflin in Scranton, Pennsylvania, in the American adaptation. The workplace environment of the office is one that is universally understood, which allowed for the central situation of the program to be easily transferred from Britain to the United States and is, perhaps, one of the reasons for its success. However, changes were made to this central situation, and both versions contain visual signifiers within the office setting that nationalize the workspace. The Scranton office contains a number of American items such as a Homer Simpson toy (which is also a reference to Greg Daniels's previous work on *The Simpsons*), bobblehead dolls, university stickers and flags, a water cooler that is the center of office gossip, and a basketball hoop in the warehouse. In the British series, the visual signifiers are less obvious, but the office is situated in the Trading Estate, carrying connotations of industrialization and urban banality, and the characters mention real aspects of Slough such as the Tudor-themed nightclub:

> Tim: "Slough's nightlife is incredible; it's got two nightclubs, it's got Chasers and New York, New York. They call it the nightclub that never sleeps. That closes at one. There was, oh my god, a themed nightclub called Henry the Eighth…It's not there anymore. But not a day goes by that I don't think about it." (I.v)

The attitudes of the office workers in each version also suggest differences between the countries. These attitudes are clearly established in the opening credits of both the British and American programs. The British series opens with the slow, doleful piano tune of "Handbags and Glad-rags." The music is accompanied by shots of the Trading Estate of Slough; there are no people to be seen, the sky is overcast, every building is gray, and we watch as cars circle the roundabout, trapped in an endless circle that reflects the monotony of life in the Slough office. In contrast, the American series opens with a lively, upbeat tune, with each of the main characters seen talking on the phone or working on a document in the office, and upon entering the town the sign "Scranton Welcomes You" comes into view. These welcoming and cheerful opening credits set a much more hopeful tone to the American adaptation, suggesting the "community" aspect of American sitcoms and also playing a vital role in attracting viewers to the series on the commercial channel NBC.

Beyond the central situation of the office workplace, the two versions of *The Office* make use of situations recognizable as belonging to either British or American culture. This is most apparent in two parallel episodes: the British "pub quiz" and the American "basketball game" episodes. These situations illustrate the differences in comedy between the two nations; both place the characters in a competitive situation, but the dynamics of each are drawn from each nation's popular culture. The British episode revolves around a trivia quiz in the local pub, an annual event in which the characters compete in teams. The local pub as well as the pub quiz are considered something of a British institution, and the situation has its basis in verbal competition and mental ability, which can be seen as a form of cultural capital in Britain. Everitt and Bowler note that "the public house…has been regarded for many years as a bastion of traditional English culture" and have called it "a significant national phenomenon—and cultural symbol." They go on to note that

> the public bar has become mythologically identified as the pub space within the agencies of mass popular culture such as British cartoons (eg. *Andy Capp*), and radio (The Bull in *The Archers*) and TV series (The Rovers Return on *Coronation Street* and The Queen Vic on *Eastenders*).[44]

The parallel American episode is based on a basketball game between Michael's office workers and those in the warehouse downstairs. Here the situation is based in physical comedy rather than verbal, and a full eight minutes of the episode is dedicated to scenes of the basketball game itself. The comedy of the episode is created from visual shots of Michael's warm-up routine, Dwight taking off his shirt, the African American office worker's inability to make any shots (after Michael's racist assumption of his talent), and the competition for Pam's attention between Jim and Roy (her fiancé). Sport is seen to be an integral part of American culture and athletic ability is held as a form of cultural capital in that nation, and therefore the inclusion of a basketball game within the sitcom clearly positions it as a recognizable signifier of American culture. According to Mike Featherstone,

> Sport is such a pervasive activity in contemporary America that to ignore it is to overlook one of the most significant aspects of this society. It is a social phenomenon which extends into education, politics, economics, art, the mass media, and even international diplomatic relations. Involvement in sport is almost considered a public duty by many Americans.[45]

In a similar vein to the British pub quiz, the basketball game is common to American culture and provides a competitive environment in which the characters can interact. These situations, therefore, work effectively within both versions of *The Office*, as they have been drawn from British and American popular culture and are familiar as a quintessential aspect of that nation's set of cultural signifiers.

Characters

A comparative analysis can be made between the four main characters of each version of *The Office* (see the appendix for the names of major characters in both versions), with each displaying characteristics that can be associated with specific notions of national identity. David Brent and Michael Scott are managers who want to impress their workers and be seen as comedians, and both announce their wish to be "a friend first, a boss second—probably an entertainer third" (I.i). They are both characters who cause acute embarrassment to those around them, but the manner and source of their actions differ. David operates within the British understanding that comedy is a form of "power" in that culture (as described previously by Gray and highlighted by James Bowman's assertion that "Dave Brent is always seen, by himself as much as by us, against the backdrop of the culture he tries and fails so utterly to live up to"[46]). David is constantly searching for approval through his performances of humor. Performing in front of the camera he pleads, "innit, Gareth, innit?" desperate to impress. David's self-important, deluded, and ultimately pathetic character is familiar and well placed within the context of the British sitcom. Like Hancock and Fawlty before him, David is a man of unachievable aspirations and has an inflated view of his own ability.

In contrast, the American boss Michael's attempts at comedy are designed not to garner respect and power from his employees but rather to entertain them, to create a "community" within the workplace. "Where was my Oprah moment?" Michael asks, and proceeds to organize a group training session in what he calls "an environment of welcoming" (I.ii). Michael's use of comedy and his interactions with employees are all designed to foster a community spirit and are an attempt to find himself friends, followers, and admirers: "Grumble, grumble, but you would follow me to the ends of the earth, grumbling all the way. Like that dwarf from *Lord of the Rings*" (I.v), he tells his workers before their basketball game. His attempts at community and "family" reflect the American sitcom tradition of a support network of characters that is not as prevalent in British sitcom.

The characters of Gareth Keenan and Dwight Schrute, as the slightly odd, powerloving assistant to the regional manager, both have volunteer jobs outside of the office that carry particular national connotations. Gareth, in the British series, is a member of the Territorial Army, and the American Dwight is a volunteer sheriff's deputy "on the weekends." Both of these positions are used for comic effect to highlight the characters' insistence on hierarchy, rules, and discipline. In the British series, much is made of Gareth's position within the volunteer army: Tim and Dawn trick him into discussing army and war techniques in terms that could be interpreted as gay, and he is continually mentioning his army knowledge and the ways in which it could be used in the office environment:

> You know the phrase softly softly catchee monkey?…I could catch a monkey—if I was starving I could. I'd make poison darts out of the poison off deadly frogs. One milligram of that poison can kill a monkey. Or a man. Prick yourself, you'll be dead within a day. Or longer. Different frogs, different times. (I.ii)

A great deal of the comedy of Gareth's character comes from the seriousness with which he views his position as lieutenant and the British audience's knowledge and understanding that he is only a member of the volunteer Territorial Army, rather than a full-time military man.

Dwight is a volunteer deputy sheriff in Lackawanna County, an American equivalent of the part-time volunteer work of the Territorial Army. This role is treated with the same reverence and importance: "It's okay here, uh, but people sometimes take advantage, because it's so relaxed. And, I'm a volunteer sheriff's deputy on the weekends, and you cannot screw around there. It's sort of one of the rules" (I.i). However, other than this parallel reference to the job in the first episode, very little mention is made of Dwight's position throughout the first season. Instead, the humor of his character comes more from his obsession with power and authority and his love of any task that provides him with this (such as choosing the office health care plan or designing the weekend work-roster). These characteristics position Dwight as the universally stereotypical hardworking office assistant, who takes his job much more seriously than necessary and is therefore a source of comedy to his coworkers and to the audience.

The characters of Tim Canterbury and Jim Halpert also draw upon certain aspects of British and American culture and of the tradition of British and American sitcom. In the British series, Tim is an intelligent and articulate young man, who seems much more capable and understanding than those around him. He aspires to something greater than his current job and talks of leaving the office to pursue a university degree in Psychology. Tim informs us that "I like ballet, I love the novels of Proust, I love the work of Alan Delon" (I.iii). Tim is trapped within his current situation, a common trait within the sitcom tradition, and this inability to move is highlighted by his cynicism and frustration in the office, often manifested in the practical jokes played on Gareth and by his disillusioned and sarcastic humor. Although he does quit his job in episode four of the first season, this grand gesture does not progress any further, and in the season finale we learn that he has instead accepted a promotion within the company. Tim's character therefore has an aura of lost hope and wasted opportunity, which serves to highlight the monotony and hopelessness of the British series as a whole.

In contrast to the quietly cultured Tim, Jim is portrayed as the "jock" figure, a character who holds an esteemed position with regards to American notions of sport and athletic ability. "Basketball was my thing in high school" (I.v), he announces, and it is unlikely that such a figure would profess a love for ballet or confess he still lives at home. Like Tim, Jim possesses the same sense of boredom and frustration at his job and carries out the same practical jokes on Dwight. However, the American series suggests a greater interest and commitment to the job than is seen in his British counterpart. In the "Diversity Day" episode, Jim informs the documentary crew of an annual phone call that secures 25 percent of his commission for the year: "I buy a mini bottle of champagne and celebrate a little. And this year, I'm pushing recycled paper on them for 1 percent more. I know, I'm getting cocky, right?" (I.ii). In this interview, Jim shows a greater interest and enthusiasm for his job than is seen in Tim through-out the whole first series of the British sitcom. Upon losing the sale to Dwight, he is returned to the familiar position of frustration and stagna-tion, thus restoring the sitcom's equilibrium. However, in the character of Jim, with his "jock" persona and assertive pursuit of a sale, there is much less of the lost hope that surrounds the British Tim.

In keeping with the typical characteristics of the American sitcom, which often incorporate romantic serial narratives (seen in *Friends* [NBC: 1994–2004], Frasier [NBC: 1993–2004], *Cheers*, and *M*A*S*H*), the love inter-est and unresolved sexual tension between Jim and Pam is introduced earlier and made more obvious than that of Tim and Dawn in the British series. This type of interrelationship is an effective method of ensuring audience loyalty to a long-running series. In the original series, Dawn does not inform us of her three-year engagement to Lee until the fourth episode of the first season:

> Lee proposed to me on Valentine's day. He didn't do it face to face, he took out one of those little ads in the paper, and I think they must have charged by the word, because it just said "Lee love Dawn, mar-riage?" Which, you know, I like, because it's not often you get some-thing which is both romantic *and* thrifty. (I.iv)

In the American series, the sexual interest between these two characters is made much more apparent, and Pam discusses her lengthy engagement to Roy in the first episode. She tells us, "I do illustrations…Jim thinks they're good." Later in the same episode, there is an interview with Jim in which he informs us of Pam's favorite flavor of yogurt. The interview then cuts to a shot of Pam and her embarrassed yet flattered reaction to this news: "Jim said mixed berries? Oh wow, he's on to me" (I.i).

Humor

Both versions of *The Office* use culturally specific humor, created from an "inside knowledge" of specific British or American sensibilities. This includes references to people or characters from popular culture and institutions that carry connotations for those in the country. The use of humor is therefore very important in the sitcom's construction of national identity, for the audience must be familiar with the "cultural code" (as Boskin termed it) to understand the comedy and the jokes. The importance of such familiarity is shown in both the British and American versions. The first episode of the British series is filled with references to the Royal Family, the charity fund-raising of Comic Relief, *Eastenders* (BBC1: 1985-), insults such as "twat" and "knob-end," the comedians "Vic and Bob," and the Territorial Army. This script, when used for the first episode of the American adaptation, was altered to include cultural references that would be recognized by the American audience. Therefore the episode contains references to Hillary Clinton, the Three Stooges, Bob Hope, Abraham Lincoln, Bono, Volunteer Deputy Sheriff, *The Jamie Kennedy Experiment* (WB: 2002–2004), and *Punk'd* (MTV: 2003–). In relocating the sitcom from Britain to the United States, such nationally specific and familiar references were adapted to ensure that the humor created from such an "inside knowledge" was retained.

In relation to humor's sociocultural function, implicit social codes and cultural understandings play a vital role in the success of comedy. Traditional sitcom gives the audience cues or signs of comedy (such as a laugh-track or the inclusion of pauses for laughter in the dialogue), but *The Office*, in its mock-documentary style, does not.[47] Therefore, an understanding of certain national and social issues becomes even more important. Class is the central social issue used in the British series of *The Office* and forms the underlying basis of much of the humor. The series addresses the traditional three-tiered class system (working, middle, and upper class) in a more complex manner than has been seen in previous British sitcoms such as *Steptoe and Son* (BBC1: 1962–1974) and *Keeping Up Appearances* (BBC1: 1990–1995), in which working-class characters strive to better their social class. In *The Office*, the audience is not sympathetic toward or aligned against any one social class; rather, the interactions and class identifications of the characters are complex and inverted. Neither the middle-class David nor Chris Finch are particularly likeable characters, but neither is the distant and removed upper-class character of Jennifer Taylor-Clarke (David's supervisor) or the working-class Lee and Glynn (a warehouse worker) with their sexually loaded and offensive jokes. The most likeable characters, such as Tim (with his plans to attend university) and Dawn (who hopes to pursue her passion for illustrating), are those who aspire to a greater standing and position in life. Such characters are "trapped" within the office; suspended above the working-class but below the comfort of the middle-class, despite their humor and personality.

David is a representation of the middle-class, continually attempting both to impress those above him and exert authority over those below, and desperate not to offend those who may jeopardize his current position. His continual desperation to be respected and asked for advice is seen throughout:

> You've seen how I react to people, make them feel good, make them think that anything's possible. If I make them laugh along the way, sue me. And I don't do it so they turn round and go "thank you David for the opportunity, thank you for the wisdom, thank you for the laughs." I do it so, one day, someone will go "there goes David Brent. I must remember to thank him." (I.vi)

He attempts to gain this respect through his comedy and humor and aspires to belong to the perceived higher class, described by Francis Gray as those who decide what is funny, and who are held in such high regard in British culture.[48] *The Office*, therefore, continues the British sitcom tradition of addressing the issue of social class, but in a manner that is much less stratified and simple, both in terms of our shifting identifications with characters and the program's complex portrayal of traditionally simple class distinctions. The sitcom bases much of its humor in the interactions and aspirations of characters of different social standings.

In the American episode "Diversity Day," the issue of race is at the centre of the situation's humor. The episode shows the arrival of a "diversity teacher," brought in by Corporate to hold a seminar after complaints are made about Michael's "Chris Rock routine." The episode revolves around Michael's lack of comprehension of the unspoken social understandings of race and racist prejudices in the United States. This is a particularly sensitive issue within the culture and one that Ben Walters has noted is "usually taboo for mainstream US sitcoms"[49] as an area of humor:

> "How come," Michael asks, "Chris Rock can do a routine, and everybody finds it hilarious and groundbreaking, then I go and do the exact same routine, same comedic timing, and people file a complaint to Corporate? Is it because I'm white and Chris is black?" (I.ii)

The national sensitivity of such an issue (as previously discussed by Herman Gray) makes Michael's response to Diversity Day all the more uncomfortable. He proceeds to organize his own activities, which include a game in which the participants must guess the race on their forehead: "Jewish," "Italian," or "black," whilst Michael circles the room as Martin

Luther King Jr. and urges the players to "stir the melting pot" (I.ii). He also makes a remark to a Mexican employee: "um, let me ask you, is there a term besides 'Mexican' that you prefer? Something less offensive?" (I.ii). The comedy of this episode of *The Office* therefore relies on Michael's complete disregard for the cultural understandings and social cues associated with the issue of race in the United States.

Although the issues of class and race are addressed throughout both versions of the sitcom, class is foremost in the British and race in the American, reflecting dominant social issues within each nation's psyche. *The Office* uses these issues to create humor around familiar topics, and an understanding of their national relevance is an important part of the success of such comedy.

Conclusion

Comparison of the British and American versions of *The Office* has demonstrated the many ways in which each has been tailored to fit the institutional, social, and cultural environment of its respective country. Both have been effectively constructed to appeal to their national audience, as they are recognizable as "belonging" to that specific nation. Such adaptation was necessary because of the national specificity of the situations, characters, and humor in the sitcom. As has become clear, although the sitcom genre is one that has had global success and is developing new forms in both countries, there still remain obvious distinctions between British and American programs. Within the situations, characters, and humor of the genre is a long tradition of national traits and characteristics that emerged in the 1950s and can still be seen in contemporary programs. As was shown, both the British original and the American adaptation remain relatively similar in terms of the central premise and the comedy verite style, but they display key differences within the components of situation, character, and humor. This has been achieved in a number of ways, including contrasting production methods and narrative structure due to institutional differences, the inclusion of references to popular culture and recognizable situations, the continuation of national character traits, the articulation of social issues relevant to that nation, and the use of such familiar issues to create humor.

Format adaptations must therefore address issues of national specificity to be successful. The adaptation of the British *The Office* into an American program was in no way certain of success, as illustrated by the failure of so many sitcoms to make the transatlantic journey. However, both versions of the program (after initially slow starts) have gone on to achieve high ratings and critical praise, winning awards in Britain and the United States. The success of the American adaptation can be seen as intimately linked to its ability to adjust to the American media environment, adopt the characteristics of the American sitcom, and incorporate the recognizable signifiers and references of American culture. Creating this "cultural proximity" between the program and the national audience is a vital element in the success of any format adaptation, highlighting the importance of national identity in the international format trade. The process of adapting a television program for a different national audience requires both an outward acknowledgement of the differences between the initial country and its destination and an inward nationalizing of the program. Successful format adaptations appear to be those that are an interpretation of the original rather than simply a copy, and are able to fit the social, cultural, and institutional context of the new country. Clearly then, despite the international nature of the format trade and the increasingly global world in which it operates, the success of the sitcom *The Office* as an original format and an adaptation suggests that articulations of national identity are as strong as ever.

Appendix

Major Characters in *The Office*

Office Position	British	American
Regional manager	David Brent *Ricky Gervais*	Michael Scott *Steve Carell*
Assistant (to the) regional manager	Gareth Keenan *Mackenzie Crook*	Dwight Schrute *Rainn Wilson*
Sales representative	Tim Canterbury *Martin Freeman*	Jim Halpert *John Kransinski*
Receptionist	Dawn Tinsley *Lucy Davis*	Pam Beesly *Jenna Fischer*
Warehouse employee and receptionist's fiancé	Lee *Joel Beckett*	Roy Anderson *David Denman*
Traveling sales representative	Chris Finch *Ralph Ineson*	Todd Packer *David Koechner*
Corporate supervisor	Jennifer Taylor-Clarke *Stirling Gallacher*	Jan Levinson-Gould *Melora Hardin*
Temp/intern	Ricky Howard *Oliver Chris*	Ryan Howard *B.J. Novak*

Notes

1. For examples of such a response, see BBC News, "Will the US Version of *The Office* Be a Hit?" March 29, 2005, http://news.bbc.co.uk/2/hi/talking_point/4381843.stm (accessed October 7, 2007); Diana Wichtel, "Staple Attraction," *The Listener*, December 2, 2006, pp. 70-71; and Gary Younge, "America Remakes *The Office*, but No One's Laughing," *The Guardian*, May 8, 2004, http://www.guardian.co.uk/international/story/0,3604,1212151,00.html (accessed June 18, 2007).

2. Josh Wolk, "Take This Job and Love It," *Entertainment Weekly*, February 24, 2006, pp. 20–21.

3. Gary Younge, "Office Intrigue Attracts the US Networks," *The Guardian*, January 24, 2003, http://media.guardian.co.uk/broadcast/story/0,881155,00.html (accessed June 18, 2007).

4. *BBC News*, "Will the US Version of *The Office* Be a Hit?"

5. *BBC Sales Company,* "*The Office* Press Kit," 2002, http://www.bbcprograms.com/pbs/catalog/THE_OFFICE/COLOR%20 PUBLICITY.pdf (accessed August 9, 2007).

6. *BBC Worldwide Press Releases*, "David Brent's Office to Appear in 60 Countries around the World," November 25, 2002, http://www.bbc.co.uk/pressoffice/bbcworldwide/ (accessed June 24, 2007).

7. Ricky Gervais, *Rickygervais.com*, 2004, http://www.rickygervais.com/notwqanda (accessed September 13, 2007). The German version of *The Office*, unlike the American and French, was considered "unofficial" as it did not acknowledge any links to the British sitcom, despite definite similarities. The program first screened in 2004, and after the BBC threatened legal action, an agreement was reached with German producer Brainpool. Season Two onwards acknowledged that the series was "inspired by *The Office* by Gervais and Merchant" in the closing credits.

8. Ben Walters, *The Office* (London: British Film Institute, 2005), 160.

9. James Hibberd, "For the Networks, Season Didn't Rate," *Hollywood Reporter,* 2008, www.hollywoodreporter.com (accessed November 22, 2008).

10. David Goetzl, "Office Politics: Turner Beefs Up Comedy Line-Up," *MediaPost Publications,* June 22, 2007, http://publications.mediapost.com/index.cfm?fuseaction=Articles.showArticle&art_aid=62802 (accessed September 13, 2007).

11. Andrew Higson defines the concept as "the shared identity of the naturalised inhabitants of a particular political-geographical space—that

is, a particular nation." Andrew Higson, "Nationality: National Identity and the Media," in *The Media: An Introduction,* ed. Adam Briggs and Paul Cobley (Essex, UK: Longman, 1998), 354-64, at 354.

12. Benedict Anderson, *Imagined Communities: Reflections on the Origin and Spread of Nationalism* (London: Verso, 1983), 6.

13. Higson, "Nationality," 354.

14. Albert Moran, *Copycat TV: Globalisation, Programme Formats and Cultural Identity* (Luton, UK: University of Luton Press, 1998), 18.

15. Albert Moran, "Television Formats in the World/The World of Television Formats," in *Television across Asia: Television Industries, Programme Formats and Globalisation,* ed. Albert Moran and Michael Keane (London: Routledge Curzon, 2004), 1–8, at 7.

16. Moran, *Copycat TV,* 21.

17. Brett Mills, *Television Sitcom* (London: British Film Institute, 2005), 9.

18. Stuart Cunningham and Elizabeth Jacka, *Australian Television and International Mediascapes* (Cambridge: Cambridge University Press, 1996).

19. Joseph D. Straubhaar, *World Television: From Global to Local* (Thousand Oaks, CA: Sage, 2007), 26.

20. Silvio Waisbord, "McTV: Understanding the Global Popularity of Television Formats," *Television & New Media* 5, no. 4 (2004): 359–83, at 372.

21. Moran, *Copycat TV,* 177.

22. Brett Mills, "Comedy Verite: Contemporary Sitcom Form," *Screen* 45, no. 1 (2004): 63–78, at 75.

23. Steve Neale and Frank Krutnik, *Popular Film and Television Comedy* (London: Routledge, 1990), 239.

24. Ibid.

25. Jane Feuer, "Narrative Form in American Network Television," in *High Theory/Low Culture: Analysing Popular Television and Film,* ed. Colin MacCabe (New York: St Martin's Press, 1986), 101–114, at 107.

26. Phil Wickham, "Sitcom: ScreenOnline," *British Film Institute,* 2007, http://www.screenonline.org.uk/tv/id/445368/index.html (accessed June 6, 2007).

27. *British Film Institute,* "ScreenOnline," 2007, www.screenonline.org.uk (accessed June 6, 2007).

28. Herman Gray, *Watching Race: Television and the Struggle for Blackness* (Minneapolis: University of Minnesota Press, 2004), 292.

29. Mills, *Television Sitcom*, 40–41.

30. Bernadette Casey, Neil Casey, Ben Calvert, Liam French, and Justin Lewis, *Television Studies: The Key Concepts* (London: Routledge, 2002), 30.

31. Mills, *Television Sitcom*, 41.

32. Ibid., 67.

33. Stella Bruzzi, "Docusoaps," in *The Television Genre Book,* ed. Glen Creeber (London: British Film Institute, 2001), 132–34, at 132.

34. Frances Gray, "Privacy, Embarrassment and Social Power: British Sitcom," in *Beyond a Joke: The Limits of Humour,* ed. Sharon Lockyer and Michael Pickering (New York: Palgrave Macmillan, 2005), 146–61, at 158.

35. Brett Mills, "Studying Comedy," in Creeber, *The Television Genre Book*, 61–62, at 61.

36. Joseph Boskin, "The Complicity of Humour: The Life and Death of Sambo," in: *The Philosophy of Laughter and Humour,* ed. John Morreall (Albany: State of New York Press, 1987), 250–64, at 257.

37. Ibid, 254.

38. Neale and Krutnik, *Popular Film and Television Comedy*, 242–43.

39. Ronald de Sousa, "When Is It Wrong to Laugh?" in Morreall, *The Philosophy of Laughter and Humour*, 226–50, at 242.

40. Konrad Lorenz, *On Aggression* (New York: Bantam, 1963), 284.

41. For all subsequent citations to *The Office*, see *The Office*, Season One DVD (U.K./BBC Version) (Middlesex, UK: BBC, 2001); and *The Office*, Season One DVD (U.S./NBC Version) (Los Angeles, Universal, 2005).

42. B. J. Novak, "The Alliance (Commentary Track)," *The Office Season One DVD* (U.S./NBC Version) (Los Angeles, Universal, 2005).

43. Walters, *The Office*, 176.

44. J. C. Everitt and I. R. Bowler, "Bitter-Sweet Conversions: Changing Times for the British Pub," *Journal of Popular Culture* 30, no. 2 (1996): 101–22, at 106.

45. Mike Featherstone, *Consumer Culture and Postmodernism* (Newbury Park, CA: Sage, 1990), 4.

46. James Bowman, "Feared, Loved, Ridiculed," *The American,* May 10, 2007, http://www.jamesbowman.net/articleDetail.asp?pubID=1827 (accessed June 14, 2007).

47. Mills, "Comedy Verite," 71–72.

48. Gray, "Privacy, Embarrassment and Social Power."

49. Walters, *The Office,* 163.

Discussion Questions

1. Identify the thesis of this article. What kinds of information do you expect in the rest of the essay based on this thesis?

2. The article spends some time discussing the differences between the main characters of each show (ex: Jim Halpert vs. Tim Canterbury). How do the members of *The Office* fulfill stereotypes of Americans? American stereotypes of the British?

3. Beeden and de Bruin claim, "each [version of *The Office*] has been tailored to fit the institutional, social, and cultural environment of its respective country." From their reading of these series, what can you tell about the institutional, social, and cultural environments of Great Britain and the US? How are they different? How is that difference reflected in the two series?

4. How does Beeden and de Bruin's claim about national identity articulation in television adaptations correspond to Takacs' ideas of national identity formation as played out in the Jessica Lynch saga?

5. Watch clips or episodes of *Absolutely Fabulous* and *Sex and the City.* What do you notice about differences in humor? How might these shows demonstrate similar notions of national identity formation?

Cynics Encouraged To Apply:
The Office As Reality Viewer Training

Christopher Kocela

Christopher Kocela is Assistant Professor of English at Georgia State University. His articles have appeared in numerous literature and popular culture journals, including *Postmodern Culture, LIT, Genders,* and *Pynchon Notes.* In this essay, Kocela discusses how the American version of *The Office* refines and adapts the "mockumentary." As you read, pay attention to the connections Kocela makes between *The Office,* reality television, and the postdocumentary.

As Brett Mills writes of the British version of *The Office* (2001–03), "by using the conventions of documentary for humour, *The Office* undermines the distinctions between sitcom and documentary, between seriousness and humour, demonstrating that the outcomes of one can be achieved through the conventions of the other" (107). Mills's description of the vanishing divide between seriousness and humor on *The Office* is indicative of that "knowing laughter" which, according to Richard Kilborn, is the objective of all mockumentary forms. Kilborn argues that mockumentary, by parodying conventional strategies of traditional documentary, strives to produce "knowing laughter": "Audiences are still entertained, but are at the same time being invited to consider some of the more serious implications of television's ever growing intrusiveness, together with the media's compulsive need to make performers out of people" (183). Yet although both British and American versions of *The Office* produce the "knowing laughter" essential to successful mockumentary, the American adaptation has evolved beyond its British original into a sustained parody and critique not only of traditional documentary conventions, but also of reality TV as well. Self-conscious references to reality programs on NBC's *The Office* are integral to the production of a kind of humor that speaks to viewers who have come to use reality TV not only as entertainment, but as a form of social bonding in an era in which the boundary between public and private, and between workplace and home, has become difficult to discern. As a result, the American *Office* redefines the concept of mockumentary for a televisual era dominated by reality programming.[1]

It's Not Business, It's Just Personal

The obsessiveness with which the American version of *The Office* references reality TV and its conventions is most conspicuously exhibited in the character of Michael Scott (Steve Carell), who repeatedly portrays himself not just as an amateur comedian for his employees (à la the

British version's David Brent [Ricky Gervais]), but also as an aspiring reality TV host. This trend emerges as early as the pilot episode, in which Michael, hoping to impress the new office temp, stages a mock firing of his secretary, Pam (Jenna Fischer), in an attempt to recreate the "candid camera" gags of shows like *The Jamie Kennedy Experiment* (2002–03) and *Punk'd* (2003–07). Even after the joke misfires and Pam is reduced to tears, Michael remains in character as program "host," revealing the truth of the situation with a mock-gleeful "You've been X-ed, punk!" Subsequent episodes reveal the more pervasive influence of reality TV on Michael's management techniques. In "The Alliance" (S1E4),[2] Michael defines his management style relative to that of Donald Trump on *The Apprentice* (2004–present): "I think the main difference between me and Donald Trump is that I get no pleasure out of saying the words, *'You're fired.'*" In "The Fight" (S2E6), Michael defeats his crony, Dwight Schrute (Rainn Wilson), in an office wrestling match and shouts, "You *are* the weakest link!" "The Carpet" (S2E14) opens with Michael's discovery that someone has soiled the floor of his office—an affront he first decides to treat as a personal test: "I'm a big *Fear Factor* fan […] so this is sort of like my audition tape." Later in the episode, unable to stand the smell any longer, he criticizes the men replacing the carpet for not working quickly enough: "*Extreme Home Makeover* put together a house in an hour. If you were on that crew, you would be fired like that." Finally, several episodes are devoted to special outings planned by Michael with his favorite reality programs in mind. At the start of "Traveling Salesmen" (S3E12), Michael calls for a group huddle and informs his staff that, in an effort to get back to roots, he has planned a day of team sales calls that he regards as a recreation of *Amazing Race*. "Survivor Man" (S4E5) takes its title and theme from the *Science Channel's* popular reality series starring Les Stroud: here Michael ventures into the Pennsylvania wilderness in order to demonstrate his ability to live off the land. Finally, "Beach Games" (S3E22) focuses on Michael's attempt to recreate a Scranton edition of *Survivor* (2000–present) for his employees. This is undoubtedly Michael's finest hour as a reality TV host ("One day. Fourteen strangers who work together. But only one survivor!"), and it drives home the way in which, for Michael, reality takes second place to reality TV: the final prize in his version of *Survivor* is his own job.[3]

Michael's use of reality TV to inspire and motivate his staff contributes to what several reviewers have portrayed as the fundamental optimism of the American version of *The Office*. As journalist Liesl Schillinger observes, where the mood of the British *Office* is "resignation mingled with self-loathing," in the American version, "passivity mingles with rueful hopefulness: an American always believes there's something to look forward to" (5).[4] Dogged by incessant threats of downsizing and closure,

Michael deploys the conventions of reality TV to raise morale and to teach lessons about the value of team play.[5] Yet more important, Michael's obsession with recreating reality game shows dramatizes the cultural fascination with trying to get "inside" the events depicted on TV—a fascination which, according to John Corner, drives the production of reality programming and the turn toward a *"postdocumentary"* age (297). In Corner's definition, *postdocumentary* does not refer to the disappearance of documentary or its claims to the factual; instead, it signals an era (our own) in which documentary tactics for producing belief in factuality or reality have been dispersed across a host of new entertainment and reality forms (297). This dispersal is itself the result of a perceived need on the part of conventional news providers to give access to the subjective experience of real events. As Corner writes: "An expanded desire for 'emotional knowledge' about events—about what it is like to be 'inside' an event, 'inside' an experience— has appeared across a number of factual genres, including news, encouraging new modes of the subjective both in visual style and speech" (291). Through its creation of a comic character obsessed with getting inside the experience of reality TV, *The Office* presents itself as a parody of what it means to live in the postdocumentary world. This parody, in turn, occasionally challenges Corner's insistence that reality TV does not betoken the death of traditional documentary or belief in reality. As Michael remarks in "Conflict Resolution" (S2E21), complaining about his boredom: "It can't always be like *The Apprentice*. On *Big Brother*, something important happens every day."

Though the specific role of reality TV in the turn toward a postdocumentary age continues to be debated (as does the term *postdocumentary* itself),[6] two effects seem especially pertinent to *The Office* and the kind of knowing laughter that the show generates. The first effect is the tendency of reality TV to normalize and legitimate surveillance. As Susan Murray and Laurie Ouellette observe:

> More and more programs rely on the willingness of "ordinary" people to live their lives in front of television cameras. We, as audience members, witness this openness to surveillance, normalize it, and in turn, open ourselves up to such a possibility. We are also encouraged to participate in self-surveillance.(6)

In keeping with this idea, Daniel Trottier argues that different genres or formats of reality TV instruct their audience members to subject themselves to different kinds of surveillance practices. "Real crime" programs like *Cops* (1989–present) and *America's Most Wanted* (1989–present) situate their audiences on a criminal-justice grid by encouraging participation in efforts to track down criminals, while makeover programs like *Queer Eye for the Straight Guy* (2003–07) broadcast "a particular relationship between subjects and a panoptic consumer apparatus" (273). The result is a partial breakdown of the public/private divide—a breakdown conducive to the second effect of reality TV relevant to *The Office*. This is the effect whereby, according to Misha Kavka, reality TV confronts us with a problem of an "ethics of emotion."

As Kavka points out, when viewers watch reality TV, they know that they are being manipulated, but they look past that fact in order to experience the emotional connection to "real" on-screen people that this type of programming affords. What viewers look for when watching reality TV is that sense of affective connection between themselves as individuals and a "collective psyche, that shared pool of feeling whose production and recognition glues individuals into a particular social body" (95).[7] To achieve this feeling, viewers are willing to forgive the blatant artificiality of the scenarios created in "intimate strangers" formats like *Survivor*, *Big Brother*, (2000–present), and *Joe Millionaire* (2003). What matters is not why a particular group of people has been gathered together, but *that* they have been gathered together in a setting that promises the rapid transformation of strangers into intimate relations. Ultimately, reality TV persuades its audience to buy in to surveillance by fostering a sense of emotional connection with that community of intimate strangers on-screen—an effect created by oscillating between group surveillance shots and individual, confessional interviews. Yet this sense of expanded media intimacy also reinforces conflicted attitudes toward the ideological message of reality TV. Kavka maintains the following about "real love" shows like *Joe Millionaire* and *The Bachelor*:

> Narratively, the ideology of requited love prevails, but in their form these programs urge us to love (or, just as possibly, to hate) without return, since we expend a great deal of emotion on people who cannot see us back. Our affective response, in other words, is excessive, and thereby in excess of the moral imperative or normatizing ideology built into the format. (102)

Although Kavka writes specifically about programs in which the purported aim is to match contestants with their "true love," the argument also applies to the crime-based and make-over formats discussed by Trottier. If reality TV normalizes panoptic surveillance by promoting a certain set of synoptic values (whether moral or commercial), the format of reality TV inevitably, though subtly, contradicts that aim. Even if, for example, one fully subscribes to the ideology of a reality make-over program and believes that a given contestant will benefit by the make-over, the very fact that viewers are encouraged to like and sympathize with this person from the outset serves as an implicit emotional argument *against* the need to change him or her. The tagline that appears on the opening title screen of *The Apprentice*—"It's Not Personal, It's Just Business"—is thus a clear mystification of the dynamics of the show's appeal as a popular incarnation of the "intimate strangers" format. The business of *The Apprentice* as reality TV is the production of the personal at the level of affect—a production in which surveillance itself plays the starring role.

Given that *The Apprentice* is the most frequently referred-to reality show on *The Office*, it is appropriate that Michael Scott's mantra regarding the relationship between business and the personal is the antithesis of Donald Trump's: "Business is always personal. It's the most personal thing in the world" ("Business School," S3E17). This statement is fundamental to understanding *The Office* as a parody of reality TV and its effects in the postdocumentary age. *The Office* as a scripted comedy produces knowing laughter about the ethical and ideological dimensions of the breakdown of the public/private divide—a breakdown that is both reflected in, and produced by, the conventions of reality TV.

Beyond the fact that the employees at Dunder Mifflin are subject to constant surveillance from the camera crew, often against their will, several episodes to date explore the theme of surveillance in the workplace. "Email Surveillance" (S2E15) is the most sustained meditation on this topic, focusing on Michael's abuse of email spyware to gather information about the private lives of his employees. This episode ends with Michael crashing a party at the home of one his salesmen, Jim Halpert (John Krasinski)—a party to which he has deliberately not been invited because, in Jim's words, "if he were there, people wouldn't be able to relax." In "Conflict Resolution" (S2E21), Michael gains access to privileged information about employee complaints and takes it upon himself to air these complaints in a public forum, hoping to heal old wounds, which, instead, are reopened by his tactlessness. Nor is Michael the only character to abuse privileged information on the show. "Health Care" (S1E3) focuses on the violations of privacy that occur when Michael's sycophantic righthand man, Dwight Schrute, is placed in charge of choosing a new health care plan for his coworkers. The climax of the episode is a board room meeting in which Dwight reads from a list of anonymously submitted medical ailments, demanding that the staff publicly identify which ailment pertains to them:

> DWIGHT. Number one—inverted penis. [*long silence*]

> MEREDITH. Could you mean vagina? Because if you do, I want that covered.

> DWIGHT. I thought your vagina was removed during your hysterectomy.

> MEREDITH. A uterus is different from a vagina. I still have a vagina.

Similarly, in "Drug Testing" (S2E26) the entire office is subjected to a spot urine test, at Dwight's instigation, when a joint is discovered in the office parking lot. When the staff objects to the testing, Toby, the human resources representative, reminds everyone, "When you sign your contract you agree to random drug testing."

Beyond exploring the issue of external surveillance, *The Office* also parodies the way in which reality TV encourages participation in *self-surveillance*. Much of the show's humor derives from the reversals that occur whenever Michael strives for political correctness. When he asks one of his employees if there is some other, "less offensive" term than "Mexican" that he might prefer to be called ("Diversity Day" S1E2), or when Michael exclaims incredulously, "I call everyone faggy! Why would anyone find that offensive?" ("Gay Witch Hunt" S3E1), laughter results, in part, from the depiction of an office manager so completely ignorant about what constitutes offensive workplace behavior. At the same time, Michael's gaffes remind viewers that the common sense he so conspicuously lacks is not common enough: nearly everyone has witnessed similar, if less extreme, examples of workplace insensitivity, and most people are on guard against inadvertently offending someone themselves. To be sure, *The Office* does not hold a monopoly on humor that pushes the envelope of political correctness, but the originality of the series lies in the way Michael's failure to internalize the normative self-surveillance necessary to workplace interaction is symptomatically registered, and compensated for, by the mockumentary format of the series itself.

Obviously whatever humor is to be found in Michael's spectacularly un-PC behavior depends on the cameras *not* dwelling on the hurt and injustice done to the victims of his insensitive remarks. A too-long close-up on Pam's tearful face after being "punk'd" in the pilot episode would render this scene patently unfunny. Instead, to promote knowing laughter at Michael's blunders, the mockumentary editors of *The Office* conspicuously police audience reaction by ensuring that Michael is able to get a word in to the viewing audience after his offensive gags and remarks have been "caught" by the film crew. Often this confessional sequence is preceded by a moment of group silence in which an office worker—usually Jim—gives a knowing look at the camera, indicating that some social norm has been violated. When, for example, Michael learns that Oscar Martinez (Oscar Nuñez), a member of the accounting staff, has complained to human resources about his use of the term "faggy," the camera cuts to his confessional explanation of when it is appropriate to use inappropriate language:

> You don't call retarded people retards. It's in bad taste. You call your friends retards when they're acting retarded. And I consider Oscar a friend. ("Gay Witch Hunt" S3E1)

Michael's faulty logic, malapropisms, and factual errors almost always undermine his efforts to justify himself, deepening the comedic effect. But in the process, these earnest "talking head" sequences also mock the way reality TV normalizes surveillance by manipulating viewer emotions. As Trottier argues, a chief function of reality programming is to "foster an understanding of surveillance as being an invaluable (or at least entertaining) component of social relations" (260). Crime and makeover reality programs accomplish this goal by drawing clear distinctions between criminal behavior and the victims subjected to it, encouraging the audience to identify with the victims. On crime shows like *America's Most Wanted* the difference between criminals and victims is legalistic, while on makeover programs like *Queer Eye for the Straight Guy* the intervention that takes place is portrayed as a rescue effort—accepted if not welcomed by the beneficiary—to save someone who has become a metaphoric victim of their own or others' "criminal" fashion negligence. In *The Office*, however, the boundary between criminals and victims is blurred not only because the camera sometimes seems to take Michael's side against the viewpoint of his offended staff members, but also because Michael himself is portrayed as a victim of managerial makeovers organized by the corporate head office to correct his political incorrectness. Even when Michael himself is not attempting to recreate reality programs like *Survivor Man* and *Amazing Race*, part of the humor of episodes like "Sexual Harrassment" (S2E2) and "Diversity Day" derives from their recreation, in the workplace, of the conventions of makeover shows like *Queer Eye for the Straight Guy*—with the vital difference that Michael is never successfully made over. Consequently, what is naturalized in *The Office* is not the social need for self-surveillance but Michael's own contradictory emotional investment in it.

On *The Office*, mixed feelings about surveillance and political correctness frequently reflect the kinds of *ideological* contradictions that Kavka identifies in her study of reality TV viewing. The ideological ramifications of Michael's conflicted attitude toward surveillance, for example, become particularly evident when he inadvertently reveals how his own managerial strategies betray his "business is personal" mantra. One such admission occurs in "The Alliance" (S1E4), in which Michael offers his own, worker-sensitive version of Donald Trump's "You're fired!": "I think if I had a catch-phrase it'd be, 'You're hired! And you can work here as long as you want!' But that's unrealistic." Even more pointedly, Michael's last words in the pilot episode of the series establish what amounts to a fundamental disconnect between belief and action regarding the "corporate family":

> My proudest moment here was not when I increased profits by
> seventeen percent, or when I cut expenses without losing a single

employee. No, no, no. It was a young Guatemalan guy, first job in the country, barely spoke English, who came to me and said, "Mr. Scott, would you be the godfather to my child?" Wow! [*Long pause.*] Didn't work out in the end. We had to let him go—he sucked. ("Pilot" S1E1)

Particularly important here is that Michael fails to see how his actions as manager undermine his "proudest moment" with the company. Unlike the British series' David Brent, Michael is not inherently deceitful; Carell's painfully earnest delivery of these lines (evoking the reality TV convention that the truth always comes out in the confessional, talking head sequences) encourages viewers to take Michael's word for his emotional investment in the moment he describes. Rather, the comedic point of this scene is Michael's failure to register a patent contradiction between what he genuinely believes and what he actually does. Despite the show's repeated emphasis on the breakdown of the public/private divide in the workplace, it is clear that, at some level, business at Dunder Mifflin is still business as usual in the sense that generating profit trumps all other considerations. Michael may be a hopeless case as manager, but he remains in his position, despite his social ineptitude, because at crucial moments he is still able to make the sale.[8] As a result, to laugh at Michael is not to laugh at just his foolish inability to police himself according to politically correct standards; it is also to laugh at the cynical corporate attitude toward political correctness that he represents as a regional manager. Michael is a comic figure because he doesn't seem to see the superficiality of his "corporate family" metaphor, yet to laugh at his naiveté is troubling because it implies a continuity between the mockumentary format of *The Office* and the ideological disconnect between belief and action that Michael displays. This continuity is driven home whenever Michael's employees are seen struggling to come up with an appropriate response to their boss's behavior—a silent struggle that, owing to the absence of canned laughter on the show, is replicated in viewers' own living rooms.

Knowing Laughter, Knowing Silence, and the Jim Halpert Shrug

Reviewers of *The Office* have made much of the fact that the producers' refusal to employ a laugh track enables long, uncomfortable silences to serve as the punch line of many of the jokes. This silence captures the sense of frustration experienced by Michael's offended and incredulous staff members, and it serves as a reminder of why they have to put up with him—because he's the boss. Yet the irony of episodes like "Email Surveillance" and "Drug Testing" is that Michael's employees not only put up with his insensitivity and invasiveness, they also encourage it. When,

in "The Dundies" (S2E1), Michael's racist performance as master of cer-
emonies for the yearly company awards dinner is booed and catcalled by
other patrons at the local *Chili's*, Michael's employees rise to his defense.
Similarly, when Michael shows up uninvited at Jim's party and comman-
deers the karaoke machine at the end of "Email Surveillance," Jim decides
to join him in a duet of "Islands in the Stream." Given the show's need to
produce laughs, these challenges to credibility make some sense, since
without Jim's shrugging submission, there would be no opportunity to
enjoy Michael's imitation of Dolly Parton's vocals. But scenes in which
Michael's employees effectively applaud his intrusive and insulting behavior also recall the earlier "knowing silences" in which their discomfort
was displayed. At the end of the day, although Michael's staff members see
through his ridiculous rhetoric about the office as family, they confirm
his corporate metaphor every time they humor him. By presenting this
troubled "applause" as, itself, a source of potentially uncomfortable humor for the viewing audience, *The Office* teaches important lessons about
the mediated nature of ideology in our cynical, postdocumentary age.

Slavoj Žižek discusses canned laughter as an example of what he describes
as the objectivity of belief (29–35). For Žižek, the function of the laugh
track on most popular shows is not to encourage emotional investment
in the program by reminding viewers when to laugh. On the contrary,
its function is to laugh *instead* of the viewer, relieving him or her of the
mental effort necessary for emotional engagement in what they're watching. Canned laughter thus exemplifies, in Žižek's view, the way that ideology functions in a fundamentally cynical world. Although most viewers
know better than to believe what they see on television, the medium
itself, via the laugh track, objectifies their belief for them by supply-
ing the appropriate viewer response as an integral part of its format. By
this line of reasoning, one does not have to believe that a particular line
from a mundane sitcom is funny; through canned laughter, the TV supplies its own laughter and inscribes its audience's ongoing participation
in whatever ideologies inform its programming content. Paradoxically,
emotional disconnection facilitates participation, revealing the fact that
ideology functions not only at the level of what we *think* but—much more
important—at the level of what we *do*. Ideology takes root in the cynical
distance between day-to-day practices and what subjects actually feel and
think about those practices. Catering to our sense that we always already
"know better" than this, ideology flourishes in an environment in which
we convince ourselves that, so long as we don't actually get sucked into
believing in what we're doing, we can go on doing it without having to
take responsibility for our actions.

In the present context Žižek's discussion of canned laughter highlights the difference between cynical participation in an age ruled by the television sitcom and in the age of reality TV. Reality TV has by and large done away with the laugh track in an effort to distance itself from the conventions associated with scripted television. Relying on viewers' empathy with the "real" people onscreen, reality TV seeks an emotionally committed audience and frequently enlists active viewer participation. Though it is possible just to watch *Big Brother* or *American Idol* (2002–present), ideal viewers (and millions of actual viewers) also contribute to the program by telephoning in and texting their votes as to which contestants should be removed from competition on a week-to-week basis. Yet this increased participation is not to be confused with a heightened belief on the part of the audience about the reality of reality TV; according to numerous theorists of reality TV, the paradox of attachment to reality programming is that most viewers are deeply cynical about what they are doing. Kavka's elegant reading of participation in reality love programs illuminates the process by which these shows enlist ongoing subscription to ideologies of surveillance by appealing to emotions that actually *contradict* those ideologies. Like Žižek's "post-ideological" subjects, reality TV fans know very well that their favorite programs are constructed and contrived, but they watch anyway. The crucial difference is that, in the case of reality TV, cynical belief is objectified not in the passive form of canned laughter but in those very activities, like voting and blogging, that constitute an essential part of the program format.

As a cross between scripted television and the conventions of reality TV, *The Office* produces a heightened awareness of the difference in emotional commitment demanded by these programming formats—a difference felt whenever knowing laughter fills the knowing silence left by the absence of the laugh track. In particular, although *The Office* does not demand the same degree of viewer participation as actual reality programs,[9] its parodic deployment of documentary/reality conventions calls attention to the way that some of these conventions now substitute for canned laughter as ideological mediators between belief and action. Beyond merely documenting Michael's conflicted attitude to his "office as family" philosophy, for example, confessional sequences in which Michael speaks alone to the camera become reflections on the way such interviews construct an emotional truth about their subjects that is predicated on the strategic positioning of the camera as a silent, impartial recorder of events. Although few are likely to believe in the possibility of absolutely unbiased reporting, the camera in talking-head sequences objectifies that belief to the extent that it seems to operate independent of biased human interpretation. Indeed, talking-head shots take their name from the depiction, in tight focus, of a single subject in monologue undisturbed by interviewers' questions or action requiring camera movement.[10] On *The Office*, such conventional techniques are both comically exaggerated and undercut. On one hand, the complete lack of any diegetic rationale for the shooting or assembly of documentary footage about Dunder Miffin's employees mocks, by exaggeration, the on-screen silence maintained by cameramen and interviewers in order to produce the illusion of the camera's impartiality.[11] Absent any controlling argument for the presence of the cameras at Dunder Mifflin, Michael's deliberate orchestration of reality TV-inspired events and performances becomes the de facto argument of the "documentary" that evolves over the course of the series. On the other hand, the cameras themselves frequently betray the illusion of their impartiality through conspicuous pans that appear as emotional or critical reactions to Michael's blunders. When, after catching one of Michael's goofs, the camera pans to Jim for a response, this movement not only substitutes, visually, for the aural interruption of canned laughter, it also lays bare the function of the surveillance camera as the dominant new technology for enabling cynical participation. In these moments, which recur frequently throughout the series, Jim's reactions (a shrug, rolling eyes, a shake of the head) reveal the way in which the camera itself actually facilitates ongoing subscription to the ideology of surveillance by providing viewers with the opportunity for dissent—in principle if not in practice.

In light of the popularity of *The Office*, Jim's shrug (and its variations[12]) stands as a privileged site of ideological critique on contemporary television. Jim clearly knows when Michael has crossed the line, and he knows, too, that Michael's attitude toward political correctness in the workplace is inherently contradictory. When, looking into the camera, Jim gives his Oliver Hardyesque "can you believe this?" shrug, viewers' sense of the injustice and foolishness of what they've been watching is confirmed. Moreover, in contrast to the talking-head sequences in which Michael *inadvertently* reveals the distance between his beliefs and his practices as regional manager, Jim is openly cynical about what he does at work. As he tells the camera early on: "Right now this is just a job. If I advance any higher in this company, then this would be my career. And, well, if this were my career, I'd have to throw myself in front of a train" ("Health Care" S1E3). Yet although no one makes cynical participation look cooler than Jim, he, like Michael and Dwight, is also a company man. Subsequent episodes show Jim not only progressing upward through the ranks of Dunder Mifflin, they also reveal that the esteem in which he is held by his superiors in the New York corporate office derives, in part, from the carefree, even dismissive attitude he affects about office politics. A decisive moment in season three is the backyard game of twenty-one Jim plays with Dunder Mifflin's chief financial officer, David Wallace (Andy Buckley), during David's own corporate party. As it turns out, David, like

Jim, "hates" these corporate functions and uses the chance to shoot hoops behind the house not only as an escape from the party, but also as an opportunity to pick Jim's brain about Michael's personal life. That Jim is willing to play ball with David here both literally and figuratively reveals the self-serving nature of his cynical attitude. In an age in which even corporate CFO's profess a fundamental disbelief in what they do, cynicism provides no basis for resisting corporate ideology. On the contrary, the arc of Jim's character development implies that cynical detachment now serves, in fact, to suture subjects more tightly to the ideologies from which they claim a critical distance. What *The Office* dramatizes, episode after episode, is the function of the reality/surveillance camera in the ideological "suturing" process. Jim looks to the camera and shrugs instead of objecting to the behavior he finds offensive in the workplace: the implication is that the camera now absolves people of the responsibility of having to confront—in the sense of actually *doing* anything about—the contradiction between their beliefs and their day-to-day practices. The dynamics of this process are central to understanding the series' mockumentary critique of reality TV. Canned laughter used to free viewers from having to respond emotionally to televised programming, inscribing their participation in the medium even while preserving their right to disagree with the programming content. But the camera eye of reality TV fixates on and celebrates emotional response of any kind, rewarding its viewers with a feeling of community that frees them from having to disagree with the shows' claims to "reality." Of course the aim of both strategies is to ensure that we keep the television on—an aim with which *The Office*, it should go without saying, is also complicit by virtue of its status as an ad-driven network show. That the series so effectively keeps us watching is a result, in part, of the many opportunities it provides for *both* emotional engagement and critical reflection.

For Walter Benjamin, the turn toward the age of mechanical reproduction was marked by the waning of the cultic aura of art and by the inculcation in the masses of a fundamentally critical view of artistic representation and social reality. A prime mover in this cultural turn was popular film, which encouraged its audience to identify with the camera eye and to adopt its "testing" approach to whatever was put before it (228–29). By contrast, the turn toward the postdocumentary age seems to be marked by reliance on the camera as a means of bracketing questions about the constructedness of the "reality" it depicts. In the wake of reality TV, which provides free training in cynical detachment to millions of homes every night, the surveillance camera has taken the place of canned laughter as the new, most culturally prevalent form of objectified communal belief. Watching reality TV, viewers feel the emotional connection to the people on-screen not because they believe in the reality of the community represented there, but because the camera believes for them. As a mockery of this now seemingly inevitable cultural development, *The Office* invites us to consider the other areas of our lives in which we, like Jim, have come to regard it as our job to shrug and keep on watching.

NOTES

1. This is not to suggest that the British version is unaware of reality programming; on the contrary, the character of David Brent, like Michael Scott, also refers to popular reality series on several occasions. But there is nothing in the British version to compare with the extended parodies of *Survivor*, *Survivor Man* (2004–present), or *Amazing Race* (2001–present) that have emerged in the second through fourth seasons of the American version. For this reason, my argument differs from that of Jeffrey Griffin, who maintains that the success of NBC's *The Office* depends on a systematic process of "format adaptation" whereby almost every feature of the British original, from setting to character to dialogue, is Americanized so as to appeal to U.S. viewers. Griffin's argument, supported by a careful comparison of the British version to the first fourteen episodes of the American adaptation, is convincing; but because it focuses on so narrow and early a sampling of the American version, it misses what has become a central feature of the U.S. adaptation—its deliberate parody of numerous aspects of reality TV.

2. Please note my shorthand method for referring to specific episodes in the series: S1E4 means season one, episode four. It is important to mention that, although Michael is clearly obsessed with reality programming, he is not the only character on the show who evidently watches a lot of reality TV. In "Health Care" (S1E3), Jim asks Pam if she watched *Trading Spouses* (2004) last night; in "Performance Review" (S2E8), Pam asks Jim if he watched *The Apprentice* last night; and Stanley thinks his being fired in "Halloween" (S2E5) is a joke about *The Apprentice*. There are too many examples to cite all of them here. Michael also makes reference to nonreality TV—in particular to much older American sitcoms and dramas (*Gilligan's Island* [1964–67], *Six Million Dollar Man* [1974–78], *Kung Fu* [1972–75]) which, it would appear, Michael watched as a child.

3. In the DVD commentary on the "Beach Games" (S3E22) episode, the producers of the series reveal that NBC's *The Office* employs the same camera crew that filmed the first two seasons of CBS's *Survivor*.

4. See Friend for a similar point about the optimism of the American version.

5. Meanwhile, for viewers of the American *Office*, analogies between the plight of our favorite characters and reality TV contestants help cut through the overwhelming sense of being trapped in one's job that defines the British version, subtly reminding us that this dysfunctional workplace "family" is purely adoptive and temporary. The much greater attention paid to the character of the temp in the American version also reinforces the optimistic notion that one can always escape an oppressive workplace environment.

6. For a history of Corner's term, including its origins and the controversy surrounding its use, see Holmes and Jermyn; see also Bignell (25–28).

7. Though Kavka's argument is theoretical and speculative in nature, her ideas are supported by surveys (like those conducted by Crew, cited hereafter) about why viewers tune in to "intimate strangers" formats.

8. The show establishes early on that Dwight, the least socially and politically aware member of the office, is the most productive salesman and generates the most revenue for the company. Michael, who was promoted to his administrative position as a result of his excellent sales record, also occasionally shows remarkable salesmanship—particularly in "The Client" (S2E7), where he outshines his own boss, Jan Levinson-Gould (Melora Hardin), in landing a difficult contract.

9. *The Office* does have an active Web presence, but the various blogs devoted to the show, some of which are maintained by the series' actors, do not directly shape its progress or content in the manner of many reality programs.

10. For a fascinating discussion of the way in which pre–reality era prime-time sitcoms interrogated "docu-real" conventions through the use of interviews, see Caldwell.

11. I refer here to the fact that the presence of the cameras at Dunder Mifflin is never explained: we don't know why the documentary crew is there in the first place nor who invited them into the workspace. Michael seems, in the pilot episode at least, to provide an introduction of the crew to the office staff, but on many occasions, his effort to hide from the cameras, rather than simply asking them to leave, suggests that the authority to halt or shape the direction of filming does not reside with him. Nor does it seem that the corporate head office has authorized the intrusion, since visitors from that office—particularly Michael's immediate superior, Jan—are at times surprised and dismayed to learn that they are on camera.

12. By "shrug" I also include the numerous bodily signals used by Jim to register dissent before the camera.

Works Cited

"The Alliance." Dir. Bryan Gordon. Writ. Michael Schur. *The Office.*

"Beach Games." Dir. Harold Ramis. Writ. Greg Daniels and Jennifer Celotta. *The Office.*

Benjamin, Walter. "The Work of Art in the Age of Mechanical Reproduction." 1936. Trans. Harry Zohn. *Illuminations: Essays and Reflections.* By Benjamin. Ed. Hannah Arendt. New York: Schocken, 1969. 217–51. Print.

Bignell, Jonathan. *Big Brother: Reality TV in the Twenty-First Century.* New York: Palgrave, 2005. Print.

"Business School." Dir. Joss Whedon. Writ. by Greg Daniels and Brent Forrester. *The Office.*

Caldwell, John. "Prime-Time Fiction Theorizes the Docu-Real." *Reality Squared: Televisual Discourse on the Real.* Ed. James Friedman. New Brunswick: Rutgers UP, 2002. 259–92. Print.

"The Carpet." Dir. Victor Nelli Jr. Writ. By Greg Daniels and Paul Lieberstein. *The Office.*

"Conflict Resolution." Dir. Charles McDougall. Writ. by Greg Daniels. *The Office.*

Corner, John. "Framing the New." Afterword. *Understanding Reality Television.* Ed. Su Holmes and Deborah Jermyn. London: Routledge, 2004. 290–99. Print.

Crew, Richard E. "Viewer Interpretations of Reality Television: How Real is *Survivor* for Its Viewers?" *How Real Is Reality TV? Essays on Representation and Truth.* Ed. David S. Escoffery. Jefferson: McFarland, 2006. 61–77. Print.

"Diversity Day." Dir. Ken Kwapis. Writ. Greg Daniels and B. J. Novak. *The Office.*

"Drug Testing." Dir. Greg Daniels. Writ. Greg Daniels and Jennifer Celotta. *The Office.*

"E-Mail Surveillance." Dir. Paul Feig. Writ. Greg Daniels and Jennifer Celotta. *The Office.*

Friend, Tad. "The Paper Chase: Office Life in Two Worlds." *New Yorker.* Condé Nast Digital, 11 Dec. 2006. Web. 14 Jan. 2008.

"Gay Witch Hunt." Dir. Ken Kwapis. Writ. Greg Daniels. *The Office.*

Griffin, Jeffrey. "The Americanization of *The Office*: A Comparison of the Offbeat NBC Sitcom and Its British Predecessor." *Journal of Popular Film and Television* 35.4 (2008): 154–63. Print.

"Health Care." Dir. Ken Whittingham. Writ. Greg Daniels and Paul Lieberstein. *The Office*.

Holmes, Su and Deborah Jermyn. "Understanding Reality TV." Introduction. *Understanding Reality Television*. Ed. Su Holmes and Deborah Jermyn. London: Routledge, 2004. 1–32. Print.

Kavka, Misha. "Love 'n the Real; or, How I Learned to Love Reality TV." *The Spectacle of the Real: From Hollywood to "Reality" TV and Beyond*. Ed. Geoff King. Bristol: Intellect, 2005. 93–103. Print.

Kilborn, Richard. *Staging the Real: Factual TV Programming in the Age of Big Brother*. Manchester: Manchester UP, 2003. Print.

Mills, Brett. "Comedy Verite: Contemporary Sitcom Form." *Screen* 45.1 (2004): 63–78. Print.

Murray, Susan and Laurie Ouellette. Introduction. *Reality TV: Remaking Television Culture*. New York: New York UP, 2004. 1–15.

Novak, B. J. and John Krasinski. "Commentary, Episode One: Pilot." *The Office: Season One*. NBC. 24 Mar. 2005–26 Apr. 2005. DVD. Universal, 2005.

The Office. Prod. Greg Daniels and Ricky Gervais. Perf. Steve Carell, Rainn Wilson, Jenna Fischer, John Krasinski, Melora Hardin, Kate Flannery, Oscar Nuñez, Paul Lieberstein, and B. J. Novak. NBC. 24 Mar. 2005–present. DVD. Universal.

"Pilot." Dir. Ken Kwapis. Writ. Ricky Gervais and Greg Daniels. *The Office*.

Schillinger, Liesl. "Foreign *Office*." *Slate*. Washington Post, Newsweek Interactive Co. LLC, 20 Sept. 2006. Web. 14 Jan. 2008.

Trottier, Daniel. "Watching Yourself, Watching Others: Popular Representations of Panoptic Surveillance in Reality TV Programs." *How Real Is Reality TV? Essays on Representation and Truth*. Ed. David S. Escoffery. Jefferson: McFarland, 2006. 259–76. Print.

Žižek, Slavoj. *The Sublime Object of Ideology*. London: Verso, 1989. Print.

Discussion Questions

1. What does Kocela mean by the "postdocumentary" age? How do mockumentary series, such as *The Office, Parks and Recreation,* and *Modern Family,* demonstrate this concept of the postdocumentary?

2. How does *The Office* critique reality television? What might you say the argument of *The Office* is?

3. Drawing on the work of other critics, Kocela characterizes the American version of *The Office* as portraying "fundamental optimism," while the British version portrays "resignation mingled with self-loathing." How do these characterizations of the two adaptations correspond with Beeden and de Bruin's reading of the series?

4. Are Michael's inappropriate comments about women and minorities more or less offensive than similar comments made by characters in *Mad Men*? Why is that? Why do we read the two shows differently?

5. Michael Scott is generally considered a likeable character, but as Kocela points out, Michael often makes inappropriate comments or remarks. Find a clip of *The Office* in which Michael is in some way offensive. Do you agree with Kocela's analysis of Michael's behavior and the purpose of the "talking heads" sequences? As a viewer, do you forgive Michael? Would you if you were the person being offended?

What's Right With Reality TV

James Poniewozik

James Poniewozik is a media and television critic for *Time*. He has also written for *Salon, Fortune, Rolling Stone,* and many other publications. As you read this article, consider the larger cultural implications of Poniewozik's arguments about our reality TV "obsession" and dissolving notions of privacy.

Ten years since the premiere of *Survivor*, the genre has gone from guilty pleasure to quintessentially American entertainment

The first thing you notice on MTV's *Jersey Shore* is the nicknames. Well, that and the hair, and the thongs, and the leathery tans, and the tattoos, and the hair gel, and the hot-tub sex, and the bar brawls, and the lustily embraced Italian-American stereotypes. But then: those nicknames. There's Nicole (Snooki) Polizzi. Mike (The Situation) Sorrentino. And most spectacularly, Jenni (Jwoww) Farley. For future copy editors of academic histories of mass media, that's two syllables, hyphen optional, and three w's, not in a row.

Like the tetragrammatic name of God, the moniker Jwoww has encoded in it everything you need to understand the world we live in today. The idea that an unknown 23-year-old from Long Island would come equipped with a tabloid-ready exclamatory nickname, like J. Lo or P. Diddy, might, in a more self-effacing era, have seemed presumptuous. Now it's just commonsense branding. If you might be on a reality show, you may as well have a name that pops and precedes you like a well-positioned set of silicone implants. (Oh, also: you should get the implants too.)

For the cast of *Jersey Shore*—gearing up to shoot Season 2 in the next few months—camera-readiness is second nature. These are the children of reality TV. In February 1992—literally a generation ago—*The Real World* introduced MTV's viewers to living in public. Ten years ago, *Survivor*—now in its 20th season—mainstreamed the idea for older viewers. The *Jersey Shore*-ites have never known a world in which hooking up drunk in a house paid for by a Viacom network was not an option. This year in the coveted post–Super Bowl time slot, CBS showcased not a new drama or sitcom but its reality series *Undercover Boss*. (The premiere attracted 38.6 million viewers, the most for a post–Super Bowl show since *Survivor: The Australian Outback* in 2001.) In March, Jerry Seinfeld returns to NBC—as producer of the reality show *The Marriage Ref*.

Reality is more than a TV genre now. It's the burgeoning career field that led Richard Heene to perpetrate the Balloon Boy hoax, and Tareq and Michaele Salahi to crash a White House dinner, Bravo TV cameras in tow. It's the content mill for the cable-tabloid-blog machine, employing human punch lines like Rod Blagojevich, the disgraced governor turned contestant on *Celebrity Apprentice*. It's everywhere. When Scott Brown won an upset Senate victory in Massachusetts, he was joined onstage by his daughter Ayla, an *American Idol* semifinalist from Season 5.

In 1992, reality TV was a novelty. In 2000, it was a fad. In 2010, it's a way of life.

The Evolution of a Genre

The summer of the first *Survivor* season, I wrote a cover story about it for this magazine. The concerns that the show's popularity raised seem so quaint now: a professor worried its success would lead to "Let's try a public execution. Let's try a snuff film." We're still waiting for those. But *Survivor* is still on—considered, together with the likes of *Idol* and *The Amazing Race*, to be relatively tame, even family-oriented entertainment.

At the time, there were a handful of reality shows on TV. Since then, we've seen 20 *Survivors*, 16 *Amazing Races* and 14 *The Bachelors*. We've seen *Chains of Love*, *Rock of Love*, *Flavor of Love* and *Conveyor Belt of Love*. *American Candidate*, *American Gladiators* and *American Inventor*. Anna Nicole, Kathy Griffin and Britney & Kevin. *Design Star*, *Rock Star*, *Nashville Star* and *Dancing with the Stars*. *Joe Millionaire*, *Average Joe* and *The Joe Schmo Show*. *Shark Tank* and *Whale Wars*, *The Mole* and *The Swan*. *Fear Factor*, *The It Factor* and *The Benefactor*. (Coming in 2011: Simon Cowell's *The X Factor*!)

You can break down reality TV roughly into two major subgenres. The first—the big competition-event show—descends from *Survivor* and includes most of reality's big hits: *Idol*, *The Bachelor*, *The Amazing Race*, *The Biggest Loser*, *Project Runway*. These shows mainstreamed reality TV for bigger, broader (and older) audiences by applying it to familiar genres: game shows, singing competitions, cook-offs, dating shows.

The other type of reality show descends from *The Real World*'s naked voyeurism. Some of these shows are about celebrities, former celebrities or pseudo celebrities. Some are about therapy, about work or about parenting. And many are just about life. Bravo's *Real Housewives* series is still spreading across the country like Cheesecake Factory franchises. (The Salahis snuggled up to the President as candidates for *The Real Housewives of D.C.*) When Jon and Kate Gosselin drew 10 million viewers to watch their marriage end on TLC, reality TV proved it wasn't going into middle age quietly.

From Personality to Persona

Big as reality TV is, it's also just a facet of a larger shift in popular culture: changing attitudes toward privacy and self-expression. If you grew up with reality TV and the Internet, your default setting is publicity, not privacy. Mark Zuckerberg, the founder of Facebook, recently argued that sharing has become the "social norm."

Zuckerberg was defending a controversial change in Facebook's privacy settings to make the company's trove of user information more valuable. Still, he has hundreds of millions of users and their college beer-bong photos proving his point every day. Facebook's competitor Twitter is a worldwide agora of valuable information and TMI. You can make your tweets private if you want, but why would you?

Thus comes what you might call the realitization of reality: the evolution of once private, or at least obscure, acts into performance. The diary becomes the blog. The home-movie collection becomes the YouTube channel. The résumé becomes the public search-result page.

And the personality becomes the persona. Every time you sign up for a new social-networking service, you make decisions about, literally, who you want to be. You package yourself—choose an avatar, pick a name, state your status—not unlike a storyteller creating a character or a publicist positioning a client. You can be professional on LinkedIn, flippant on Facebook and epigrammatic on Twitter. What's more, each of these representations can be very different and yet entirely authentic. Like a reality producer in a video bay, you edit yourself to fit the context.

In the workplace, for more than a decade, job-insecure Americans have been told to cultivate "the brand called you." Decide what your strengths are. Focus on your core competencies. Be aware of the bullet points of your identity. The message of both business and leisure today is, Distinguish between the actual and the for-public-consumption self.

Put all these factors together, and reality TV's endless stream of candidates seems inevitable. Every winter, *American Idol*'s audition rounds attract a deluge of self-created characters, who have the formula for getting on national TV down to a science. "I'm the crazy accordion lady/ This is my song," yowls a blue-haired young woman cradling a squeeze-box. The advanced descendants of the costumed screwballs who tried to get Monty Hall's attention on *Let's Make a Deal*, today's reality performance artists put on virtual costumes—the Bitch, the Horndog, the Drama Queen—to get noticed. In reality TV, privacy and even likability are commodities that can be traded for something more valuable.

Which is? Reality TV is now a valid career choice. *The New York Times* estimated that at any given time, there are 1,000 people on air as reality TV stars. (That may not seem like a huge number, but compared with, let's say, full-time TV critics, it's quite a healthy field.) For a few talented individuals—say, *Idol*'s Kelly Clarkson or the cooks of *Top Chef*—this has made possible actual real-life opportunity. Jennifer Hudson lost on *Idol* but won an Oscar as an actress. Elisabeth Hasselbeck went from eating bugs on *Survivor* to chewing out Joy Behar on *The View*.

And for others, it has enabled a life of lucrative famousness for famousness. Members of the cast of *The Hills*, for instance, reportedly earn up to $90,000 an episode; the *Real Housewives*, about $30,000. *Hills* star Heidi Montag has released an album, launched a clothing line, even, God help us, co-written a book. Co-star Audrina Patridge at one point received $10,000 to party at a nightclub for two hours. Reality star Kim Kardashian reportedly nets $10,000 for each product she endorses on Twitter. How much money did you make in the last 30 seconds?

Will Offend for Fame

Of course, you don't reach that level of success without working for it. Kardashian, for instance, didn't get her show until a sex tape of her and an R&B singer became public. Which is another lesson of reality TV: outrageousness pays.

And the more reality TV there is, the more outrageous you have to be to break out. Nadya Suleman, or Octomom, parlayed a horrifyingly dangerous multiple birth into a reality special, ending up—like her apparent model, Angelina Jolie—on the cover of *Star* magazine, showing off "My New Bikini Body! How I Did It!" Richard Heene convinced the world that his 6-year-old son was hurtling toward his death in a balloon. But as the veteran of ABC's *Wife Swap* knew, the show he was pitching—eccentric storm-chasing scientist and his wacky family—wouldn't even raise an eyebrow on a cable schedule.

But what message is it all sending? The viralization of people like *American Idol*'s General Larry (Pants on the Ground) Platt and William Hung before him has led to the charge that reality TV invites us to laugh at little people for sport. The fame of *Jersey Shore*'s tanning-bed casualties and others brings the critique that reality TV celebrates violence, sluttiness (male and female) and other bad behavior.

These charges are so contradictory as to cancel each other out. How, exactly, can reality TV mock its participants and celebrate them at the same time? In fact, the audience's relation to reality shows is more complicated. People don't watch *Jersey Shore* because they consider the Situation a role model. It's entertaining because the show is basically satire, a pumped-up spoof of bigger-is-better American culture. (Quoth Jwoww: "I see a bunch of, like, gorilla juice heads, tall, completely jacked, steroid, like multiple growth hormone—that's, like, the type I'm attracted to.")

One of the biggest proponents of the idea that reality TV appeals to the worst in us is … reality TV. Case in point, Susan Boyle. When she showed up, unpolished and dowdy, and blew the doors off *Britain's Got Talent* in her singing audition, it was hailed as a sign that we were finally getting sick of the ugly, snarky culture of reality TV. Did you see her wipe the smirk off Simon Cowell's face? The judges were ready to laugh at her, but she showed them that looks aren't everything! Well, yes, except that Boyle's entire "subversion" of reality TV was set up, framed and milked by a reality show.

Reality shows showcase plenty of bad behavior, but they also presume a heavy moralism on the part of the audience. *Survivor* is known for its self-rationalizing, situational ethics. Anything you do to win can be justified as playing the game. But part of the reason fans become involved in the show is that they get invested in the good guys and bad guys.

Look at the title of *Survivor's* 10th-anniversary season, starting this month: "Heroes vs. Villains"—that is, those who played decently vs. those who "just played the game." Plenty of fans were entertained by Richard Hatch, who lied his way to the first-season title (often while buck naked). But a million dollars and one tax-evasion conviction later, do they admire him?

The main dangers of reality TV aren't to the viewers but to the participants and those around them. The Heenes were lucky the Balloon Boy hoax was just embarrassing and not deadly. But the sleaziest, and saddest, aspect of their whole story was the implication that their kids were being raised to think it was all a normal thing that people do to help the family business. As Falcon Heene blurted to his dad on *Larry King Live*, "You guys said that we did this for the show."

DJ Adam Goldstein, a.k.a. DJ AM, died last year of an overdose resulting from a drug relapse—while making a reality show about drug abuse for MTV that brought him close to his old temptations. NBC's *The Biggest Loser* casts ever heftier contestants and subjects them to ever-more-stressful challenges, to the point where it seems a competitive-eating reality show would be healthier. Sometimes it's the producers, not the viewers, who could use the reminder that it's not O.K. to do whatever it takes to win the (ratings) game.

Why Reality TV Is Us

But there's more to reality TV than fame-crazy lunatics, 'roid-raging meatheads and silicone drama queens wearing little more than craftily deployed censors' pixelation. A decade after *Survivor*, reality TV has become too vast and diverse a genre to be defined by any one set of especially lousy shows. And for all of everyone's worries 10 years ago, reality TV hasn't crowded "quality shows" off the air. The past 10 years of scripted shows—*The Wire, Battlestar Galactica, The Office, Mad Men*—are the strongest TV has ever had. (One genre that reality may be crowding out is soap operas. *As the World Turns* is ending, as did *Guiding Light*, their appeal supplanted by the immersive serial dramas *of Jon & Kate,* among others.)

In the best cases, reality and scripted television have reached a kind of symbiosis. It's not just that reality shows have learned to structure themselves like sitcoms and dramas. Many of the best TV shows of the '00s lift heavily from reality TV or would have been impossible without it.

Lost, for instance, began as an attempt to create a drama version of *Survivor*. Several of TV's best comedies—the American and British versions of *The Office, Parks and Recreation, Arrested Development* and *Modern Family*—have borrowed directly from reality TV's format of vérité filmmaking and "confessional" interviews with the characters.

Maybe the best example yet of the reality-fiction alliance is Fox's high school choir spoof *Glee*, which, in essence, is *American Idol* in teen-dramedy form. It is a literal re-creation of the pop appeal of *Idol* (just like *Idol*'s, *Glee*'s songs fly to the top of iTunes on a weekly basis). And it's also a critique of the *American Idol* culture that made it possible. In the words of Rachel (Lea Michele), "Nowadays, being anonymous is worse than being poor."

The best reality shows can be much more engrossing, complex and diverse than your average TV cop show. Last year *The Amazing Race* included the team of bisexual screenwriter Mike White and his gay minister father Mel White, giving a more nuanced, less stereotypical portrayal of both sexual orientation and faith than most big-network dramas would.

The past decade has seen experiments like documentary maker Morgan Spurlock's *30 Days* for FX, a brilliant trading-places switcheroo. (For instance, an anti-immigration militant spent a month living the life of an illegal alien.) *Wife Swap* is an intriguing show about American subcultures (homeschoolers, political activists, etc.) and the natural tendency of parents to secretly judge one another. TLC's *19 Kids and Counting*, about the fecund Duggars, may be an extreme-parenting freak show, but it's also a series about the life of a deeply religious family, a rare subject for TV dramas today.

Even MTV, home of *Jersey Shore*, has the high-minded *16 and Pregnant* (which often features working-class families, who scarcely exist in network drama nowadays); *The Buried Life*, about four friends who travel the world helping people accomplish things they want to do before they die; and *My Life as Liz*, a sort of reality *My So-Called Life* about a high school outcast in small-town Texas.

Are any of these MTV shows as big or as widely hyped as *Jersey Shore* (which got nearly 5 million viewers for its season finale)? No. But that is on you and me, not on reality TV. And even in the cheesiest reality shows, there is an aspirational quality, a democratic quality, a quality that's— yeah, I'll say it—American. "American" in the sense that what is true of countries is true of TV genres: their worst traits are inseparable from their best ones.

In the basic criticism of reality TV—that it makes people famous for nothing rather than rewarding hard work—is a Puritan streak that is as old as Plymouth Rock: Seek thou not the Folly of Celebrity, but apply thyself with Humility to thy Industry! Well, that's one strain of American values. But there are other American ideas that reality TV taps into: That everybody should have a shot. That sometimes being real is better than being polite. That no matter where you started out, you can hit it big, get lucky and reinvent yourself. In her own way, Jwoww is as American a character as the nobody Jay Gatsby heading east and changing his name.

And most important, that you can find something interesting in the lives of people other than celebrities, lawyers and doctors. In CBS's new *Undercover Boss*, executives go incognito to work in entry-level jobs in their companies. In the premiere, Larry O'Donnell, president and COO of Waste Management, picks up litter and cleans toilets. He learns that a woman driving a garbage route has to pee in a coffee can to keep on schedule; trash sorters are docked two minutes' pay for every minute they're late from their half-hour lunch. He's horrified; he's humbled; he vows to help his workers out.

There's plenty to criticize in *Undercover Boss*. The show is moving but it's also manipulative and infuriating. Yes, O'Donnell hands out raises and rewards to the nice people we've met. It makes him (and us) feel good. But company-wide—economy-wide—there's no reason to believe things will get better for the overstressed workers who didn't get on TV.

But here's the thing: you, watching the show, have the tools to come to that conclusion. You've held a job. You know how companies work. And one thing reality TV has trained people to do is to be savvy about its editing. That's how people watch reality TV: you can doubt it, interrogate it, talk back to it, believe it, or not.

And either way, what you're left with is a prime-time TV show about topical concerns, at a time when people would like to see some humility in our CEOs; a show, like Discovery's *Dirty Jobs*, about toilet cleaners and garbage pickers and other people that "quality TV" rarely takes notice of; a show, at heart, about how absolutely crazy-hard ordinary people work.

You also—in the worn-out but cheerful employees—see a testimony to the incredible camera-readiness of the American public. How did O'Donnell manage to work unsuspected among his employees? He told them he was "Randy," a host making a reality show, natch, about entry-level jobs.

And what could be more natural than that? What could be more normal, in an age of ubiquitous media, than to take a stranger for a ride on your garbage truck and complain about your supervisors to the cameras? TV calls, and you must answer. It is as if, as a society, we had been singing in front of a mirror for generations, only to discover that now the mirror can actually see us. And if we are really lucky, it might just offer us a show.

Discussion Questions

1. What is Poniewozik's argument, or main idea? Do you agree with him? Why or why not?

2. "Like the tetragrammatic name of God, the moniker Jwoww has encoded in it everything you need to understand the world we live in today." If you read only that statement, what would you assume about "the world we live in today?"

3. According to Poniewozik, "even in the cheesiest reality shows, there is an aspirational quality, a democratic quality, a quality that's—yeah, I'll say it—American. 'American' in the sense that what is true of countries is true of TV genres: their worst traits are inseparable from their best ones." What, then, would you consider to be the US's best traits? Our worst? Are these connected? How?

4. Both articles about reality TV discuss the dissolving boundaries of the public and the private. In what areas of your life have public and private overlapped?

5. Kocela says reality television "provides free training in cynical detachment to millions of homes every night," and that we identify and connect with reality television actors "not because [we] believe in the reality of the community represented there, but because the camera believes for [us]." How do these readings of reality television align with the arguments made by Poniewozik? How do they conflict?

6. Poniewozik argues for what is right with our reality television obsession. How might the Jessica Lynch saga illustrate what's wrong with it?

Survival of the Stereotypical: A Study of Personal Characteristics and Order of Elimination on Reality Television

Bryan E. Denham, Richelle N. Jones

Bryan E. Denham and Richelle N. Jones take a scientific approach to their study of stereotypes in reality television. Like many articles of this type, "Survival of the Stereotypical" includes a Review of Literature, Methods, Results, and Discussion section. As you read, consider whether this structure influences your acceptance of the argument.

Since the advent of television, people have enjoyed watching the dubious adventures of others. From Ralph and Alice Kramden to Homer and Marge Simpson, television viewers have laughed at personal foibles and followed satirical storylines in situation comedies. In recent years, however, the relatively light humor of these fictitious programs has given way to more severe and cynical forms of entertainment, such as the humiliation and ultimate elimination of contestants on "reality" television programs. While it surely is not inappropriate to enjoy programs that entertain audiences with plot twists and surprise maneuvers, weekly television shows that feature competitions to "survive," to serve as an executive apprentice to a famous business mogul, or to become the next major pop star, may be important to analyze given their routine selections of "winners" and "losers." If contestant patterns exist—that is, if reality programs perpetuate the same kinds of stereotyping that other programs do (Greenberg and Brand 273–314; Greenberg, Mastro and Brand 333–351 ; Potter 82–85)—then groups whose members seem to be eliminated first and most conspicuously on a regular basis may not find reality programming entertaining; instead, they might find the entire genre offensive and base.

Reality television has become ubiquitous in primetime, and the programs featuring competitions boast followings in the tens of millions (Nabi et al. 304). Yet, the genre also stands to reproduce many cultural stereotypes through its various contests. As examples, older contestants may appear "eccentric, infirm, stubborn, and foolish" (Potter 85), while female competitors may appear physically inferior to their male counterparts, who would appear more prepared to compete and lead others (see Lawrence and Jewett 129–133; Vera and Gordon 113–125). Contestants of color might be characterized for their physical prowess, in addition to being sexualized or portrayed as happy-go-lucky (Davis and Harris 154–169; Greenberg and Brand 273–314; Kraszewski 179–196). Indeed, as this paper will reveal, contestants on reality programs frequently tend to be stereotyped by age, gender and race, among other factors, and the programs thus may affect the perceptions of viewers who do not realize the extent to which they, too, stereotype others based on group characteristics (Gorham 229–247; Shugart 79–100). Shugart, for instance, describes how reality court programs reinforce dominant conceptions of discipline through representations of class and race/ethnicity, noting, astutely, that court programs have relatively little to do with legal situations and "more to do with the exposure, review, and discipline of the participants' very lifestyles and behaviors, which are consequently inscribed as the locus and logic for the issues that bring them before the courts" (84).

Like primetime dramas, reality programs offer ongoing stories for audience members to follow, but unlike dramas, viewers get to watch "real people" realize lifelong dreams or make fools of themselves in front of millions. Because the programs are not scripted and do not employ directors, *per se*, viewers may draw conclusions about the competitions as if contestants were unaware that anyone was watching, let alone filming. Additionally, viewers may be naïve when it comes to casting decisions; that is, they may not realize that producers sometimes cast certain contestants precisely *because* those contestants satisfy a stereotype (Haralovich and Trosset 75–96). Casting decisions also may reflect the extent to which contestants stand to generate revenue apart from actual broadcasts – from what Bignell describes as "spin-off products, tie-in books and DVDs, mobile phone text updates and sponsorship of programmes" (22).

This article examines personal characteristics and order of elimination on three reality television programs: *Survivor*, *The Apprentice* and *American Idol*. The paper examines whether programs that purport to give every contestant an opportunity for success appear to do so, or whether the programs merely help to preserve the status quo and the cultural assumptions therein. Given the relatively modest amount of scholarship on reality programming, the paper seeks to help fill a void, adding a content study to existing research.

Review of Literature

Although one could argue that the known presence of a video camera fundamentally alters "reality," more than 40 television series since 2000 have been characterized by the term "reality television" (Deery 2). Programs have included *Survivor, Fear Factor, Temptation Island, The Apprentice, American Idol* and *Big Brother*, among others, giving media audiences captivating stories to follow and broadcast corporations fortunes to collect. As an example, as Deery points out (3), it took CBS the equivalent of one minute in advertising revenues to recoup the $1 million prize it offered a victor on Survivor, the final episode of which (in season one) drew 51.7 million viewers (Nabi et al. 304). With that many people watching, it becomes important to consider the images and representations emanating from such programs, especially since producers tout the programs as "real," thus implying that behaviors observed during a given episode are essentially the same as those one would observe "in reality."

Deery sheds light on why studying contestant characteristics and order of elimination might be worthwhile, and potentially meaningful toward understanding cultural stereotyping in broadcast content: "Reality TV represents, among other things, the triumph of the market, the notion that everyone as well as everything has a price and that people will do pretty much anything for money…Audiences tune in to see how far the process has advanced, whereas producers capitalize on the spectacle of greed to generate their own profits" (2). Deery discusses how the target audiences for reality television show little interest in subjects of intellectual import, opting instead for "sensational, uneditorialized, intimate action in the personal, confessional, or therapeutic mode" (4). If, in fact, that is the case, one might expect the producers of reality programs to recruit contestants who represent extremes, such that audience members will grow fond of certain characters and develop a dislike of others. Exploiting cultural differences—and especially cultural stereotypes—likely assists in that process, a process that can be grounded, in part, in disposition theory (Bryant and Miron 549–582; Oliver 507–524; Zillmann 225–239).

In advancing disposition theory, Zillmann suggests that audience enjoyment of a media production is contingent upon audience members' affective dispositions toward characters in the production, as well as the outcomes those characters experience (225–239). "Simply stated," Raney explains, "the theory predicts that enjoyment increases when liked characters experience positive outcomes or when disliked characters experience negative ones. Conversely, enjoyment suffers when liked characters experience negative outcomes and/or disliked characters experience positive ones" (350). Discussing this theory of media enjoyment, Raney notes that audience members tend to form alliances with characters in dramas and that enjoyment tends to increase with the opportunity to make a moral judgment. Because the contestant pool on many reality television programs tends to be heterogeneous, viewers have the opportunity to form alliances with certain characters, supporting those characters a bit more each week, and at the same time, hoping that contestants opposite the favored ones fare poorly—perhaps to the point of utter humiliation.

Disposition theory has been applied to several genres, but because reality television is a relatively new phenomenon, it has not served as a conceptual framework for this type of programming. Further, because disposition theory focuses on the viewing experience, as opposed to production choices, its fundamental assertions are mentioned in this paper primarily to inform the process by which reality television engages audience members. To become engaged in a media production, viewers need to care about the characters they observe—at least to some extent—and one way producers might go about "hooking" viewers is by maximizing perceived differences among the contestants and, in some cases, exploiting their lifestyles. As Shugart argues, backgrounds and behaviors of reality television participants assist in contextualizing the predicaments in which the contestants find themselves. "Writers design dramatic stories to have realistic characters that viewers can identify with and realistic trials to create greater arousal," Shapiro and Chock explain. "At the end, good things happen to characters who are liked and bad things to disliked characters, which gives a positive valence to emotional arousal" (186). Creating rivalries thus stands to capture the attention of viewers, and the greater the number of viewers, the greater the advertising revenues (Podlas 141–172).

In discussing the extent to which audience members consider elements of media productions "real," Shapiro and Chock point to perceived *typicality* (166). Specifically, the more typical the characteristics' of individuals and situations are, the more "real" they may appear to audience members. Gorham explains what is at stake when productions capitalize on this notion, advancing (stereo)typical images in the interest of profit maximization and little else:

> Racial stereotypes in the media can influence our interpretations of media content in a way that supports dominant racial myths. By automatically priming racial stereotype-congruent interpretations of subsequent media texts, and by doing so repeatedly and consistently, stereotypes in the media can maintain unjust, harmful, and dominant understandings of race by influencing the way individuals interpret media texts (244).

Through the work of Omi and Winant, as well as that of Hunt, and Bonilla-Silva, media stereotypes of race, in particular, can be contextualized in broader social terms. For instance, suggesting that social structures and everyday experiences are *organized* through race, Omi and Winant note that "Temperament, sexuality, intelligence, athletic ability, aesthetic preferences, and so on are presumed to be fixed and discernable from the palpable mark of race" (60). Additionally, consistent with the notion of *typicality* posited by Shapiro and Chock (166), Hunt writes about *race as representation* (19). In commenting on Omi and Winant, as well as the earlier scholarship of Prager (99–119), Hunt observes that "what we *know* about race at any given point in time is composed of commonsense ideologies, expectations, rules of etiquette—representations. And these representations are linked to important economic, political and cultural forces—forces which shape, *and are shaped by*, the shifting meanings undergirding racial categories" (19). Finally, Bonilla-Silva notes that in a given society, "After racial stratification is established, race becomes an independent criterion for vertical hierarchy" (45). Moreover, "Races, like other social categories such as class and gender, are socially constructed and thus permanently unstable categories of human identity and action. Yet after they emerge in any society, they organize a hierarchical order with definite social relations of domination and subordination" (62).

Addressing both race and gender, Vera and Gordon explored the presence of "white messiahs" in film, noting how these autonomous and brave characters frequently come to the aid of vulnerable people of color (113–125). Media representations, the authors explain, do not merely mimic—or seek to mimic—reality but in fact may suggest new ways of acting, feeling and thinking, and while audiences may dismiss media representations as "entertainment," societal messages contained in such productions may have lasting effects (for additional discussion, see Bennett 408–425; Dubrofsky 39–56; Ferris et al. 490–510; Annette Hill 79–107; Alice Hill 191–211; Nabi et al. 421–447; Roberti 117–134). "In the United States," Vera and Gordon suggest, "whites have seen themselves as the norm while seeing racial others as all alike. Whites have seen and portrayed people of color in distorted ways that spread negative images throughout our culture and, via our media, throughout the world" (114). (Editor's note: See also Richard Dyer's seminal 1989 film studies essay, "White.") As Cohen suggests, when one adds age to race and gender representations, even more severe stereotyping may occur:

> Aging creates 'double marginality' for women who experience ageism and sexism and 'triple jeopardy' when racism, ageism, and sexism intersect. From card shops to policy decisions, and from media images to popular culture, older women have been objectified and devalued... While this devaluation affects both men as well as women, there is clearly a difference with older women. Three examples of how older women are diminished in this society include: making older women invisible, emphasizing youthful beauty over mature looks, and minimizing older women's sexuality (601).

With regard to reality television, Patkin observed animosity between younger and older contestants on *Survivor: Africa* (15). Animosity developed, Patkin suggests, when older contestants did not keep pace with the physical tasks assigned to group members. From the standpoint of exploiting differences, this tension between younger and older contestants on reality television appears to reflect organizational cultures more generally. As an example, in a cross-cultural study, McCann and Giles observed younger workers to perceive older employees as more negative, non-accommodating and self-centered, regardless of the culture at hand (1); television thus stands to reproduce cultural assumptions while purporting to expose instances of flawed thinking and stereotyping (Cavender 155–172; Foster 270–289).

In sum, stereotypes that seep into media productions stand to impact the viewer regardless of whether the viewer realizes it, or even whether the viewer disagrees with the stereotypes (Gorham 229–247). But reality television frequently travels well beyond subtlety and into the domain of outright humiliation. Contestants often are eliminated from reality programs one by one, and with assistance from "surviving" contestants, audience members are both tacitly and overtly encouraged to detest the eliminated contestants because of apparent shortcomings; after all, if the individuals were "stronger" or "brighter," none of this would be happening.

Methods

In considering programs to evaluate, we based our decision, first, on a definition of "reality-based television programming" offered by Nabi et al. (2003):

> Programs that film real people as they live out events (contrived or otherwise) in their lives, as these events occur. Such programming is characterized by several elements: (a) people portraying themselves (i.e., not actors or public figures performing roles), (b) filmed at least in part in their living or working environment rather than on a set, (c) without a script, (d) with events placed in a narrative context, (e) for the primary purpose of entertainment (304).

Given this definition, in addition to reasons that follow, we chose to examine contestant characteristics and order of elimination on three programs: *Survivor, The Apprentice,* and *American Idol.* We selected these three programs, in particular, because of their respective popularity and because each one has a different means of contestant evaluation/elimination. These differences may offer insights on techniques used by producers to retain "demographically preferred" contestants (Podlas 141–172). Additionally, examining programs with differing methods may shed light on more overt manipulation, which Boone discusses in the context of *Survivor.* "Clearly one component on *Survivor* that involves deception is the voting process. Though contestants discuss voting options openly, the voting is done individually and no one is assured that any other contestant will honor an agreement to vote a specific way" (103). Podlas identifies lawsuits that have been filed by contestants who characterized their respective contests as rigged. One of the most common complaints. Podlas explains, concerns the practice of "selective editing," whereby producers manipulate what actually transpires by omitting certain scenes, and in some cases, showing scenes out of order to shed positive light on popular contestants. Thus, on *Survivor*, even though contestants vote one another off the island, as it were, editors may construct stories to appeal to certain demographics. When audience members cast votes to eliminate contestants, selective editing has the potential to undercut the integrity of a program entirely.

The premise of *Survivor* is for contestants to outlast the elements and one another, and it is the contestants, themselves, who control the order of elimination. Contestants stay "alive" based on the extent to which they contribute to the overall "survival" of the group, with one contestant voted out each week. Scholars suggest that while "survival" skills certainly assist contestants in remaining on the program, the real key to success is managing the "social milieu," establishing (perceived) trustworthiness and "likeability" (Boone 97–110; Godard 73–96; Wingenbach 132–150). Such attributes are important because contestants eliminated from competition select the ultimate victor; contestants thus may be "resurrected" to determine who wins both the prize money and future endorsement opportunities.

Contestants on *The Apprentice* compete with one another toward landing a job as CEO of an organization owned by real estate magnate Donald Trump. On this program. Trump, himself, decides on which candidates can continue to compete and which he must let go with his now famous line, "You're fired" (Kinnick and Parton 429–456). In choosing a protégé. Trump, of course, must satisfy the interests of network executives, namely their interest in maximizing profits by collecting millions of dollars in advertising.

The third program in the study, *American Idol*, is a talent search in which television audience members vote on which contestants they want to continue. Before audience members get to cast their votes, however, contestants must advance beyond preliminary rounds, in which judges decide on 24 finalists (12 from each gender). In the preliminary stages, judges wield considerable power in deciding which contestants stand to help build ratings and which should be dismissed and perhaps embarrassed on national television. As Bignell observes, those who "win," or at least make it to the final rounds, tend to be those who stand to make the networks monies beyond the actual competition. DVD, CD and book sales are three examples.

In selecting programs with differing approaches toward contestant elimination, we sought to examine potential instances of humiliation in more than one setting, as humiliation, Hartling and Luchetta suggest, is often connected with broader practices of social control (259–278). They note that humiliation occurs when someone in a position of power launches a deliberate attack on another, and for purposes of the current paper, the important point is that humiliation is an attack on identity—something that is not readily changeable (Hartling and Luchetta 259–278). We thus considered it important to examine instances in which individuals from different gender, race and age cohorts were "kicked off" or "fired" from their respective contests—or whether they appeared as contestants at all.

Because any one season of these programs could have been anomalous, we analyzed three seasons of *Survivor* (i.e., *Borneo, Outback* and *Africa*), the first two seasons of *The Apprentice*, and the first three seasons of *American Idol*, creating a total candidate pool of 116. We coded each candidate for three demographic variables: Gender, race, and age. Race categories included African American, Hispanic, Middle Eastern, Asian American, Caucasian, and Other, allowing that some of these terms reflect ethnicity more than race. We included Middle Eastern as a category in order to examine whether Middle Eastern contestants appeared to experience heightened levels of animosity given recent world events. As Potter may have anticipated in describing the dearth on television of Asians, Hispanics, Native Americans and members of other minority groups, such as those from the Middle East, only African Americans and Caucasians appeared in sufficient numbers to warrant statistical analyses (81). We thus categorized members of minority groups apart from African Americans as "Other," offering an early finding that the populations in our study appeared to resemble those in other TV genres; apart from African Americans, few members of minority groups competed on the programs.

As Potter reports, 80% of all characters on television are white, and males outnumber females three to one (81). While the 16% of black characters on television eclipses the 12% population figure, Hispanics constitute just 2% of TV characters while composing 9% of the U.S. population (Potter 81). Asian Americans and Native Americans, combined, account for less than 1% of characters on television, and importantly, approximately 75% of all television characters are between ages 20 and 50; in the real world, just one-third of the population falls between those ages (Potter 81). Finally, just 2% of characters on television are over age 65, compared to 11% in the actual population (Potter 81). Thus, television tends to distort demographic realities, and in regard to race, we found that to be the case early on.

In terms of age, we consulted program websites—specifically, the online biographies of competitors—to categorize competitors in one of the following age brackets: 16–20, 21–25, 26–30, 31–35, 36–40, and 41+. For exploratory purposes, we also recorded marital status, sexuality of competitors (if stated), nature of occupation, and hair color. We included the variable addressing hair color because of scholarship suggesting that females on television often have blonde hair, which is associated stereotypically with glamour (Davis 325–332; Glascock 656–669). Additionally, as Potter notes, another stereotype is the "dumb blonde, who is superficial, cares only about physical appearance and dress styles, and has no common sense" (83).

With respect to statistical analyses, we recorded the order in which all contestants (n=116) departed their respective programs, listing the contestants in order and indicating alongside their first names their age, race and gender. We ran basic frequency analyses in describing the individuals included in the study and used cross-tabulation and chi square tests, where appropriate, in exploring whether differences existed across age, race, and gender in terms of the programs on which contestants appeared. In terms of how these analyses informed cultural stereotypes, while the overall number of African American characters on television has eclipsed actual population figures (Potter 81), African Americans have nevertheless been depicted on television as less likely to be employed or less likely to be in professional occupations (Glascock 90–100). African Americans historically have been stereotyped as entertainers (e.g., athletes, musicians), while Caucasians have been portrayed more as stoic individuals in white-collar occupations (Greenberg and Brand 273–314). Finally, African Americans have been portrayed as younger than Caucasians (Baptista-Fernandez and Greenberg 13–21) as well as disproportionately overweight (Kaufman 37–46). The following section reports the results of our study, indicating whether reality television stands to reproduce common cultural stereotypes.

Results

Beginning with a descriptive report, 81 (69.8%) of 116 contestants in this study were Caucasian, followed by 22 (19%) African Americans and 13 (11.2%) individuals from other minority groups. The sample consisted of 56 (48.3%) males and 60 (51.7%) females, and the two genders showed relative parity across age. Overall, 12 competitors (10.3%) appeared in the 16–20 age bracket, 41 (35.3%) appeared in the 21–25 bracket, with 28 (24.1 %) in the 26–30 range, 13 (11.2%) in the 31–35 bracket, 9 (7.8%) in the 36–40 range and 13 (11.2%) in the 41–plus.

With regard to marital status, 78 competitors (67.2%) indicated they were single, followed by 22 (19%) who said married, and 16 (13.8%) whose status could not be determined. Just three of 26 competitors (11.5%) who revealed their sexuality said they were gay or lesbian. Nearly one in two

competitors (56 of 116; 48.3%) held white-collar positions, compared
with 19 (16.4%) in blue-collar jobs, 15 (12.9%) students, six (5.2%) re-
tirees, and 20 (17.3%) undetermined. The appearance variable related to
hair color is reported later.

Race. As the collapsed frequencies and row percentages in Table 1 indicate, African Americans made 22 appearances, nearly six in 10 of which
were on *American Idol.* Despite having more than three times as many
competitors overall, just two more Caucasians (n=15) than African
Americans (n= 13) participated on *American Idol.* Among other minorities, 46.2% appeared on *American Idol,* compared to just 18.5% of
Caucasians. Mirroring that, about one in three Caucasians appeared on
The Apprentice, compared to fewer than one in five African Americans.
Additionally, Caucasians appeared in much higher numbers on *Survivor,*
and the differences observed in Table 1 were highly significant,
$^2(4, n = 116) = 16.43, p < .01.$

Table 1. Cross-tabulation of race by reality television program

	American Idol	Survivor	Apprentice	Total
African-American	13	5	4	22
	59.1%	22.7%	18.2%	100%
Other	6	3	4	13
	46.2%	23.1%	30.7%	100%
Caucasian	15	40	26	81
	18.5%	49.4%	32.1%	100%
Total	34	48	34	116
	29.3%	41.4%	29.3%	100%

Gender. Table 2 reveals a relatively even dispersion of men and women
across the three television programs. Overall, 19 (31.7%) of 60 female
appearances came on *American Idol,* compared to 24 (40.0%) and 17
(28.3%), respectively, on *Survivor* and *The Apprentice.* No differences in
Table 2 showed significance, $^2(2, n = 116) = .24$, p= ns.

Table 2. Cross-tabulation of gender by reality television program

	American Idol	Survivor	Apprentice	Total
Male	15	24	17	56
	26.8%	42.9%	30.3%	100%
Female	19	24	17	60
	31.7%	40.0%	28.3%	100%
Total	34	48	34	116
	29.3%	41.4%	29.3%	100%

Age. Table 3, a cross-tabulation of age across the three reality television programs, offers some noteworthy findings. Here, all contestants in the first age bracket appeared on *American Idol*, as did 53.7% of contestants in the second bracket. Contestants must be between ages 16 and 25 to appear on *American Idol*, and one could certainly expect minors to appear exclusively on that program. Nonetheless, one might have expected more contestants from the second bracket to appear elsewhere. Mirroring that pattern, not a single competitor aged 41 or over appeared on *The Apprentice*, and just two (22.2%) of nine competitors ages 36 to 40 appeared on that program. Most of the older contestants appeared on *Survivor*. Because Table 3 contains seven cells with zero observations, we did not compute chi square.

Table 3. Cross-tabulation of age by reality television program

	American Idol	Survivor	Apprentice	Total
16–20	12	0	0	12
	100%	0%	0%	100%
21–25	22	13	6	41
	53.7%	31.7%	14.6%	100%
26–30	0	12	16	28
	0%	42.9%	57.1%	100%
31–35	0	3	10	13
	0%	23.1%	76.9%	100%
36–40	0	7	2	9
	0%	81.8%	18.2%	100%
41–plus	0	13	0	13
	0%	100%	0%	100%
Total	34	48	34	116
	29.3%	41.4%	29.3%	100%

Appearance. Table 4, a cross-tabulation of gender across hair color, reveals that the majority of female contestants had brown hair, as opposed to blonde. Yet, the table also reveals that, compared with male competitors, higher percentages of women had blonde and brown hair, respectively, and fewer had black.

Table 4. Cross-tabulation of gender by hair color

	Blonde	Brown	Red	Gray	Black	Other	Total
Male	4	30	2	5	14	1	56
	7.1%	53.6%	3.6%	8.9%	25.0%	1.8%	100%
Female	10	39	1	4	3	3	60
	16.6%	65.0%	1.7%	6.7%	5.0%	5.0%	100%
Total	14	69	3	9	17	4	116
	12.1%	59.5%	2.6%	7.8%	14.7%	4.9%	100%

Elimination. In examining the order in which competitors were eliminated from their respective programs, several interesting patterns emerged. Beginning with *The Apprentice*, both winners were white males, with an African American male, Kwame, finishing second the first season and a white female, Jennifer M., finishing second in year two. While an African American male, Kevin, was one of the last competitors cut in the second season, African American females finished nowhere near the final rounds, nor did other minorities of either gender, with the possible exception of Ivana, an Asian American who departed relatively late in the game in the second competition. Notably, Ivana was "fired" for stripping, and her dismissal may have reflected how Asian women are stereotyped as sexual provocateurs, and how women, in general, tend to be sexualized through mass media. Moreover, Omarosa, an African American female from the first season, not only did not advance into the final rounds, but in the months following her departure, she served as the brunt of skits and/or jokes on programs such as *Saturday Night Live* and *The Tonight Show with Jay Leno*, her confidence in her identity a primary source of entertainment.

An examination of the data from *American Idol* reveals a pattern largely opposite that of *The Apprentice*, in that African Americans—one male and one female—won two of three competitions. African Americans and members of other minorities could be seen throughout the lists of competitors, with no apparent patterns of elimination. In examining the first and second seasons, it is worth noting that Kelly (Clarkson), who won the competition in year one, and Clay (Aiken), who finished as runner-up to Ruben Studdard in year two, have become celebrities; both are white.

It remains to be seen whether Ruben or Fantasia Barrino, who won the third competition, will, at some point, receive the degree of adulation enjoyed by Kelly and Clay. (Editor's note: One might also observe that Jennifer Hudson, an eliminated African American contestant, has since won an Oscar for a role in a musical, *Dream Girls.*)

Finally, in examining the data from the three *Survivor* competitions, one of the most conspicuous patterns involves age. Looking at *Survivor Borneo*, the first two competitors eliminated from competition were Sonja, a 63-year-old white female, and B.B., a 64-year-old white male. That same pattern held on *Survivor Outback*, with Debb, a 45-year-old white female, and Maralyn, a 51-year-old white female, departing first and third, respectively. On *Survivor Africa*, several of the older competitors were among the first ones eliminated, but because the third season included more competitors from the older age brackets, several "lasted" until the final rounds, when Lex, a 38-year-old white male, and Ethan, a 27-year-old white male, took over. Thus, with a few notable exceptions, "old folks" tended to depart the *Survivor* programs relatively early in the process.

Discussion

This study has demonstrated that, in many respects, reality television reproduces cultural stereotypes and societal expectations and assumptions. Beginning with the race demographic, African Americans appeared the most frequently—and enjoyed the most success—on *American Idol*, an entertainment talent contest. African Americans enjoyed little success on *The Apprentice*, and they scarcely appeared on the Survivor programs. An implication of such patterns is the perpetuation of stereotypes about African Americans and their capacity to entertain people of all races. White males, it would appear, tend to make stronger executives, where "serious" work and "difficult" decisions must be made (Kinnick and Parton 429–456). Data revealed, somewhat remarkably, that while the study included more than three times as many whites as African Americans, just two more whites than Blacks appeared on *American Idol*. More than four in five white competitors appeared on the other two programs, compared to approximately three in five African Americans who appeared on *American Idol*. It should be noted, of course, that reality television programs do not exist in a vacuum; that is, they must satisfy the commercial interests of their respective networks, and one way of doing so is to ensure that women and contestants from minority groups are retained for much of a given season. Large numbers of women and minorities are less likely to quit watching when they can identify with certain contestants, as disposition theory would suggest. Still, stereotypes appeared manifest in the programs we studied.

Indeed, as Torres and Charles note in summarizing the perceptions of African American college students about how their white peers view them, "The most popular stereotype is that Blacks are entertainers—generally more musically and/or athletically inclined than whites. Implicit in this perception is that Blacks are also less equipped for more cerebral pursuits" (122). Still, at the end of the proverbial day, it may be the white entertainers (e.g., Clarkson and Aiken) who receive longer-term monetary benefits. In sum, the two programs *American Idol* and *The Apprentice*, through both winners and program distributions of African Americans and other minorities, appear to have perpetuated the cultural stereotype of African Americans as entertainers and as individuals not equipped for the tasks of an executive in an office boardroom. On *The Apprentice*, for instance, Omarosa appeared overly emotional and somewhat defiant, leading her to be satirized on other television programs.

The *Survivor* programs shed stereotypical light on what it means to grow old in American society (Cohen 599–620). Competitors on these programs purportedly had to demonstrate to one another how important each was to the overall "survival" of the group, and as one might expect, the older competitors—especially older women—were not deemed terribly important. Thus, the *Survivor* programs appear to have perpetuated the age-old patterns of Hollywood, namely that men grow more distinguished with age, thus continuing to star in movies in their seventies and eighties, while women simply grow older (Cohen 599–620; Roth 189–202). As Cohen posits, "To be old in our society is to be devalued. To be old and female is to experience double oppression" (599). It should be noted, though, that *Survivor Africa*, while ironically including just one African American competitor, did include an older cross-section of competitors than did the two previous competitions.

With regard to appearance, this study did not find evidence that a majority of women on reality television tend to have blonde hair and thus appear more glamorous or urbane. Of course, that may be the result of how reality programs come together. Producers look for interesting people (i.e., those who can help to generate high ratings), and in assembling reality "casts," they likely try to locate competitors who appear opposite one another along variables such as appearance and personality. Such casting assists viewers in building alliances with certain competitors while growing to dislike others. As indicated, Omarosa, an African-American who appeared on the first season of *The Apprentice*, became fodder for late-night comedians and actor Maya Rudolph on *Saturday Night Live*. Appearing on "Weekend Update" as Omarosa, Rudolph spoke of her strength as a proud African American woman, and as she spoke, various objects, such as dry-wall and a bowling ball, landed on her head from above the set. Looking back to the segment of this paper addressing embarrassment, while many people insist that they are laughing *with* the person in a humiliating predicament, they likely are laughing *at* the person and the stereotypical behaviors therein.

Future research on reality television might address how (and if) the demographics of reality programs change as the programs become more popular, thus commanding larger sums in advertising. Studies should continue to compare the types of programs on which competitors from various races and ethnicities compete, for as the current study has demonstrated, the aggregate numbers can mask show-specific patterns. Ecological fallacies such as these can in turn mask stereotypical assumptions and the exploitation of those assumptions for the entertainment of millions—and the monetary gain of a few. Ultimately, reality television offers a clear window through which to examine cultural stereotypes and the consequences those stereotypes yield for members of different groups.

Works Cited

Baptista-Fernandez, Pilar, and Bradley S. Greenberg. "The Context, Characteristics and Communication Behaviors of Blacks on Television." *Life on Television.* Ed. Bradley S. Greenberg. Norwood, NJ: Ablex, 1980.13–21.

Bennett, Jeffrey A. "In Defense of Gaydar: Reality Television and the Politics of the Glance." *Critical Studies in Media Communication* 23 (2006): 408–425.

Bignell, Jonathan. *Big Brother: Reality TV in the 21st Century.* New York: Palgrave, 2005.

Bonilla-Silva, Eduardo. *White Supremacy & Racism in the Post-Civil Rights Era.* Boulder, CO: Lymie Rienner Publishers, 2001.

Boone, R. Thomas. "The Nonverbal Communication of Trustworthiness: A Necessary *Survivor* Skill." *Survivor Lessons: Essay on Communication and Reality Television.* Ed. Matthew J. Smith and Andrew F. Wood. Jefferson, NC: McFarland & Company, 2003. 97–110.

Bryant, Jennings, and Dorina Miron. "Entertainment as Media Effect." *Media Effects: Advances in Theory and Research* (2nd ed.). Ed. Jennings Bryant and Dolf Zillmann. Mahwah, NJ: Erlbaum, 2002. 549–582.

Cavender, Gray. "In Search of Community of Reality TV: *America's Most Wanted* and *Survivor*." *Understanding Reality Television.* Ed. Su Holmes and Deborah Jermyn. London: Routledge, 2004. 155–172.

Cohen, Harriett L. "Developing Media Literacy Skills to Challenge Television's Portrayal of Older Women." *Educational Gerontology* 28 (2002): 599–620.

Davis, Donald M. "Portrayals of Women in Prime-Time Network Television: Some Demographic Characteristics." *Sex Roles* 23 (1990): 325–332.

Davis, Laurel R., and Othello Harris. "Race and Ethnicity in U.S. Sports Media." *MediaSport*. Ed. Lawrence A. Wenner. London: Routledge, 1998. 154–169.

Deery, June. "Reality TV as Advertainment." *Popular Communication* 2 (2004): 1–20.

Dubrofsky, Rachel. "The Bachelor: Whiteness in the Harem." *Critical Studies in Media Communication* 23 (2006): 39–56.

Dyer, Richard. "White." *Screen* 29.4 (1989): 44–64.

Ferris, Amber L., Sandi W Smith, Bradley S. Greenberg, and Stacy L. Smith. "The Content of Reality Dating Shows and Viewer Perceptions of Dating." *Journal of Communication* 57 (2007): 490–510.

Foster, Derek. "'Jump in the Pool': The Competitive Culture of *Survivor* for Networks." *Understanding Reality Television*. Ed. Su Holmes and Deborah Jermyn. London: Routledge, 2004. 270–289.

Glascock, Jack. "Gender Roles on Prime-Time Network Television: Demographics and Behaviors." *Journal of Broadcasting and Electronic Media* 45 (2001): 656–669.

Glascock, Jack. "Gender, Race and Aggression in Newer TV Networks' Primetime Programming." *Communication Quarterly* 5 (2003): 90–100.

Godard, Ellis. "The Social Geometry of Reality Shows." *Survivor Lessons: Essays on Communication and Reality Television*. Ed. Matthew J. Smith and Andrew F. Wood. Jefferson, NC: McFarland & Company, 2003. 73–96.

Gorham, Bradley W. "Stereotypes in the Media: So What?" *The Howard Journal of Communications* 10 (1999): 229–247.

Greenberg, Bradley S., and Jeffrey E. Brand. "Minorities and the Mass Media: 1970s to 1990s." *Media Effects: Advances in Theory and Research*. Ed. Jennings Bryant and Dolf Zillmann. Hillsdale, NJ: Erlbaum, 1994. 273–314.

Greenberg, Bradley S., Dana Mastro, and Jeffrey E. Brand. "Minorities and the Mass Media: Television into the 21st Century." *Media Effects: Advances in Theory and Research* (2nd ed). Ed. Jennings Bryant and Dolf Zillmann. Mahwah, NJ: Erlbaum, 2002. 333–351.

Haralovich, Mary Beth, and Michael W. Trosset. "'Expect the Unexpected': Narrative Pleasure and Uncertainty Due to Chance in *Survivor*." *Reality TV: Remaking Television Culture*. Ed. Susan Murray and Laurie Ouelette. New York: NYU Press, 2004. 75–96.

Hartling, Linda M., and Tracy Luchetta. "Humiliation: Assessing the Impact of Derision, Degradation and Debasement." *The Journal of Primary Prevention* 19 (1999): 259–278.

Hill, Alice. "Viewers Perceptions of Reality Programs." *Communication Quarterly* 54 (2006): 91–211.

Hill, Annette. *Reality TV: Audiences and Popular Factual Television*. London: Routledge, 2005.

Hunt, Darnell M. *Screening the Los Angeles 'Riots': Race, Seeing, and Resistance*. Cambridge: Cambridge University Press, 1997.

Kaufman, Lois. "Prime-Time Nutrition." *Journal of Communication* 30 (1980): 37–46.

Kinnick, Katherine, and Sabrena R. Parton. "Workplace Communication." *Business Communication Quarterly* 68 (2005): 429–456.

Kraszewski, Jon. "Country Hicks and Urban Cliques: Mediating Race, Reality, and Liberalism on MTV's *The Real World*." *Reality TV: Remaking Television Culture*. Ed. Susan Murray and Laurie Ouelette. New York: New York University Press, 2004. 179–196.

Lawrence, John S., and Robert Jewett. *The Myth of the American Superhero*. Grand Rapids, MI: William B. Eerdmans Publishing Company, 2002.

Mastro, Dana, and Bradley S. Greenberg. "The Portrayal of Racial Minorities on Prime Time Television." *Journal of Broadcasting and Electronic Media* 44 (2000): 690–703.

McCann, Robert M., and Howard Giles. "Age-Differentiated Communication in Organizations: Perspectives from Thailand and the United States." *Communication Research Reports* 24 (2001): 1–12.

Nabi, Robin L., Erica N. Biely, Sara J. Morgan, and Carmen R. Stitt. "Reality-Based Television Programming and the Psychology of its Appeal." *Media Psychology* 5 (2003): 303–330.

Nabi, Robin L., Carmen R. Stitt, Jeff Halford, and Keli L. Finnerty. "Emotional and Cognitive Predictors of the Enjoyment of Reality-Based and Fictional Television Programming." *Media Psychology* 8 (2006): 421–447.

Oliver, Mary Beth. "Individual Differences in Media Effects." *Media Effects: Advances in Theory and Research.* Ed. Jennings Bryant and Dolf Zillmann. Mahwah, NJ: Erlbaum, 2002. 507–524.

Omi, Michael, and Howard Winant. *Racial Formation in the United States from the 1960s to the 1990s.* New York: Routledge, 1994.

Patkin, Terri Toles. "Individual and Cultural Identity in the World of Reality Television." *Survivor Lessons: Essays on Communication and Reality Television.* Ed. Matthew J. Smith and Andrew F. Wood. Jefferson, NC: McFarland & Company, 2003. 13–26.

Podlas, Kimberlianne. "Primetime Crimes: Are Reality Television Programs 'Illegal Contests' in Violation of Federal Law." *Cardozo Arts and Entertainment Law Journal* 25 (2007): 141–172.

Potter, W. James. *Media Literacy.* Thousand Oaks, CA: Sage, 2005.

Prager, Jeffrey. "American Racial Ideology as Collective Representation." *Ethnic and Racial Studies* 5 (1992): 99–119.

Raney, Arthur. "Expanding Disposition Theory: Reconsidering Character Liking, Moral Evaluations, and Enjoyment." *Communication Theory* 14 (2004): 348–369.

Roberti, Jonathan W. "Demographic Characteristics and Motives of Individuals Viewing Reality Dating Shows." *Communication Review* 10 (2007): 117–134.

Roth, Elaine. "Momophobia: Incapacitated Mothers and Their Adult Children in 1990's Films." *Quarterly Review of Film and Video* 22 (2005): 189–202.

Shapiro, Michael. A., and T. Makana Chock. "Psychological Processes in Perceiving Reality." *Media Psychology* 5 (2003): 163–198.

Shugart, Helene A. "Ruling Class: Disciplining Class, Race, and Ethnicity in Television Reality Court Shows." *Howard Journal of Communications* 17 (2006): 79–100.

Torres, Kimberly C., and Camille Z. Charles. "Metastereotypes and the Black-White Divide." *Du Bois Review: Social Science Research on Race* 1 (2004): 115–149.

Vera, Hernan, and Andrew M. Gordon. "The Beautiful American: Sincere Fictions of the White Messiah in Hollywood Movies." *White Out: The Continuing Significance of Racism.* Ed. Ashley W. Doane and Eduardo Bonilla-Silva. New York: Routledge, 2003. 113–125.

Wingenbach, Ed. "Survivor, Social Change, and the Impediments to Political Rationality: Reality Television as Social Science Experiment." *Survivor Lessons: Essays on Communication and Reality Television.* Ed. Matthew J. Smith and Andrew F. Wood. Jefferson, NC: McFarland & Company, 2003. 132–150.

Zillmann, Dolf. "The Experimental Exploration of Gratifications from Media Entertainment." *Media Gratifications Research: Current Perspectives.* Ed. Karl E. Rosengren, Lawrence A. Wenner, and Philip Palmgreen. Beverly Hills, CA: Sage, 1985. 225–239.

Discussion Questions

1. What do Denham and Jones mean by a content study? What methods do they employ to conduct this study? Do you find their results persuasive? Why or why not?

2. Consider the network TV shows, like *The Office*, that are based on or influenced by reality television. Do the characters on the network shows fulfill any reality TV stereotypes?

3. Who do you find more relatable: the characters on *The Office* or a reality show? Which do you care about more? Why? What about the characters in *Mad Men*?

4. What are some similarities between the multiple documentaries about the rescue of Private Jessica Lynch and reality television? How do these demonstrate Poniewozik's notion that reality television proves our nation's "worst traits are inseparable from their best ones"?

5. Relate Denham and Jones's discussion of stereotypes in reality television with portrayals of stereotypes discussed in the articles by Takacs, Baird, and Kocela. Why might we be more forgiving when reality television producers and audiences stereotype their characters than we are when the media or fictional characters do the same?

6. Chose a reality show you watch (or have seen). What stereotypes do you see in this show? Why do you think those particular stereotypes are seen in this show?

TELEVISION AND CULTURAL STUDIES

Library Resources

There is one database, **Film and Television Literature Index (FTLI)** that will provide the best information for a college or graduate level paper regarding television and cultural studies. FTLI can be found in the alphabetical list of databases under the column *Find Articles* on the library home page.

FTLI is produced by EBSCO publishing and provides a comprehensive bibliographic database of indices and abstracts for over 300 publications concerning film and television scholarship and writing. Designed for students, scholars, and general readers, the OSU library has coverage from 1988 to the present. Some journal articles will be available full text, but some will not so be sure to make use of your Interlibrary Loan privileges when needed.

When you click on **FTLI** within the alphabetical list of databases, you will be taken to EBSCO to conduct your search. Clicking on **FTLI** brings up a screen with a set of boxes and search field options.

If you aren't sure what you want to write about, try typing "television" in the first line and "cultural studies" in the second line. This will call up several results; browsing titles and abstracts might give you some ideas for more specific topics. If you have an idea of what you want to write about, try narrowing your search with phrases such as "reality television" and "gender" or "sitcoms" and "race representation." If the articles are not available in full-text, use the "Find Articles" button to see if the articles are available elsewhere, or request the article through Interlibrary Loan.

Other useful databases include JSTOR, Project Muse, and Academic Search Premier.

Further Readings

Allen, Robert C., and Annette Hill, eds. *The Television Studies Reader.* New York: Routledge, 2004.

Anderson, Tim J. "As if History Was Merely a Record: The Pathology of Nostalgia and the Figure of the Recording in Contemporary Popular Cinema." *Music, Sound, and the Moving Image* 2.1 (2008): 51–76.

Benjamin, Walter. *The Work of Art in the Age of Mechanical Reproduction.* Trans J. A. Underwood. London: Penguin UK, 2008.

Braudy, Leo, and Marshall Cohen, eds. *Film Theory and Criticism: Introductory Readings.* 7th ed. New York: Oxford UP, 2009.

Dickstein, Morris. "The Home and the World." *Dissent* 51.1 (2004): 111–15.

—. "The Politics of the Thriller." *Dissent* 53.2 (2006): 89–92.

Durham, Meenakshi Gigi, and Douglas M. Kellner, eds. *Media and Cultural Studies: KeyWorks.* Rev. ed. Malden, MA: Blackwell, 2006.

Katz, Elihu, and Paddy Scannell, eds. *The End of Television? Its Impact on the World (So Far).* The ANNALS of the American Academy of Political and Social Science 625.1 (2009).

Mittell, Jason. *Television and American Culture.* New York: Oxford UP, 2010.

Newcomb, Horace, ed. *Television: The Critical View.* 7th ed. New York: Oxford UP, 2006.

Sontag, Susan. "Notes on 'Camp.'" *Partisan Review,* 1964.

Warshow, Robert. *The Immediate Experience: Movies, Comics, Theatre, and Other Aspects of Popular Culture.* Cambridge: Harvard UP, 2002.

LITERACY AND MULTICULTURALISM

College of Education

Introduction

Oklahoma State University's College of Education is home to more than 3,000 students and a host of nationally recognized programs. In addition to traditional courses in K–12 education, the College offers a range of courses from athletic training to aviation and aerospace education. The faculty members often combine their research interests with active participation in various outreach programs like organizing tutoring programs, or enrichment and math camps for public school children. This section focuses on one of those research areas: literacy education. In a country where people are becoming more and more aware of shockingly low levels of literacy, literacy education has become a topic of intense scrutiny. The College's dedication to improving literacy education is demonstrated in its involvement with national and international organizations which promote literacy. In fact, Dr. Barbara J. Walker, a reading education professor in the College, has recently been installed as the president of the International Reading Association.

One of the professors who teaches and conducts research in this field is Dr. Susan Parsons. Her interest in the impact of diversity on literacy education coincides with a national debate which influences both research in educational theories and teaching practices in the classroom. In this chapter, you will read a number of articles reflecting a wide range of approaches to questions centered on literacy education and multiculturalism. Frederick Douglass's account of the ways in which he had to teach himself to read and write is a seminal text that articulates the power dynamics inherent in the acquisition of literacy. These dynamics are further explored in articles by Peggy McIntosh and Paulo Freire, who trace fundamental ways in which the learning environment of the classroom is connected to the larger world. Peggy Moore-Hart's research highlights ways in which technological developments can be used to promote multicultural awareness in a classroom. Finally, E. D. Hirsch's essay highlights some of the controversies and critical debates in the field.

Whether you hope to be a teacher one day, or will have a child or children for whom you want the best education, or simply care about the next generation, the readings in this unit will raise questions you'll want to consider.

Rama Janamanchi

Interview with Dr. Susan Parsons

Dr. Parsons kindly agreed to sit down with Rama Janamanchi and Patricia MacVaugh to share some of her thoughts and expertise on teacher education, literacy, and multiculturalism. Here are some excerpts from that interview.

What are some of the current major issues in the field of education?

One of the very interesting issues in Teacher Education right now is the on-going push to get rid of Teacher Education. There is a dialogue now about what people need to know to teach. Inherent in the national legislation at this point—inherent in the moves to privatize or to go with alternative certification—is this idea that teachers only need content knowledge and that knowledge about how to teach is superfluous, is "fluffy." You see, for instance, in the legislation, as part of "No Child Left Behind," that for teachers to be recognized as highly qualified and in order for them to stay in the classroom, those teachers must have a content major. So, for instance, special education teachers are struggling because they teach content across the board. They have to get highly certified in all the different areas they teach.

Another major issue is the relationship between theory and practice. Many students come in and want to learn step by step—"Here's what you do," "Here are your materials." We work to teach them that they need to understand purpose, to understand how children develop and learn, and to understand this complex theoretical base so that they can make choices about method and don't just go with the wind. They need to evaluate what's good for children and what fits with how children learn.

If you look at classroom structure, if you look at the curriculum as text, it didn't just happen. It's not just there and neutral. Every decision made in that school, in that classroom, positions the people in that classroom in a certain way, puts certain people of power and their choices in one place and marginalizes others. So, we're trying to get students to go back and look at that critically.

What has led to your interest in literacy and diversity?

Practice. The fact that again and again, as we work with our students, we kept bumping up against this issue. When I first came to OSU, and I walked into my entry level literacy class and gave them a book by Eve Bunting called *Day Laborers in the Southwest*, one of my students kept saying "Well, *they* all do this," and "*They* all do that." I was trying to disrupt that language and the student was having great difficulty. I tried to front load the literature with diversity issues, and the same semester, another student came to me and said, "Why are we reading all of these books about racism? We took care of that in the 60s." These were not comments that were meant to be sarcastic or rude; they were just coming from the students' very, very good hearts, and they were genuinely wondering why we were doing this kind of thing. So, I think very early on that sparked my interest in how to prepare teachers that don't have experience with diversity to teach in a world that is so far beyond them. Promoting literacy in classrooms that have children from diverse backgrounds really is an issue that stretches to the broader community, so I thought it was pretty significant that we needed to start asking these questions.

What are some of your expectations for students who come in to your classes?

We expect them to have some scholarly awareness, to be able to research. We expect them to be able to write, and to write themselves into knowing, and I think that's a big important issue because, ideally, we're working with them on developing themselves as teachers. I think that a scholarly attitude toward life is really important; teachers need to be scholars. We've got two years to deal with this really complex world and to get them analyzing and responding. If they're not thinkers and questioners when they begin, then they've got more of a struggle.

When you said you want students to write their way in to knowing, what sort of writing are you thinking about?

I am definitely thinking about scholarly exploration, this idea of being able to take a question, find different voices, different perspectives and put it together, to gather information and make it meaningful—not just to report it but to connect it. Also, for me—and I'm a literacy professor—writing into knowing means learning how to write, learning who you are, learning to use various voices, and learning to approach various audiences. Student writers need to be actively making decisions and move beyond getting the assignment turned in; they need to become aware of their learning process and aware of what they need to know as they go.

What are some key readings you would recommend to those interested in literacy and multiculturalism?

One is Shirley Brice-Heath's work *Ways with Words*, an ethnographic study of two communities in South Carolina, which shows how literacy develops in those communities and illuminates why when these kids come to school and don't succeed, it wasn't about them not being literate; it's that their literacy looks different. Another is Peggy McIntosh's essay, "White Privilege."

Are there specific academic venues that you would like your students to be aware of, and to read, to get a sense of where current issues are in terms of education?

I almost always send them to our major professional association Web sites, and they are excellent. The International Reading Association, <www.reading.org>, gives you suggested articles, position statements dealing with controversy, and a wealth of material; that's always a good place to start. The site has themed lists that are really helpful. Another is the Web site for the National Council of Teachers of English <http://www.ncte.org/>; in particular the discussions that they're having on diversity are just outstanding in terms of resources.

Dr. Parsons, thank you very much for your time.

A Narrative of the Life of Frederick Douglass, Chapter VII

Frederick Douglass

The following excerpt is taken from Frederick Douglass's *Narrative of the Life of Frederick Douglass, An American Slave, Written by Himself* (1855). Douglass, who was born in slavery and eventually escaped to freedom, became a very influential figure in the antislavery movement through his effective speeches and writing. He was also a strong supporter of women's rights movements. In chapter seven of his *Narrative*, Douglass tells the story of the means and motivations behind his learning to read and write, powerfully illustrating the political and ideological dimensions of literacy acquisition in a slave society.

I lived in Master Hugh's family about seven years. During this time, I succeeded in learning to read and write. In accomplishing this, I was compelled to resort to various stratagems. I had no regular teacher. My mistress, who had kindly commenced to instruct me, had, in compliance with the advice and direction of her husband, not only ceased to instruct, but had set her face against my being instructed by any one else. It is due, however, to my mistress to say of her, that she did not adopt this course of treatment immediately. She at first lacked the depravity indispensable to shutting me up in mental darkness. It was at least necessary for her to have some training in the exercise of irresponsible power, to make her equal to the task of treating me as though I were a brute.

My mistress was, as I have said, a kind and tenderhearted woman; and in the simplicity of her soul she commenced, when I first went to live with her, to treat me as she supposed one human being ought to treat another. In entering upon the duties of a slaveholder, she did not seem to perceive that I sustained to her the relation of a mere chattel, and that for her to treat me as a human being was not only wrong, but dangerously so. Slavery proved as injurious to her as it did to me. When I went there, she was a pious, warm, and tenderhearted woman. There was no sorrow or suffering for which she had not a tear. She had bread for the hungry, clothes for the naked, and comfort for every mourner that came within her reach. Slavery soon proved its ability to divest her of these heavenly qualities. Under its influence, the tender heart became stone, and the lamblike disposition gave way to one of tiger-like fierceness. The first step in her downward course was in her ceasing to instruct me. She now commenced to practise her husband's precepts. She finally became even more violent in her opposition than her husband himself. She was not satisfied with simply doing as well as he had commanded; she seemed anxious to do better. Nothing seemed to make her more angry than to see me with a newspaper. She seemed to think that here lay the danger. I have had her rush at me with a face made all up of fury, and snatch from me a news-paper, in a manner that fully revealed her apprehension. She was an apt woman; and a little experience soon demonstrated, to her satisfaction, that education and slavery were incompatible with each other.

From this time I was most narrowly watched. If I was in a separate room any considerable length of time, I was sure to be suspected of having a book, and was at once called to give an account of myself. All this, how-ever, was too late. The first step had been taken. Mistress, in teaching me the alphabet, had given me the *inch*, and no precaution could prevent me from taking the *ell*.

The plan which I adopted, and the one by which I was most successful, was that of making friends of all the little white boys whom I met in the street. As many of these as I could, I converted into teachers. With their kindly aid, obtained at different times and in different places, I finally succeeded in learning to read. When I was sent of errands, I always took my book with me, and by going one part of my errand quickly, I found time to get a lesson before my return. I used also to carry bread with me, enough of which was always in the house, and to which I was always welcome; for I was much better off in this regard than many of the poor white children in our neighborhood. This bread I used to bestow upon the hungry little urchins, who, in return, would give me that more valu-able bread of knowledge. I am strongly tempted to give the names of two or three of those little boys, as a testimonial of the gratitude and affection I bear them; but prudence forbids;—not that it would injure me, but it might embarrass them; for it is almost an unpardonable offence to teach slaves to read in this Christian country. It is enough to say of the dear lit-tle fellows, that they lived on Philpot Street, very near Durgin and Bailey's ship-yard. I used to talk this matter of slavery over with them. I would sometimes say to them, I wished I could be as free as they would be when they got to be men. "You will be free as soon as you are twenty-one, *but I am a slave for life!* Have not I as good a right to be free as you have?" These words used to trouble them; they would express for me the liveliest sympathy, and console me with the hope that something would occur by which I might be free.

I was now about twelve years old, and the thought of being a *slave for life* began to bear heavily upon my heart. Just about this time, I got hold of a book entitled "The Columbian Orator." Every opportunity I got, I used to read this book. Among much of other interesting matter, I found in it a dialogue between a master and his slave. The slave was represented as having run away from his master three times. The dialogue represented the conversation which took place between them, when the slave was retaken the third time. In this dialogue, the whole argument in behalf of slavery was brought forward by the master, all of which was disposed of by the slave. The slave was made to say some very smart as well as impressive things in reply to his master—things which had the desired though unexpected effect; for the conversation resulted in the voluntary emancipation of the slave on the part of the master.

In the same book, I met with one of Sheridan's mighty speeches on and in behalf of Catholic emancipation. These were choice documents to me. I read them over and over again with unabated interest. They gave tongue to interesting thoughts of my own soul, which had frequently flashed through my mind, and died away for want of utterance. The moral which I gained from the dialogue was the power of truth over the conscience of even a slaveholder. What I got from Sheridan was a bold denunciation of slavery, and a powerful vindication of human rights. The reading of these documents enabled me to utter my thoughts, and to meet the arguments brought forward to sustain slavery; but while they relieved me of one difficulty, they brought on another even more painful than the one of which I was relieved. The more I read, the more I was led to abhor and detest my enslavers. I could regard them in no other light than a band of successful robbers, who had left their homes, and gone to Africa, and stolen us from our homes, and in a strange land reduced us to slavery. I loathed them as being the meanest as well as the most wicked of men. As I read and contemplated the subject, behold! that very discontentment which Master Hugh had predicted would follow my learning to read had already come, to torment and sting my soul to unutterable anguish. As I writhed under it, I would at times feel that learning to read had been a curse rather than a blessing. It had given me a view of my wretched condition, without the remedy. It opened my eyes to the horrible pit, but to no ladder upon which to get out. In moments of agony, I envied my fellow-slaves for their stupidity. I have often wished myself a beast. I preferred the condition of the meanest reptile to my own. Any thing, no matter what, to get rid of thinking! It was this everlasting thinking of my condition that tormented me. There was no getting rid of it. It was pressed upon me by every object within sight or hearing, animate or inanimate. The silver trump of freedom had roused my soul to eternal wakefulness. Freedom now appeared, to disappear no more forever. It was heard in every sound, and seen in every thing. It was ever present to torment me with a sense of my wretched condition. I saw nothing without seeing it, I heard nothing without hearing it, and felt nothing without feeling it. It looked from every star, it smiled in every calm, breathed in every wind, and moved in every storm.

I often found myself regretting my own existence, and wishing myself dead; and but for the hope of being free, I have no doubt but that I should have killed myself, or done something for which I should have been killed. While in this state of mind, I was eager to hear any one speak of slavery. I was a ready listener. Every little while, I could hear something about the abolitionists. It was some time before I found what the word meant. It was always used in such connections as to make it an interesting word to me. If a slave ran away and succeeded in getting clear, or if a slave killed his master, set fire to a barn, or did any thing very wrong in the mind of a slaveholder, it was spoken of as the fruit of *abolition*. Hearing the word in this connection very often, I set about learning what it meant. The dictionary afforded me little or no help. I found it was "the act of abolishing;" but then I did not know what was to be abolished. Here I was perplexed. I did not dare to ask any one about its meaning, for I was satisfied that it was something they wanted me to know very little about. After a patient waiting, I got one of our city papers, containing an account of the number of petitions from the north, praying for the abolition of slavery in the District of Columbia, and of the slave trade between the States. From this time I understood the words *abolition* and *abolitionist*, and always drew near when that word was spoken, expecting to hear something of importance to myself and fellow-slaves. The light broke in upon me by degrees. I went one day down on the wharf of Mr. Waters; and seeing two Irishmen unloading a scow of stone, I went, unasked, and helped them. When we had finished, one of them came to me and asked me if I were a slave. I told him I was. He asked, "Are ye a slave for life?" I told him that I was. The good Irishman seemed to be deeply affected by the statement. He said to the other that it was a pity so fine a little fellow as myself should be a slave for life. He said it was a shame to hold me. They both advised me to run away to the north; that I should find friends there, and that I should be free. I pretended not to be interested in what they said, and treated them as if I did not understand them; for I feared they might be treacherous. White men have been known to encourage slaves to escape, and then, to get the reward, catch them and return them to their masters. I was afraid that these seemingly good men might use me so; but I nevertheless remembered their advice, and from that time I resolved to run away. I looked forward to a time at which it would be safe for me to escape. I was too young to think of doing so immediately; besides, I wished to learn how to write, as I might have occasion to write my own pass. I consoled myself with the hope that I should one day find a good chance. Meanwhile, I would learn to write.

The idea as to how I might learn to write was suggested to me by being in Durgin and Bailey's ship-yard, and frequently seeing the ship carpenters, after hewing, and getting a piece of timber ready for use, write on the timber the name of that part of the ship for which it was intended. When a piece of timber was intended for the larboard side, it would be marked thus—"L." When a piece was for the starboard side, it would be marked thus—"S." A piece for the larboard side forward, would be marked thus—"L. F." When a piece was for starboard side forward, it would be marked thus—"S. F." For larboard aft, it would be marked thus—"L. A." For starboard aft, it would be marked thus—"S. A." I soon learned the names of these letters, and for what they were intended when placed upon a piece of timber in the ship-yard. I immediately commenced copying them, and in a short time was able to make the four letters named. After that, when I met with any boy who I knew could write, I would tell him I could write as well as he. The next word would be, "I don't believe you. Let me see you try it." I would then make the letters which I had been so fortunate as to learn, and ask him to beat that. In this way I got a good many lessons in writing, which it is quite possible I should never have gotten in any other way. During this time, my copy-book was the board fence, brick wall, and pavement; my pen and ink was a lump of chalk. With these, I learned mainly how to write. I then commenced and continued copying the Italics in Webster's Spelling Book, until I could make them all without looking on the book. By this time, my little Master Thomas had gone to school, and learned how to write, and had written over a number of copy-books. These had been brought home, and shown to some of our near neighbors, and then laid aside. My mistress used to go to class meeting at the Wilk Street meetinghouse every Monday afternoon, and leave me to take care of the house. When left thus, I used to spend the time in writing in the spaces left in Master Thomas's copy-book, copying what he had written. I continued to do this until I could write a hand very similar to that of Master Thomas. Thus, after a long, tedious effort for years, I finally succeeded in learning how to write.

Discussion Questions

1. Look at the particular metaphors Douglass uses to describe his responses or to explain his mistress's actions. Connect these to Parsons et al.'s analysis of metaphors in preservice teachers.

2. Compare and/or contrast Douglass's chapter and Freire's personal narratives of literacy acquisition. What parallels and/or contrasts can be drawn?

3. According to Hirsch and other writers in this chapter, literacy is not a neutral skill, but rather always a "political decision" or act. What political and ideological dimensions, what power struggles, are evident in Douglass's efforts to acquire literacy?

4. Despite the expanse of time that separates the writers, Douglass and McIntosh both offer clear challenges to spoken and unspoken assumptions of racial privilege. What parallels and/or distinctions can you draw between the two texts?

The Importance of the Act of Reading

Paulo Freire

Paulo Freire challenges traditional pedagogical models that he believes dehuman-
ize students into "banks," or repositories of facts. Freire's theory of informal education
seeks to value students' individual experience as part of the learning process. Since
his death in 1997, Freire's influence continues through his advocates, including the
Paulo Freire Institute at UCLA. In this article, Freire shares early memories to show that
his pre-literate perceptions of his childhood surroundings helped shape the cognitive moves he would later bring to reading. For Paulo Freire, literacy begins not with
learning to understand written texts, but with the individual's earliest perceptions of
the world.

In attempting to write about the importance of reading, I must say something about my preparation…something about the process of writing
this [text], which involved a critical understanding of the act of reading.
Reading does not consist merely of decoding the written word or language; rather, it is preceded by and intertwined with knowledge of the
world. Language and reality are dynamically interconnected. The understanding attained by critical reading of a text implies perceiving the relationship between text and context.

As I began writing about the importance of the act of reading, I felt myself drawn enthusiastically to rereading essential moments in my own
practice of reading, the memory of which I retained from the most remote experiences of childhood, from adolescence, from young manhood,
when critical understanding of the act of reading took shape in me. In
writing this [chapter], I put objective distance between myself and the
different moments at which the act of reading occurred in my experience:
first, reading the world, the tiny world in which I moved; afterward, reading the word, not always the word-world in the course of my schooling.

Recapturing distant childhood as far back as I can trust my memory,
trying to understand my act of *reading* the particular world in which I
moved, was absolutely significant for me. Surrendering myself to this effort, I re-created and relived in the text I was writing the experiences I
lived at a time when I did not yet read words.

I see myself then in the average house in Recife, Brazil, where I was born,
encircled by trees. Some of the trees were like persons to me, such was
the intimacy between us. In their shadow I played, and in those branches
low enough for me to reach I experienced the small risks that prepared
me for greater risks and adventures. The old house—its bedrooms, hall,
attic, terrace (the setting for my mother's ferns), backyard—all this was

my first world. In this world I crawled, gurgled, first stood up, took my first steps, said my first words. Truly, that special world presented itself to me as the arena of my perceptual activity and therefore as the world of my first reading. The *texts*, the *words*, the *letters* of that context were incarnated in a series of things, objects, and signs. In perceiving these I experienced myself, and the more I experienced myself, the more my perceptual capacity increased. I learned to understand things, objects, and signs through using them in relationship to my older brothers and sisters and my parents.

The *texts*, *words*, *letters* of that context were incarnated in the song of the birds—tanager, flycatcher, thrush—in the dance of the boughs blown by the strong winds announcing storms; in the thunder and lightning; in the rainwaters playing with geography, creating lakes, islands, rivers, streams. The *texts*, *words*, *letters* of that context were incarnated as well in the whistle of the wind, the clouds in the sky, the sky's color, its movement; in the color of foliage, the shape of leaves, the fragrance of flowers (roses, jasmine); in tree trunks; in fruit rinds (the varying color tones of the same fruit at different times—the green of a mango when the fruit is first forming, the green of a mango fully formed, the greenish-yellow of the same mango ripening, the black spots of an overripe mango—the relationship among these colors, the developing fruit, its resistance to our manipulation, and its taste). It was possibly at this time, by doing it myself and seeing others do it, that I learned the meaning of the verb *to squash*.

Animals were equally part of that context—the same way the family cats rubbed themselves against our legs, their mewing of entreaty or anger; the ill humor of Joli, my father's old black dog, when one of the cats came too near where he was eating what was his. In such instances, Joli's mood was completely different from when he rather playfully chased, caught, and killed one of the many opossums responsible for the disappearance of my grandmother's fat chickens.

Part of the context of my immediate world was also the language universe of my elders, expressing their beliefs, tastes, fears, and values which linked my world to a wider one whose existence I could not even suspect.

In the effort to recapture distant childhood, to understand my act of reading the particular world in which I moved, I re-created, relived the experiences I lived at a time when I did not yet read words. And something emerged that seems relevant to the general context of these reflections: my fear of ghosts. During my childhood, the presence of ghosts was a constant topic of grown-up conversation. Ghosts needed darkness or semidarkness in order to appear in their various forms—wailing the pain of their guilt; laughing in mockery; asking for prayers; indicating where their cask was hidden. Probably I was seven years old, the streets of the neighborhood where I was born were illuminated by gaslight. At nightfall, the elegant lamps gave themselves to the magic wand of the lamplighters. From the door of my house I used to watch the thin figure of my street's lamplighter as he went from lamp to lamp in a rhythmic gait, the lighting taper over his shoulder. It was a fragile light, more fragile even than the light we had inside the house; the shadows overwhelmed the light more than the light dispelled the shadows.

There was no better environment for ghostly pranks than this. I remember the nights in which, enveloped by my own fears, I waited for time to pass, for the night to end, for dawn's demilight to arrive, bringing with it the song of the morning birds. In morning's light my night fears sharpened my perception of numerous noises, which were lost in the brightness and bustle of daytime but mysteriously underscored in the night's deep silence. As I became familiar with my world, however, as I perceived and understood it better by *reading* it, my terrors diminished.

It is important to add that *reading* my world, always basic to me, did not make me grow up prematurely, a rationalist in boy's clothing. Exercising my boy's curiosity did not distort it, nor did understanding my world cause me to scorn the enchanting mystery of that world. In this I was aided rather than discouraged by my parents.

My parents introduced me to reading the word at a certain moment in this rich experience of understanding my immediate world. Deciphering the word flowed naturally from *reading* my particular world; it was not something superimposed on it. I learned to read and write on the ground of the backyard of my house, in the shade of the mango trees, with words from my world rather than from the wider world of my parents. The earth was my blackboard, the sticks my chalk.

When I arrived at Eunice Vascancello's private school, I was already literate. Here I would like to pay heartfelt tribute to Eunice, whose recent passing profoundly grieved me. Eunice continued and deepened my parents' work. With her, reading the word, the phrase, and the sentence never entailed a break with reading the *world*. With her, reading the word meant reading the *word-world*.

Not long ago, with deep emotion, I visited the home where I was born. I stepped on the same ground on which I first stood up, on which I first walked, began to talk, and learned to read. It was that same world that first presented itself to my understanding through my reading it. There I saw again some of the trees of my childhood. I recognized them without difficulty. I almost embraced their thick trunks—young trunks in my childhood. Then, what I like to call a gentle or well-behaved nostalgia, emanating from the earth, the trees, the house, carefully enveloped me. I left the house content, feeling the joy of someone who has reencountered loved ones.

Continuing the effort of rereading fundamental moments of my childhood experience, of adolescence and young manhood — moments in which a critical understanding of the importance of the act of reading took shape in practice—I would like to go back to a time when I was a secondary school student. There I gained experience in the critical interpretation of texts I read in class with the Portuguese teacher's help, which I remember to this day. Those moments did not consist of mere exercises, aimed at our simply becoming aware of the existence of the page in front of us, to be scanned, mechanically and monotonously spelled out, instead of truly read. Those moments were not *reading lessons* in the traditional sense, but rather moments in which texts, including that of the young teacher Jose Pessoa, were offered to us in our restless searching.

Sometime afterward, as a Portuguese teacher in my twenties, I experienced intensely the importance of the act of reading and writing—basically inseparable —with first-year high school students. I never reduced syntactical rules to diagrams for students to swallow, even rules governing prepositions after specific verbs, agreement of gender and number, contractions. On the contrary, all this was proposed to the student's curiosity in a dynamic and living way, as objects to be discovered within the body of texts, whether the student's own or those of established writers, and not as something stagnant whose outline I described. The students did not have to memorize the description mechanically, but rather learn its underlying significance. Only by learning the significance could they know how to memorize it, to fix it. Mechanically memorizing the description of an object does not constitute knowing the object. That is why reading a text as pure description of an object (like a syntactical rule), and undertaken to memorize the description, is neither real reading nor does it result in knowledge of the object to which the text refers.

I believe much of teachers' insistence that students read innumerable books in one semester derives from a misunderstanding we sometimes have about reading. In my wanderings throughout the world there were not a few times when young students spoke to me about their struggles with extensive bibliographies, more to be *devoured* than truly read or studied, "reading lessons" in the old-fashioned sense, submitted to the students in the name of scientific training, and of which they had to give an account by means of reading summaries. In some bibliographies I even read references to specific pages in this or that chapter from such and such a book, which had to be read: "pages 15–37."

Insistence on a quantity of reading without internalization of texts proposed for understanding rather than mechanical memorization reveals a magical view of the written word, a view that must be superseded. From another angle, the same view is found in the writer who identifies the potential quality of his work, or lack of it, with the quantity of pages he has written. Yet one of the most important documents we have—Marx's "Theses on Feuerbach"—is only two and a half pages long.

To avoid misinterpretation of what I'm saying, it is important to stress that my criticism of the magical view of the word does not mean that I take an irresponsible position on the obligation we all have— teachers and students—to read the classic literature in a given field seriously in order to make the texts our own and to create the intellectual discipline without which our practice as teachers and students is not viable.

But to return to that very rich moment of my experience as a Portuguese teacher: I remember vividly the times I spent analyzing the work of Gilberto Freyre, Lins do Rego, Graciliano Ramos, Jorge Amado. I used to bring the texts from home to read with students, pointing out syntactical aspects strictly linked to the good taste of their language. To that analysis I added commentaries on the essential differences between the Portuguese of Portugal and the Portuguese of Brazil.

I always saw teaching adults to read and write as a political act, an act of knowledge, and therefore a creative act. I would find it impossible to be engaged in a work of mechanically memorizing vowel sounds, as in the exercise "ba-be-bi-bo-bu, la-le-li-lo-lu." Nor could I reduce learning to read and write merely to learning words, syllables, or letters, a process of teaching in which the teacher *fills* the supposedly *empty* heads of learners with his or her words. On the contrary, the student is the subject of the process of learning to read and write as an act of knowing and of creating. The fact that he or she needs the teacher's help, as in any pedagogical situation, does not mean that the teacher's help nullifies the student's creativity and responsibility for constructing his or her own written language and for reading this language.

When, for instance, a teacher and a learner pick up an object in their hands, as I do now, they both feel the object, perceive the felt object, and are capable of expressing verbally what the felt and perceived object is. Like me, the illiterate person can *feel* the pen, perceive the pen, and say *pen*. I can, however, not only feel the pen, perceive the pen, and say *pen*, but also write *pen* and, consequently, read *pen*. Learning to read and write means creating and assembling a written expression for what can be said orally. The teacher cannot put it together for the student; that is the student's creative task.

I need go no further into what I've developed at different times in the complex process of teaching adults to read and write. I would like to return, however, to one point referred to elsewhere in this book because of its significance for the critical understanding of the act of reading and writing, and consequently for the project I am dedicated to—teaching adults to read and write.

Reading the world always precedes reading the word, and reading the word implies continually reading the world. As I suggested earlier, this movement from the word to the world is always present; even the spoken word flows from our reading of the world. In a way, however, we can go further and say that reading the word is not preceded merely by reading the world, but by a certain form of *writing* it or *rewriting* it, that is, of transforming it by means of conscious, practical work. For me, this dynamic movement is central to the literacy process.

For this reason I have always insisted that words used in organizing a literacy program come from what I call the "word universe" of people who are learning, expressing their actual language, their anxieties, fears, demands, and dreams. Words should be laden with the meaning of the people's existential experience, and not of the teacher's experience. Surveying the word universe thus gives us the people's words, pregnant with the world, words from the people's reading of the world. We then give the words back to the people inserted in what I call "codifications," pictures representing real situations. The word *brick*, for example, might be inserted in a pictorial representation of a group of bricklayers constructing a house.

Before giving a written form to the popular word, however, we customarily challenge the learners with a group of codified situations, so they will apprehend the word rather than mechanically memorize it. Decodifying or *reading* the situations pictured leads them to a critical perception of the meaning of culture by leading them to understand how human practice or work transforms the world. Basically, the pictures of concrete situations enable the people to reflect on their former interpretation of the world before going on to read the word. This more critical reading of the prior, less critical reading of the world enables them to understand their indigence differently from the fatalistic way they sometimes view injustice.

In this way, a critical reading of reality, whether it takes place in the literacy process or not, and associated above all with the clearly political practices of mobilization and organization, constitutes an instrument of what Antonio Gramsci calls "counterhegemony."

To sum up, reading always involves critical perception, interpretation, and *rewriting* of what is read.

Discussion Questions

1. By poetically describing the environment of his childhood, what points does Freire make about literacy, learning, and teaching?

2. What is Freire arguing when he makes the distinction between "mechanically and monotonously" scanning a page and "truly" reading it?

3. How do you think Freire might respond to the multicultural literacy projects that Moore-Hart describes and advocates?

4. Freire, like Hirsch, posits that literacy is always shaped by one's particular cultural background and experiences; compare and/or contrast the conclusions they draw from this shared observation.

Cultural Literacy

E. D. Hirsch, Jr.

Most essays in this chapter focus on culturally inclusive ways to help students achieve literacy in English. University of Virginia professor emeritus E. D. Hirsch argues that literacy for students in the United States requires familiarity with prominent facts and ideas of Western culture in addition to the ability to recognize words. Hirsch asserts that lack of familiarity with Western literature, art, and history can put students at a disadvantage when they try to communicate in Western society, and that any multicultural curriculum must balance the "two equally American traditions of unity and diversity."

For the past twelve years I have been pursuing technical research in the teaching of reading and writing. I now wish to emerge from my closet to declare that technical research is not going to remedy the national decline in our literacy that is documented in the decline of verbal SAT scores. We already know enough about methodology to do a good job of teaching reading and writing. Of course we would profit from knowing still more about teaching methods, but better teaching techniques alone would produce only a marginal improvement in the literacy of our students. Raising their reading and writing levels will depend far less on our methods of instruction (there are many acceptable methods) than on the specific contents of our school curricula. Commonsensical as this proposition might seem to the man in the street, it is regarded as heresy by many (I hope by ever fewer) professional educators. The received and dominant view of educational specialists is that the specific materials of reading and writing instruction are interchangeable so long as they are "appropriate," and of "high quality."

But consider this historical fact. The national decline in our literacy has accompanied a decline in our use of common, nation-wide materials in the subject most closely connected with literacy, "English." From the 1890s to 1900 we taught in English courses what amounted to a national core curriculum. As Arthur Applebee observes in his excellent book *Tradition and Reform in the Teaching of English*, the following texts were used in those days in more than 25 percent of our schools: *The Merchant of Venice, Julius Caesar*, "First Bunker Hill Oration," *The Sketch Book, Evangeline*, "The Vision of Sir Launfal," "Snow-Bound," *Macbeth*, "The Lady of the Lake," *Hamlet*, "The Deserted Village," Gray's "Elegy," "Thanatopsis," *As You Like It*. Other widely used works will strike a resonance in those who are over fifty: "The Courtship of Miles Standish," "Il Penseroso," *Paradise Lost*, "L'Allegro," "Lycidas," *Ivanhoe, David Copperfield, Silas Marner*, etc., etc. Then in 1901 the College Entrance

Examinations Board issued its first "uniform lists" of texts required to be known by students in applying to colleges. This core curriculum, though narrower, became even more widespread than the earlier canon. Lest anyone assume that I shall urge a return to those particular texts, let me at once deny it. By way of introducing my subject, I simply want to claim that the decline in our literacy and the decline in commonly shared knowledge that we acquire in school are causally related facts. Why this should be so and what we might do about it are my twin subjects.

That a decline in our national level of literacy has occurred few will serious doubt. The chief and decisive piece of evidence for it is the decline in verbal SAT scores among the white middle class. (This takes into account the still greater lowering of scores caused by an increased proportion of poor and minority students taking the tests.) Now scores on the verbal SAT show a high correlation with reading and writing skills that have been tested independently by other means. So, as a rough index to the literacy levels of our students, the verbal SAT is a reliable guide. That is unsurprising if we accept the point made by John Carroll and others that the verbal SAT is chiefly a vocabulary test, for no one is surprised by a correlation between a rich vocabulary and a high level of literacy. A rich vocabulary is not a purely technical or rote-learnable skill. Knowledge of words is an adjunct to knowledge of cultural realities signified by words, and to whole domains of experience to which words refer. Specific words go with specific knowledge. And when we begin to contemplate how to teach specific knowledge, we are led back inexorably to the contents of the school curriculum, whether or not those contents are linked, as they used to be, to specific texts.

From the start of our national life, the school curriculum has been an especially important formative element of our national culture. In the schools we not only tried to harmonize the various traditions of our parent cultures, we also wanted to strike out on our own within the dominant British heritage. Being rebellious children, we produced our own dictionary, and were destined, according to Melville, to produce our own Shakespeare. In this self-conscious job of culture making, the schools played a necessary role. That was especially true in the teaching of history and English, the two subjects central to culture making. In the nineteenth century we held national conferences on school curricula. We formed the College Board, which created the "uniform lists" already referred to. The dominant symbol for the role of the school was the symbol of the melting pot.

But from early times we have also resisted this narrow uniformity in our culture. The symbol of the melting pot was opposed by the symbol of the stew pot, where our national ingredients kept their individual characteristics and contributed to the flavor and vitality of the whole. That is the doctrine of pluralism. It has now become the dominant doctrine in our schools, especially in those subjects, English and history, that are closest to culture making. In math and science, by contrast, there is wide agreement about the contents of a common curriculum. But in English courses, diversity and pluralism now reign without challenge. I am persuaded that if we want to achieve a more literate culture than we now have, we shall need to restore the balance between these two equally American traditions of unity and diversity. We shall need to restore certain common contents to the humanistic side of the school curriculum. But before we can make much headway in that direction, we shall also need to modify the now-dominant educational principle that holds that any suitable materials of instruction can be used to teach the skills of reading and writing. I call this the doctrine of educational formalism.

The current curriculum guide to the study of English in the state of California is a remarkable document. In its several pages of advice to teachers I do not find the title of a single recommended work. Such "curricular guides" are produced on the theory that the actual contents of English courses are simply vehicles for inculcating formal skills, and that contents can be left to local choice. But wouldn't even a dyed-in-the-wool formalist concede that teachers might be saved time if some merely illustrative, non-cumpulsory titles were listed? Of course; but another doctrine, in alliance with formalism, conspires against even that concession to content—the doctrine of pluralism. An illustrative list put out by the state would imply official sanction of the cultural and ideological values expressed by the works on the list. The California Education Department is not in the business of imposing cultures and ideologies. Its business is to inculcate "skills" and "positive self concepts," regardless of the students' cultural backgrounds. The contents of English should be left to local communities.

This is an attractive theory to educators in those places where spokesmen for minority cultures are especially vocal in their attack on the melting-pot idea. That concept, they say, is nothing but cultural imperialism (true), which submerges cultural identities (true) and gives minority children a sense of inferiority (often true). In recent years such attitudes have led to attacks on teaching school courses exclusively in standard English; in the bilingual movement (really a monolingual movement) it has led to attacks on an exclusive use of the English language for instruction. This kind of political pressure has encouraged a retreat to the extreme and untenable educational formalism reflected in the California curriculum guide.

What the current controversies have really demonstrated is a truth that is quite contrary to the spirit of neutrality implied by educational formalism. Literacy is not just a formal skill; it is also a political decision. The decision to want a literate society is a value-laden one that carries costs as well as advantages. English teachers by profession are committed to the ideology of literacy. They cannot successfully avoid the political implications of that ideology by hiding behind the skirts of methodology and research. Literacy implies specific contents as well as formal skills. Extreme formalism is misleading and evasive. But allow me to illustrate that point with some specific examples.

During most of the time that I was pursuing research in literacy I was, like others in the field, a confirmed formalist. In 1977 I came out with a book on the subject, *The Philosophy of Composition*, that was entirely formalistic in outlook. One of my arguments, for instance, was that the effectiveness of English prose as an instrument of communication gradually increased, after the invention of printing, through a trial-and-error process that slowly uncovered some of the psycholinguistic principles of efficient communication in prose. I suggested that freshmen could learn in a semester what earlier writers had taken centuries to achieve, if they were directly taught those underlying psycholinguistic principles. (With respect to certain formal structures of clauses, this idea still seems valid.) I predicted further that we could learn how to teach those formal principles still more effectively if we pursued appropriately controlled pedagogical research.

So intent was I upon this idea that I undertook some arduous research into one of the most important aspects of writing pedagogy—evaluation. After all, in order to decide upon the best methods of inculcating the skills of writing, it was essential to evaluate the results of using the different teaching methods. For that we needed non-arbitrary, reliable techniques for evaluating student writing. In my book I had made some suggestions about how we might do this, and those ideas seemed cogent enough to a National Endowment for the Humanities panel to get me a grant to go forward with the research. For about two years I was deeply engaged in this work. It was this detailed engagement with the realities of reading and writing under controlled conditions that caused me finally to abandon my formalistic assumptions. (Later I discovered that experimentation on a much bigger scale had brought Richard C. Anderson, the premier scholar in reading research, to similar conclusions.)

The experiments that changed my mind were, briefly, these: To get a non-arbitrary evaluation of writing, we decided to base our evaluations on actual audience effects. We devised a way of comparing the effects of well-written and badly written versions of the same paper. Our method was to pair off two large groups of readers (about a hundred in each group), each of which, when given the *same* piece of writing, would read it collectively with the same speed and comprehension. In other words, we matched the reading skills of these two large groups. Then, when one group was given a good version and the other given a degraded version, we measured the overall effect of these stylistic differences on speed and accuracy of comprehension. To our delight, we discovered that good style did make an appreciable difference, and that the degree of difference was replicable and predictable. So far so good. But what became very disconcerting about these results was that they came out properly only when the subjects of the papers were highly familiar to our audiences. When, later in the experiments, we introduced unfamiliar materials, the results were not only messy, they were "counterintuitive," the term of art for results that go against one's expectations. (Real scientists generally like to get counterintuitive results, but we were not altogether disinterested onlookers and were dismayed.) For what we discovered was that good writing makes very little difference when the subject is unfamiliar. We English teachers tend to believe that a good style is all the more helpful when the content is difficult, but it turns out that we are wrong. The reasons for this unexpected result are complex, and I will not pause to discuss them at length, since the important issues lie elsewhere.

Briefly, good style contributes little to our reading of unfamiliar material because we must continually backtrack to test out different hypotheses about what is being meant or referred to. Thus, a reader of a text about Grant and Lee who is unsure just who Grant and Lee are would have to get clues from later parts of the text, and then go back to re-read earlier parts in the light of surer conjectures. This trial-and-error backtracking with unfamiliar material is so much more time-consuming than the delays caused by a bad style alone that style begins to lose its importance as a factor in reading unfamiliar material. The contribution of style in such cases can no longer be measured with statistical confidence.

The significance of this result is, first of all, that one cannot, even in principle, base writing evaluations on audience effects—the only non-arbitrary principle that makes any sense. The reading skill of an audience is not a constant against which prose can be reliably measured. Audience reading skills vary unpredictably with the subject matter of the text. Although we were trying to measure our prose samples with the yardstick of paired audiences, the contrary had, in effect, occurred; our carefully contrived prose samples were measuring the background knowledge of our audiences. For instance, if the subject of a text was "Friendship," all audience pairs, everywhere we gave the trials, exhibited the same differentials. Also, for all audiences, if the subject was "Hegel's Metaphysics," the differential between good and bad writing tended to disappear. Also, so long as we used university audiences, a text on Grant and Lee gave the same sort of appropriate results as did a text on friendship. But for one community college audience (in, no less, Richmond, Virginia) "Grant and Lee" turned out to be as unfamiliar as "Hegel's Metaphysics"—a complacency-shattering result.

While the variability of reading skills within the same person was making itself disconcertingly known to me, I learned that similar variability was showing up in formal writing skills—and for the same reasons. Researchers at the City University of New York were finding that when a topic is unfamiliar, writing skill declines in all of its dimensions—including grammar and spelling—not to mention sentence structure, parallelism, unity, focus, and other skills taught in writing courses. One part of the explanation for such results is that we all have limited attention space, and cannot pay much heed to form when we are devoting a lot of our attention to unfamiliar content. But another part of the explanation is more interesting. Part of our skill in reading and in writing is skill not just with linguistic structures but with words. Words are not purely formal counters of language; they represent large underlying domains of content. Part of language skill is content skill. As Apeneck Sweeney profoundly observed: "I gotta use words when I talk to you."

When I therefore assert that reading and writing skills are content-bound, I mean also to make the corollary assertion that important aspects of reading and writing skills are *not* transferable. Of course some skills *are* carried over from task to task; we know that broad strategies of reading and writing can become second nature, and thereby facilitate literary skills at all levels. But the content-indifferent, how-to approach to literacy skills is enormously oversimplified. As my final example of this, I shall mention an ingenious experiment conducted by Richard C. Anderson and his colleagues at the University of Illinois. It, too, was an experiment with paired audiences and paired texts. The texts were two letters, each describing a wedding, each of similar length, word-familiarity, sentence complexity, and number of idea units. Each audience was similarly paired according to age, educational level, marital status, sex, professional specialty, etc. Structurally speaking, the texts were similar and the audiences were similar. The crucial variables were these: one letter described a wedding in America, the other a wedding in India. One audience was American, the other Indian. Both audiences read both letters. The results were that the reading skills of the two groups—their speed and accuracy of comprehension—were very different in reading the two linguistically similar letters. The Americans read about an American wedding skillfully, accurately, and with good recall. They did poorly with the letter about the Indian wedding. The reverse was the case with the group of Indian readers. Anderson and his colleagues concluded that reading is not just a linguistic skill, but involves translinguistic knowledge beyond the abstract sense of words. They suggested that reading involves both "linguistic-schemata" (systems of expectation) and "content-schemata" as well. In short, the assumptions of educational formalism are incorrect.

Every writer is aware that the subtlety and complexity of what can be conveyed in writing depends on the amount of relevant tacit knowledge that can be assumed in readers. As psycholinguists have shown, the explicitly stated words on the page often represent the smaller part of the literary transaction. Some of this assumed knowledge involves such matters as generic conventions, that is, what to expect in a business letter, a technical report, a detective story, etc. An equally significant part of the assumed knowledge—often a more significant part—concerns tacit knowledge of the experiential realities embraced by the discourse. Not only have I gotta use words to talk to you, I gotta assume you know *something* about what I am saying. If I had to start from scratch, I couldn't start at all.

We adjust for this in the most casual talk. It has been shown that we always explain ourselves more fully to strangers than to intimates. But, when the strangers being addressed are some unknown collectivity to whom we are writing, how much shall we then need to explain? This was one of the most difficult authorial problems that arose with the advent of printing and mass literacy. Later on, in the eighteenth century, Dr. Johnson confidently assumed he could predict the knowledge possessed by a personage whom he called "the common reader." Some such construct is a necessary fiction for every writer in every literate culture and subculture. Even a writer for an astrophysics journal must assume a "common reader" for the subculture being addressed. A newspaper writer must also assume a "common reader" but for a much bigger part of the culture, perhaps for the literate culture as a whole. In our own culture, Jefferson wanted to create a highly informed "common reader," and he must have assumed the real existence of such a personage when he said he would prefer newspapers without government to government without newspapers. But, without appropriate, tacitly shared background knowledge, people cannot understand newspapers. A certain extent of shared, canonical knowledge is inherently necessary to a literate democracy.

For this canonical information I have proposed the term "cultural literacy." It is the translinguistic knowledge on which linguistic literacy depends. You cannot have the one without the other. Teachers of foreign languages are aware of this interdependency between linguistic proficiency and translinguistic, cultural knowledge. To get very far in reading or writing French, a student must come to know facets of French culture quite different from his own. By the same token, American children learning to read and write English get instruction in aspects of their own national culture that are as foreign to them as French. National culture always has this "foreignness" with respect to family culture alone. School materials contain unfamiliar materials that promote the "acculturation" that is a universal part of growing up in any tribe or nation. Acculturation into a national literate culture might be defined as learning what the "common reader" of a newspaper in a literate culture could be expected to know. That would include knowledge of certain values (whether or not one accepted them), and knowledge of such things as (for example) the First Amendment, Grant and Lee, and DNA. In our own culture, what should these contents be? Surely our answer to that should partly define our school curriculum. Acculturation into a literate culture (the minimal aim of schooling; we should aim still higher) could be defined as the gaining of cultural literacy.

Such canonical knowledge could not be fixed once and for all. "Grant and Lee" could not have been part of it in 1840, or "DNA" in 1940. The canon changeth. And in our media-paced era, it might change from month to month—faster at the edges, more slowly at the center, and some of its contents would be connected to events beyond our control. But much of it is within our control and is part of our traditional task of culture making. One reassuring feature of our responsibilities as makers of culture is the implicit and automatic character of most canonical cultural knowledge; we get it through the pores. Another reassuring aspect is its vagueness. How much do I *really* have to know about DNA in order to comprehend a newspaper text directed to the common reader? Not much. Such vagueness in our background knowledge is a feature of cultural literacy that Hilary Putnam has analyzed brilliantly as "the division of linguistic labor." An immensely literate person, Putnam claims that he does not know the difference between a beech tree and an elm. Still, when reading those words he gets along acceptably well because he knows that under the division of linguistic labor somebody in the culture could supply more precise knowledge if it should be needed. Putnam's observation suggests that the school curriculum can be vague enough to leave plenty of room for local choice regarding what things shall be studied in detail, and what things shall be touched on just far enough to get us by. This vagueness in cultural literacy permits a reasonable compromise between lockstep, Napoleonic prescription of texts on the one side, and extreme laissez-faire pluralism on the other. Between these two extremes we have a national responsibility to take stock of the contents of schooling.

Although I have argued that a literate society depends upon shared information, I have said little about what that information should be. This is chiefly a political question. Estimable cultures exist that are ignorant of Shakespeare and the First Amendment. Indeed, estimable cultures exist that are entirely ignorant of reading and writing. On the other hand, no culture exists that is ignorant of its own traditions. In a literate society, culture and cultural literacy are nearly synonymous terms. American culture, always large and heterogeneous, and increasingly lacking a common acculturative curriculum, is perhaps getting fragmented enough to lose its coherence as a culture. Television is perhaps our only national curriculum, despite the justified complaints against it as a partial cause of the literacy decline. My hunch is that this complaint is overstated. The decline in literacy skills, I have suggested, is mainly a result of cultural fragmentation. Within black culture, for instance, blacks are more literate than whites, a point that was demonstrated by Robert L. Williams, as I learned from a recent article on the SAT by Jay Amberg (THE AMERICAN SCHOLAR, Autumn 1982). The big political question that has to be decided is whether we *want* a broadly literate culture that unites our cultural fragments enough to allow us to write to one another and read what our fellow citizens have written. Our traditional, Jeffersonian answer has been yes. But even if that political decision remains the dominant one, as I very much hope, we still face the much more difficult political decision of choosing the contents of cultural literacy.

The answer to this question is not going to be supplied by theoretical speculation and educational research. It will be worked out, if at all, by discussion, argument, and compromise. Professional educators have understandably avoided this political arena. Indeed, educators should *not* be left to decide so momentous an issue as the canonical contents of our culture. Within a democracy, educational technicians do not want and should not be awarded the function that Plato reserved for philosopher kings. But who is making such decisions at a national level? Nobody, I fear, because we are transfixed by the twin doctrines of pluralism and formalism.

Having made this technical point where I have some expertise, I must now leave any pretense of authority, except as a parent and citizen. The question of guidance for our national school curriculum is a political question on which I have only a citizens's opinion. For my own part, I wish we could have, a National Board of Regents— our most successful and admirable body for educational leadership. This imposing body of practical idealists is insulated by law from short-term demagogic pressures. It is a pluralistic group, too, with representation for minority as well as majority cultures. Its influence for good may be gauged by comparing the patterns of SAT scores in New York with those in California, two otherwise comparable states. To give just one example of the Regents' leadership in the field of writing, they have instituted a requirement that no New Yorker can receive a high school diploma before passing a statewide writing test that requires three types of prose composition.

Of course I am aware that the New York Regents have powers that no National Board in this country could possibly gain. But what a National Board could hope to achieve would be the respect of the country, a respect that could give it genuine influence over our schools. Such influence, based on leadership rather than compulsion, would be quite consistent with our federalist and pluralist principles. The Board, for instance, could present broad lists of suggested literary works for the different grades, lists broad enough to yield local freedom but also to yield a measure of commonality in our literary heritage. The teachers whom I know, while valuing their independence, are eager for intelligent guidance in such matters.

But I doubt that such a Curriculum Board would ever be established in this country. So strong is our suspicion of anything like a central "ministry of culture," that the Board is probably not a politically feasible idea. But perhaps a consortium of universities, or of national associations, or of foundations could make ongoing recommendations that arise from broadly based discussions of the national curriculum. In any case, we need leadership at the national level, and we need specific guidance.

It would be useful, for instance, to have guidance about the *words* that high school graduates ought to know—a lexicon of cultural literacy. I am thinking of a special sort of lexicon that would include not just ordinary dictionary words, but would also include proper names, important phrases, and conventions. Nobody likes word lists as objects of instruction; for one thing, they don't work. But I am not thinking of such a lexicon as an object of instruction. I am thinking of it rather as a guide to objects of instruction. Take the phrase "First Amendment," for instance. That is a lexical item that can hardly be used without bringing in a lot of associated information. Just what *are* the words and phrases that our school graduates should know? Right now, this seems to be decided by the makers of the SAT, which is, as I have mentioned, chiefly a vocabulary test. The educational technicians who choose the words that appear on the SAT are already the implicit makers of our national curriculum. Is then the Educational Testing Service our hidden National Board of Education? Does it sponsor our hidden national curriculum? If so, the ETS is rather to be praised than blamed. For if we wish to raise our national level of literacy, a hidden national curriculum is far better than no curriculum at all.

Where does this leave us? What issues are raised? If I am right in my interpretation of the evidence—and I have seen no alternative interpretation in the literature—then we can only raise our reading and writing skills significantly by consciously redefining and extending our cultural literacy. And yet our current national effort in the schools is largely run on the premise that the best way to proceed is through a culturally neutral, skills-approach to reading and writing. But if skill in writing and in reading comes about chiefly through what I have termed cultural literacy, then radical consequences follow. These consequences are not merely educational but social and political in their scope—and that scope is vast. I shall not attempt to set out these consequences here, but it will be obvious that acting upon them would involve our dismantling and casting aside the leading educational assumptions of the past half century.

Discussion Questions

1. In his article, Hirsch coins the term "cultural literacy." What does he mean by this, how does he define and illustrate it, and what arguments does he ground in this concept?

2. Hirsch claims that a "doctrine of pluralism" dominates in U.S. schools; what does he mean by this description, and what does he propose as an alternative?

3. For Hirsch, reading comprehension depends not only on linguistic skill but also on broader cultural knowledge. Explain what he means by this and what conclusions he draws from this assessment.

4. How might Hirsch's "cultural literacy" and Moore-Hart's "multicultural literacy" work to achieve similar goals, and how might a teacher incorporate both in the classroom?

5. Part of what one learns in college is how to communicate in an academic community—whether this means writing essays, making posters, or verbal presentations. What kinds of translinguistic knowledge have you acquired (or hope to acquire) as you go through college? Think about the specific formats (articles, reviews of field, lectures, or discussions) in which such knowledge is offered. How has that format affected your success in learning?

White Privilege: Unpacking The Invisible Knapsack

Peggy McIntosh

Peggy McIntosh has written extensively on multicultural concerns in culture and education, and she currently serves as the associate director of the Wellesley College Center for Research on Women. Additionally, McIntosh's *National S.E.E.D. Project on Inclusive Curriculum* provides seminars for teachers who want to bring gender and cultural equality to the classroom. Her article, "White Privilege: Unpacking the Invisible Knapsack," seeks to make readers more broadly aware of racial and gender barriers embedded in American culture.

> I was taught to see racism only in individual
> acts of meanness, not in invisible systems
> conferring dominance on my group.

Through work to bring materials from women's studies into the rest of the curriculum, I have often noticed men's unwillingness to grant that they are overprivileged, even though they may grant that women are disadvantaged. They may say they will work to improve women's status, in the society, the university, or the curriculum, but they can't or won't support the idea of lessening men's. Denials that amount to taboos surround the subject of advantages that men gain from women's disadvantages. These denials protect male privilege from being fully acknowledged, lessened, or ended.

Thinking through unacknowledged male privilege as a phenomenon, I realized that, since hierarchies in our society are interlocking, there was most likely a phenomenon of white privilege that was similarly denied and protected. As a white person, I realized I had been taught about racism as something that puts others at a disadvantage, but had been taught not to see one of its corollary aspects, white privilege, which puts me at an advantage.

I think whites are carefully taught not to recognize white privilege, as males are taught not to recognize male privilege. So I have begun in an untutored way to ask what it is like to have white privilege. I have come to see white privilege as an invisible package of unearned assets that I can count on cashing in each day, but about which I was "meant" to remain oblivious. White privilege is like an invisible weightless knapsack of special provisions, maps, passports, codebooks, visas, clothes, tools, and blank checks.

Describing white privilege makes one newly accountable. As we in women's studies work to reveal male privilege and ask men to give up some of their power, so one who writes about having white privilege must ask, "Having described it, what will I do to lessen or end it?"

After I realized the extent to which men work from a base of unacknowledged privilege, I understood that much of their oppressiveness was unconscious. Then I remembered the frequent charges from women of color that white women whom they encounter are oppressive. I began to understand why we are justly seen as oppressive, even when we don't see ourselves that way. I began to count the ways in which I enjoy unearned skin privilege and have been conditioned into oblivion about its existence.

My schooling gave me no training in seeing myself as an oppressor, as an unfairly advantaged person, or as a participant in a damaged culture. I was taught to see myself as an individual whose moral state depended on her individual moral will. My schooling followed the pattern my colleague Elizabeth Minnich has pointed out: whites are taught to think of their lives as morally neutral, normative, and average, and also ideal, so that when we work to benefit others, this is seen as work that will allow "them" to be more like "us."

Daily Effects of White Privilege

I decided to try to work on myself at least by identifying some of the daily effects of white privilege in my life. I have chosen those conditions that I think in my case attach somewhat more to skin-color privilege than to class, religion, ethnic status, or geographic location, though of course all these other factors are intricately intertwined. As far as I can tell, my African American coworkers, friends, and acquaintances with whom I come into daily or frequent contact in this particular time, place, and line of work cannot count on most of these conditions.

1. I can, if I wish, arrange to be in the company of people of my race most of the time.

2. If I should need to move, I can be pretty sure of renting or purchasing housing in an area that I can afford and in which I would want to live.

3. I can be pretty sure that my neighbors in such a location will be neutral or pleasant to me.

4. I can go shopping alone most of the time, pretty well assured that I will not be followed or harassed.

5. I can turn on the television or open to the front page of the paper and see people of my race widely represented.

6. When I am told about our national heritage or about "civilization," I am shown that people of my color made it what it is.

7. I can be sure that my children will be given curricular materials that testify to the existence of their race.

8. If I want to, I can be pretty sure of finding a publisher for this piece on white privilege.

9. I can go into a music shop and count on finding the music of my race represented, into a supermarket and find the staple foods that fit with my cultural traditions, into a hairdresser's shop and find someone who can deal with my hair.

10. Whether I use checks, credit cards, or cash, I can count on my skin color not to work against the appearance of financial reliability.

11. I can arrange to protect my children most of the time from people who might not like them.

12. I can swear, or dress in second-hand clothes, or not answer letters without having people attribute these choices to the bad morals, the poverty, or the illiteracy of my race.

13. I can speak in public to a powerful male group without putting my race on trial.

14. I can do well in a challenging situation without being called a credit to my race.

15. I am never asked to speak for all the people of my racial group.

16. I can remain oblivious of the language and customs of persons of color, who constitute the world's majority, without feeling in my culture any penalty for such oblivion.

17. I can criticize our government and talk about how much I fear its policies and behavior without being seen as a cultural outsider.

18. I can be pretty sure that if I ask to talk to "the person in charge" I will be facing a person of my race.

19. If a traffic cop pulls me over, or if the IRS audits my tax return, I can be sure I haven't been singled out because of my race.

20. I can easily buy posters, postcards, picture books, greeting cards, dolls, toys, and children's magazines featuring people of my race.

21. I can go home from most meetings of organizations I belong to feeling somewhat tied in rather than isolated, out of place, outnumbered, unheard, held at a distance, or feared.

22. I can take a job with an affirmative action employer without having coworkers on the job suspect that I got it because of race.

23. I can choose public accommodation without fearing that people of my race cannot get in or will be mistreated in the places I have chosen.

24. I can be sure that if I need legal or medical help my race will not work against me.

25. If my day, week, or year is going badly, I need not ask of each negative episode or situation whether it has racial overtones.

26. I can choose blemish cover or bandages in "flesh" color that more or less match my skin.

Elusive and Fugitive

I repeatedly forgot each of the realizations on this list until I wrote it down. For me white privilege has turned out to be an elusive and fugitive subject. The pressure to avoid it is great, for in facing it I must give up the myth of meritocracy. If these things are true, this is not such a free country; one's life is not what one makes it; many doors open for certain people through no virtues of their own.

In unpacking this invisible knapsack of white privilege, I have listed conditions of daily experience that I once took for granted. Nor did I think of any of these perquisites as bad for the holder. I now think that we need a more finely differentiated taxonomy of privilege, for some of these varieties are only what one would want for everyone in a just society, and others give license to be ignorant, oblivious, arrogant, and destructive.

I see a pattern running through the matrix of white privilege, a pattern of assumptions that were passed on to me as a white person. There was one main piece of cultural turf; it was my own turf, and I was among those who could control the turf. My skin color was an asset for any more I was educated to want to make. I could think of myself as belonging in major ways and of making social systems work for me. I could freely disparage, fear, neglect, or be oblivious to anything outside of the dominant cultural forms. Being of the main culture, I could also criticize it fairly freely.

In proportion as my racial group was being made confident, comfortable, and oblivious, other groups were likely being made unconfident, uncomfortable, and alienated. Whiteness protected me from many kinds of hostility, distress, and violence, which I was being subtly trained to visit, in turn, upon people of color.

For this reason, the word "privilege" now seems to me misleading. We usually think of privilege as being a favored state, whether earned or conferred by birth or luck. Yet some of the conditions I have described here work systematically to overempower certain groups. Such privilege simply confers dominance because of one's race or sex.

Earned Strength, Unearned Power

I want, then, to distinguish between earned strength and unearned power conferred systemically. Power from unearned privilege can look like strength when it is in fact permission to escape or to dominate. But not all of the privileges on my list are inevitably damaging. Some, like the expectation that neighbors will be decent to you, or that your race will not count against you in court, should be the norm in a just society. Others, like the privilege to ignore less powerful people, distort the humanity of the holders as well as the ignored groups.

We might at least start by distinguishing between positive advantages, which we can work to spread, and negative types of advantage, which unless rejected will always reinforce our present hierarchies. For example, the feeling that one belongs within the human circle, as Native Americans say, should not be seen as privilege for a few. Ideally it is an unearned entitlement. At present, since only a few have it, it is an unearned advantage for them. This paper results from a process of coming to see that some of the power that I originally saw as attendant on being a human being in the United States consisted in unearned advantage and conferred dominance.

I have met very few men who are truly distressed about systemic, unearned male advantage and conferred dominance. And so one question for me and others like me is whether we will be like them, or whether we will get truly distressed, even outraged, about unearned race advantage and conferred dominance, and, if so, what we will do to lessen them. In any case, we need to do more work in identifying how they actually affect our daily lives. Many, perhaps most, of our white students in the United States think that racism doesn't affect them because they are not people of color; they do not see "whiteness" as a racial identity. In addition, since race and sex are not the only advantaging systems at work, we need similarly to examine the daily experience of having age advantage, or ethnic advantage, or physical ability, or advantage related to nationality, religion, or sexual orientation.

Difficulties and dangers surrounding the task of finding parallels are many. Since racism, sexism, and heterosexism are not the same, the advantages associated with them should not be seen as the same. In addition, it is hard to disentangle aspects of unearned advantage that rest more on social class, economic class, race, religion, sex, and ethnic identity than on other factors. Still, all of the oppressions are interlocking, as the members of the Combahee River Collective pointed out in their "Black Feminist Statement" of 1977.

One factor seems clear about all of the interlocking oppressions. They take both active forms, which we can see, and embedded forms, which as a member of the dominant group one is taught not to see. In my class and place, I did not see myself as a racist because I was taught to recognize racism only in individual acts of meanness by members of my group, never in invisible systems conferring unsought racial dominance on my group from birth.

Disapproving of the systems won't be enough to change them. I was taught to think that racism could end if white individuals changed their attitudes. But a "white" skin in the United States opens many doors for whites whether or not we approve of the way dominance has been conferred on us. Individual acts can palliate, but cannot end, these problems.

To redesign social systems we need first to acknowledge their colossal unseen dimensions. The silences and denials surrounding privilege are the key political tool here. They keep the thinking about equality or equity incomplete, protecting unearned advantage and conferred dominance by making these subjects taboo. Most talk by whites about equal opportunity seems to me now to be about equal opportunity to try to get into a position of dominance while denying that systems of dominance exist.

It seems to me that obliviousness about white advantage, like obliviousness about male advantage, is kept strongly inculturated in the United States so as to maintain the myth of meritocracy, the myth that democratic choice is equally available to all. Keeping most people unaware that freedom of confident action is there for just a small number of people props up those in power and serves to keep power in the hands of the same groups that have most of it already.

Although systemic change takes many decades, there are pressing questions for me and, I imagine, for some others like me if we raise our daily consciousness on the perquisites of being light-skinned. What will we do with such knowledge? As we know from watching men, it is an open question whether we will choose to use unearned advantage to weaken hidden systems of advantage, and whether we will use any of our arbitrarily awarded power to try to reconstruct power systems on a broader base.

Discussion Questions

1. McIntosh opens her article with a discussion about male-female power relations before moving on to issues of race. How does she make the connection between these issues? What assumptions does she make, and what are some ways in which these assumptions might be challenged? Given that many teachers (particularly in elementary schools) are women, how does McIntosh's article deal with that particular confluence of power?

2. Select a few specific points of invisible racial privilege listed by McIntosh. To what extent do you agree with her claims, and/or to what extent do her characterizations of racial privilege accord with your own experience?

3. How do McIntosh's arguments about racial privilege bear on questions of literacy and multiculturalism in the classroom? How can her arguments be connected to the questions of curriculum and teaching methodology raised by other authors in this unit?

4. McIntosh argues that many whites equate equal opportunity with "equal opportunity to try to get into a system of dominance while denying that systems of dominance exist." What does she mean by this? Can educators reconcile Mcintosh's views with Hirsch's argument for a curriculum that includes knowledge about Western culture?

Literature Study Groups: Literacy Learning "With Legs"

Sue Christian Parsons, Kouider Mokhtari, David Yellin, Ryan Orwig

Ryan Orwig's task was to go into an existing classroom at an urban school with significantly low reading scores and conduct book clubs with the students once a week. An experienced teacher and graduate student, Ryan was a graduate research assistant in a partnership of teachers, administrators, and university faculty working together to create a dynamic learning community aimed at increasing students' literacy learning and motivation to read and write. Ryan wrote:

> Perhaps I was naive, but when I started teaching the book club at an urban, low-income school I knew there would be many challenges. However, the one that struck me immediately was the fact that, even when they did read, these students had no experience discussing material and connecting it to their lives. As they explained it, they simply read what was assigned (sometimes) and answered the questions (if they had time). Reading was something that was forced upon them, and it had no connection to their lives whatsoever.

Approaching the task with some degree of trepidation, Ryan soon found that engaging the students in meaningful dialogue about books that mattered to them revealed very different kinds of students from the disconnected ones he had first observed. Books became dog-eared as readers returned to them again and again to support an argument. Students engaged in heated dialogue about big ideas like justice and the nature of guilt and innocence in the court system—a topic encountered in the text but swiftly connected to and debated in the arena of their own lives. Ryan reports that one student literally woke up, abandoning her usual habit of snoozing during class to engage in the literature study group. They began, as the poet W. H. Auden described it, giving "passionate attention" (Peterson & Eeds, 1990, p. 12) to a text—and such attention is a powerful force to becoming fully and actively literate.

Literature study and the middle school learner

Early adolescence can be a difficult and tumultuous time for students. Both boys and girls have serious concerns about being accepted by their peers, about their physical development, their attractiveness to the opposite sex, their success in athletics, and their academic performance in the classroom (Atwell, 1998). As the poet John Ciardi put it, "You don't have to suffer to be a poet; adolescence is enough suffering for anyone" (quoted in Atwell, p. 51). Such are the middle grades years.

For some middle grades teachers and administrators, the young adolescent is seen in terms of predictable challenges to authority. Hence, the emphasis is on running a tight ship. Middle grades schools are highly organized institutions with many rules to be observed, punishments for every imaginable infraction, and lots of homework. "Keep them busy, really busy all of the time," it is often argued, "and you will have fewer discipline problems." This is easier said than done with an age group whose moods swing from one extreme to another almost hourly—*I hate math; I love Mr. So and So; I'll never speak to you again*—and whose passions are seemingly boundless.

With such emphasis on controlling students, enforcing rules, and dealing with the ever-changing emotions and passions of adolescents, a middle grades school can easily become, as Atwell (1998) puts it, a stifling place or "holding tank." Teachers and administrators alike sometimes forget that for the individual child, middle school is rarely about math or science or social studies. School, as John Goodland (1984) illustrated in his classic book, *A Place Called School*, is about friendships, relationships, and the social needs of young people. Any middle grades program that ignores these needs will face adolescents in a continuous struggle with authority and, too often, on the verge of dropping out of school completely.

Turning Points: Preparing American Youth for the 21st Century stressed that many adolescents feel lost, separated from the major institutions of society, and emotionally adrift in terms of their present or future goals (Carnegie Council on Adolescent Development, 1989). The authors noted, however, that middle school programs can be a viable force for reengaging young people and providing them with a purpose. Engaging in rich and meaningful ways with books that have real appeal for young adolescents is one way to help capture the enthusiasm that these same students brought to their schools only a few short years before and, in so doing, to maximize the power of their learning.

What's in a name?

Book clubs. Literature circles. Literature study groups. The terms are bandied about sometimes interchangeably and sometimes with implied distinctions about how and for what purposes they are conducted. What these groups have in common, though, is the gathering of a small group of peer readers to share insights about a common text. Literature study groups, in general, are characterized by (a) flexible grouping (usually determined by a reader's choice of a given book at a given time); (b) participant-centered dialogue (participant insights determine the direction of the dialogue; the teacher takes on the role of facilitator and expert participant rather than director of discussion); and (c) embeddedness in a strong, meaning-centered curriculum in which learners read and write copiously for real purposes. Examples of such curriculum frameworks may be found in the work of Raphael, Pardo, and Highfield (2002) and Peterson and Eeds (1990), among others, and are easily adaptable across grade levels and subject areas (Dale, 1999; Noll, 1994; Roberts, 1998; Wilkinson & Kido, 1997). Indeed, some of the strongest foundational work in this pedagogy was conducted at the middle level (Eeds & Wells, 1989; Peterson & Eeds, 1990; Smith, 1990, 1995, 1997).

What makes such engagements particularly well-suited to middle grades learners is that literature studies are highly effective in developing reading ability, knowledge about literature, and critical and analytic thinking (Faust, Cockrill, Hancock, & Isserstedt, 2005). Moreover, they accomplish these things in such a way that students are aware of their own growth. Literature studies provide space for students' voices to be heard, valuing their meanings, concerns, and insights. As Peterson and Eeds (2007) pointed out, "Story is an exploration and illumination of life" (p. 18). Students in these studies are learning about literacy and becoming proficient at it; and they are learning about life—their own lives, lived among others. It is learning that matters significantly.

Learning "with legs": Literature study as generative learning

Literature study, done well, fosters generative learning. Wittrock (1992) described generative learning as a process that involves actively building connections between what we know and understand to new ideas and experiences to make meaning and suggest further action. In a practical sense, we see generative learning as learning that is so effective and engaging, it causes us to want to know more. Generative learning experiences propel us to deeper understandings and applications for further learning. The child who participates in a productive literature study session leaves that session a different reader—more aware of the possibilities for interpreting texts, more in tune with the significance that texts may have to his own life, and more confident in his or her ability to make meaning from texts. Generative learning experiences connect to and build upon the learner's life experiences and those things that are of value to her. They provide space for interpretation and personal ownership. Perhaps most important, generative learning experiences intrigue, bringing the learner to wonder and to want to know and experience more and more. Generative learning has impetus and energy to propel the learner to new experiences, new explorations. It is, in short, "learning with legs."

Beliefs about teaching and learning

Every choice a teacher makes in a classroom is grounded in and reflective of beliefs about teaching and learning. More important, the choices teachers make about how to teach communicate to the learner the very nature of what is to be learned. The choice to engage learners with literature study, like all instructional choices a teacher makes, stems from and reflects certain beliefs about literacy and learning. We posit several of these beliefs here as a framework for discussing what a teacher's choice to implement literature study groups says about readers and the act of reading.

1. Reading is an active, interpretive engagement in which the reader brings meaning to and takes meaning from the text. In such a transactional view of reading (Rosenblatt, 1978), the meaning does not lie static in the text waiting for us to retrieve it. Rather, meaning is constructed in a transaction between the reader and the text, so both are equally important in determining it. The reader brings meaning to the text—background knowledge (about the text and about life), experiences, attitudes, beliefs, and understandings—and takes meaning from the text. Each transaction between a certain reader and a text results, then, in a unique reading of that text.

2. Reading is a vigorous meaning-making act, and the recognition of this fact leads us to hold a deep respect for readers. Too often, we teach in ways that relegate learners to passive recipients of others' ideas. We tell them what to read, we ask them questions that matter to us (or to the textbook authors or test makers), and we close the book after the reading to move to a skill lesson that we have decided connects in some way to the story they have read. Such engagements portray the reader as one who is dependent on others to determine what matters and portray the act of reading as something that is removed from the reader's life. The goal of reading, then, is to get through it and get it right according to someone else's idea of what is right, rather than living through and within a text, interpreting, connecting with, and wondering about it.

3. Dialogue is powerful pedagogy (Peterson & Eeds, 2007). As Ralph Peterson (1986) pointed out, dialogue goes beyond discussion. It is a more passionate, often unruly, and amazingly powerful form of communication. Dialogue is the unicorn to discussion's horse, as mercurial as it is serviceable, and capable of introducing us to worlds beyond those we had anticipated entering. While discussion is directed talk, usually focused on a specific goal or instructional point to be made and moderated by one person, dialogue calls for full-contact engagement by all participants, with respectful attention to listening and understanding multiple viewpoints. It is through

dialogue that the social transactions occur that bring us to understand ourselves, and others, more deeply. It is also through dialogue that learners develop rich and applicable insights into literature and the concomitant act of authoring, insights that accompany readers to their next encounter with a book or with the blank page. Dialogue enriches the quality of that engagement.

Through dialogue with others who have read the same book, readers often begin to see new and intriguing aspects of the text. They experience new perspectives beyond what their experiences showed them the first time through. Readers naturally begin to talk about literary elements like plot and characterization and symbol and mood, because they are the fiber from which the story cloth is woven. When readers talk about a story, they talk about story elements. Readers often come to understand these elements within the context of a story well before they can actually name them. When they do name those elements in this meaningful, purposeful context, the terms really make sense. Thus, readers understand and can use this new knowledge to gain deeper insights when they read (and write) again.

4.   Story matters (Junker, 1998). The time we take to read and talk about literature, and the energy we spend "entertaining a text" (Smith, 1990), is well worth it. It is not an add-on to the curriculum or an instructional filler. Instead, it is central to a curriculum that seeks to go beyond the gathering of facts and bits to foster meaningful connections and authentic applications. Indeed, what do we teach that does not have the ultimate purpose of helping our students understand themselves and the world around them? Isn't the central purpose of education to entice learners to ponder who they should be in the world and how they should help that world? Talking together about richly crafted stories helps readers develop perspective, empathy, and compassion. "Bumping up against ideologies" (Taylor, as cited in Evans, 1996) in texts reflecting multiple perspectives and diverse experiences leads learners to interrogate their own experiences and beliefs, resulting in development of strong, cogent, and articulated belief systems. Exploring challenges and possibilities in literary worlds may foster hope and a sense of empowerment. In stories, we find ourselves, including our possible selves, reflected in like characters with like experiences and standing out in stark relief against others. Good stories bring us to ask, "What might be?"—an important question for all of us to grapple with, but one that gets to the very core of the young adolescent's journey.

Practical considerations for conducting literature study

Selecting books

Ideally, the foremost consideration in selecting books for literature study is to find books that offer, as Bonnie Raitt famously sang, "something to talk about" (Eikhard, 1985). Book selections for middle grades learners should be about things that matter to young adolescents who are discovering themselves and making their marks upon the world. Such selections should offer layers of meaning, rich in symbol and metaphor, that leave sufficient room for personal interpretation. They should build on powerful, generative themes that simultaneously relate to readers' lives and illuminate broader truths beyond their own personal experiences. Generative themes may be defined as central, often universal, truths that are woven throughout a story. Examples of generative themes include, but are certainly not limited to, transience and resilience (life changes, people adapt, love and hope endure), interconnectedness (what we do affects others and the world we live in), perspective (mine is not the only way of being in the world), and grace (all people make mistakes and are given the chance to go on and do better).

Great stories for literature study should feature characters "in whom children can see themselves—as they are—and whose situations and choices allow children to extend their view of possibilities—how they might be" (Junker, 1998, p. 192). And they must, especially for the young adolescent, offer something to chew on besides a blatant, didactic message that leaves the reader no room to contemplate or argue but, rather, only to accept or reject someone else's stance (Junker, 1998, 1999).

Particularly well-suited for middle grades students are books that invite readers to take a critical stance on issues and ideas central to their own lives and the society in which they live (Leland & Harste, 2002). Such texts tend to foster passionate and, therefore, deeply engaging dialogue, and they also propel students to explore and apply ideas from the text to change the world around them.

It is also important for teachers to select texts representing a variety of genres. Contemporary realistic fiction is a natural choice for many middle grades readers, inviting them to understand the universality of human experiences and offering, at once, the chance not to be so alone and the chance to become more empathetic and tolerant. Historical fiction, and some biographies, afford the same possibilities, but offer a view of shared human experience that spans the ages, helping students understand that for generations people have experienced love and hurt and longing and joy, have felt isolated, have made mistakes, have mattered and made a difference in the world, and that each of us is part of this continuing experience. Fantasy and science fiction, genres with wide appeal for this age group (and, often, not so wide appeal for their teachers), may offer the richest truths and possibilities for meaningful connections with students' lives. Well-written fantasy features meticulously crafted worlds that, by removing us from obvious connections to lived experiences, allow us to consider bigger questions of life, such as "What is it that makes us human?" and "What really matters?" Consider, for example, Lois Lowry's (1993) *The Giver,* Nancy Fanner's (2002) *The House of the Scorpion,* or Eloise McGraw's (1996) *The Moorchild.* Such books also allow readers to ponder universal forces, such as good and evil, and the place they occupy in all of us, as in J. K. Rowling's (1999, 2000, 2001) phenomenally popular Harry Potter series or Madeline L'Engle's (1962) classic *A Wrinkle in Time* and its trilogy partners. Nonfiction texts for literature study offer intriguing possibilities for exploring information analytically and from a variety of perspectives, but the texts need to be well chosen to afford room for wondering, as discussed above.

Selecting groups

Student choice is central to effective literature studies, as each participant needs the opportunity to work with a text that matters to him or her. The process begins with the introduction of a set of quality books and an invitation to students to choose the ones of greatest interest. With a little negotiation, students can form small groups for study. Groups should consist of four to six members. Having too few members in a group often results in not enough perspectives to feed rich dialogue, while having too many sometimes silences members.

Though readers tend to select books that match their ability levels, ultimately, selection should be driven by interest; readers should be allowed to select books that are beyond their abilities to navigate independently. It is our belief that readers should not be discouraged from tackling any text they find interesting; indeed, assisting a student with text access before the study may have a strong learning benefit in the end. A reader who struggles to get through a text, then experiences it more fully through dialogue, may return to that text and read it again, each time assimilating it more fully, more fluently, and with more enjoyment.

Preparing for study

We believe it is important for participants to read the chosen work entirely before coming to the literature study dialogue session. Every book is constructed as a whole, and to discuss it in part is to experience the book much as the mice in Ed Young's (1992) *Seven Blind Mice* experience an elephant. In this retelling of an ancient Indian tale, the mice's territory is invaded by a mysterious "something." Mouse by mouse, they go out to investigate. One, who feels the elephant's tail, returns to report that the "something" is a rope. Another mouse, who investigates the leg, asserts that the "something" is a pillar, and so on. It is not until the final mouse covers every inch of the elephant that the mice can come to understand what is truly in front of them. A book that is addressed piece by piece is a very different animal from one that is experienced in its entire, carefully connected form.

To get each member to the literature study session fully prepared, it is important to offer both organizational and instructional support. The teaching done here not only maximizes the effectiveness of the literature study but also prepares students to perform more effectively in other aspects of school and life. Teachers should provide each group with a target date for the dialogue session and assist each reader in drawing up a reading plan. A reading plan should take into account the length of the book, a comfortable reading speed, and outside factors such as the student's overall course load. A simple calendar can facilitate the process, listing dates leading up to the study with reading goals (number of pages or chapters) noted for each date. With some instruction early in the year, many students will become adept at organizing themselves, while others may need continuing support throughout the year.

Students also need guidance to organize their conceptual understanding of literature. Useful strategies here include teaching students to keep reading logs in which they record their reactions and questions regularly as they read and scheduling stopgap teacher-student discussion sessions to discuss progress and insights. Such sessions are especially helpful for readers who have more difficulty navigating texts on their own. Technological resources like e-mail and online discussion boards are particularly helpful in dealing with the limited time for teacher-student interaction afforded by many middle grades school schedules. Finally, we must mention the use of the marvelously low-tech sticky note as a conceptual organizer. We use them to mark points of interest in a text, such as anything that grabs us or makes us wonder or that we want to be sure to share. A word or phrase jotted onto the sticky note can help a reader remember just what was so interesting about the passage.

Conducting the sessions

The teacher's role
One central belief guiding literature study practice is that each participant's interpretations and insights matter. This same respect is afforded to teacher and student. The teacher reads the same book the students read (not an annotation nor a teacher's version with notes dictating what to think and what to tell students to think) and reads it as a reader—noticing, wondering, and making personal determinations about what matters.

When meeting with students, the teacher then shares those insights and adds respectfully to the dialogue based on those understandings. It is important to note that being an authentic participant does not mean abdicating the role of teacher; rather, the teacher models how to engage in dialogue and offers up expanded possibilities for interpretation.

Supporting literary learning

Literature study groups in the middle grades maybe teacher- or student-led. While both configurations have real value, one real benefit of having the teacher lead the group, especially in the beginning of the year, is to support the development of literary insights through the study. Wolfe (2004) notes five critical lenses through which learners may examine a text: (1) generic criticism—taking into account the author's experiences and intents; (2) formal criticism—examining closely how "textual elements work together to create a unified whole" (p. 24); (3) text-to-text criticism—gaining insight into the text by comparing it to other texts related by genre, author, or theme; (4) transactional criticism—consciously connecting the reader's life experiences with the text; (5) sociocultural criticism—interrogating the text "in terms of whose perspectives, values, and norms are voiced and whose views are silenced" (p. 24). Certain texts may encourage particular types of analysis. For instance, a text in which readers see their own lives or encounter an idea about which they are passionate may move them toward transactional analysis or sociocultural analysis, while a book with exceptionally strong characterization may foster formal analysis of the author's use of that element. An expert teacher sharing personal insights and modeling various types of response will greatly increase students' abilities and propensities to consider varied aspects of and possibilities for engaging with a text. It is important to reiterate that the teacher's role is not to direct or prescribe talk but to participate as an expert, offering up insights and possibilities that build on and support students' own significant contributions. Ideally, as students become more and more adept at noticing from a literary perspective, groups will become increasingly supported and sustained by the students. Part of the teacher's role, then, is to teach students to take over the facilitator role as the year progresses, eventually settling on a mix of both student-facilitated and teacher-facilitated experiences.

The focus question: Taking it deeper

One way of guiding participants to go deeper into analyzing and understanding a text is to design the study session employing a group-determined focus question. This technique works best when one book is discussed for at least two sessions. During the initial session, one participant (usually the teacher, if the session is teacher-led) serves as a metalistener, engaging fully in the dialogue but also noting central comments and trends. At the end of the session, the group members revisit their dialogue with the help of the metalistener and formulate a question to take back to the text for further exploration.

Just as the book shapes the dialogue—a strongly character-driven story, for instance, might engender much talk about characterization—the dialogue shapes the question. Participants might note, in reviewing their progress, that they have made several intriguing points about religious symbolism in the seemingly secular book *The House of the Scorpion* (Farmer, 2002) and, because of this, might determine to go back to the text and explore more fully Farmer's use of such symbolism. The discussion during the next class session would begin with that topic, providing more focus and taking the students deeper into the elements of the story. It is important that the focus question be taken as a starting point for dialogue in the second session, not as an opportunity for reporting participant "answers" to the question.

The broader context

The most effective literature studies do not happen in a vacuum. In classrooms where literature study is implemented effectively, members of the classroom community enthusiastically talk about the stories they are reading. Teachers obviously read and enjoy reading. They talk about what they read. They note aloud interesting aspects of a text, letting their expertise shine and encouraging others to notice as well. Effective teachers in literature study groups are inquiring readers first, and they actively foster environments that encourage their students to engage texts in the same ways. Extensive reading by students is not just encouraged in these classrooms; it is actively facilitated as teachers and other faculty members introduce great books and make them easily available to other readers, and they put structures in place for peers to review and exchange responses to the texts they read (Peterson & Eeds, 2007). Talk about books permeates day-to-day life. Learners (adult and adolescent) read and read and read, without quizzes or reports, making their own choices without the constraints of assigned levels or topics, telling each other about great books, passing them about, lounging about with books, swapping favorites like trading cards, and putting aside books that fail to grab them. These are practical and highly desirable goals.

Writing, too, is of central importance in supporting effective literature study groups, and literature study groups help develop writers more acutely aware of the authoring craft. The writing environment, like the reading environment described above, should be an active community of adolescent and adult writers, marked by extensive opportunities to produce meaningful texts and focused effort to refine texts for authentic purposes.

Teaching reading through literature study groups has an inquiry focus. It stands to reason, therefore, that when a broader curriculum values and fosters an inquiry stance to learning, then wondering, analyzing, and problem-solving become the ways learners approach tasks in any area. Like inquiry-based pedagogy in all subject areas, literature study develops critical thinking and an active, empowered, and interested approach to learning and life.

One curricular model

In *Book Club: A Literature-Based Curriculum*, Raphael, Pardo, and Highfield (2002) described a framework for exploring literature in which student-led discussions are the central component upon which all else depends. They separated book clubs into five complementary components that can be arranged in various ways depending on the teacher's needs. In the first component, *opening community share*, the teacher starts with a brief lesson in which a specific skill or strategy is taught to the whole class and is related to the coming reading and writing. During the second component, *reading*, students take time to read, either independently, with support, or in a group. During the third component, *writing*, students write in their journals or logs. Finally, they move into the fourth component, *groups*. Here, in small groups, they participate in discussions about the book, the length of the conversation depending on the students' age and experience. All the while, the teacher circulates to moderate, add input, redirect, and help struggling students. After the first four components are complete, the teacher draws all the groups back into a whole-class discussion that serves as a culminating phase—*closing community share*. Here, students share insights, struggles, or connections made in the small-group discussions. This is a flexible model for literature study that teachers should alter to fit their classes' needs.

A place for every learner

The middle grades years, perhaps more than any others, are marked by wild variances in development (especially physical and emotional) and interests. They are also a time of significant academic variances, which take on profound importance as students begin to make strong statements about who they are and who they will be. The instructional and research partners in the study noted a positive impact on literacy learning for the previously low-performing students in those classrooms. Michael, one of those students, noted that, because of his book club experiences, writing began to come more easily for him: 'Now, when teachers ask me to write, I just start going and going, like we do in here. Before, I'd just fake it. I didn't know what to do. Now, it's easy." Ryan, his group leader, added, "I think the ideas were always in him. Now, for the first time, he is in a classroom format that allows him the opportunity to express himself." It is that very opportunity that allows literature study to work for students at all levels. Literature study, with its attention to interpretation, voice, and choice, is uniquely suited for meeting the needs of this dynamic age group, allowing each young adolescent student, whether struggling or sailing, to engage meaningfully, appropriately, and effectively in learning.

Author note

This project was funded in part by a grant from the U.S. Department of Education's GEAR UP program (Gaining Early Awareness and Readiness for Undergraduate Programs).

Extensions

The authors contend that literature study in the middle grades should be based on books that matter to students. Consider forming an inquiry group of students, teachers, and media specialists in your school to identify texts that may matter to students and make plans to acquire those texts if they are not in your school library.

References

Atwell, N. (1998). *In the middle: New understanding about writing, reading, and learning.* Portsmouth, NH: Boynton/Cook.

Carnegie Council on Adolescent Development. (1989). *Turning points: Preparing American youth for the 21st century: The report of the task force on education of young adolescents.* Washington, DC: Carnegie Corporation.

Eeds, M., & Wells, D. (1989). Grand conversations: An exploration of meaning construction in literature study groups. *Research in the Teaching of English, 23*(10), 4–29.

Eikhard, S. (1985). Something to talk about. Performed by B. Raitt, *Luck of the draw.* U.S.A.: Capitol Records.

Evans, K. S. (1996). A closer look at literature discussion groups: The influence of gender on student response and discourse. *The New Advocate, 9*(3), 183–196.

Farmer, N. (2002). *The house of the scorpion.* New York: Atheneum Books for Young Readers.

Faust, M., Cockrill, J., Hancock, C., & Isserstedt, H. (2005). *Student book clubs: Improving literature instruction in middle and high school.* Norwood, MA: Christopher-Gordon.

Gallo, D. (2006a). Bold books for teenagers: The very best possibilities. *The English Journal, 95*(4), 108–111.

Gallo, D. (2006b). Bold books for teenagers: The very best possibilities, Part 2. *The English Journal, 95*(5), 107–110.

Goodlad, J. I. (2004). *A place called school: Twentieth anniversary edition.* New York: McGraw-Hill.

Junker, M. S. (1998). Searching for the moral: Moral talk in children's literature study groups. (Doctoral dissertation, Arizona State University, 1998). *Dissertation Abstracts International* 59(11), 4062.

Leland, C., & Harste, J. (2002). Critical literacy. In A. McClure & J. Kristo (Eds.), *Adventuring with books: A booklist.* Urbana, IL: National Council of Teachers of English.

L'Engle, M. (1962). *A wrinkle in time.* New York: Ariel Books.

Lowry, L. (1993). *The giver.* Boston, MA: Houghton Mifflin.

McGraw, E.J. (1996). *The Moorchild.* New York: Margaret K. McElderry Books.

Peterson, R, (1986). Importance of dialogue. Handout distributed in Washington District Writing Practices Institute, Phoenix, AZ.

Peterson, R., & Eeds, M. (2007). *Grand conversations: Literature groups in action.* New York: Scholastic.

Peterson, R., & Eeds, M. (1990). *Grand conversations: Literature groups in action.* New York: Scholastic.

Raphael, T. E., Pardo, L. S., & Highfield, K. (2002). *Book club: A literature-based curriculum.* Lawrence, MA: Small Planet.

Roberts, S. K. (1998). Using literature study groups to construct meaning in an undergraduate reading course. *Journal of Teacher Education, 49,* 366–371.

Rosenblatt, L. (1978). *The reader, the text, the poem: The transactional theory of the literary work.* Carbondale, IL: Southern Illinois University Press.

Rowling, J. K. (1999). *Harry Potter and the prisoner of Azkaban.* New York: Arthur A. Levine Books.

Rowling, J. K. (2000). *Harry Potter and the Chamber of Secrets.* New York: Scholastic.

Rowling, J. K. (2001). *Harry Potter*. London: Bloomsbury Children's.

Smith, K. (1990). Entertaining a text: A reciprocal process. In K. Short & K. M. Pierce (Eds.), *Talking about books* (pp. 17–31). Portsmouth, MA: Heinemann.

Smith, K. (1995). Bringing children and literature together in the elementary classroom. *Primary Voices K–6, 3*(2), 23–32.

Smith, K. (1997). A retrospective from the classroom: One teacher's view. *New Advocate, 10*(1), 15–30.

Wilkinson, P., & Kido, E. (1997). Literature and cultural awareness: Voices from the journal. *Language Arts, 74*, 255–264.

Wittrock, M. C. (1992). Generative learning processes of the brain. *Educational Psychologist, 27*, 531–541.

Wolf, S. A. (2004). Interpreting literature with children. Mawah, NJ: Erlbaum.

Young, E. (1992). *Seven blind mice*. New York: Philomel Books.

Appendix
Resources for Selecting Books for Middle Grades Literature Study Groups

The following easily accessible professional resources can assist teachers in selecting engaging texts for middle grades literature study groups.

- The Association for Library Service to Children (a division of the American Library Association) provides lists of notable and award-winning books appropriate for this age group. (http://www.ala.org/ala/mgrps/divs/alsc/awardsgrants/bookmedia/index.cfm). Note especially the Children's Notables lists that are divided into leveled categories, including books suggested for middle level and older readers.

- Middle school readers may vary widely in both reading level and maturity. For your more mature and capable readers, consider the recommendations and award recipients from the Young Adult Library Services Association (http://www.ala.org/ala/mgrps/divs/yalsa/ yalsa.cfm).

- Don Gallo has written a series of articles for *The English Journal* addressing "bold books" for classroom and personal reading. We suggest reading each of the pieces in this series, but two installments, Gallo (2006a) and Gallo (2006b), are of particular interest here.

- The suggested book list at the end of *Grand Conversations: Literature Study Groups in Action* by Peterson & Eeds (2007) provides sound recommendations of books that foster literature study dialogue and serves as a model for the kinds of books to select.

- A brief but powerful chapter in *Adventuring with Books: A Booklist for PreK–Grade 6* (Leland & Harste, 2002) addresses books that foster critical dialogue. The specific books they suggest are appropriate for a wide range of readers, including those with reading abilities below that expected in middle school, but hold appeal for even older and more mature readers. Their list of criteria for selecting books that foster critical dialogue is, we believe, a vital guide for any educator.

Discussion Questions

1. Parsons et al.'s article begins with an account of "Ryan Orwig's task." What do we, as readers, learn about the paper's stance from the introduction's emphasis on Orwig? What do we learn about Orwig's attitudes and assumptions toward his job?

2. How do Parsons et al. characterize "middle grades schools" as institutions? Do the paper's authors have a stance regarding these institutions? What purpose does this characterization serve in the article?

3. The paper's authors place a great deal of emphasis on the importance of the idea of authenticity in the teaching of literature. How do Parsons et al. talk about authenticity in the essay? Why do you think they find authenticity so important to the acts of reading and talking about literature?

4. Parsons et al. base some of their pedagogy on the idea of learning "with legs," or generative learning. What is generative learning? Have you had a learning experience that you would describe as generative? Describe it.

5. In a discussion of choosing books when teaching literature, Parsons et al. state that "Book selections for middle grades learners should be about things that matter to young adolescents who are discovering themselves and making their marks upon the world…" Look at the rest of this quote on page 314. Using these "guidelines," select a book that might be an effective text for a middle grade's school literature class. Explain your selection, drawing on the ideas of Parsons et al.

6. How do Parsons et al. imagine the role of the teacher in an ideal classroom? What benefits might emerge from a teacher acting in this role? What difficulties might students and the teacher encounter?

7. In the "Author Note" for this essay, Parsons et al. indicate that their project "was funded in part by a grant from the U.S. Department of Education's GEAR UP program." Go online and find out what the GEAR UP program is. Does having an understanding of this program change how you read the article? Think about Deborah Brandt's article in this textbook; who or what might be considered the sponsor of literacy in this essay?

Sponsors of Literacy

Deborah Brandt

In his sweeping history of adult learning in the United States, Joseph Kett describes the intellectual atmosphere available to young apprentices who worked in the small, decentralized print shops of antebellum America. Because printers also were the solicitors and editors of what they published, their workshops served as lively incubators for literacy and political discourse. By the mid-nineteenth century, however, this learning space was disrupted when the invention of the steam press reorganized the economy of the print industry. Steam presses were so expensive that they required capital outlays beyond the means of many printers. As a result, print jobs were outsourced, the processes of editing and printing were split, and, in tight competition, print apprentices became low-paid mechanics with no more access to the multi-skilled environment of the craftshop (Kett 67–70). While this shift in working conditions may be evidence of the deskilling of workers induced by the Industrial Revolution (Nicholas and Nicholas), it also offers a site for reflecting upon the dynamic sources of literacy and literacy learning. The reading and writing skills of print apprentices in this period were the achievements not simply of teachers and learners nor of the discourse practices of the printer community. Rather, these skills existed fragilely, contingently within an economic moment. The pre-steam press economy enabled some of the most basic aspects of the apprentices' literacy, especially their access to material production and the public meaning or worth of their skills. Paradoxically, even as the steam-powered penny press made print more accessible (by making publishing more profitable), it brought an end to a particular form of literacy sponsorship and a drop in literate potential.

The apprentices' experience invites rumination upon literacy learning and teaching today. Literacy looms as one of the great engines of profit and competitive advantage in the 20th century: a lubricant for consumer desire; a means for integrating corporate markets; a foundation for the deployment of weapons and other technology; a raw material in the mass production of information. As ordinary citizens have been compelled into these economies, their reading and writing skills have grown sharply more central to the everyday trade of information and goods as well as to the pursuit of education, employment, civil rights, status. At the same time, people's literate skills have grown vulnerable to unprecedented turbulence in their economic value, as conditions, forms, and standards of literacy achievement seem to shift with almost every new generation of learners. How are we to understand the vicissitudes of individual literacy development in relationship to the large-scale economic forces that set the routes and determine the wordly worth of that literacy?

The field of writing studies has had much to say about individual literacy development. Especially in the last quarter of the 20th century, we have theorized, researched, critiqued, debated, and sometimes even managed to enhance the literate potentials of ordinary citizens as they have tried to cope with life as they find it. Less easily and certainly less steadily have we been able to relate what we see, study, and do to these larger contexts of profit making and competition. This even as we recognize that the most pressing issues we deal with—tightening associations between literate skill and social viability, the breakneck pace of change in communications technology, persistent inequities in access and reward—all relate to structural conditions in literacy's bigger picture. When economic forces are addressed in our work, they appear primarily as generalities: contexts, determinants, motivators, barriers, touchstones. But rarely are they systematically related to the local conditions and embodied moments of literacy learning that occupy so many of us on a daily basis.[1]

This essay does not presume to overcome the analytical failure completely. But it does offer a conceptual approach that begins to connect literacy as an individual development to literacy as an economic development, at least as the two have played out over the last ninety years or so. The approach is through what I call sponsors of literacy. Sponsors, as I have come to think of them, are any agents, local or distant, concrete or abstract, who enable, support, teach, model, as well as recruit, regulate, suppress, or withhold literacy—and gain advantage by it in some way. Just as the ages of radio and television accustom us to having programs *brought* to us by various commercial sponsors, it is useful to think about who or what underwrites occasions of literacy learning and use. Although the interests of the sponsor and the sponsored do not have to converge (and, in fact, may conflict) sponsors nevertheless set the terms for access to literacy and wield powerful incentives for compliance and loyalty. Sponsors are a tangible reminder that literacy learning throughout history has always required permission, sanction, assistance, coercion, or, at minimum, contact with existing trade routes. Sponsors are delivery systems for the economies of literacy, the means by which these forces present themselves to—and through—individual learners. They also represent the causes into which people's literacy usually gets recruited.[2]

For the last five years I have been tracing sponsors of literacy across the 20th century as they appear in the accounts of ordinary Americans recalling how they learned to write and read. The investigation is grounded in more than 100 in-depth interviews that I collected from a diverse group of people born roughly between 1900 and 1980. In the interviews, people explored in great detail their memories of learning to read and write across their lifetimes, focusing especially on the people, institutions, materials, and motivations involved in the process. The more I worked with these accounts, the more I came to realize that they were filled with references to sponsors, both explicit and latent, who appeared in formative roles at the scenes of literacy learning. Patterns of sponsorship became an illuminating site through which to track the different cultural attitudes people developed toward writing vs. reading as well as the ideological congestion faced by late-century literacy learners as their sponsors proliferated and diversified (see my essays on "Remembering Reading" and "Accumulating Literacy"). In this essay I set out a case for why the concept of sponsorship is so richly suggestive for exploring economies of literacy and their effects. Then, through use of extended case examples, I demonstrate the practical application of this approach for interpreting current conditions of literacy teaching and learning, including persistent stratification of opportunity and escalating standards for literacy achievement. A final section addresses implications for the teaching of writing.

Sponsorship

Intuitively, *sponsors* seemed a fitting term for the figures who turned up most typically in people's memories of literacy learning: older relatives, teachers, priests, supervisors, military officers, editors, influential authors. Sponsors, as we ordinarily think of them, are powerful figures who bankroll events or smooth the way for initiates. Usually richer, more knowledgeable, and more entrenched than the sponsored, sponsors nevertheless enter a reciprocal relationship with those they underwrite. They lend their resources or credibility to the sponsored but also stand to gain benefits from their success, whether by direct repayment or, indirectly, by credit of association. *Sponsors* also proved an appealing term in my analysis because of all the commercial references that appeared in these 20th-century accounts—the magazines, peddled encyclopedias, essay contests, radio and television programs, toys, fan clubs, writing tools, and so on, from which so much experience with literacy was derived. As the 20th century turned the abilities to read and write into widely exploitable resources, commercial sponsorship abounded.

In whatever form, sponsors deliver the ideological freight that must be borne for access to what they have. Of course, the sponsored can be oblivious to or innovative with this ideological burden. Like Little Leaguers who wear the logo of a local insurance agency on their uniforms, not out of a concern for enhancing the agency's image but as a means for getting to play ball, people throughout history have acquired literacy pragmatically under the banner of others' causes. In the days before free, public schooling in England, Protestant Sunday Schools warily offered basic reading instruction to working-class families as part of evangelical duty.

To the horror of many in the church sponsorship, these families insistently, sometimes riotously demanded of their Sunday Schools more instruction, including in writing and math, because it provided means for upward mobility. [3] Through the sponsorship of Baptist and Methodist ministries, African Americans in slavery taught each other to understand the Bible in subversively liberatory ways. Under a conservative regime, they developed forms of critical literacy that sustained religious, educational, and political movements both before and after emancipation(Cornelius). Most of the time, however, literacy takes its shape from the interests of its sponsors. And, as we will see below, obligations toward one's sponsors run deep, affecting what, why, and how people write and read.

The concept of sponsors helps to explain, then, a range of human relationships and ideological pressures that turn up at the scenes of literacy learning—from benign sharing between adults and youths, to euphemized coercions in schools and workplaces, to the most notorious impositions and deprivations by church or state. It also is a concept useful for tracking literacy's materiel: the things that accompany writing and reading and the ways they are manufactured and distributed. Sponsorship as a sociological term is even more broadly suggestive for thinking about economies of literacy development. Studies of patronage in Europe and *compradrazgo* in the Americas show how patron-client relationships in the past grew up around the need to manage scarce resources and promote political stability (Bourne; Lynch; Horstman and Kurtz). Pragmatic, instrumental, ambivalent, patron-client relationships integrated otherwise antagonistic social classes into relationships of mutual, albeit unequal dependencies. Loaning land, money, protection, and other favors allowed the politically powerful to extend their influence and justify their exploitation of clients. Clients traded their labor and deference for access to opportunities for themselves or their children and for leverage needed to improve their social standing. Especially under conquest in Latin America, *compradrazgo* reintegrated native societies badly fragmented by the diseases and other disruptions that followed foreign invasions. At the same time, this system was susceptible to its own stresses, especially when patrons became clients themselves of still more centralized or distant overlords, with all the shifts in loyalty and perspective that entailed (Horstman and Kurtz 13–14).

In raising this association with formal systems of patronage, I do not wish to overlook the very different economic, political, and educational systems within which U.S. literacy has developed. But where we find the sponsoring of literacy, it will be useful to look for its function within larger political and economic arenas. Literacy, like land, is a valued commodity in this economy, a key resource in gaining profit and edge. This value helps to explain, of course, the lengths people will go to secure literacy for themselves or their children. But it also explains why the powerful work so persistently to conscript and ration the powers of literacy. The competition to harness literacy, to manage, measure, teach, and exploit it, has intensified throughout the century. It is vital to pay attention to this development because it largely sets the terms for individuals' encounters with literacy. This competition shapes the incentives and barriers (including uneven distributions of opportunity) that greet literacy learners in any particular time and place. It is this competition that has made access to the right kinds of literacy sponsors so crucial for political and economic well being. And it also has spurred the rapid, complex changes that now make the pursuit of literacy feel so turbulent and precarious for so many.

In the next three sections, I trace the dynamics of literacy sponsorship through the life experiences of several individuals, showing how their opportunities for literacy learning emerge out of the jockeying and skirmishing for economic and political advantage going on among sponsors of literacy. Along the way, the analysis addresses three key issues: (1) how, despite ostensible democracy in educational chances, stratification of opportunity continues to organize access and reward in literacy learning; (2) how sponsors contribute to what is called "the literacy crisis," that is, the perceived gap between rising standards for achievement and people's ability to meet them; and (3) how encounters with literacy sponsors, especially as they are configured at the end of the 20th century, can be sites for the innovative rerouting of resources into projects of self-development and social change.

Sponsorship and Access

A focus on sponsorship can force a more explicit and substantive link between literacy learning and systems of opportunity and access. A statistical correlation between high literacy achievement and high socio-economic, majority-race status routinely shows up in results of national tests of reading and writing performance.[4] These findings capture yet, in their shorthand way, obscure the unequal conditions of literacy sponsorship that lie behind differential outcomes in academic performance. Throughout their lives, affluent people from high-caste racial groups have multiple and redundant contacts with powerful literacy sponsors as a routine part of their economic and political privileges. Poor people and those from low-caste racial groups have less consistent, less politically secured access to literacy sponsors—especially to the ones that can grease their way to academic and economic success. Differences in their performances are often attributed to family background (namely education and income of parents) or to particular norms and values operating within different ethnic groups or social classes. But in either case, much more is usually at work.

As a study in contrasts in sponsorship patterns and access to literacy, consider the parallel experiences of Raymond Branch and Dora Lopez, both of whom were born in 1969 and, as young children, moved with their parents to the same, mid-sized university town in the midwest.[5] Both were still residing in this town at the time of our interviews in 1995. Raymond Branch, a European American, had been born in southern California, the son of a professor father and a real estate executive mother. He recalled that his first grade classroom in 1975 was hooked up to a mainframe computer at Stanford University and that, as a youngster, he enjoyed fooling around with computer programming in the company of "real users" at his father's science lab. This process was not interrupted much when, in the late 1970s, his family moved to the midwest. Raymond received his first personal computer as a Christmas present from his parents when he was twelve years old, and a modem the year after that. In the 1980s, computer hardware and software stores began popping up within a bicycle-ride's distance from where he lived. The stores were serving the university community and, increasingly, the high-tech industries that were becoming established in that vicinity. As an adolescent, Raymond spent his summers roaming these stores, sampling new computer games, making contact with founders of some of the first electronic bulletin boards in the nation, and continuing, through reading and other informal means, to develop his programming techniques. At the time of our interview he had graduated from the local university and was a successful freelance writer of software and software documentation, with clients in both the private sector and the university community.

Dora Lopez, a Mexican American, was born in the same year as Raymond Branch, 1969, in a Texas border town, where her grandparents, who worked as farm laborers, lived most of the year. When Dora was still a baby her family moved to the same midwest university town as had the family of Raymond Branch. Her father pursued an accounting degree at a local technical college and found work as a shipping and receiving clerk at the university. Her mother, who also attended technical college briefly, worked part time in a bookstore. In the early 1970s, when the Lopez family made its move to the midwest, the Mexican-American population in the university town was barely one per cent. Dora recalled that the family had to drive seventy miles to a big city to find not only suitable groceries but also Spanish-language newspapers and magazines that carried information of concern and interest to them. (Only when reception was good could they catch Spanish-language radio programs coming from Chicago, 150 miles away.) During her adolescence, Dora Lopez undertook to teach herself how to read and write in Spanish, something, she said, that neither

her brother nor her U.S.-born cousins knew how to do. Sometimes, with the help of her mother's employee discount at the bookstore, she sought out novels by South American and Mexican writers, and she practiced her written Spanish by corresponding with relatives in Colombia. She was exposed to computers for the first time at the age of thirteen when she worked as a teacher's aide in a federally funded summer school program for the children of migrant workers. The computers were being used to help the children to be brought up to grade level in their reading and writing skills. When Dora was admitted to the same university that Raymond Branch attended, her father bought her a used word processing machine that a student had advertised for sale on a bulletin board in the building where Mr. Lopez worked. At the time of our interview, Dora Lopez had transferred from the university to a technical college. She was working for a cleaning company, where she performed extra duties as a translator, communicating on her supervisor's behalf with the largely Latina cleaning staff. "I write in Spanish for him, what he needs to be translated, like job duties, what he expects them to do, and I write lists for him in English and Spanish," she explained.

In Raymond Branch's account of his early literacy learning we are able to see behind the scenes of his majority-race membership, male gender, and high-end socioeconomic family profile. There lies a thick and, to him, relatively accessible economy of institutional and commercial supports that cultivated and subsidized his acquisition of a powerful form of literacy. One might be tempted to say that Raymond Branch was born at the right time and lived in the right place—except that the experience of Dora Lopez troubles that thought. For Raymond Branch, a university town in the 1970s and 1980s provided an information-rich, resource-rich learning environment in which to pursue his literacy development, but for Dora Lopez, a female member of a culturally unsubsidized ethnic minority, the same town at the same time was information- and resource-poor. Interestingly, both young people were pursuing projects of self-initiated learning, Raymond Branch in computer programming and Dora Lopez in biliteracy. But she had to reach much further afield for the material and communicative systems needed to support her learning. Also, while Raymond Branch, as the son of an academic, was sponsored by some of the most powerful agents of the university (its laboratories, newest technologies, and most educated personnel), Dora Lopez was being sponsored by what her parents could pull from the peripheral service systems of the university (the mail room, the bookstore, the second-hand technology market). In these accounts we also can see how the development and eventual economic worth of Raymond Branch's literacy skills were underwritten by late-century transformations in communication technology that created a boomtown need for programmers and software writers.

Dora Lopez's biliterate skills developed and paid off much further down the economic-reward ladder, in government-sponsored youth programs and commercial enterprises, that, in the 1990s, were absorbing surplus migrant workers into a low-wage, urban service economy.[6] Tracking patterns of literacy sponsorship, then, gets beyond SES shorthand to expose more fully how unequal literacy chances relate to systems of unequal subsidy and reward for literacy. These are the systems that deliver large-scale economic, historical, and political conditions to the scenes of small-scale literacy use and development.

This analysis of sponsorship forces us to consider not merely how one social group's literacy practices may differ from another's, but how everybody's literacy practices are operating in differential economies, which supply different access routes, different degrees of sponsoring power, and different scales of monetary worth to the practices in use. In fact, the interviews I conducted are filled with examples of how economic and political forces, some of them originating in quite distant corporate and government policies, affect people's day-to-day ability to seek out and practice literacy. As a telephone company employee, Janelle Hampton enjoyed a brief period in the early 1980s as a fraud investigator, pursuing inquiries and writing up reports of her efforts. But when the breakup of the telephone utility reorganized its workforce, the fraud division was moved two states away and she was returned to less interesting work as a data processor. When, as a seven-year-old in the mid-1970s, Yi Vong made his way with his family from Laos to rural Wisconsin as part of the first resettlement group of Hmong refugees after the Vietnam War, his school district—which had no ESL programming—placed him in a school for the blind and deaf, where he learned English on audio and visual language machines. When a meager retirement pension forced Peter Hardaway and his wife out of their house and into a trailer, the couple stopped receiving newspapers and magazines in order to avoid cluttering up the small space they had to share. An analysis of sponsorship systems of literacy would help educators everywhere to think through the effects that economic and political changes in their regions are having on various people's ability to write and read, their chances to sustain that ability, and their capacities to pass it along to others. Recession, relocation, immigration, technological change, government retreat all can—and do—condition the course by which literate potential develops.

Sponsorship and the Rise in Literacy Standards

As I have been attempting to argue, literacy as a resource becomes available to ordinary people largely through the mediations of more powerful sponsors. These sponsors are engaged in ceaseless processes of positioning and repositioning, seizing and relinquishing control over meanings and materials of literacy as part of their participation in economic and political competition. In the give and take of these struggles, forms of literacy and literacy learning take shape. This section examines more closely how forms of literacy are created out of competitions between institutions. It especially considers how this process relates to the rapid rise in literacy standards since World War II. Resnick and Resnick lay out the process by which the demand for literacy achievement has been escalating, from basic, largely rote competence to more complex analytical and interpretive skills. More and more people are now being expected to accomplish more and more things with reading and writing. As print and its spinoffs have entered virtually every sphere of life, people have grown increasingly dependent on their literacy skills for earning a living and exercising and protecting their civil rights. This section uses one extended case example to trace the role of institutional sponsorship in raising the literacy stakes. It also considers how one man used available forms of sponsorship to cope with this escalation in literacy demands.

The focus is on Dwayne Lowery, whose transition in the early 1970s from line worker in an automobile manufacturing plant to field representative for a major public employees union exemplified the major transition of the post-World War II economy—from a thing-making, thing-swapping society to an information-making, service-swapping society. In the process, Dwayne Lowery had to learn to read and write in ways that he had never done before. How his experiences with writing developed and how they were sponsored—and distressed—by institutional struggle will unfold in the following narrative.

A man of Eastern European ancestry, Dwayne Lowery was born in 1938 and raised in a semi-rural area in the upper midwest, the third of five children of a rubber worker father and a homemaker mother. Lowery recalled how, in his childhood home, his father's feisty union publications and left-leaning newspapers and radio shows helped to create a political climate in his household. "I was sixteen years old before I knew that goddamn Republicans was two words," he said. Despite this influence, Lowery said he shunned politics and newspaper reading as a young person, except to read the sports page. A diffident student, he graduated near the bottom of his class from a small high school in 1956 and, after a stint in the Army, went to work on the assembly line of a major automobile manufacturer. In the late 1960s, bored with the repetition of spraying primer paint on the right door checks of 57 cars an hour, Lowery traded in his night shift at the auto plant for a day job reading water meters in a municipal utility department. It was at that time, Lowery recalled, that he rediscovered newspapers, reading them in the early morning in his department's break room. He said:

> At the time I guess I got a little more interested in the state of things within the state. I started to get a little political at that time and got a little more information about local people. So I would buy [a metropolitan paper] and I would read that paper in the morning. It was a pretty conservative paper but I got some information.

At about the same time Lowery became active in a rapidly growing public employees union, and, in the early 1970s, he applied for and received a union-sponsored grant that allowed him to take off four months of work and travel to Washington, D.C. for training in union activity. Here is his extended account of that experience:

> When I got to school, then there was a lot of reading. I often felt bad. If I had read more [as a high-school student] it wouldn't have been so tough. But they pumped a lot of stuff at us to read. We lived in a hotel and we had to some extent homework we had to do and reading we had to do and not make written reports but make some presentation on our part of it. What they were trying to teach us, I believe, was regulations, systems, laws. In case anything in court came up along the way, we would know that. We did a lot of work on organizing, you know, learning how to negotiate contracts, contractual language, how to write it. Gross National Product, how that affected the Consumer Price Index. It was pretty much a crash course. It was pretty much crammed in. And I'm not sure we were all that well prepared when we got done, but it was interesting.

After a hands-on experience organizing sanitation workers in the west, Lowery returned home and was offered a full-time job as a field staff representative for the union, handling worker grievances and contract negotiations for a large, active local near his state capital. His initial writing and rhetorical activities corresponded with the heady days of the early 1970s when the union was growing in strength and influence, reflecting in part the exponential expansion in information workers and service providers within all branches of government. With practice, Lowery said he became "good at talking," "good at presenting the union side," "good at slicing chunks off the employer's case." Lowery observed that, in those years, the elected officials with whom he was negotiating often lacked the sophistication of their Washington-trained union counterparts. "They were part time people," he said. "And they didn't know how to calculate. We got things in contracts that didn't cost them much at the time but were going to cost them a ton down the road." In time, though, even small municipal and county governments responded to the public employees' growing power by hiring specialized attorneys to represent them in grievance and contract negotiations. "Pretty soon," Lowery observed, "ninety percent of the people I was dealing with across the table were attorneys."

This move brought dramatic changes in the writing practices of union reps, and, in Lowery's estimation, a simultaneous waning of the power of workers and the power of his own literacy. "It used to be we got our way through muscle or through political connections," he said. "Now we had to get it through legalistic stuff. It was no longer just sit down and talk about it. Can we make a deal?" Instead, all activity became rendered in writing: the exhibit, the brief, the transcript, the letter, the appeal. Because briefs took longer to write, the wheels of justice took longer to turn. Delays in grievance hearings became routine, as lawyers and union reps alike asked hearing judges for extensions on their briefs. Things went, in Lowery's words, "from quick, competent justice to expensive and long term justice."

In the meantime, Lowery began spending up to 70 hours a week at work, sweating over the writing of briefs, which are typically fifteen to thirty-page documents laying out precedents, arguments, and evidence for a grievant's case. These documents were being forced by the new political economy in which Lowery's union was operating. He explained:

> When employers were represented by an attorney, you were going to have a written brief because the attorney needs to get paid. Well, what do you think if you were a union grievant and the attorney says, well, I'm going to write a brief and Dwayne Lowery says, well, I'm not going to. Does the worker somehow feel that their represen-tation is less now?

To keep up with the new demands, Lowery occasionally traveled to major cities for two or three-day union-sponsored workshops on arbitration, new legislation, and communication skills. He also took short courses at a historic School for Workers at a nearby university. His writing instruc-tion consisted mainly of reading the briefs of other field reps, especially those done by the college graduates who increasingly were being assigned to his district from union headquarters. Lowery said he kept a file drawer filled with other people's briefs from which he would borrow formats and phrasings. At the time of our interview in 1995, Dwayne Lowery had just taken an early and somewhat bitter retirement from the union, re-placed by a recent graduate from a master's degree program in Industrial Relations. As a retiree, he was engaged in local Democratic party poli-tics and was getting informal lessons in word processing at home from his wife.

Over a 20-year period, Lowery's adult writing took its character from a particular juncture in labor relations, when even small units of government began wielding (and, as a consequence, began spreading) a "legalistic" form of literacy in order to restore political dominance over public workers. This struggle for dominance shaped the kinds of literacy skills required of Lowery, the kinds of genres he learned and used, and the kinds of literate identity he developed. Lowery's rank-and-file experience and his talent for representing that experience around a bargaining table became increasingly peripheral to his ability to prepare documents that could compete in kind with those written by his formally-educated, professional adversaries. Face-to-face meetings became occasions mostly for a ritualistic exchange of texts, as arbitrators generally deferred decisions, reaching them in private, after solitary deliberation over complex sets of documents. What Dwayne Lowery was up against as a working adult in the second half of the 20th century was more than just living through a rising standard in literacy expectations or a generalized growth in professionalization, specialization, or documentary power—although certainly all of those things are, generically, true. Rather, these developments should be seen more specifically, as outcomes of ongoing transformations in the history of literacy as it has been wielded as part of economic and political conflict. These transformations become the arenas in which new standards of literacy develop. And for Dwayne Lowery—as well as many like him over the last 25 years—these are the arenas in which the worth of existing literate skills become degraded. A consummate debater and deal maker, Lowery saw his value to the union bureaucracy subside, as power shifted to younger, university-trained staffers whose literacy credentials better matched the specialized forms of escalating pressure coming from the other side.

In the broadest sense, the sponsorship of Dwayne Lowery's literacy experiences lies deep within the historical conditions of industrial relations in the 20th century and, more particularly, within the changing nature of work and labor struggle over the last several decades. Edward Stevens Jr. has observed the rise in this century of an "advanced contractarian society" (25) by which formal relationships of all kinds have come to rely on "a jungle of rules and regulations" (139). For labor, these conditions only intensified in the 1960s and 1970s when a flurry of federal and state civil rights legislation curtailed the previously unregulated hiring and firing power of management. These developments made the appeal to law as central as collective bargaining for extending employee rights (Heckscher 9). I mention this broader picture, first, because it relates to the forms of employer backlash that Lowery began experiencing by the early 1980s and, more important, because a history of unionism serves as a guide for a closer look at the sponsors of Lowery's literacy.

These resources begin with the influence of his father, whose membership in the United Rubber Workers during the ideologically potent 1930s
and 1940s, grounded Lowery in class-conscious progressivism and its
favorite literate form: the newspaper. On top of that, though, was a pragmatic philosophy of worker education that developed in the U.S. after
the Depression as an anti-communist antidote to left-wing intellectual
influences in unions. Lowery's parent union, in fact, had been a central
force in refocusing worker education away from an earlier emphasis
on broad critical study and toward discrete techniques for organizing
and bargaining. Workers began to be trained in the discrete bodies of
knowledge, written formats, and idioms associated with those strategies.
Characteristic of this legacy, Lowery's crash course at the Washington-
based training center in the early 1970s emphasized technical information, problem solving, and union-building skills and methods. The
transformation in worker education from critical, humanistic study to
problem-solving skills was also lived out at the school for workers where
Lowery took short courses in the 1980s. Once a place where factory workers came to write and read about economics, sociology, and labor history,
the school is now part of a university extension service offering workshops—often requested by management—on such topics as work restruc-
turing, new technology, health and safety regulations, and joint labor-
management cooperation.[7] Finally, in this inventory of Dwayne Lowery's
literacy sponsors, we must add the latest incarnations shaping union
practices: the attorneys and college-educated co-workers who carried into
Lowery's workplace forms of legal discourse and "essayist literacy."[8]

What should we notice about this pattern of sponsorship? First, we can
see from yet another angle how the course of an ordinary person's literacy
learning—its occasions, materials, applications, potentials—follows the
transformations going on within sponsoring institutions as those institutions fight for economic and ideological position. As a result of wins, loss-
es, or compromises, institutions undergo change, affecting the kinds of
literacy they promulgate and the status that such literacy has in the larger
society. So where, how, why, and what Lowery practiced as a writer—and
what he didn't practice—took shape as part of the post-industrial jockeying going on over the last thirty years by labor, government, and industry.
Yet there is more to be seen in this inventory of literacy sponsors. It ex-
poses the deeply textured history that lies within the literacy practices of
institutions and within any individual's literacy experiences. Accumulated
layers of sponsoring influences—in families, workplaces, schools, memory—carry forms of literacy that have been shaped out of ideological and
economic struggles of the past. This history, on the one hand, is a sustaining resource in the quest for literacy. It enables an older generation to
pass its literacy resources onto another. Lowery's exposure to his father's

newspaper-reading and supper-table political talk kindled his adult passion for news, debate, and for language that rendered relief and justice. This history also helps to create infrastructures of opportunity. Lowery found crucial supports for extending his adult literacy in the educational networks that unions established during the first half of the 20th century as they were consolidating into national powers. On the other hand, this layered history of sponsorship is also deeply conservative and can be maladaptive because it teaches forms of literacy that oftentimes are in the process of being overtaken by new political realities and by ascendent forms of literacy. The decision to focus worker education on practical strategies of recruiting and bargaining— devised in the thick of Cold War patriotism and galloping expansion in union memberships—became, by the Reagan years, a fertile ground for new forms of management aggression and cooptation.

It is actually this lag or gap in sponsoring forms that we call the rising standard of literacy. The pace of change and the place of literacy in economic competition have both intensified enormously in the last half of the 20th century. It is as if the history of literacy is in fast forward. Where once the same sponsoring arrangements could maintain value across a generation or more, forms of literacy and their sponsors can now rise and recede many times within a single life span. Dwayne Lowery experienced profound changes in forms of union-based literacy not only between his father's time and his but between the time he joined the union and the time he left it, twenty-odd years later. This phenomenon is what makes today's literacy feel so advanced and, at the same time, so destabilized.

Sponsorship and Appropriation In Literacy Learning

We have seen how literacy sponsors affect literacy learning in two powerful ways. They help to organize and administer stratified systems of opportunity and access, and they raise the literacy stakes in struggles for competitive advantage. Sponsors enable and hinder literacy activity, often forcing the formation of new literacy requirements while decertifying older ones. A somewhat different dynamic of literacy sponsorship is treated here. It pertains to the potential of the sponsored to divert sponsors' resources toward ulterior projects, often projects of self-interest or self-development. Earlier I mentioned how Sunday School parishioners in England and African Americans in slavery appropriated church-sponsored literacy for economic and psychic survival. "Misappropriation" is always possible at the scene of literacy transmission, a reason for the tight ideological control that usually surrounds reading and writing instruction. The accounts that appear below are meant to shed light on the dynamics of appropriation, including the role of sponsoring agents in that process. They are also meant to suggest that diversionary tactics in literacy learning may be invited now by the sheer proliferation of literacy activity in contemporary life. The uses and networks of literacy criss-cross through many domains, exposing people to multiple, often amalgamated sources of sponsoring powers, secular, religious, bureaucratic, commercial, technological. In other words, what is so destabilized about contemporary literacy today also makes it so available and potentially innovative, ripe for picking, one might say, for people suitably positioned. The rising level of schooling in the general population is also an inviting factor in this process. Almost everyone now has some sort of contact, for instance, with college educated people, whose movements through workplaces, justice systems, social service organizations, houses of worship, local government, extended families, or circles of friends spread dominant forms of literacy (whether wanted or not, helpful or not) into public and private spheres. Another condition favorable for appropriation is the deep hybridity of literacy practices extant in many settings. As we saw in Dwayne Lowery's case, workplaces, schools, families bring together multiple strands of the history of literacy in complex and influential forms. We need models of literacy that more astutely account for these kinds of multiple contacts, both in and out of school and across a lifetime. Such models could begin to grasp the significance of re-appropriation, which, for a number of reasons, is becoming a key requirement for literacy learning at the end of the 20th century.

The following discussion will consider two brief cases of literacy diversion. Both involve women working in subordinate positions as secretaries, in print-rich settings where better educated male supervisors were teaching them to read and write in certain ways to perform their clerical duties. However, as we will see shortly, strong loyalties outside the workplace prompted these two secretaries to lift these literate resources for use in other spheres. For one, Carol White, it was on behalf of her work as a Jehovah's Witness. For the other, Sarah Steele, it was on behalf of upward mobility for her lower middle-class family.

Before turning to their narratives, though, it will be wise to pay some attention to the economic moment in which they occur. Clerical work was the largest and fastest growing occupation for women in the 20th century. Like so much employment for women, it offered a mix of gender-defined constraints as well as avenues for economic independence and mobility. As a new information economy created an acute need for typists, stenographers, bookkeepers and other office workers, white, American-born women and, later, immigrant and minority women saw reason to pursue high school and business-college educations. Unlike male clerks of the 19th century, female secretaries in this century had little chance for advancement. However, office work represented a step up from the farm or

the factory for women of the working class and served as a respectable occupation from which educated, middle-class women could await or avoid
marriage (Anderson, Strom). In a study of clerical work through the first
half of the 20th century, Christine Anderson estimated that secretaries
might encounter up to 97 different genres in the course of doing dictation
or transcription. They routinely had contact with an array of professionals, including lawyers, auditors, tax examiners, and other government
overseers (52–53). By 1930, 30% of women office workers used machines
other than typewriters (Anderson 76) and, in contemporary offices, clerical workers have often been the first employees to learn to operate CRTs
and personal computers and to teach others how to use them. Overall, the
daily duties of 20th-century secretaries could serve handily as an index to
the rise of complex administrative and accounting procedures, standard-
ization of information, expanding communication, and developments in
technological systems.

With that background, consider the experiences of Carol White and
Sarah Steele. An Oneida, Carol White was born into a poor, single-parent
household in 1940. She graduated from high school in 1960 and, between
five maternity leaves and a divorce, worked continuously in a series of
clerical positions in both the private and public sectors. One of her first
secretarial jobs was with an urban firm that produced and disseminated
Catholic missionary films. The vice-president with whom she worked
most closely also spent much of his time producing a magazine for a national civic organization that he headed. She discussed how typing letters
and magazine articles and occasionally proofreading for this man taught
her rhetorical strategies in which she was keenly interested. She described
the scene of transfer this way:

> [My boss] didn't just write to write. He wrote in a way to make his
> letters appealing. I would have to write what he was writing in this
> magazine too. I was completely enthralled. He would write about
> the people who were in this [organization] and the different works
> they were undertaking and people that died and people who were
> sick and about their personalities. And he wrote little anecdotes.
> Once in a while I made some suggestions too. He was a man who
> would listen to you.

The appealing and persuasive power of the anecdote became especially
important to Carol White when she began doing door-to-door missionary work for the Jehovah's Witnesses, a pan-racial, millenialist religious
faith. She now uses colorful anecdotes to prepare demonstrations that she
performs with other women at weekly service meetings at their Kingdom
Hall. These demonstrations, done in front of the congregation, take the
form of skits designed to explore daily problems through Bible principles.

Further, at the time of our interview, Carol White was working as a municipal revenue clerk and had recently enrolled in an on-the-job training seminar called Persuasive Communication, a two-day class offered free to public employees. Her motivation for taking the course stemmed from her desire to improve her evangelical work. She said she wanted to continue to develop speaking and writing skills that would be "appealing," "motivating," and "encouraging" to people she hoped to convert.

Sarah Steele, a woman of Welsh and German descent, was born in 1920 into a large, working-class family in a coal mining community in eastern Pennsylvania. In 1940, she graduated from a two-year commercial college. Married soon after, she worked as a secretary in a glass factory until becoming pregnant with the first of four children. In the 1960s, in part to help pay for her children's college educations, she returned to the labor force as a receptionist and bookkeeper in a law firm, where she stayed until her retirement in the late 1970s.

Sarah Steele described how, after joining the law firm, she began to model her household management on principles of budgeting that she was picking up from one of the attorneys with whom she worked most closely. "I learned cash flow from Mr. B_____," she said. "I would get all the bills and put a tape in the adding machine and he and I would sit down together to be sure there was going to be money ahead." She said that she began to replicate that process at home with household bills. "Before that," she observed, "I would just cook beans when I had to instead of meat." Sarah Steele also said she encountered the genre of the credit report during routine reading and typing on the job. She figured out what constituted a top rating, making sure her husband followed these steps in preparation for their financing a new car. She also remembered typing up documents connected to civil suits being brought against local businesses, teaching her, she said, which firms never to hire for home repairs. "It just changes the way you think," she observed about the reading and writing she did on her job. "You're not a pushover after you learn how business operates."

The dynamics of sponsorship alive in these narratives expose important elements of literacy appropriation, at least as it is practiced at the end of the 20th century. In a pattern now familiar from the earlier sections, we see how opportunities for literacy learning—this time for diversions of resources—open up in the clash between long-standing, residual forms of sponsorship and the new: between the lingering presence of literacy's conservative history and its pressure for change. So, here, two women— one Native American and both working-class—filch contemporary literacy resources (public relations techniques and accounting practices) from more educated, higher-status men. The women are emboldened in these acts by ulterior identities beyond the workplace: Carol White with faith and Sarah Steele with family. These affiliations hark back to the first sponsoring arrangements through which American women were gradually allowed to acquire literacy and education. Duties associated with religious faith and child rearing helped literacy to become, in Gloria Main's words, "a permissable feminine activity" (579). Interestingly, these roles, deeply sanctioned within the history of women's literacy—and operating beneath the newer permissible feminine activity of clerical work—become grounds for covert, innovative appropriation even as they reinforce traditional female identities.

Just as multiple identities contribute to the ideologically hybrid character of these literacy formations, so do institutional and material conditions. Carol White's account speaks to such hybridity. The missionary film company with the civic club vice president is a residual site for two of literacy's oldest campaigns—Christian conversion and civic participation—enhanced here by 20th-century advances in film and public relations techniques. This ideological reservoir proved a pleasing instructional site for Carol White, whose interests in literacy, throughout her life, have been primarily spiritual. So literacy appropriation draws upon, perhaps even depends upon, conservative forces in the history of literacy sponsorship that are always hovering at the scene of acts of learning. This history serves as both a sanctioning force and a reserve of ideological and material support.

At the same time, however, we see in these accounts how individual acts of appropriation can divert and subvert the course of literacy's history, how changes in individual literacy experiences relate to larger scale transformations. Carol White's redirection of personnel management techniques to the cause of the Jehovah's Witnesses is an almost ironic transformation in this regard. Once a principal sponsor in the initial spread of mass literacy, evangelism is here rejuvenated through late-literate corporate sciences of secular persuasion, fund-raising, and bureaucratic management that Carol White finds circulating in her contemporary workplaces. By the same token, through Sarah Steele, accounting practices associated with corporations are, in a sense, tracked into the house, rationalizing and standardizing even domestic practices. (Even though Sarah Steele did not own an adding machine, she penciled her budget figures onto adding-machine tape that she kept for that purpose.) Sarah Steele's act of appropriation in some sense explains how dominant forms of literacy migrate and penetrate into private spheres, including private consciousness. At the same time, though, she accomplishes a subversive diversion of literate power. Her efforts to move her family up in the middle class involved not merely contributing a second income but also, from her desk as a bookkeeper, reading her way into an understanding of middle-class economic power.

Teaching and the Dynamics of Sponsorship

It hardly seems necessary to point out to the readers of *CCC* that we haul a lot of freight for the opportunity to teach writing. Neither rich nor powerful enough to sponsor literacy on our own terms, we serve instead as conflicted brokers between literacy's buyers and sellers. At our most worthy, perhaps, we show the sellers how to beware and try to make sure these exchanges will be a little fairer, maybe, potentially, a little more mutually rewarding. This essay has offered a few working case studies that link patterns of sponsorship to processes of stratification, competition, and reappropriation. How much these dynamics can be generalized to classrooms is an ongoing empirical question.

I am sure that sponsors play even more influential roles at the scenes of literacy learning and use than this essay has explored. I have focused on some of the most tangible aspects—material supply, explicit teaching, institutional aegis. But the ideological pressure of sponsors affects many private aspects of writing processes as well as public aspects of finished texts. Where one's sponsors are multiple or even at odds, they can make writing maddening. Where they are absent, they make writing unlikely. Many of the cultural formations we associate with writing development— community practices, disciplinary traditions, technological potentials— can be appreciated as make-do responses to the economics of literacy, past and present. The history of literacy is a catalogue of obligatory relations. That this catalogue is so deeply conservative and, at the same time, so ruthlessly demanding of change is what fills contemporary literacy learning and teaching with their most paradoxical choices and outcomes.[9]

In bringing attention to economies of literacy learning I am not advocating that we prepare students more efficiently for the job markets they must enter. What I have tried to suggest is that as we assist and study individuals in pursuit of literacy, we also recognize how literacy is in pursuit of them. When this process stirs ambivalence, on their part or on ours, we need to be understanding.

Acknowledgments

This research was sponsored by the NCTE Research Foundation and the Center on English Learning and Achievement. The Center is supported by the U.S. Department of Education's Office of Educational Research and Improvement, whose views do not necessarily coincide with the author's. A version of this essay was given as a lecture in the Department of

English, University of Louisville, in April 1997. Thanks to Anna Syvertsen and Julie Nelson for their help with archival research. Thanks too to colleagues who lent an ear along the way: Nelson Graff, Jonna Gjevre, Anne Gere, Kurt Spellmeyer, Tom Fox, and Bob Gundlach.

Notes

1. Three of the keenest and most eloquent observers of economic impacts on writing teaching and learning have been Lester Faigley, Susan Miller, and Kurt Spellmeyer.

2. My debt to the writings of Pierre Bourdieu will be evident throughout this essay. Here and throughout I invoke his expansive notion of "economy," which is not restricted to literal and ostensible systems of money making but to the many spheres where people labor, invest, and exploit energies—their own and others'—to maximize advantage. See Bourdieu and Wacquant, especially 117–120 and Bourdieu, Chapter 7.

3. Thomas Laqueur (124) provides a vivid account of a street demonstration in Bolton, England, in 1834 by a "pro-writing" faction of Sunday School students and their teachers. This faction demanded that writing instruction continue to be provided on Sundays, something that opponents of secular instruction on the Sabbath were trying to reverse.

4. See, for instance, National Assessments of Educational Progress in reading and writing (Applebee et al.; and "Looking").

5. All names used in this essay are pseudonyms.

6. I am not suggesting that literacy that does not "pay off" in terms of prestige or monetary reward is less valuable. Dora Lopez's ability to read and write in Spanish was a source of great strength and pride, especially when she was able to teach it to her young child. The resource of Spanish literacy carried much of what Bourdieu calls cultural capital in her social and family circles. But I want to point out here how people who labor equally to acquire literacy do so under systems of unequal subsidy and unequal reward.

7. For useful accounts of this period in union history, see Heckscher; Nelson.

8. Marcia Farr associates "essayist literacy" with written genres esteemed in the academy and noted for their explictness, exactness, reliance on reasons and evidence, and impersonal voice.

9. Lawrence Cremin makes similar points about education in general
    in his essay "The Cacophony of Teaching." He suggests that complex
    economic and social changes since World War Two, including the
    popularization of schooling and the penetration of mass media, have
    created "a far greater range and diversity of languages, competencies,
    values, personalities, and approaches to the world and to its educa-
    tional opportunities" than at one time existed. The diversity most of
    interest to him (and me) resides not so much in the range of different
    ethnic groups there are in society but in the different cultural for-
    mulas by which people assemble their educational— or, I would say,
    literate—experience.

Works Cited

Anderson, Mary Christine. "Gender, Class, and Culture: Women
Secretarial and Clerical Workers in the United States, 1925–1955." Diss.
Ohio State U, 1986.

Applebee, Arthur N., Judith A. Langer, and Ida V.S. Mullis. *The Writing
Report Card: Writing Achievement in American Schools.* Princeton: ETS,
1986.

Bourdieu, Pierre. *The Logic of Practice.* Trans. Richard Nice. Cambridge:
Polity, 1990.

Bourdieu, Pierre and Loic J. D. Wacquant. *An Invitation to Reflexive
Sociology.* Chicago: Chicago UP, 1992.

Bourne, J. M. *Patronage and Society in Nineteenth-Century England.*
London: Edward Arnold, 1986.

Brandt, Deborah. "Remembering Reading, Remembering Writing." *CCC*
45 (1994): 459–79.

———. "Accumulating Literacy: Writing and Learning to Write in the
20th Century." *College English* 57 (1995): 649–68.

Cornelius, Janet Duitsman. *'When I Can Ready My Title Clear': Literacy,
Slavery, and Religion in the Antebellum South.* Columbia: U of South
Carolina, 1991.

Cremin, Lawrence. "The Cacophony of Teaching." *Popular Education and
Its Discontents.* New York: Harper, 1990.

Faigley, Lester. "Veterans' Stories on the Porch." *History, Reflection and
Narrative: The Professionalization of Composition, 1963–1983.* Eds. Beth
Boehm, Debra Journet, and Mary Rosner. Norwood: Ablex, in press.

Farr, Marcia. "Essayist Literacy and Other Verbal Performances." *Written Communication* 8 (1993): 4–38.

Heckscher, Charles C. *The New Unionism: Employee Involvement in the Changing Corporation.* New York: Basic, 1988.

Hortsman, Connie and Donald V. Kurtz. *Compradrazgo in Post-Conquest Middle America.* Milwaukee: Milwaukee-UW Center for Latin America, 1978.

Kett, Joseph F. *The Pursuit of Knowledge Under Difficulties: From Self Improvement to Adult Education in America 1750–1990.* Stanford: Stanford UP, 1994.

Laqueur, Thomas. *Religion and Respectability: Sunday Schools and Working Class Culture 1780–1850.* New Haven: Yale UP, 1976.

Looking at How Well Our Students Read: The 1992 National Assessment of Educational Progress in Reading. Washington: US Dept. of Education, Office of Educational Research and Improvement, Educational Resources Information Center, 1992.

Lynch, Joseph H. *Godparents and Kinship in Early Medieval Europe.* Princeton: Princeton UP, 1986.

Main, Gloria L. "An Inquiry Into When and Why Women Learned to Write in Colonial New England." *Journal of Social History* 24 (1991): 579–89.

Miller, Susan. *Textual Carnivals: The Politics of Composition.* Carbondale: Southern Illinois UP, 1991.

Nelson, Daniel. *American Rubber Workers & Organized Labor, 1900–1941.* Princeton: Princeton UP, 1988.

Nicholas, Stephen J. and Jacqueline M. Nicholas. "Male Literacy, 'Deskilling,' and the Industrial Revolution." *Journal of Interdisciplinary History* 23 (1992): 1–18.

Resnick, Daniel P., and Lauren B. Resnick. "The Nature of Literacy: A Historical Explanation." *Harvard Educational Review* 47 (1977): 370–85.

Spellmeyer, Kurt. "After Theory: From Textuality to Attunement With the World." *College English* 58 (1996): 893–913.

Stevens, Jr., Edward. *Literacy, Law, and Social Order.* DeKalb: Northern Illinois UP, 1987.

Strom, Sharon Hartman. *Beyond the Typewriter: Gender, Class, and the Origins of Modern American Office Work, 1900–1930.* Urbana: U of Illinois P, 1992.

Discussion Questions

1. Brandt begins her essay with a description of how print shops changed with the invention of the steam press. What does this historical information say about literacy, learning, and economics? Additionally, what rhetorical functions might this information serve in the development of Brandt's argument?

2. The first of Brandt's interview subjects whom we learn about in this essay are Raymond Branch and Dora Lopez. Despite a number of similarities in the interview subjects' lives, Branch and Lopez develop in very different ways. Who or what might be considered the sponsors of these individuals' literacies, and how did these sponsorships directly and indirectly shape Branch's and Lopez's experiences?

3. Brandt focuses much of her discussion of literacy sponsorship around the real-life experiences of her interview subjects. What does Brandt's argument gain from this strategy? How does the use of these interviews limit Brandt's argument?

4. What does Brandt mean when she discusses "misappropriation" or "literacy diversion" in the context of sponsorship?

5. In discussing patron-client relationships, Brandt mentions "patronage in Europe" and "*compradrazgo* in the Americas." What are these concepts, how do they work, and how do they relate to the idea of sponsorship?

6. Take a moment and consider the sponsors of your own literacy. Consider your formal education, religious institutions, and other groups to which you've belonged or been involved with while making your list. Select one of these sponsors and investigate its role in sponsoring literacy. How did this sponsor shape your own literacy? Is the sponsor recognized by others as a sponsor of literacy? How did this sponsorship help you? Limit you?

7. Some schools in the United States rely on corporate sponsorship for funding, effectively putting corporations in the role of sponsors within public schools. Investigate this phenomena and consider the implications this sponsorship might have on literacy and learning. What positive and/or negative effects could this form of sponsorship have on students? How is this controversy being addressed in the field of education?

8. Consider Freire's and Hirsch's essays in this chapter. Who or what might Freire cite as sponsors of his literacy? Who or what might sponsor the type of literacy described by Hirsch?

LITERACY AND MULTICULTURALISM

Library Resources

There is one database, **ERIC**, which can provide most of the information needed for a college or graduate level paper. ERIC can be found in the alphabetical list of databases under the column *Find Articles*, as was done for the database **ProQuest**.

ERIC is produced by the Educational Resources Information Center, containing over 950,000 abstracts on education research and practice. ERIC covers two types of literature:

Journals indexed and abstracted include scholarly and professional journals and practitioner magazines. Articles are generally peer reviewed.

Documents include non-journal literature, such as full text curriculum guides, theses, conference papers, standards, reports, book chapters, etc. Not peer reviewed.

When you click on **ERIC** within the alphabetical list of databases, you have a choice of three vendors. "via EBSCO" is the preferred method to search since this vendor produces other databases you may use later. Clicking on **ERIC (via EBSCO)** brings up a screen with a set of boxes you can type in subject or keyword terms.

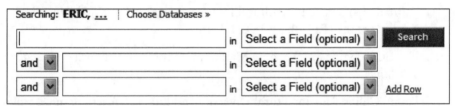

Type in the term "multiculturalism" in the first line and "literacy" in the second line. Hit the "Search" button. Results for journal and magazine articles, book chapters and other ERIC documents are displayed with the newest citations displayed first. If the full text or PDF is not available follow the button to find the articles electronically.

Additional information on this topic can be found at the Mary L. Williams Curriculum Materials Library (CML), located in the basement of Willard Hall. The CML, a branch library, provides reference and readers' advisory assistance primarily for students and faculty of the Teacher Education Unit of the College of Education, the Human Development and Family Science Department of the College of Human Environmental Sciences and local educators. Reference staff are available there to help you with any of your research needs or questions.

Further Readings

Brock, Cynthia H., Dorothy K. Moore and Laura Parks. "Exploring Pre-service Teachers Literacy Practices with Children from Diverse Backgrounds: Implications for Teacher Educators." *Teaching and Teacher Education* 27 (2007): 898–915. Print.

de Courcy, Michèle. "Disrupting Preconceptions: Challenges to Pre-service Teachers' Beliefs About ESL Children." *Journal of Multilingual & Multicultural Development* 28.3 (2007):188–203. Print.

Home Page. *International Reading Association.* International Reading Association. 1996–2008. Web. 28 May 2008. <http://www.reading.org/>

Kilman, Carrie. "Gates of Change." *Teaching Tolerance.* Spring 2007: 44–52. Print.

Kozol, Jonathon. "Still Separate, Still Unequal: America's Educational Apartheid." *Harper's Magazine.* 1 Sep 2005: 41–54. Print.

Home Page. *National Council of Teachers of English.* NCTE. 1998–2008. Web. 28 May 2008. <http://www.ncte.org/>

Pattnaik, Jyotsna. "Multicultural Literacy Starts at Home." *Childhood Education* 80.1 (Fall 2003): 18–24. Print.

Pazkonas, Lynda S. "Teaching Mathematics through Cultural Quilting." *Teaching Children Mathematics* 9.5 (2003): 250–251. Print.

Potter, Gillian. "Sociocultural Diversity and Literacy Teaching in Complex Times: The Challenges for Early Childhood Educators." *Childhood Education* 84.2 (2007–08): 64–69. Print.

Yates, H. Marguerite and Vikki K. Collins. "How One School Made the Pieces Fit: Elementary School Builds on a Learning Community to Lift the Achievement for Black Students in Reading and Math." *The Journal of Staff Development* 27.4 (2006): 30–35. Print.

CONSERVATION AND CONSCIOUSNESS

Department of Biosystems and Agricultural Engineering, College of Engineering, Architecture, and Technology

Introduction

Regardless of whether you prefer the term "climate change" or "global warming," or perhaps you think the whole "green movement" is one big ploy to push political agendas and make a quick buck in the process, this chapter offers multiple voices on one of today's hottest topics that will have you questioning the stability of the world as you know it. At the heart of this chapter is the necessity to raise awareness and promote action. Sophie Uliano points out, "The problem lies in our lack of understanding about the sources of our everyday necessities." Thus, this chapter is fittingly titled "Conservation and Consciousness." You will find simple suggestions for changes you can make as an individual on a daily basis to global repercussions that shed light on issues that must be addressed by human civilization as a whole.

We live in a society that constantly bombards us with green initiatives. Although some initiatives raise genuine concerns, many of them are merely ephemeral marketing tools. The easy response is to ignore the issue entirely. Bill McKibben and Mike Tidwell, however, harshly warn against this type of reaction. The various articles you will read focus on both the ecological and economic repercussions of consumer consumption, and corporate as well as government malfeasance. Though the authors differ in their opinions on the ways in which individuals, governments, and corporations must be held responsible and must take action against this growing epidemic, each article suggests ways in which readers can raise their awareness of the issues surrounding conservation.

This chapter also highlights a research project conducted by Dr. Bellmer, a faculty member in the Robert M. Kerr Food and Agricultural Products Center and also OSU's Department of Biosystems and Agricultural Engineering (BAE). The BAE department is housed in the College of Engineering, Architecture, and Technology (CEAT) and is home to important teaching and research programs involving development of biobased products and bioenergy, value-added food processing, and conservation of natural resources. The final report in this chapter shows one example of the extensive research being conducted in this department to support conservation and consciousness.

Interview with Dr. Danielle Bellmer

Dr. Bellmer graciously answered some interview questions posed by Jessica Glover. The following excerpts share some of her thoughts and expertise in Food and Bioprocessing, particularly research in developing a soda waste alternative.

I think first-year students will want to know what led to your interest in developing a soda waste alternative. Can you explain how the idea came to fruition?

The soda waste fermentation project actually started when a gentleman from Lamco Recycling contacted me asking about what we could do with the soft drink waste that he was collecting. Their company was paid to dispose of truckloads of soda bottling waste, and basically they would adjust the pH and then send it to the wastewater treatment plant for disposal. He was aware that the sugar content potentially had value as a fermentation substrate, and he learned of my name from a previous research project involving ethanol production.

After that inquiry, we began initial testing largely based on curiosity. Our goal was to simply determine how easily soft drinks could be fermented to ethanol. The initial experiments were conducted as part of a freshman class project, and after seeing positive results, we continued testing.

What is the next step in your research/writing process?

Our initial testing has shown that for most soft drinks, fermentation of the sugars to ethanol is relatively easy and results in high sugar conversion efficiency. We are currently working on a scientific publication from the initial testing. The next steps will involve a more detailed analysis of process parameters, with the goal of optimizing fermentation time and efficiency. This information will be necessary for a more thorough evaluation of the economic feasibility of the entire process.

What is the final goal for your research and hard work?

The ultimate goal for this work is for an Oklahoma bottling company to establish a process for utilizing their waste for energy production. This would allow them to turn a waste liability into an energy asset. The process appears to be technically feasible and relatively simple; hopefully the economic evaluation results will be positive as well.

Have you ever felt overwhelmed while trying to achieve this goal? If so, what has kept you motivated?

I would guess that everyone feels overwhelmed at various times in work and in life. The best advice I have is to break the large, overwhelming tasks into smaller pieces, and tackle one piece at a time. Prioritizing goals also helps to ensure that the most important aspects of a project get accomplished first.

Obviously, your work has the potential to reduce the amount of waste that bottling plants in Oklahoma generate. How do you think your research will be received outside the academy?

Utilization of waste products is, by its very nature, applied research; and one of the main functions of the Food and Agricultural Products Center is applied research for the benefit of Oklahoma businesses. Quite frankly, this is a project that people outside the academic community are more excited about than people inside the academic community. It is certainly not rocket science, but could potentially be very beneficial for some local businesses. In processing industries, and in particular food processing industries, there are many opportunities for improvement in efficiency if we consider utilization of various waste streams. As energy and waste disposal both become more expensive, the motivation for improvement in efficiency will also increase.

Are there any other issues you feel passionately about or that you are currently working on?

Yes! I am very passionate about the need for sustainable, alternative energy sources that we can produce here in the United States. Renewable energy will be one of the most critical issues facing this generation for several reasons including economical, environmental, and national security factors. Economically, we are spending billions of dollars in other countries for energy imports. Those are dollars that could be spent at home if we had alternative sources of energy available locally. Environmentally, we know that burning fossil fuels is emitting carbon into the atmosphere that has been sequestered underground for millions of years, and the potential negative impacts of that carbon are still being revealed. The national security issue is probably the biggest motivational factor for me. Most people don't realize the level of vulnerability that exists for countries such as ours that import a large percentage of their energy needs. A serious disruption in our energy supply would likely result in economic and political chaos as well as huge negative impacts on our daily lives. The only way to decrease this vulnerability is to produce our own sources of energy.

In addition, there is a finite supply of petroleum resources. Most scientists don't agree on when the supply will run out, but they know that it will. As the resources are diminished and the extraction process becomes more difficult, the price will increase. The dangers of our dependence on oil are not new, but the level of concern seems to rise and fall with gas prices. I hope that we (as a country) don't wait too long before we get serious about finding alternative sources of energy.

A specific area of alternative energy research that I have been involved in is the use of sweet sorghum as a bioenergy feedstock. Sweet sorghum is a crop similar to sugar cane, but it can grow in temperate climates including many regions of the U.S. The juice that is pressed from sweet sorghum stalks contains sugars which can be directly fermented, making it one of the simplest ways to produce fuels such as ethanol. Other advantages of sweet sorghum as a feedstock include its relatively low water and nutrient requirements and its drought tolerance. I have spent several years studying the use of sweet sorghum and I believe it has great potential as a future renewable energy feedstock.

Do you have any thoughts on the growing trend in America to "Go Green"? Can you elaborate on this trend and any possible changes you foresee in the future, particularly regarding Food & Agricultural research?

There is a growing interest in business and production practices that incorporate sustainability. Increasingly, I believe that we will see companies requiring their supply chain partners to demonstrate continuous improvements in sustainability within their organizations. Within the food processing industry we're beginning to see "green" improvements such as biodegradable packaging, buying raw materials locally, and greater use of renewable energy. As the general public becomes more aware, industry will use it as a marketing tool. We don't realize it, but we vote every day with our feet, and with our pocketbooks. As consumers, we provide endorsement and acceptance of products and business practices through our purchases.

What other issues are being researched within the Food & Agricultural Products Research & Technology Center?

Research projects at the FAPC cover a wide array of topics involving the general improvement of the quality, safety and profitability of the food and agricultural products industries. Some of the general areas covered in addition to renewable energy include:

> Food Microbiology—the fate of pathogenic microorganisms during processing
>
> Cereal Chemistry—quality control and value-added processing of cereal grains
>
> Oilseed Processing—development of new uses for oilseed crops

Meat Processing—improving quality and value of meat products

Fruit & Vegetable Processing—new product development from fruits/vegetables

Food Engineering—food process and equipment design and improvement

Agribusiness Economics—economic evaluation and business planning

How can OSU students get involved with research projects related to your field?

Many faculty in Biosystems and Agricultural Engineering as well as faculty and staff within the Food and Agricultural Products Center hire undergraduate students to help with research projects. Students majoring in Biosystems Engineering, Food Engineering, Food Science, and related fields will generally be given preference, but we also hire other majors. If you're interested in a part-time job, stop by a professor's office, or send an email indicating your interest.

What can students do to reduce waste and conserve resources during their very busy schedules while enrolled in college?

I think we can all find opportunities to decrease waste and conserve energy in our everyday lives. Some simple ways that we can all help:

Recycle everything, from aluminum cans to cardboard boxes.

Carpool as often as possible.

Turn the lights (and electronics) off when you leave a room.

Replace incandescent bulbs with compact fluorescent light bulbs.

Don't let water run needlessly. . . . We waste a lot of water.

Check the temperature of your hot water heater.

Set your thermostat up a few degrees in the summer and down in the winter.

Thank you for answering our questions!

"One touch of nature makes the whole world kin." —William Shakespeare

Gorgeously Green Lifestyle Checklist

Sophie Uliano

Sophie Uliano, the ultimate "Green Goddess," is the author of three guidebooks for "gorgeously green" lifestyles. Uliano also has a website (gorgeouslygreen.com) which offers tips for living green daily, from "lean and green diets" to an "eco-friendly dream getaway." The following is a questionnaire from her *New York Times* bestseller, *Gorgeously Green: 8 Simple Steps to an Earth-Friendly Life*. Uliano emphasizes that readers must simply become a little more aware of the way they live so they can make small steps toward living "a simply gorgeous life." Answer the following questions to explore the many ways that you can start practicing earth-friendly living.

(Yes/No Answers)

Your Beauty

1. Do you know what the ingredients are in your cosmetics?
2. Do you ever read the labels on your lotions and creams?
3. Do you know what is in your nail polish?
4. Do you use drugstore hair dye?
5. Do you buy your products from a department store?
6. Do you believe labels that say "natural" or "organic"?

Your Home

1. Do you know what energy-efficient appliances are?
2. Do you buy energy-efficient appliances?
3. Do you know what compact fluorescent light bulbs (CFLs) are?
4. Do you buy CFLs?
5. Do you purchase paper items made from recycled or postconsumer material?
6. Have you ever cleaned your refrigerator coils?
7. Do you shut things off when not using them?
8. Do you unplug appliances and chargers when not using them?
9. Is your thermostat set at 68 degrees Fahrenheit or lower?
10. Is your air conditioner set at 78 degrees Fahrenheit or higher?
11. Is your water heater wrapped?

12. Do you use space heaters?

13. Do you purchase green energy?

14. Do you use your washer/dryer almost every day?

15. Do you ever air-dry your clothes?

16. Do you take your clothes to a regular dry-cleaner?

17. Do you have low-flow toilets and showers?

18. Do you use recycled trash bags?

19. Are you aware of how many bags of trash you generate weekly?

20. Do you use toxic cleaners in your home?

21. Do you chuck used batteries in the trash?

22. Do you know what volatile organic compounds (VOCs) are?

23. Are VOCs present in your home?

24. Have you ever visited a hazardous waste facility?

25. Do you have green houseplants in your home?

26. Do all members of your family try to conserve water?

Your Yard
1. Do you have a garden?

2. Do you grow herbs?

3. Do you know about native plants?

4. Do you grow native plants?

5. Do you use lawn fertilizers?

6. Do you use garden pesticides?

7. Is your garden organic?

8. Do you irrigate your lawn every day?

9. Do you hose your driveway to clean it off?

Your Ride
1. Do you drive an energy-efficient car?

2. If not, are you considering purchasing one?

3. Do you ever carpool?

4. Do you use a reusable mug?

5. Do you drive to the store every day?

6. Do you own a bicycle?

7. When you change your oil, do you recycle it?

8. Do you check your tire pressure once a week?

9. Do you wash your car at home?

Your Shopping

1. Do you buy organic cotton clothes or bed linens?

2. Do you buy clothes not made with sweatshop labor?

3. Do you try to eat locally grown food?

4. Do you eat organic food?

5. Do you try to buy things with less packaging?

6. Do you shop at farmer's markets?

7. Do you buy from small local stores?

8. Do you avoid factory farmed meats?

9. Do you buy organic produce?

10. Do you buy Fair-Trade items?

11. Do you purchase genetically modified organism (GMO)-free food?

12. Do you purchase antibiotic- and hormone-free dairy?

Your Desires

1. Do you wish to become healthier?

2. Do you want to become more vibrant?

3. Do you want to live according to your deepest values?

4. Do you want to feel exhilarated?

5. Are you ready to become Gorgeously Green?

Discussion Questions

1. By reviewing the list of questions that Sophie Uliano asks, what can you tell about her perspective and the audience she is writing to?

2. Once you have answered all of the questions, review your answers. Did you answer "yes" or "no" to most questions? Were there certain categories where you answered "yes" more frequently? How could you make simple changes in your daily habits to change a few answers to "yes"?

3. After taking time to examine this checklist, do one or two questions stand out to you? Perhaps it raises an issue that you are unfamiliar with or one that you would like to know more about. Over the next week, follow up on this topic. Gather information about the particular question you underscored and prepare a brief presentation to deliver to your classmates. Your goal should be to raise consciousness about this particular topic.

4. Do you notice any areas that Uliano's checklist does not highlight? How do you think her goals compare to other environmentalists in this chapter? How might her general concept to take simple steps toward green living be used to tackle global environmental issues?

Truth in Architecture

Joe Myers

Community Spotlight On OSU's North Classroom Building

Established in 1890 as a land grant college and agricultural research station, Oklahoma State University was originally designed on a 1910 formal concept of green space quadrangles that had classroom, research and faculty buildings placed both symmetrically and axially. This design was expanded in 1928 into the Bennett Plan (named for then OSU President Henry G. Bennett), which drew heavily on the Harvard University building and campus design, in an effort to establish Oklahoma State University as the "Harvard of the West." This design continues to influence the appearance of the campus today.

In 2004, OSU began investigating a new campus development plan. By 2006, this had evolved into the Master Plan 2025 titled "Achieving Greatness: Celebrating Tradition, Enhancing Identity and Place," a comprehensive twenty-year plan that will build "on the historic traditions of the planning and architecture of the campus, provide opportunities to enhance identity and place by addressing Points of Entry, Connections, Landmarks and Growth" (Long-Range Facilities Planning).

The North Classroom Building at the corner of Hall of Fame and Monroe Street is not only an example of the Master Plan 2025 moving right on schedule, but represents one of the newest, "greenest" buildings on campus. Upon its opening in January 2009, at a cost of 15 million dollars, the North Classroom Building offered 14 classrooms with 36–48 seats, two 125 seat auditoriums, a student Success Center with study areas (that can be reserved) and the Roots café. Niles Jones with the Oklahoma State University Long-Range Facilities Planning office offered key insight into the process that his office went through when designing the building. "If you notice, we were very cognizant of 'green technology' in our planning and incorporated cutting edge expertise that at the time of design and construction was not part of mandatory LEED Certification (Leadership in Energy & Environmental Design) of buildings today." Jones pointed out that key design elements, such as chimneys, were incorporated, though no fireplaces exist in the building—they are used to route out essential venting (heating, bathroom, etc.) so that a functional aesthetic is achieved. This extended to the dormers (small attic windows) on the roof, as well. The east-facing dormers operate as additional venting, while the west-facing dormers are open to allow daylight into the building. Energy efficient lighting that can be remotely activated, coupled with large, low e-value, argon-filled, double-pane glass offers increased natural light with a reduction in heat gain within the building. This combined with "fritted" glass (outward facing reflective dots) on the south and west sides of the building aid in light capture and heat reduction. The inset for the first floor, along the south and west side of the building, that results in the covered walkway overhang, was incorporated to increase available light while vastly reducing heat capture within the Student Success Center and Roots Café.

Established by the United States Green Building Council, LEED is an internationally recognized green building certification system, providing third-party verification that a building or community was designed and built using strategies aimed at improving performance across all the metrics that matter most: energy savings, water efficiency, CO_2 emissions reduction, improved indoor environmental quality, and stewardship of resources and sensitivity to their impacts (USGBC.org). To incorporate the LEED Certification mandates into the construction meant that the North Classroom Building had to be located on a public transportation path, must have bike racks, utilize the highest efficiency HVAC (Heating/Ventilation/Air Conditioning), low flow toilets and show a demonstrated return on investment within five years of opening that offsets the increased cost of construction. By designing in this "green" fashion, students at Oklahoma State University are the beneficiaries of truth in architecture that will be incorporated into all future construction and expansion, such as the Student Union renovations that will be completed in 2012.

Waste Not, Want Not

Bill McKibben

Bill McKibben is a leading environmentalist and author of dozens of books about the environment. He is a founder of the grassroots climate campaign 350.org, which has coordinated 15,000 rallies in 189 countries since 2009. In this brief article, McKibben fiercely tackles controversial topics such as the excesses of the American lifestyle, global warming, and the war in Iraq while calling out Congress, Wal-Mart, Barack Obama, and even the average Joe Consumer.

ONCE A YEAR OR SO, it's my turn to run recycling day for our tiny town. Saturday morning, 9 to 12, a steady stream of people show up to sort out their plastics (No. 1, No. 2, etc.), their corrugated cardboard (flattened, please), their glass (and their returnable glass, which goes to benefit the elementary school), their Styrofoam peanuts, their paper, their cans. It's quite satisfying—everything in its place.

But it's also kind of disturbing, this waste stream. For one, a town of 550 sure generates a lot—a trailer load every couple of weeks. Sometimes you have to put a kid into the bin and tell her to jump up and down so the lid can close.

More than that, though, so much of it seems utterly unnecessary. Not just waste, but wasteful. Plastic water bottles, one after another—80 million of them get tossed every day. The ones I'm stomping down are being "recycled," but so what? In a country where almost everyone has access to clean drinking water, they define waste to begin with. I mean, you don't have a mug? In fact, once you start thinking about it, the category of "waste" begins to expand, until it includes an alarming percentage of our economy. Let's do some intellectual sorting:

There's old-fashioned waste, the dangerous, sooty kind. You're making something useful, but you're not using the latest technology, and so you're spewing particulates into the air, or maybe sewage into the water. You wish to keep doing it, because it's cheap, and you block any regulation that might interfere with your right to spew. This is the kind of waste that's easy to attack; it's obvious and obnoxious and a lot of it falls under the Clean Air Act and Clean Water Act and so on. There's actually less of this kind of waste than there used to be—that's why we can swim in most of our rivers again.

There's waste that comes from everything operating as it should, only too much so. If carbon monoxide (carbon with one oxygen atom) exemplifies pollution of the first type, then carbon dioxide (carbon with two oxygen atoms) typifies the second. Carbon monoxide poisons you in your garage and turns Beijing's air brown, but if you put a catalytic converter on your tailpipe it all but disappears. Carbon dioxide doesn't do anything to you directly—a clean-burning engine used to be defined as one that released only CO_2 and water vapor—but in sufficient quantity it melts the ice caps, converts grassland into desert, and turns every coastal city into New Orleans.

There's waste that comes from doing something that manifestly doesn't need doing. A hundred million trees are cut every year just to satisfy the junk-mail industry. You can argue about cutting trees for newspapers, or magazines, or Bibles, or symphony scores—but the cascade of stuffporn that arrives daily in our mailboxes? It wastes forests, and also our time. Which, actually, is precious—we each get about 30,000 days, and it makes one a little sick to calculate how many of them have been spent opening credit card offers.

Or think about what we've done with cars. From 1975 to 1985, fuel efficiency for the average new car improved from 14 to 28 miles per gallon. Then we stopped worrying about oil and put all that engineering talent to work on torque. In the mid-1980s, the typical car accelerated from 0 to 60 mph in 14.5 seconds. Today's average (even though vehicles are much heavier) is 9.5 seconds. But it's barely legal to accelerate like that, and it makes you look like an idiot, or a teenager.

Then there's the waste that comes with doing something maybe perhaps vaguely useful when you could be doing something actually useful instead. For instance: Congress is being lobbied really, really hard to fork over billions of dollars to the nuclear industry, on the premise that it will fight global warming. There is, of course, that little matter of nuclear waste—but lay that aside (in Nevada or someplace). The greater problem is the wasted opportunity: That money could go to improving efficiency, which can produce the same carbon reductions for about a fifth of the price.

Our wasteful habits wouldn't matter much if there were just a few of us—a Neanderthal hunting band could have discarded six plastic water bottles apiece every day with no real effect except someday puzzling anthropologists. But the volumes we manage are something else. Chris Jordan is the photographer laureate of waste—his most recent project, "Running the Numbers," uses exquisite images to show the 106,000 aluminum cans Americans toss every 30 seconds, or the 1 million plastic cups distributed on US airline flights every 6 hours, or the 2 million plastic beverage bottles we run through every 5 minutes, or the 426,000 cell phones we discard every day, or the 1.14 million brown paper supermarket bags we use each hour, or the 60,000 plastic bags we use every 5 seconds, or the 15 million sheets of office paper we use every 5 minutes, or the 170,000 Energizer batteries produced every 15 minutes. The simple amount of stuff it takes—energy especially—to manage this kind of throughput makes it daunting to even think about our waste problem. (Meanwhile, the next time someone tells you that population is at the root of our troubles, remind them that the average American uses more energy between the stroke of midnight on New Year's Eve and dinner on January 2 than the average, say, Tanzanian consumes in a year. Population matters, but it really matters when you multiply it by proximity to Costco.)

Would you like me to go on? Americans discard enough aluminum to rebuild our entire commercial air fleet every three months—and aluminum represents less than 1 percent of our solid waste stream. We toss 14 percent of the food we buy at the store. More than 46,000 pieces of plastic debris float on each square mile of ocean. And—oh, forget it.

These kinds of numbers get in the way of figuring out how much we really waste. In recent years, for instance, 40 percent of Harvard graduates have gone into finance, consulting, and business. They had just spent four years with the world's greatest library, some of its finest museum collections, an unparalleled assemblage of Nobel-quality scholars, and all they wanted to do was go to lower Manhattan and stare into computer screens. What a waste! And when they got to Wall Street, of course, they figured out extravagant ways to waste the life savings of millions of Americans, which in turn required the waste of taxpayer dollars to bail them out, money that could have been spent on completely useful things: trains to get us where we want to go—say, new national parks.

Perhaps the only kind of waste we've gotten good at cutting is the kind we least needed to eliminate: An entire industry of consultants survives on telling companies how to get rid of inefficiencies—which generally means people. And an entire class of politicians survives by railing about government waste, which also ends up meaning programs for people: Health care for poor children, what a boondoggle.

Want to talk about government waste? We're going to end up spending north of a trillion dollars on the war in Iraq, which will go down as one of the larger wastes of money—and lives—in our history. But we spend more than half a trillion a year on the military anyway, more than the next 10 nations combined. That almost defines profligacy.

We've gotten away with all of this for a long time because we had margin, all kinds of margin. Money, for sure—we were the richest nation on Earth, and when we wanted more we just borrowed it from China. But margin in other ways as well: We landed on a continent with topsoil more than a foot thick across its vast interior, so the fact that we immediately started to waste it with inefficient plowing hardly mattered. We inherited an atmosphere that could buffer our emissions for the first 150 years of the Industrial Revolution. We somehow got away with wasting the talents of black people and women and gay folks.

But our margin is gone. We're out of cash, we're out of atmosphere, we're out of luck. The current economic carnage is what happens when you waste—when the CEO of Merrill Lynch thinks he needs a $35,000 commode, when the CEO of Tyco thinks it would be fun to spend a million dollars on his wife's birthday party, complete with an ice sculpture of Michelangelo's *David* peeing vodka. The melted Arctic ice cap is what you get when everyone in America thinks he requires the kind of vehicle that might make sense for a forest ranger.

Getting out of the fix we're in—if it's still possible—requires in part that we relearn some very old lessons. We were once famously thrifty: Yankee frugality, straightening bent nails, saving string. We used to have a holiday, Thrift Week, which began on Ben Franklin's birthday: "Beware of little expenses; a small leak will sink a great ship," said he. We disapproved of frippery, couldn't imagine wasting money on ourselves, made do or did without. It took a mighty effort to make us what we are today—in fact, it took a mighty industry, advertising, which soaks up plenty more of those Harvard grads and represents an almost total waste.

In the end, we built an economy that depended on waste, and boundless waste is what it has produced. And the really sad part is, it felt that way, too. Making enough money to build houses with rooms we never used, and cars with engines we had no need of, meant wasting endless hours at work. Which meant that we had, on average, one-third fewer friends than our parents' generation. What waste that! "Getting and spending, we lay waste our powers," wrote Wordsworth. We can't say we weren't warned.

The economic mess now transfixing us will mean some kind of change. We can try to hang on to the status quo—living a Wal-Mart life so we can buy cheaply enough to keep the stream of stuff coming. Or we can say uncle. There are all kinds of experiments in postwaste living springing up: Freecycling, and Craigslisting, and dumpster diving, and car sharing (those unoccupied seats in your vehicle—what a waste!), and open sourcing. We're sharing buses, and going to the library in greater numbers. Economists keep hoping we'll figure out a way to revert—that we'll waste a little more, and pull us out of the economic doldrums. But the psychological tide suddenly runs the other way.

We may have waited too long—we may have wasted our last good chance. It's possible the planet will keep warming and the economy keep sinking no matter what. But perhaps not—and we seem ready to shoot for something nobler than the hyperconsumerism that's wasted so much of the last few decades. Barack Obama said he would "call out" the nation's mayors if they wasted their stimulus money. That's the mood we're in, and it's about time.

Running the Numbers looks at Contemporary American culture through the austere lens of statistics. Chris Jordan states, "My hope is that images representing these quantities might have a different effect than the raw numbers alone.…This project visually examines these vast and bizarre measures of our society, in large intricately detailed prints assembled from thousands of smaller photographs.

www.**chrisjordan**.com/current_set2.php

The **U.S. Environmental Protection Agency's mission** is to protect human health and the environment. EPA submitted the **FY 2011–2015 Strategic Plan** on September 30, 2010 to the Congress and to the Office of Management and Budget.

According to the EPA, "The Plan identifies the measurable environmental and human health outcomes the public can expect over the next five years and describes how we intend to achieve those results. The Plan represents a commitment to our core values of science, transparency, and the rule of law in managing our programs."

http://www.epa.gov/planandbudget/strategicplan.html

Discussion Questions

1. Bill McKibben describes many different types of "waste." Review the article and list as many as you can. How do the types of waste differ? What are the impacts of each? What do these wastes mean for our culture?

2. McKibben states, "Population matters, but it *really* matters when you multiply it by proximity to Costco." What do you make of McKibben's assertion that as of now, growth is an inherent component of America's economy? Can you imagine a world where economic growth isn't sought? What do you think would have to happen for that to be feasible?

3. McKibben is known for his hard-hitting commentary on American consumption and corruption. Underline the statements you found to be most extreme, and consider why they stood out to you. Be prepared to share your comments with other class members.

4. This article is littered (so to speak) with statistics, outside references, and bold arguments. Follow up on one aspect of McKibben's essay by conducting Internet research. Write a short summary of what you examined.

5. Compare McKibben's official website (billmckibben.com) with Sophie Uliano's website (gorgeouslygreen.com). Be sure to consider audience and tone. In what ways are their goals similar? How are they different? Which author do you find more effective in making the point that conservation and consciousness must be addressed?

6. In McKibben's latest book, *Eaarth: Making a Life on a Tough New Planet*, he argues that we have waited too long to stop the advance of global warming, and massive change is not only unavoidable but already underway. Research and write a two page review of the global ecological changes that you noted since this essay was published in 2009. What weather-related disasters have accompanied these changes? Have global efforts to take dramatic action been effective? Why or why not?

Where I Lived, and What I Lived For

Henry David Thoreau

The following is an excerpt from "Where I Lived, and What I Lived For," the second chapter of Henry David Thoreau's *Walden; or, Life in the Woods. Walden* describes a two-year period in Thoreau's life from March 1845 to September 1847. From the Fourth of July, the author retired from town to live alone at Walden Pond. Much of *Walden's* material was derived from his journals which can be read as a reflection upon simple living in harmony with natural surroundings.

We must learn to reawaken and keep ourselves awake, not by mechanical aids, but by an infinite expectation of the dawn, which does not forsake us in our soundest sleep. I know of no more encouraging fact than the un-questionable ability of man to elevate his life by a conscious endeavor. It is something to be able to paint a particular picture, or to carve a statue, and so to make a few objects beautiful; but it is far more glorious to carve and paint the very atmosphere and medium through which we look, which morally we can do. To affect the quality of the day, that is the highest of arts. Every man is tasked to make his life, even in its details, worthy of the contemplation of his most elevated and critical hour. If we refused, or rather used up, such paltry information as we get, the oracles would dis-tinctly inform us how this might be done.

I went to the woods because I wished to live deliberately, to front only the essential facts of life, and see if I could not learn what it had to teach, and not, when I came to die, discover that I had not lived. I did not wish to live what was not life, living is so dear; nor did I wish to practice resigna-tion, unless it was quite necessary. I wanted to live deep and suck out all the marrow of life, to live so sturdily and Spartan-like as to put to rout all that was not life, to cut a broad swath and shave close, to drive life into a corner, and reduce it to its lowest terms, and, if it proved to be mean, why then to get the whole and genuine meanness of it, and publish its mean-ness to the world; or if it were sublime, to know it by experience, and be able to give a true account of it in my next excursion. For most men, it ap-pears to me, are in a strange uncertainty about it, whether it is of the devil or of God, and have *somewhat hastily* concluded that it is the chief end of man here to "glorify God and enjoy him forever."

Still we live meanly, like ants; though the fable tells us that we were long ago changed into men; like pygmies we fight with cranes; it is error upon error, and clout upon clout, and our best virtue has for its occasion a su-perfluous and evitable wretchedness. Our life is frittered away by detail. An honest man has hardly need to count more than his ten fingers, or in extreme cases he may add his ten toes, and lump the rest. Simplicity, simplicity, simplicity! I say, let your affairs be as two or three, and not a hundred or a thousand; instead of a million count half a dozen, and keep your accounts on your thumb-nail. In the midst of this chopping sea of civilized life, such are the clouds and storms and quicksands and thousand-and-one items to be allowed for, that a man has to live, if he would not founder and go to the bottom and not make his port at all, by dead reckoning, and he must be a great calculator indeed who succeeds. Simplify, simplify. Instead of three meals a day, if it be necessary eat but one; instead of a hundred dishes, five; and reduce other things in proportion. Our life is like a German Confederacy, made up of petty states, with its boundary forever fluctuating, so that even a German cannot tell you how it is bounded at any moment. The nation itself, with all its so-called internal improvements, which, by the way are all external and superficial, is just such an unwieldy and overgrown establishment, cluttered with furniture and tripped up by its own traps, ruined by luxury and heedless expense, by want of calculation and a worthy aim, as the million households in the land; and the only cure for it, as for them, is in a rigid economy, a stern and more than Spartan simplicity of life and elevation of purpose. It lives too fast. Men think that it is essential that the *Nation* have commerce, and export ice, and talk through a telegraph, and ride thirty miles an hour, without a doubt, whether *they* do or not; but whether we should live like baboons or like men, is a little uncertain. If we do not get out sleepers, and forge rails, and devote days and nights to the work, but go to tinkering upon our *lives* to improve *them*, who will build railroads? And if railroads are not built, how shall we get to heaven in season? But if we stay at home and mind our business, who will want railroads? We do not ride on the railroad; it rides upon us. Did you ever think what those sleepers are that underlie the railroad? Each one is a man, an Irishman, or a Yankee man. The rails are laid on them, and they are covered with sand, and the cars run smoothly over them. They are sound sleepers, I assure you. And every few years a new lot is laid down and run over; so that, if some have the pleasure of riding on a rail, others have the misfortune to be ridden upon. And when they run over a man that is walking in his sleep, a supernumerary sleeper in the wrong position, and wake him up, they suddenly stop the cars, and make a hue and cry about it, as if this were an exception. I am glad to know that it takes a gang of men for every five miles to keep the sleepers down and level in their beds as it is, for this is a sign that they may sometime get up again.

Why should we live with such hurry and waste of life? We are determined to be starved before we are hungry. Men say that a stitch in time saves nine, and so they take a thousand stitches today to save nine tomorrow. As for *work*, we haven't any of any consequence. We have the Saint Vitus' dance, and cannot possibly keep our heads still. If I should only give a few pulls at the parish bell-rope, as for a fire, that is, without setting the bell, there is hardly a man on his farm in the outskirts of Concord, notwithstanding that press of engagements which was his excuse so many times this morning, nor a boy, nor a woman, I might almost say, but would forsake all and follow that sound, not mainly to save property from the flames, but, if we will confess the truth, much more to see it burn, since burn it must, and we, be it known, did not set it on fire—or to see it put out, and have a hand in it, if that is done as handsomely; yes, even if it were the parish church itself. Hardly a man takes a half-hour's nap after dinner, but when he wakes he holds up his head and asks, "What's the news?" as if the rest of mankind had stood his sentinels. Some give directions to be waked every half-hour, doubtless for no other purpose; and then, to pay for it, they tell what they have dreamed. After a night's sleep the news is as indispensable as the breakfast. "Pray tell me anything new that has happened to a man anywhere on this globe"—and he reads it over his coffee and rolls, that a man has had his eyes gouged out this morning on the Wachito River; never dreaming the while that he lives in the dark unfathomed mammoth cave of this world, and has but the rudiment of an eye himself.

Discussion Questions

1. Henry David Thoreau's *Walden* was published in 1854. Do you consider his message to be a palpable influence even for today's American mindset? Name three Americans that reflect the same attitudes toward self-sufficiency and simple living.

2. Thoreau was known as a Transcendentalist. Research this philosophy. What are your initial thoughts about this 19th century American movement? Write a short overview comparing transcendentalism's core beliefs with the current surge to go green.

3. What does Thoreau mean when he writes, "We do not ride on the railroad; it rides upon us"? In what ways can you apply this same sentiment to contemporary American society?

4. Thoreau's dictum "simplify, simplify" speaks to the culture of waste described by McKibben. What differences do you see in Thoreau's approach? Whose approach do you see as most persuasive?

5. Spend a little time looking up Thoreau's biography and try to understand why he chose to retreat from civilization. Do you see any benefits from his decision? Would you ever consider choosing a similar lifestyle? What unique challenges would you face in doing so in 21st century America?

Into the Wild

Into the Wild is a 1996 non-fiction book written by Jon Krakauer. It is an expansion of Krakauer's 9,000-word article on Christopher McCandless titled "Death of an Innocent," which appeared in the January 1993 issue of *Outside*. The book was adapted into a 2007 movie of the same name directed by Sean Penn with Emile Hirsch starring as McCandless.

You can watch a preview and clips of the video at www.intothewild.com.

After reviewing McCandless's experience, do you think he was merely "looking for adventure" by traveling to Alaska? In what ways are Thoreau and McCandless similar? How do their quests differ?

A New Beginning

Joe Myers

Community Spotlight on OSU's Botanical Garden and Arboretum

Located just north of Highway 51 and Sangre Road, visitors will find the Oklahoma State University Botanical Garden and Arboretum, home to the OETA television show *Oklahoma Gardening*. Operating since its inception in 1935, the arboretum functions as both an outdoor classroom and laboratory for agriculture extension research. In 2005, a new twenty-five year master plan was unveiled that will transform the 100 acre facility into the Integrated Environmental Research and Education Site or IERES, pronounced 'Iris'. The mission for the Oklahoma State University IERES is to be one of the most comprehensive collections of environmentally sensitive and energy efficient practices in Oklahoma and the Great Plains, providing programs for academic and public education as well as multidisciplinary research.

June of 2011 will usher in the grand opening of the new main gate along Highway 51, between Stillwater Creek and Cow Creek, and the entry drive flanked by a double row of sycamore trees leading to the updated parking facilities. "We sought input from many different groups of people during the planning process. Some of the participants included K-12 and college students, OSU faculty and administration, public school teachers from within and outside Stillwater, city employees, the Chamber of Commerce, OSUBG Ambassadors, and representatives from our OBG member gardens," said Dr. Dale Maronek, Head of the Department of Horticulture and Landscape Architecture and Director of the OSU Botanical Garden.

The vision for IERES includes a living laboratory where visitors discover the world of plants; a gathering place that accommodates a range of activities, from learning to recreation to community events and celebrations; and a place of refuge for people seeking peace, solitude and contemplation. All of this will be accomplished while the Botanical Garden conducts research, disseminates information, and provides educational programs that stimulate and encourage the appreciation, conservation, and utilization of plants by the people of Oklahoma. The garden, when completed, is designed to accommodate about 100,000 visitors per year.

IERES will address a variety of urban riparian and natural resource issues using an integrated system that demonstrates appropriately designed, sustainable, attractive, and energy efficient landscape practices/applications.

These practices will include pollution mitigation, stream bank stabilization measures, habitat preservation, stormwater management systems addressing erosion control, ground water recharge using porous surfaces, and water capture/reuse/redistribution/conservation. Partnerships with State and Federal agencies, corporations, and scientists in plant, engineering and environmental sciences will provide a capacity to efficiently plan, design, build and manage development, preserve critical resources, enhance quality of life and promote economic sustainability. Currently unavailable in the Midwest, this one-stop facility will serve a multi-state area by illustrating individual and comprehensive integrated landscape applications for a variety of environmental Best Management Practices.

Once fully operational, the IERES will feature an energy efficient and environmentally friendly "green cottage." This facility will serve as a prototype for area and residential developers trying to gain a competitive edge in today's soaring energy market while playing an important role in resource/landscape management, environmental planning and water reuse. Featuring a variety of landscape and engineering practices that address stormwater mitigation (bioretention, pervious pavements, vegetative filter, etc.), and the site will become a national asset that accommodates plant, landscape, and sustainable research efforts to capture, reuse and recharge precious water resources. A hub for academic, municipal and public education programs, the "green cottage" will demonstrate and promote successful integration of required energy infrastructure, conservation and landscape planning within a community. Careful attention will be given to "green" construction materials and methods. An adjacent Utility Garden containing native heat and drought resistant plants and landscape features will highlight various ways to screen unsightly structures through appropriate construction, plant utilization and planting strategies.

Finally, while educating city leaders, industry employees, students, and citizens, the IERES will offer excellent opportunities to enjoy the natural landscape of Oklahoma. A trail built along an enhanced riparian corridor will connect to Stillwater's existing trail system, linking the public to natural areas, cultivated ornamental display gardens, landscape construction/application gardens, prairie landscapes and learning stations that explain environmental components of the IERES system.

Directions to OSU Botanical Garden

Home to *Oklahoma Gardening* Studio Grounds
From Highway 51 & Sangre Road, 1/2 mile north, 1/4 mile east, south side of the road.

Oklahoma Gardening studio grounds is located inside the OSU Botanical Garden.

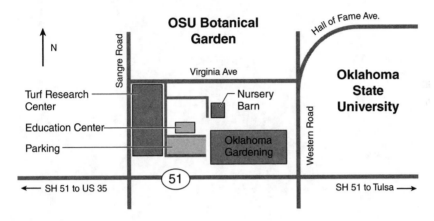

Open House
Open the 1st & 3rd Saturdays May through October, 9 a.m. until 3 p.m.

Guided Tours
For groups of 8 or more call 405-744-5404.
Available days & times are: M-T-Th-F, 8:30 a.m.–4 p.m.

If you are visiting after 5 p.m. or the weekend other than the "Open House" days and times, we recommend that you park across the road to the north and use the walk through gates. This may keep one from becoming locked within the arboretum. Thank you for your assistance!

Visitors are welcome to visit the gardens from sunrise to sunset.

The gardens are now under video surveillance.

The Great Horse-Manure Crisis of 1894

Stephen Davies

Stephen Davies is the academic director at the Institute of Economic Affairs in London. The following essay was posted to *The Freeman: Ideas on Liberty* in September 2004. The magazine is the flagship publication of the Foundation for Economic Education which reports on the ideals of free society and the "consequences and contradictions that inevitably result from collectivism, interventionism, and the welfare state." In the following essay, Davies comments on human integrity and the economic incentives that drive societal change.

We commonly read or hear reports to the effect that "If trend X continues, the result will be disaster." The subject can be almost anything, but the pattern of these stories is identical. These reports take a current trend and extrapolate it into the future as the basis for their gloomy prognostications. The conclusion is, to quote a character from a famous British sitcom, "We're doomed, I tell you. We're doomed!" Unless, that is, we mend our ways according to the author's prescription. This almost invariably involves restrictions on personal liberty.

These prophets of doom rely on one thing—that their audience will not check the record of such predictions. In fact, the history of prophecy is one of failure and oversight. Many predictions (usually of doom) have not come to pass, while other things have happened that nobody foresaw. Even brief research will turn up numerous examples of both, such as the many predictions in the 1930s—about a decade before the baby boom began—that the populations of most Western countries were about to enter a terminal decline. In other cases, people have made predictions that have turned out to be laughably overmodest, such as the nineteenth-century editor's much-ridiculed forecast that by 1950 every *town* in America would have a telephone, or Bill Gates's remark a few years ago that 64 kilobytes of memory is enough for anyone.

The fundamental problem with most predictions of this kind, and particularly the gloomy ones, is that they make a critical, false assumption: that things will go on as they are. This assumption in turn comes from overlooking one of the basic insights of economics: that people respond to incentives. In a system of free exchange, people receive all kinds of signals that lead them to solve problems. The prophets of doom come to their despondent conclusions because in their world, nobody has any kind of creativity or independence of thought—except for themselves of course.

A classic example of this is a problem that was getting steadily worse about a hundred years ago, so much so that it drove most observers to despair. This was the great horse-manure crisis.

Nineteenth-century cities depended on thousands of horses for their daily functioning. All transport, whether of goods or people, was drawn by horses. London in 1900 had 11,000 cabs, all horse-powered. There were also several thousand buses, each of which required 12 horses per day, a total of more than 50,000 horses. In addition, there were countless carts, drays, and wains, all working constantly to deliver the goods needed by the rapidly growing population of what was then the largest city in the world. Similar figures could be produced for any great city of the time.*

The problem of course was that all these horses produced huge amounts of manure. A horse will on average produce between 15 and 35 pounds of manure per day. Consequently, the streets of nineteenth-century cities were covered by horse manure. This in turn attracted huge numbers of flies, and the dried and ground-up manure was blown everywhere. In New York in 1900, the population of 100,000 horses produced 2.5 million pounds of horse manure per day, which all had to be swept up and disposed of. (See Edwin G. Burrows and Mike Wallace, *Gotham: A History of New York City to 1898* [New York: Oxford University Press, 1999]).

In 1898 the first international urban-planning conference convened in New York. It was abandoned after three days, instead of the scheduled ten, because none of the delegates could see any solution to the growing crisis posed by urban horses and their output.

The problem did indeed seem intractable. The larger and richer that cities became, the more horses they needed to function. The more horses, the more manure. Writing in the *Times* of London in 1894, one writer estimated that in 50 years every street in London would be buried under nine feet of manure. Moreover, all these horses had to be stabled, which used up ever-larger areas of increasingly valuable land. And as the number of horses grew, ever-more land had to be devoted to producing hay to feed them (rather than producing food for people), and this had to be brought into cities and distributed—by horse-drawn vehicles. It seemed that urban civilization was doomed.

Crisis Vanished

Of course, urban civilization was not buried in manure. The great crisis vanished when millions of horses were replaced by motor vehicles. This was possible because of the ingenuity of inventors and entrepreneurs such as Gottlieb Daimler and Henry Ford, and a system that gave them the freedom to put their ideas into practice. Even more important, however, was the existence of the price mechanism. The problems described earlier meant that the price of horse-drawn transport rose steadily as the cost of feeding and housing horses increased. This created strong incentives for people to find alternatives.

No doubt in the Paleolithic era there was panic about the growing exhaustion of flint supplies. Somehow the great flint crisis, like the great horse-manure crisis, never came to pass.

The closest modern counterpart to the late nineteenth-century panic about horse manure is agitation about the future course of oil prices. The price of crude oil is rising, partly due to political uncertainty, but primarily because of rapid growth in China and India. This has led to a spate of articles predicting that oil production will soon peak, that prices will rise, and that, given the central part played by oil products in the modern economy, we are facing intractable problems. We're doomed!

What this misses is that in a competitive market economy, as any resource becomes more costly, human ingenuity will find alternatives.

We should draw two lessons from this. First, human beings, left to their own devices, will usually find solutions to problems, but only if they are allowed to; that is, if they have economic institutions, such as property rights and free exchange, that create the right incentives and give them the freedom to respond. If these are absent or are replaced by political mechanisms, problems will not be solved.

Second, the sheer difficulty of predicting the future, and in particular of foreseeing the outcome of human creativity, is yet another reason for rejecting the planning or controlling of people's choices. Above all, we should reject the currently fashionable "precautionary principle," which would forbid the use of any technology until proved absolutely harmless.

Left to themselves, our grandparents solved the great horse-manure problem. If things had been left to the urban planners, they would almost certainly have turned out worse.

*See Joel Tarr and Clay McShane, "The Centrality of the Horse to the Nineteenth Century American City," in Raymond Mohl, ed., *The Making of Urban America* (New York: SR Publishers, 1997), pp. 105–30. See also Ralph Turvey, "Work Horses in Victorian London" at www.turvey.demon. co.uk.

Discussion Questions

1. If you had to summarize Stephen Davies' main argument in this article, how would you do so? What kinds of assumptions are made by Davies about his audience? How does he relate his tone and attitude to his overall argument?

2. Davies' article describes the problems that resulted from the sheer number of horses in cities during the nineteenth century. Review the textbox on page 367 entitled "Running the Numbers." Visit Chris Jordan's website and consider the visual argument Jordan is making with his art. List the multiple consequences that might result from the quantity of waste products that Jordan presents. What alternatives can you think of to cause this 21st century waste crisis to vanish?

3. Visit *The Freeman* website at http://www.thefreemanonline. org/. Find the above article posted in Volume 54, Issue 7. Read the comments posted by readers and write a one page response.

4. If Davies and McKibben were in a room together, they would no doubt disagree. Create a conversation between them. How might they agree that today's situation is different than the horse-manure crisis of 1894? How might Davies assert that they are the same?

5. Davies calls attention to "prophets of doom" that rely on their audience's failure to follow up on predictions. Review the various voices of environmentalism in this unit and their predictions. Then, conduct brief Internet research in which you locate one of the "numerous examples" of past predictions that have failed to come to fruition or that no one foresaw.

Going Broke By Going Green

Obama Administration energy policies are impairing our jobs, revenues, economy and health

Bishop Harry Jackson, Jr., Niger Innis

This article was posted to CFACT News on *January 14, 2011*. Bishop Harry Jackson, Jr. and Niger Innis are co-chairs of the *Affordable Power Alliance*, a humanitarian coalition of civil rights, minority, small business, senior citizen and faith-based organizations that champion access to reliable, affordable energy. In this article they expose the negative effects of going green.

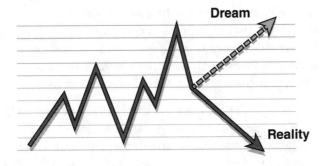

President Obama's healthcare program came under intense scrutiny in 2010. As we enter 2011, we need to open our eyes to what is really going on behind his green energy propaganda, as well. To some, it may not seem as desperate an issue as healthcare, but it will grow to become just as devastating to those citizens among us who are poor, because access to affordable energy affects everything we do.

The administration's green policies are being thrust into a precarious American economy. Every "green scenario" shows raised energy costs across the board. Not only will the average person pay more for energy; many will lose their jobs as the forced transition to alternative power sources rocks the stability of current energy-producing and energy-using companies.

Skyrocketing energy prices and lost jobs also mean millions of otherwise healthy Americans are subjected to new health threats: higher air conditioning, heating, transportation and other energy bills. For those who cannot afford the increased costs, this can mean death from heat stroke and hypothermia; reduced budgets for healthy food, proper healthcare, home and car repairs, college, retirement, and charitable giving; and psychological depression that accompanies economic depression.

Land withdrawals and leasing and permitting delays don't just lock up vast energy storehouses. They kill jobs, eliminate billions in government bonus, rent, royalty and tax revenues—and force us to spend other billions to import more oil that we could produce right here at home.

The White House agenda represents a double power grab. It usurps state, local and private sector control over energy prices and generation, and gives it to unelected Washington bureaucrats. It also seizes our reliable, affordable energy, and replaces it with expensive, intermittent power.

While many Americans are duped into thinking renewable energy sources are the ticket to a clean world, they have not looked at the downside to these energy sources. Replacing fossil fuel power with coerced renewable energy means millions of acres will be covered with turbines and solar panels, and built with billions of tons of concrete, steel, copper, fiberglass and rare earth metals. It means millions of acres of forest and crop land will be converted to farming for inefficient biofuels that also require vast inputs of water, pesticides, fertilizers and hydrocarbon fuels.

Moreover, wind and solar facilities work only 10–30 percent of the time, compared to 90–95 percent for coal, gas and nuclear power plants. Even worse, prolonged cold is almost invariably associated with high atmospheric pressure, and thus very little wind. On December 21, 2010—one of the coldest days on record for Yorkshire, England (undoubtedly due to global warming)—the region's coal, gas and nuclear power plants generated 53,000 megawatts of electricity; its wind turbines provided a measly 20 MW, or 0.04% of the total. The same high pressure, no wind scenario happens on the hottest summer days.

"Renewable" and "clean" energy projects received $30 billion in subsidies under the gargantuan stimulus bill. They got another $3 billion in the "lame duck" tax deal. Federal wind power subsidies are $6.44 per million BTUs—dozens of times what coal and natural gas receive, to generate 1/50 of the electricity that coal does. At current and foreseeable coal and gas prices, wind (and solar) simply cannot compete.

As to "green" jobs, Competitive Enterprise Institute energy analyst Chris Horner calculates that the stimulus bill's subsidies for wind and solar mean taxpayers are billed $475,000 for each job created. Texas Comptroller Susan Combs reports that property tax breaks for wind projects in her state cost nearly $1.6 million per job. "Green energy" is simply unsustainable, environmentally and economically.

President Obama and EPA Administrator Lisa Jackson may be convinced that we face a manmade climate change crisis, and unacceptable health risks from power plant and refinery emissions. However, their "climate science" is little more than a self-proving theory: no matter what happens—hotter or colder, wetter or drier, more storms or fewer—it's "proof" of global warming.

Thousands of scientists say there is yet no real evidence that we face such a crisis, and most coal-fired power plants and refineries have already reduced their harmful emissions to the point that only the most sensitive or health-impaired would be harmed.

The problem is not runaway global warming. It is a runaway and unaccountable federal bureaucracy.

Putting the green power grab into even sharper focus are these eye-opening comments from two "socially responsible" CEOs, who have lobbied the Congress, EPA and White House intensely for cap-tax-and-trade, far tougher emission policies and still more subsidies. We thank the *Wall Street Journal* for bringing them to our attention.

EPA's regulations "increase operating costs for coal-fired generators and ultimately increase the price of energy" for families and companies that need electricity, observed Exelon CEO John Rowe. "The upside for Exelon is unmistakable. Exelon's clean [mostly nuclear] generation will continue to grow in value in a relatively short time. We are of course positioning our portfolio to capture that value."

"Even without legislation in Congress, EPA is marching forward in terms of regulating carbon dioxide," noted Lewis Hay, CEO of NextEra Energy, America's largest producer of wind and solar power. "That puts us in a very good position."

The *Journal* summarized the situation succinctly in a recent editorial: "The EPA is abusing environmental law to achieve policy goals that the democratic process rejected, while also engineering a transfer of wealth from the 25 states in the Midwest and South that get more than 50 percent of their electricity from coal. The industry beneficiaries [of these destructive regulations] then pretend that this agenda is nothing more than a stroll around Walden Pond, when it's really about lining their own pockets."

It is time to face reality. Misnamed "green energy" policies severely undermine any opportunity America may have to rebuild her economy. Perpetuating current jobless rates would be just the tip of the iceberg if we follow the path that EPA and the White House have laid in front of us.

Let your legislators know that you do not support the White House's current green programs. We cannot afford to go broke trying to go green.

Discussion Questions

1. According to Bishop Harry Jackson, Jr. and Niger Innis, what are the consequences of going green? Do you agree or disagree with their argument? What values do these authors hold?

2. Jackson and Innis claim: "The problem is not runaway global warming. It is a runaway and unaccountable federal bureaucracy." After reviewing this statement closely, do you agree or disagree with them that these issues might be mutually exclusive?

3. Visit CFACT.org online. Review the organization's statement of purpose. What perspective does the Committee For a Constructive Tomorrow bring to the current conversations on today's global challenges? Do you consider this to be a credible source? Why or why not?

4. Jackson and Innis are very suspicious of any government plan to improve the environment. What might they think about Uliano's personal strategy? Write a one page response and be prepared to support your opinion during class discussion.

5. Hone in on one of the statements made in this article. Research and test the validity of the argument made. For example, Jackson and Innis begin this article by stating, "President Obama's healthcare program came under intense scrutiny in 2010." Research what this healthcare program consisted of and in what ways it was scrutinized. Write a two page response to the statement you analyzed. Evaluate whether or not your research supports that particular claim.

Snap into Action for the Climate
The terrifying new speed of global warming and our last chance to stop it

Mike Tidwell

Mike Tidwell is founder and director of the Chesapeake Climate Action Network, "a grassroots nonprofit dedicated to raising awareness about the impacts and solutions associated with global warming in Maryland, Virginia, and DC." Tidwell is the author of *The Ravaging Tide: Strange Weather, Future Katrinas, and the Coming Death of America's Coastal Cities* and *Bayou Farewell: The Rich Life and Tragic Death of Louisiana's Cajun Coast.*

RECORD HEAT and wind and fire displace nearly one million Southern Californians. Record drought in Atlanta leaves the city with just a few more months of drinking water. Arctic ice shrinks by an area twice the size of Texas in *one* summer. And all over the world—including where you live—the local weather borders on unrecognizable. It's way too hot, too dry, too wet, too weird wherever you go.

All of which means it's time to face a fundamental truth: the majority of the world's climate scientists have been totally wrong. They've failed us completely. Not concerning the basics of global warming. Of course the climate is changing. Of course humans are driving the process through fossil fuel combustion and deforestation. No, what the scientists have been wrong about—and I mean really, *really* wrong—is the speed at which it's all occurring. Our climate system isn't just "changing." It's not just "warming." It's *snapping*, violently, into a whole new regime right before our eyes. A fantastic spasm of altered weather patterns is crashing down upon our heads right now.

The only question left for America is this: can we snap along with the climate? Can we, as the world's biggest polluter, create a grassroots political uprising that emerges as abruptly as a snap of the fingers? A movement that demands the clean-energy revolution in the time we have left to save ourselves? I think we can do it. I hope we can do it. Indeed, the recent political "snap" in Australia, where a devastating and unprecedented drought made climate change a central voting issue and so helped topple a Bush-like government of deniers, should give us encouragement.

But time is running out fast for a similar transformation here.

A CLIMATE SNAP? REALLY? It sounds so much like standard fearmongering and ecohyperbole. But here's proof: One of the most prestigious scientific bodies in the world, the group that just shared the Nobel Peace Prize with Al Gore for its climate work, predicted fourteen months ago that unchecked global warming could erase *all* of the Arctic Ocean's summertime ice as early as 2070. Then, just two months later, in April 2007, a separate scientific panel released data indicating that the 2070 mark was way off, suggesting that ice-free conditions could come to the Arctic as early as the summer of 2030. And as if this acceleration weren't enough, yet another prediction emerged in December 2007. Following the year's appalling melt season, in which vast stretches of Arctic ice the size of Florida vanished almost weekly at times, a credible new estimate from the U.S. Naval Postgraduate School in Monterey, California, indicated there could be zero—*zero*—summer ice in the Arctic as early as 2013.

Five precious years. An eye-blink away.

So the Arctic doomsday prediction has gone from 2070 to 2013 in just eleven months of scientific reporting. This means far more than the likely extinction of polar bears from drowning and starvation. A world where the North Pole is just a watery dot in an unbroken expanse of dark ocean implies a planet that, well, is no longer planet Earth. It's a world that is destined to be governed by radically different weather patterns. And it's a world that's arriving, basically, tomorrow, if the U.S. Naval Postgraduate School has it right.

How could this be happening to us? Why is this not dominating every minute of every presidential debate?

Actually it's the so-called feedback loops that have tripped up scientists so badly, causing the experts to wildly misjudge the speed of the climate crash. Having never witnessed a planet overheat before, no one quite anticipated the geometric rate of change. To cite one example, when that brilliantly white Arctic ice melts to blue ocean, it takes with it a huge measure of solar reflectivity, which increases sunlight absorption and feeds more warmth back into the system, amplifying everything dramatically. And as northern forests across Canada continue to die en masse due to warming, they switch from being net absorbers of CO_2 to net emitters when forest decomposition sets in. And as tundra melts all across Siberia, it releases long-buried methane, a greenhouse gas twenty times more powerful than even CO_2. And so on and so on and so on. Like the ear-splitting shriek when a microphone gets too close to its amplifier, literally dozens of major feedback loops are screeching into place worldwide, all at the same time, ushering in the era of runaway climate change.

"Only in the past five years, as researchers have learned more about the way our planet works, have some come to the conclusion that changes probably won't be as smooth or as gradual as [previously] imagined," writes Fred Pearce in his new book *With Speed and Violence: Why Scientists Fear Tipping Points in Climate Change.* "We are in all probability already embarked on a roller coaster ride of lurching and sometimes brutal change."

GLOBAL WARMING is no longer a hundred-year problem requiring a hundred-year solution. It's not even a fifty-year problem. New data and recent events clearly reveal it's a right-here, right-now, white-hot crisis requiring dramatic and comprehensive resolution in the next twenty to thirty years, with drastic but achievable changes in energy consumption required *immediately*. But even a near-total abandonment of fossil fuels might not be enough to save us, given how fast the planet is now warming.

So the rising whisper even among many environmentalists is this: we might also have to develop some sort of life-saving atmospheric shield. In a controversial but decidedly plausible approach called geo-engineering, we could do everything from placing giant orbiting mirrors in outer space to seeding the atmosphere with lots of sulfur dioxide, basically becoming a "permanent human volcano." More on this in a moment.

But first, if there's any good news surrounding the sudden and unexpected speed of global warming it is this: it's nobody's fault. New evidence shows that we were almost certainly locked into a course of violent climate snap well before we first fully understood the seriousness of global warming back in the 1980s. Even had we completely unplugged everything twenty years ago, the momentum of carbon dioxide buildup already occurring in the atmosphere clearly would have steered us toward the same disastrous results we're seeing now.

So we can stop blaming ExxonMobil and Peabody Coal and the father-son Bush administrations. Their frequently deceitful lobbying and political stalling over the past twenty years didn't wreck the climate. The atmosphere was already wrecked well before the first Bush took office. These staunch conservatives simply created a "solution delay" that we can—and must—overcome in a very short time.

The tendency toward denial is still very much with us, of course. From this point forward, however, there can be no hesitation and no absolution. In a world of obvious climate snap, any obstruction, any delay, from any quarter, is hands down a crime against humanity.

AMID THE SUDDEN need to rethink everything ASAP comes another piece of good news: the clean-energy solutions to global warming grow more economically feasible and closer at hand with each passing year. Europeans, with a standard of living equal to ours, already use *half* the energy per capita as Americans. If we just adopted Europe's efficiency standards we'd be halfway to fixing our share of the problem in America.

We can't do this? We can pilot wheeled vehicles on Mars and cross medical frontiers weekly and invent the iPhone, but we can't use energy as efficiently as Belgium does today? Or Japan, for that matter? We can, of course. Wind power is the fastest growing energy resource in the world, and a car that runs on nothing but prairie grass could soon be coming to a driveway near you.

But to achieve these changes fast enough, the American people need a grassroots political movement that goes from zero to sixty in a matter of months, a movement that demands the sort of clean-energy policies and government mandates needed to transform our economy and our lives. We need a mass movement of concerned voters that "snaps" into place overnight—as rapidly as the climate itself is changing. Skeptics need only remember that we've experienced explosive, purposeful change before—quickly mobilizing to defeat Nazism in the '40s, casting off statutory Jim Crowism in a mere decade.

What just took place in Australia could be seen as a dress rehearsal for what might soon happen here in America. The underlying factors couldn't be more similar. A historic drought (similar to current conditions in the U.S. Southwest and Southeast) with an established scientific link to global warming had become so bad by 2007 that 25 percent of Australia's food production had been destroyed and every major city was under emergency water restrictions. The conservative incumbent government, meanwhile, had denied the basic reality of global warming for a decade, refusing to sign the Kyoto Protocol. But voters were increasingly traumatized by the drought and increasingly educated. (Proportionally, twice as many Aussies watched Al Gore's *An Inconvenient Truth* as Americans.) Against this backdrop, Labor Party candidate Kevin Rudd made climate change one of his topmost issues, talking about it constantly as he campaigned toward a landslide victory. It was good politics. The electorate had snapped into place and so had Rudd. His first official act in November was to sign Kyoto and commit his nation to a major clean-energy overhaul.

That time must come soon to America. November 4, 2008, would be a nice start date. And when we go, we must go explosively. Voters, appalled by the increasingly weird weather all across America—weather soon to be made worse by the bare Arctic Ocean and other feedback loops—must finally demand the right thing, laughing all the way to the polls over the recent congressional bill requiring 35 mpg cars by 2020. By 2015, we need to have cut electricity use by at least one third and be building nothing less than 50 *mpg* cars. *And* constructing massive and graceful wind farms off most of our windy seacoasts.

That's *our* snap. That's our glorious feedback loop, with political will and technological advances and market transformations all feeding off each other for breathtaking, runaway change.

BUT WILL IT BE ENOUGH? As inspiring and unifying and liberating as this World War II–like mobilization will be for our nation, it sadly will not. Getting off carbon fuels—though vital and mandatory—won't steer us clear of climate chaos. We've delayed action far too long for that tidy resolution. Carbon dioxide lingers in the atmosphere for up to a hundred years, and there's already more than enough up there to erase all the "permanent" ice in the Arctic.

This leaves us with a huge decision to make. Either we fatalistically accept the inability of clean energy alone to save us, resigning ourselves to the appalling climate pain and chaos scientists say are coming, or we take one additional awesome step: we engineer the climate. Specifically, human beings must quickly figure out some sort of mechanical or chemical means of reflecting a portion of the sun's light away from our planet, at least for a while. Whether you're comfortable with this idea or not, trust me, the debate is coming, and we'll almost certainly engage in some version of this risky but necessary tinkering.

First of all, forget the giant mirrors in space. Too difficult and expensive. And all those lofty notions of machines that suck CO_2 out of the atmosphere? At best, they are many years away, with significant cost hurdles and engineering challenges still to be resolved. More likely, we'll engage in some combination of cruder efforts, including painting every rooftop and roadway and parking lot in the world white to replace some of the Arctic ice's lost capacity for solar reflectivity.

After that, all roads pretty much lead to Mount Pinatubo in the Philippines. In 1991 that volcano erupted, spewing enough light-reflecting sulfur dioxide and dust into the atmosphere to cool the entire planet by one degree Fahrenheit for two full years. Could humans replicate this effect long enough to give our clean-energy transformation a chance to work? Can we artificially cool the Earth, using sulfur dioxide, even while the atmosphere remains full of greenhouse gases? Several very smart climate scientists, including Ralph Cicerone, current president of the U.S. National Academy of Sciences, think the idea is plausible enough to investigate thoroughly right now as a possible "emergency option" for future policymakers.

Ironically, we could "harvest" ample supplies of sulfur from modern coal-burning power plants, where it is a byproduct. In liquid form, sulfur could then be added—ironically, again—to jet fuel, allowing passenger aircraft worldwide to seed the atmosphere per scientific calibrations. In theory, we could even use powerful army artillery to shoot sulfur canisters into the atmosphere. But supply and delivery would likely be less of a challenge than the inevitable side effects, including an uptick in acid rain. And then there are the unknown and unintended consequences of subjecting the atmosphere to a multidecade or perhaps multicentury Mount Pinatubo effect. We would need an urgent research effort to assess the possible negative impacts of this process so we can devote resources to ameliorating at least the anticipated outcomes.

But the answer to the question *Can human beings artificially cool the planet?* is almost certainly yes. That answer, I realize, poses a terrible conundrum for conservationists like me who understand it's precisely this sort of anthropocentrism and technological arrogance that got us into the mess we're in. But like it or not, we are where we are. And I, for one, can't look my ten-year-old son in the eye and, using a different sort of ideological arrogance, say, *No, don't even try atmospheric engineering. We've learned our lesson. Just let catastrophic global warming run its course.*

What kind of lesson is that? I'd rather take my chances with global engineering and its possible risks than accept the *guarantee* of chaotic warming. As respected climate scientist Michael MacCracken has said, "Human beings have been inadvertently engineering the climate for 250 years. Why not carefully *ad*vertently engineer the climate for a while?"

SO HERE WE ARE, stripped of exaggeration and rhetoric, and hard pressed by the evidence right before our eyes. Our destiny will be decided, one way or another, in the next handful of years, either by careful decision-making or paralyzing indecision. We stand at a crossroads in human and planetary history. Or as my southern grandfather used to say, "The fork has finally hit the grits."

Try as I might, I truly can't imagine the Arctic Ocean completely free of ice by 2013, nor can I extrapolate all the appalling implications, from the end of wheat farming in Kansas to more record-breaking heat waves in Chicago. It truly is a terrifying time to be alive. But also exhilarating. As the Reverend Martin Luther King Jr. once said, "I know, somehow, that only when it is dark enough, can you see the stars."

The part of the picture that I can see is our own snap. I can see potent political change coming to America with our nation passionately joining the Kyoto process. I can see layers and layers of *solution* feedback loops that follow. I can see national policies that freeze and then quickly scale back the use of oil, coal, and natural gas. I see multitudes of Americans finally inspired to conserve at home, their money-saving actions feeding and amplifying the whole process. I then see consumer and governmental demand unleashing the genius of market systems and technological creativity, accelerating everything until we as a society are moving at geo-metric speed too, just like the climate, and suddenly our use of dirty fuels simply disappears.

Snap!

I can see my son coming of age in a world where the multiplier benefits of clean energy go far beyond preserving a stable climate. No more wars for oil. No more mountaintops removed for coal. A plummet in childhood asthma. A more secure, sustainable, and prosperous economy. Although there are surely dark times ahead, I can see him living through them, living deep into the twenty-first century, when most of the lingering green-house gases will have finally dissipated from our atmosphere, allowing an orderly end to the geo-engineering process.

Best of all, I see spiritual transformation ahead. We simply cannot make the necessary changes without being changed ourselves. Of this I am sure. With every wind farm we build, with every zero-emission car we engineer, we will remember our motivation as surely as every Rosie the Riveter knew in the 1940s that each rivet was defeating fascism. A deep and explicit understanding of sustainability will dawn for the first time in modern human history, moving from energy to diet to land use to globalization.

We will know, finally, that to live in permanent peace and prosperity we must live in a particular way, adhering to a particular set of truths about ourselves and our planet. To borrow from the great architect William McDonough, we will finally become native to this world. We will have lived through the climate threat, *evolved* through it, and our new behavior will emanate from the very core of our humanity.

> "The universe is not required to be in perfect harmony with the human ambition." —Carl Sagan

Discussion Questions

1. The title of Mike Tidwell's essay is "Snap Into Action for the Climate." After reading this essay, what do you think Tidwell meant by that title? Were you motivated to take any personal action for the climate? Explain why or why not.

2. Think about Tidwell's predictions for the future. Compare his "doom and gloom" introduction with his brighter vision presented at the end of his essay. Why did he choose to present the material in this order? Was his approach effective? Do you feel frightened about the future or hopeful after reading this article? Both?

3. Tidwell's essay was published in the May/June issue of *Orion Nature Quarterly*. Visit *Orion*'s website at www.orionmagazine. org. Compare this magazine and website with that of *Mother Jones*, the organization that published Bill McKibben's essay. In what ways are their goals similar? How are they different? Which do you find more effective for a general audience?

4. Imagine if Bill McKibben and Mike Tidwell had dinner with Bishop Harry Jackson, Jr. and Niger Innis. The topic of global warming inevitably enters their conversation. Write a three-page scenario where each author voices his prediction for the future. Perhaps even have Sophie Uliano make an appearance. Feel free to throw in a little humor to spice up the evening!

The CSR 2.0 Principle of Scalability: The Limits of Ethical Consumerism

Wayne Visser

Wayne Visser is Founder and Director of the think-tank CSR International and the author/editor of twelve books. The following is an excerpt from his latest book, *The Age of Responsibility: CSR 2.0 and the New DNA of Business*.

Case 7: Lee Scott and Wal-Mart

"Rapacious behemoth," "aggressive," "bully," and "evil empire" are just some of the public epithets Wal-Mart had acquired by the time Harold Lee Scott Junior took over as President and CEO in 2000. *Fortune* magazine said "the firm had what could be charitably described as an 'us-versus-them' mentality, in which 'us' was Wal-Mart and 'them' was everybody else, from critics to the competition, the government, and yes, sometimes even its own employees. The company's public image as a rapacious behemoth reflected that." *Business Week* reported a "mounting socio-political backlash to Wal-Mart's size and aggressive business practices" and urged Wal-Mart to "stop the bullying…stop squeezing employees and suppliers and charge customers a little more."

The source of all these jibes and accusations can be traced to two killer facts. One, ever since founder Sam Walton opened the company's first store in Arkansas in 1962, Wal-Mart has been all about discount operations—low cost and low price. And two, from its humble beginnings, Wal-Mart mushroomed into the largest company in the world—a $405 billion giant with over 2 million employees, serving customers more than 200 million times each week at more than 8,400 retail units under 55 different banners in 15 countries around the world. There is nothing about Wal-Mart that can be described as small, other than its prices.

"When it comes to price, it's hard to beat Wal-Mart," admits *Business Week*, "but the 'everyday low prices' come at a high cost to its employees." The result has been dozens of lawsuits brought by employees claiming to be overworked and underpaid, including "the mother of sex discrimination class actions," which alleges the company discriminated against 1.6 million women. In fact, there are two union-funded activist organizations, Wakeup Wal-Mart and Wal-Mart Watch, that exist for the sole purpose of criticizing Wal-Mart. And that's just on labour issues.

When it comes to green issues, "the name 'Wal-Mart' has always triggered a shudder," says *Grist* magazine. The company has been charged with "exacerbating suburban sprawl, burning massive quantities of oil via its

10,000-mile supply chain, producing mountains of packaging waste, polluting waterways with runoff from its construction sites, and encouraging gratuitous consumption." The litany of alleged sins doesn't end there either— putting small companies out of business, maltreating suppliers, offering inferior employee benefits, the list goes on and on.

The point is that when Scott took charge, and for at least the first five years of his reign, Wal-Mart was under siege, with a siege mentality to fit. "We would put up the sandbags and get out the machine guns," Scott recalls. "If somebody criticized us, my first thought was, 'Why don't they like us?' Or 'What could we do to them?' versus now, when I think, 'Could the criticism have some truth?'" *Fortune* later concluded that "Scott had apparently learned that the best way to respond to an attacker was not with an attack of one's own, but to embrace them." And embrace them he did, to the extent that his journey to openness—alongside that of Wal-Mart—is today one of the most remarkable leadership stories of our time. So what happened? And why, and how?

It seems some of the seminal credit must go to one of Sam Walton's sons and to the NGO, Conservation International (CI). Rob Walton, Chairman of Wal-Mart's Board of Directors since 1992, is a lover of the outdoors and found himself in February 2004 on a ten-day trip to Costa Rica, hosted by Peter Seligmann, co-founder and CEO of CI. After pointing out the destructive havoc that fleets of fishing boats were wreaking on the delicate Costa Rican marine habitat, legend has it that Seligmann looked the Wal-Mart chairman in the eye and said, "We need to change the way industry works. And you can have an influence." Rob was moved and promised to introduce Seligmann to Scott.

The timing was serendipitous, as Scott had just concluded a review of Wal-Mart's legal and public relations problems, and it wasn't a pretty picture. The discrimination lawsuit had been certified as a federal class action, new stores were blocked by activists in Los Angeles, San Francisco, and Chicago, and the company had just forked out millions to regulators for air and water pollution infringements. The findings of two recent studies only made matters worse: one that showed that Wal-Mart's spending on health benefits for its employees was 30% less than the average of its retail peers, and another by McKinsey, concluded that up to 8% of shoppers had stopped patronizing the store because of its increasingly tarnished reputation.

The watershed meeting took place without fanfare in June 2004, with Rob Walton, Scott, Seligmann, Glenn Prickett (also of CI), and Jib Ellison, a river-rafting guide turned management consultant. Whatever was said, it convinced Scott to dip Wal-Mart's toes into green waters. No doubt it helped that CI's board included former Intel chairman Gordon Moore,

BP chief executive John Browne, and former Starbucks CEO Orin Smith, and that CI were already advising Starbucks on fairtrade issues and McDonald's on sustainable agriculture and fishing. Whatever the reasons, Scott commissioned Ellison's management consulting firm BluSkye to measure Wal-Mart's total environmental impact.

It was a bold move, but it quickly paid off. BluSkye found that, for example, by eliminating excessive packaging on its Kid Connection private-label line of toys, Wal-Mart could save $2 million a year in shipping costs, 3,800 trees, and one million barrels of oil. And on its fleet of 7,200 trucks, rather than letting the truck engine idle during the drivers' mandatory ten-hour breaks, it could save $26 million a year in fuel costs by installing auxiliary power units to heat/cool the cabs. In short, Wal-Mart had belatedly discovered the win-win world of eco-efficiency, which WBCSD had been promoting since 1992. "As we headed down this first path in our sustainability journey and started to see these results, we really got excited," recalls Scott.

If the truth be told, these initiatives were neither radical nor especially high impact in the context of Wal-Mart's global footprint. And Scott could easily have stopped there, having gained the PR benefits and the easy-picking cost savings. Fortunately, however, fate intervened. On 29 August 2005, Hurricane Katrina hit the Louisiana coast and devastated New Orleans. "Katrina was one of the worst disasters in the history of the United States," reflected Scott, "but it also brought out the best in our company…We responded by doing what we do best: We empowered our people and leveraged our presence and logistics to deliver the supplies that hurricane victims so desperately needed. Hurricane Katrina changed Wal-Mart forever. And it changed us for the better. We saw our full potential—with absolute clarity—to serve not just our customers, but our communities, our countries, and even the world. We saw our opportunity and our responsibility. In the aftermath of the storm, we asked ourselves: How can we be that company—the Wal-Mart we were during Katrina—all the time? Sustainability became a big part of the answer."*

And so began one of the most unexpected and remarkable stories of corporate transformation. Scott soon announced three radical goals: (1) to be supplied 100% by renewable energy; (2) to create zero waste; and (3) to sell products that sustain people and the environment. Admittedly they are described as "aspirational" with no timelines attached, but if they get anywhere close, or even halfway there, they will have been a major catalyst for the post-industrial revolution. Already, we see the Wal-Mart effect of scalability in action in three areas: fish, cotton and light bulbs. Let's look at each in turn.

---

* From the 2007 London Lecture of HRH Prince of Wales's Business and the Environment Programme.

Wal-Mart plans to purchase *all* of its wild-caught fresh and frozen fish for the US market from Marine Stewardship Council (MSC) certified fisheries by 2011. They are also working with Global Aquaculture Alliance (GAA) and Aquaculture Certification Council (ACC) to certify that all foreign shrimp suppliers adhere to Best Aquaculture Practice standards in the US by 2011. By 2009, they were already halfway there. Speaking to the *Wall Street Journal,* George Chamberlain, president of the Aquaculture Alliance put the move in perspective: "The endorsement drew attention; Wal-Mart buys more shrimp than any other US company, importing 20,000 tons annually—about 3.4% of US shrimp imports. With Wal-Mart's nod, we went from trying to convince individual facilities to become certified to having long waiting lines."

Scott also made a commitment to phase out chemically treated textile crops. By 2008, Wal-Mart was the largest buyer of organic cotton, with more than 10 million pounds purchased annually. They are also the world's largest purchaser of conversion cotton—cotton grown without chemicals, but waiting to be certified as organic. Scott is under no illusions about the ripple effects: "Cotton farmers can now invest in organic farming because they have the certainty and stability of a major buyer. Through leadership and purchasing power, all of us can create new markets for sustainable products and services. We can drive innovation. We can build acceptance. All we need is the will to step out and make the difference."

Another product Scott targeted for greening was lightbulbs. A compact fluorescent light bulb (CFL) has clear advantages over the widely used incandescent light—it uses 75% less electricity, lasts ten times longer, produces 450 pounds fewer greenhouse gases from power plants, and saves consumers $30 over the life of each bulb. But it is eight times as expensive as a traditional bulb, gives off a harsher light, and has a peculiar appearance. As a result, the CFL bulbs only ever achieved 6% penetration, B.W. (Before Wal-Mart). To tip the scales in favour of CFLs, Wal-Mart set the goal of selling 100 million energy-saving bulbs. Success would mean total sales of CFLs in the US would double, saving Americans $3 billion in electricity costs and avoiding the need to build additional power plants for the equivalent of 450,000 new homes.

To ram home the point about Wal-Mart's mighty sway, according to the *New York Times,* when they proposed this audacious goal, lightbulb manufacturers, who sell millions of incandescent lights at Wal-Mart, immediately expressed reservations. In a December 2005 meeting with executives from General Electric, Wal-Mart's largest bulb supplier, "the message from GE was, "Don't go too fast. We have all these plants that produce traditional bulbs." The response from the Wal-Mart buyer was uncompromising: "We are going there. You decide if you are coming with us." Unsurprisingly, GE decided to tool up and scale up to meet the demand.

Today, these and other initiatives are all part of Wal-Mart's sustainability 360° programme. Compounding the scalability effect is the fact that Wal-Mart plans to take its more than 100,000 suppliers along with it on this sustainability journey. In 2009, it announced the creation of a "worldwide sustainable product index." Step 1 was providing each of its suppliers with a survey of 15 simple, but powerful, questions to evaluate their own company's sustainability in four areas: energy and climate; natural resources; material efficiency; and people and community. Step 2 is to develop a global database of information on the lifecycle of products, to be shared on a public platform. And step 3 will be to translate the findings into a simple, convenient, easy-to-understand rating, so customers can make choices and consume in a more sustainable way.

Wal-Mart is not second-guessing what these assessment, measurement and information systems will look like. However, it has said that by 2012, all direct import suppliers will be required to source 95% of their production from factories that receive one of Wal-Mart's two highest ratings in audits for environmental and social practices, including standards of product safety, quality and energy efficiency. In February 2010, it also committed to reducing 20 million metric tons of carbon pollution from its products' lifecycles and supply chains over the next five years. That's equivalent to eliminating the annual greenhouse gas emissions from 3.8 million cars by 2015.

To be sure, Wal-Mart still has plenty of critics—of its Sustainability Index, its labour practices, its supply chain performance and its Goliath tactics. But—to borrow from the Marvel comic-adapted movie *Transformers*— it is getting harder and harder to cast Wal-Mart as the evil Megatron (part of the Deceptacon race) and far more plausible to see it as Optimus Prime, an awesomely powerful yet ultimately well-intentioned Transformer. The moral of the Wal-Mart story is that it is making sustainability and responsibility scalable. Scott's take on it is that "more than anything else, we see sustainability as mainstream… We believe working families should not have to choose between a product they can afford and a sustainable product." That is nothing short of the CSR holy grail, and the jury is still very much out—especially since Scott stepped down in 2009—but if anyone can tip us into the Age of Responsibility, it's the new "sustainability super-power" Wal-Mart.

Discussion Questions

1. Review this article and highlight the "three radical goals" announced by Scott and the three targeted products that were used as part of Wal-Mart's Sustainability 360° program. Are these new goals, standards, and steps required for their "worldwide sustainability product index" making enough of an impact? After writing a brief explanation of why or why not, share your answer with one or two classmates. How are your responses similar? In what areas do your answers differ? Try to persuade your peers to agree with your assessment.

2. In another section of his book *The Age of Responsibility*, Wayne Visser writes, "What makes Wal-Mart such a good example of scalability is not just its size, but the principles underlying its actions, such as mainstreaming sustainability, measuring total impacts, empowering customers, working with suppliers and setting audacious goals. The lesson of history is that the 'ethical consumer' is the enemy of progress!" In your opinion, is Wal-Mart merely presenting a responsible front to the world to ease the conscience of well-to-do Western consumers?

3. In Dr. Bellmer's interview at the beginning of this unit she states, "We don't realize it, but we vote every day with our feet, and with our pocketbooks." After reading Visser's excerpt on the limits of ethical consumerism, consider how you are "voting." Do you consider your daily consumption habits to be responsible?

4. Visit a local Wal-Mart. Evaluate the layout of the store and the different marketing tactics Wal-Mart uses to promote ethical consumption: organic, fair-trade, eco-friendly, locally made/grown products, etc. Also, assess the price points and quality of these products with other comparable merchandise sold in the store. Write a two page report of your findings and be prepared to present this for your classmates.

Use of Soft Drink Waste for Ethanol Production:
A Preliminary Report

Danielle Bellmer, F. Holbrook, J. Lim

Danielle Bellmer is an associate professor of Biosystems Engineering at Oklahoma State University and is also a faculty member in the Robert M. Kerr Food and Agricultural Products Center. Flint Holbrook and Jonathan Lim, a biosystems and agricultural engineering sophomore, work with Dr. Bellmer to investigate the sticky side of the soda industry that many of us have never thought about. This report offers an overview of the extensive research behind their innovative use for soft drink waste alternative.

Introduction

Food processing industries generate large amounts of waste, including both liquid and solid waste. This represents a significant opportunity to reclaim valuable products and byproducts from the waste streams. Bottling plants generate liquid waste as a result of problems on the production line, improper packaging issues, or product that becomes outdated. Currently the waste product is sent to wastewater treatment plants for disposal. In order to dispose of the product, they must increase the pH of the soda and then are able to send it to the municipal wastewater treatment plant, in limited quantities.

Waste soda contains carbohydrates that are potentially valuable for energy production. Soft drinks contain high fructose corn syrup, with a sugar content of 12–15% fructose. This sugar could be a valuable feedstock for production of ethanol. However, the soft drink products also contain other compounds which may inhibit the fermentation process such as phosphoric acid, citric acid, caffeine, salt, preservatives, and added coloring. If the existing sugars could be easily converted to ethanol without being inhibited by the other ingredients, this could be a valuable waste handling alternative for bottling plants.

Objectives

The main objective of this study was to determine the ease and efficiency of fermentation of soft drink waste to produce ethanol. Specific objectives were to determine whether pH adjustment is necessary, whether added nutrients are required, and determine the sugar conversion efficiency for several common sodas.

Methods

Fermentation

A series of experiments was conducted to test the ease of fermentation of soft drink waste. Four types of soda were compared, including Pepsi, Coke, Sprite, and Mountain Dew. The tests were performed in 400 ml plastic fermentation containers with fitted tubes for airlocks, as shown in Figure 1. Before fermentation, each soda was allowed to go flat to simulate its delivery as a waste product. Standard distillers yeast (Superstart) was inoculated at a level of 0.26 g/l for all experiments. Yeast was hydrated in 10 ml warm water for 20 minutes prior to inoculation. Distillers' nutrients (ammonium phosphate) were used at varying levels based on experimental design. Each fermentation batch was allowed to ferment for seven days to ensure a complete reaction.

pH Adjustment

The initial pH of the soft drinks ranged from 2.28 to 3.0. For the pH adjusted samples, calcium carbonate was added to the samples to reach a pH of approximately 5.0. This required between .15 and .43 g calcium carbonate, depending on the sample.

Experimental Design

In the first experiment, a full factorial design was used to evaluate the effects of pH adjustment and nutrient addition on fermentation efficiency. Two levels of pH adjustment were tested, including no adjustment (natural pH) and pH adjustment to approximately 5.0. Two levels of nutrients were also evaluated, including no nutrient addition and the use of 0.8 mg/ml ammonium phosphate. All tests were conducted in triplicate. Total number of samples included 4 soft drinks × 2 pH levels × 2 nutrient levels × 3 replicates for a total of 48 fermentation samples.

In the second experiment, the effect of nutrient load was evaluated. Four different levels of ammonium phosphate were tested, including 0, .2, .4, and .8 mg/ml. Samples were tested at their natural pH levels, and soft drinks included Coke, Sprite, Pepsi, and a mixture containing 25% each of Coke, Sprite, Pepsi, and Mountain Dew.

Ethanol Analysis

Upon the completion of fermentation, the alcohol potential of each fermented sample was measured using a hydrometer (based on density differences before and after fermentation). Ten ethanol measurements made using the hydrometer were also validated by an HPLC, and ethanol readings made using the hydrometer were found to be within +/- 1% of HPLC readings. All data points reported represent the average of three replicates.

Figure 1. Fermentation container setup.

Results and Discussion

As shown in Figure 2, all four types of soft drink were capable of being fermented into ethanol. Under ideal conditions, with both pH adjustment and nutrient addition, Mountain Dew had the greatest ethanol yield. However, with no pH adjustment, Mountain Dew produces very little ethanol. For three of the four products (Coke, Pepsi, and Sprite) ethanol yields were very similar (~ 6%) with and without pH adjustment in the presence of nutrients, indicating that pH adjustment was not necessary. With no nutrient addition and no pH adjustment, none of the soft drinks produced much ethanol. In the absence of nutrients, pH adjustment resulted in production of some ethanol for all 4 products, but it was a lower yield (3.5%–4.5% ethanol) than that achieved with added nutrients.

It is hypothesized that the reason Mountain Dew behaved differently than the other three soft drinks tested was because of the presence of sodium benzoate, a preservative found in Mountain Dew. The preservative would inhibit yeast fermentation at low pH levels, but its effect is greatly reduced at higher pH. This would explain why the Mountain Dew produced very little ethanol when the pH was not increased.

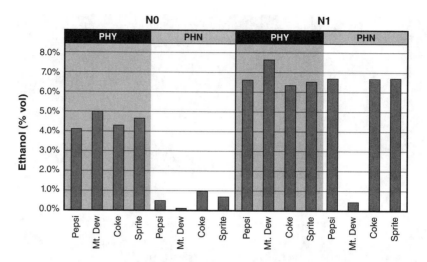

Figure 2. Yield of ethanol for 4 soft drinks (Pepsi, Mountain Dew, Coke, Sprite) as affected by pH adjustment and nutrient addition. PHY=pH adjustment to ~5.0, PHN = no pH adjustment, N0 = no nutrient addition, N1=nutrients added at 0.8 mg/ml.

The ability of yeasts to produce ethanol from the available sugar can be expressed as the sugar conversion efficiency, which is the amount of ethanol produced divided by the theoretical ethanol yield from sugar. The theoretical maximum amount of ethanol that can be produced from hexose sugars is 0.51g ethanol/g sugar. Table 1 shows the initial total sugar content, the theoretical ethanol yield, the maximum ethanol yield achieved, and the sugar conversion efficiency for each of the four soft drinks tested. It can be seen that Mountain Dew has the highest initial sugar content, and therefore the highest theoretical ethanol yield, at 66.3 g/l. Ethanol yields measured with the hydrometer are in percent volume, and had to be converted to weight percent in the table. Resulting sugar conversion efficiencies were between 84 and 91%.

Table 1. Initial sugar content, ethanol yield, and maximum sugar conversion efficiency for the four soft drinks tested.

Soft Drink	Initial Total Sugar Content	Theoretical Ethanol Yield	Maximum Ethanol Yield Achieved	Sugar Conversion Efficiency
Coke	111 g/l	56.61 g/l	48.9 g/l (6.2% vol)	86.4%
Pepsi	115 g/l	58.65 g/l	49.6 g/l (6.3% vol)	84.6%
Sprite	106 g/l	54.06 g/l	48.9 g/l (6.2% vol)	90.5%
Mountain Dew	130 g/l	66.3 g/l	57.5 g/l (7.3% vol)	86.7%

Figure 3 shows the effect of nutrient level on ethanol production for Pepsi, Sprite, Coke, and a mixture containing 25% each of Pepsi, Sprite, Coke, and Mountain Dew. Samples were not adjusted for pH, hence there was no need to test Mountain Dew alone since previous results showed very little ethanol production under those conditions. Results show that at 0.2 mg/ml ammonium phosphate addition, great improvement is made in ethanol production compared to no nutrient addition. But a continued increase in nutrient levels shows diminishing returns, with not much difference between the 0.2, 0.4, and 0.8 mg/ml levels. As expected, the soft drink mixture behaves similarly to the other three products.

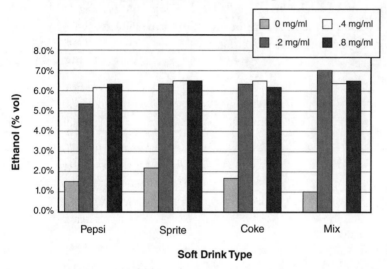

Figure 3. Yield of ethanol with nutrient levels ranging from 0–0.8 mg/ml ammonium phosphate and no pH adjustment. The soft drink Mix contains 25% of each (Coke, Pepsi, Sprite, Mountain Dew).

Conclusions

Fermentation of soft drink wastes is possible, with sugar conversion efficiencies from 85–90% under favorable conditions. All four soft drinks tested appear to require nutrient addition. With no pH adjustment and no nutrient addition, very little ethanol is produced. The amount of nutrient required for complete fermentation is between 0.2–0.4 mg/ml, and higher levels of nutrients do not result in increased yields. Mountain Dew behaves differently than the other three soft drinks, and requires pH adjustment for successful fermentation. This may be due to the presence of sodium benzoate, a preservative found in Mountain Dew but not in the other soft drinks.

The potential use of soft drink waste as a feedstock for fuel production could have both environmental and economic benefits. It could eliminate a current waste stream, and provide an alternative source of energy at the same time.

Flashback

During WWII, Walt Disney Studios produced cartoon clips distributed by the War Activities Committee Motion Picture Industry. Watch *Out of the Frying Pan and Into the Fire* (1942) on YouTube to see how Minnie and Pluto learn about the importance of conservation and recycling.

Discussion Questions

1. Consider the way in which information is organized in Dr. Bellmer's report. What kind of audience is being addressed? Why would this method be most effective for reaching that particular audience?

2. Dr. Bellmer's conclusion is very focused on specific results. What further implications can you imagine as a result of this research? Be prepared to share your answer with your classmates.

3. Using the OSU library's database of scholarly journals online, find two other studies on waste. Compare and contrast these studies with the one conducted by Dr. Bellmer. Write a two page assessment of these three studies.

4. Visit a local business (perhaps a restaurant, hotel, gas station, etc.), and interview people about their thoughts on improving various waste streams and the potential value for the production of ethanol. Follow up with questions on how they practice conservation in their daily *business* routine. Does their company have an environmental program in place? Does their company carry environmental friendly certifications or memberships in green industry associations?

5. Review the "Flashback" textbox and watch *Out of the Frying Pan and Into the Fire*. Explain why conservation of waste kitchen fats was so vital during WWII. Is this merely American propaganda with a green twist? What connections can you make between the conservation concepts in Bellmer's report and the Disney cartoon?

CONSERVATION AND CONSCIOUSNESS

Library Resources

You may find sufficient numbers of journal and magazine articles in **ProQUEST**. To find additional research articles use **JSTOR**. This database can be found in the alphabetical list of databases under the column *Find Articles*, as was done for the database **ProQUEST**.

JSTOR contains **PDF** articles from over 1,000 research and peer-reviewed journals. Many of these journals are available from the 1800s to 1900s to the present and cover many disciplines. When you click on **JSTOR** within the alphabetical list of databases, a screen appears in which you type in your keywords or subject terms:

Type in the terms "climate change" in the line, and hit the blue "search" button for results. Results for journal articles are displayed based on relevancy determination. The more times your terms you typed are in the article, the higher ranking of the journal article. To see the abstract of the article click on the **Summary** link below the title of the article. If the abstract is applicable to your research, click on the **PDF** link for the full article.

If the results from **JSTOR** are too broad you may have to add an extra term. Go back to the original search screen and type in another term like "greenhouse gases" or "greenhouse effect" with the original subject terms you typed. Hit the blue "search" button again and you should have fewer results. As with any database, if you need assistance or additional help, talk to a reference desk librarian.

Further Readings

Carson, Rachel. *Silent Spring*. Boston, Houghton Mifflin, 1962. Print.

Mahatma Ghandi: The Essential Writings. New York: Oxford UP, 2008. Print.

Marx, Leo. *The Machine in the Garden: Technology and the Pastoral Ideal in America*. New York: Oxford UP, 1964. Print.

McKibben, Bill. *Eaarth: Making a Life on a Tough New Planet*. New York: Times Books, 2010. Print.

—. *The Global Warming Reader*. New York: OR Books, 2011. Print.

Packer, Barbara. "The Transcendentalists." *The Cambridge History of American Literature*, vol. 2, 1820–1865 (1995): 329–604.

Pooley, Eric. *The Climate War: True Believers, Power Brokers, and the Fight to Save the Earth*. New York: Hyperion, 2010. Print.

Tauber, Alfred I. *Henry David Thoreau and the Moral Agency of Knowing*. Berkley: University of California Press, 2001. Print.

Thoreau, Henry David. *Walden and Civil Disobedience*. New York: Barnes & Noble Classics, 2003. Print.

Tidwell, Mike. *The Ravaging Tide: Strange Weather, Future Katrinas, and the Coming Death of America's Coastal Cities*. New York: Free Press, 2006. Print.

Uliano, Sophie. *Do It Gorgeously: How to Make Less Toxic, Less Expensive, and More Beautiful Products*. New York: Hyperion, 2010. Print.

—. *The Gorgeously Green Diet: How to Live Lean and Green*. New York: Dutton, 2009. Print.

Visser, Wayne. *Landmarks for Sustainability: Events and Initiatives that have Changed Our World*. Sheffield, Greenleaf Publishing, 2009. Print.

—. *The Age of Responsibility: CSR 2.0 and the New DNA of Business*. United Kingdom: Jon Wiley & Sons, 2011. Print.

APPENDIX

Additional Interviews
with OSU Faculty

In order to help provide a better picture of the kinds of research done at Oklahoma State, several professors volunteered to answer questions for this volume. We include these here, hoping that many might find them useful for this course or for future study at OSU.

Dr. Jennifer Borland, Assistant Professor, Art History

Tell us a little bit about your field. Give us a broad definition.

Let's approach this through the lens of the writing and think about it in contrast with how other fields approach writing. Fundamentally, Art History deals with visual material in some capacity or another. Some would even say that what they do is a history of visual culture as opposed to a history of art. Depending upon the time and place being discussed, the concept of art in the way we think about it today may not have existed. The things that you are looking at are objects with functions, objects with purposes other than just simply "art for art's sake." Thinking about as broad a visual field as possible material for someone who studies in Art History is important. The approaches that are especially important in Art History, and that Art History can offer other fields, is learning the language to talk about what you see, and that can have usefulness for somebody who deals with Screen Studies to somebody who is going to be a doctor and has to look at cells in a microscope and be able to say this cell is more oval and this one is more circular. We are really trying to train them to look closely and to be able to talk about what they see, learning a kind of visual language to articulate that in a coherent fashion, and be able to say something meaningful based on what you see.

So can you tell us a little about your specific areas of research?

I mostly work on Medieval Europe. I have worked in a variety of different media and geographic and temporal periods, but generally speaking, Europe between the 12th and 14th centuries, and I tend to be really interested in issues of gender and also audience and reception. I'm often looking at representations of people or how bodies are portrayed in various kinds of images and what that might say about cultural perceptions of the body or gender at that particular time. I am currently working on a group of medical manuscripts, but the images that they have in them are not diagrams. They are rather images of doctor-patient engagements. I am interested in how those images relate to the text of that manuscript and also how they might illuminate other ideas about the perception of the body at that particular time.

How has the field changed over the years?

There was a shift in the 70s and 80s towards thinking more about cultural history and social history, the context in which images are made—so moving away from what we might call connoisseurship where all you really do is look at the object itself and try to parse out the iconography and therefore make an argument about it—to thinking about the broader reach of images, how images played a role in that broader society whenever that was. Then, also, theoretical approaches were incorporated, thinking about things like gender, queer theory, feminism, psychoanalysis, or post-colonialism. I also think that within studies of visual culture is a really interesting move toward thinking about experience of the images. What does it mean that people encounter these in their different contexts? How does that encounter get controlled or manipulated by the image?

So what kinds of writing are done in your discipline?

Mostly scholarly articles published in journals and books, but, because Art History converges with museums and galleries, writing would also potentially include museum or gallery catalogues, museum brochures, wall texts, all the different kinds of writing that you might write for the public in a museum or gallery context. Also, potentially, exhibition reviews, reviews of a particular artist's work, in a more conventional news publication are written. Online we are seeing more exhibition reviews as well as discussions of artistic debates, and museum texts end up on websites as well.

What are some writing assignments your students might encounter?

It might range from a fairly extensive 10–15 page research paper to shorter formal or visual analysis papers where you actually go to one of the museums locally and make an effort to talk about a particular or single work of art in a paper. They might also do something like response papers to the readings that we do, especially if there are additional readings. A number of my classes—and I think this is the case with many of my colleagues in the program—include reading articles outside survey textbooks, and the best way to get students to understand those readings is to have them write about them. I do tend to avoid a lot of really extensive research papers except for in specialized courses for majors because I would rather have students learn how to talk about an object rather than spend a lot of time trying to find what other people might have to say about it. At a fundamental level, that first set of skills is more important and more applicable to a range of students, but in our program we do have a one credit course that majors take as attached to a regular lecture course where they write a more extensive research paper.

So besides what we have discussed here, what are some issues in your field that would be interesting to a first-year student?

There is some compelling stuff out there going on in the art world that has to do with art controversy. An artist whose work was removed from an exhibition in the National Gallery recently or someone like Stephen Colbert doing these great little segments on what makes art art, for example. There are some interesting things going on in popular culture that engage with that question of what is art, what does it mean to call something art, what does it mean if an artist is intentionally trying to avoid mainstream art and do work on the fringes. But a lot of those issues are contemporary, so then the question is how can you ask those questions about more historical material. When you do that, it really helps to make links if you can to more recent artwork and finds ways to make that older material more relevant to a range of students. To me, that question of what is art is one that's an exciting question to get students engaged with even though I don't think there is an answer or just one answer. But it seems to be a question that gets people really thinking about why this field exists.

What are some specific writing skills you value?

I would say that all writing skills are valuable. But, I would say that what we try to foster is finding a way to articulate what you see. The visual observations a student makes can be their evidence for a thesis or argument and to start thinking about an argument not just as a position that you are either for or against and here's the reasons why, but to actually nuance that a little bit more and be able to say that I want to be able to make this particular assertion of my interpretation of an image and the way I'm going to convince you of my interpretation is by using this visual material as evidence. The idea that you can actually make a thesis out of something relatively amorphous and your own view is hard for students to sometimes grasp, but at the same time, that isn't just an opinion, it's based on something, and convincing them that the visual or the textual can be the evidence. What's nice about learning the tools of formal analysis or visual analysis is that you don't need to do any extra research. You don't need to know anything about the artist's biography. You don't need to know the context in which it was made necessarily. Those things might inform a visual analysis, but what's great about it is that it really is this tight controlled thing where you don't have to know a lot to be able to talk about it. It really helps to look at something closely and then work your way through it, to not just describe it as an abstract piece and then be done with it, but to actually be able to say what's going on, how the elements are working against one another. Students are always saying, "I can't possibly write three pages on this," and I tell them, "Keep looking. Absolutely you can." Giving yourself time to explore all those elements is really useful, too. A good sense of knowing how to organize an argument is also quite valuable. Basic grammatical skills and things like that are also very useful. One thing that I come back to again and again is forcing really precise language from the students. "Beautiful," "interesting," and other very vague words get used a lot. Why are you saying that it is interesting? What is interesting about it? What are the elements you are reading as beautiful? How is the artist choosing these very specifically to communicate that idea to you? I try to get them to go beyond the language that they are inclined to use initially, to get them to think about word choice and language.

If you could choose one book or text that all your students would have read before taking their first course in Art History, what would it be?

I generally assign Anne D'Alleva *Look! Art History Fundamentals* to all my introductory classes. It is a little less dense than Sylvan Barnet, *A Short Guide to Writing about Art,* which is much more specific. They are both about writing about art. They give you a great synopsis of the different kinds of writing that we do in Art History and tips about writing a formal analysis paper. They both have samples of essays included. They have tips about how to write essay questions for exams. A lot of these things are tools that would be really helpful in a lot of different fields. I still send students to these texts even when they are seniors writing their last big research paper. You have to keep going back to these texts. It is kind of like the Art History's version of Strunk and White.

Dr. Duane Gill, Professor, Department of Sociology

Can you tell us a little bit about the broader field of Sociology? What are some of the specific concerns?

Sociology is a broad field, looking at human groups, human interactions, ways in which humans structure society, ways in which society has influenced humans. We study a wide variety of human activities. We often focus on issues of stratification. Groups have different access to power, property, and prestige, and that is structured in society. Within that context we're interested in looking at issues such as race, gender, age, various social statuses that feed into different access to power and stratification. We address the basic institutions of society, such as the family, politics, economics, education, mass media, and the workplace.

Can you tell us a little about your specific areas of research?

My primary area of work is in the area of disasters, and I approach it a little differently than traditional disaster sociologists. Traditionally, disaster sociologists come from a background of social organization, looking at how societies organize themselves, in particular, how do communities organize themselves, and—in the area of collective behavior—how do people come together or groups form to get things done? My approach to disasters is from an environmental perspective. I'm more interested in looking at how disasters impact the environment and disrupt the relationship between individuals and communities and the environment. So, much of my work looks at what's called technological disasters, which are disasters caused by a breakdown in technology and/or the human organizations that control that technology. A classic example is the oil spill in the Gulf of Mexico, which was a result of technological failure and the failure of the organization—the people on the rig drilling the oil— to adequately and properly control that technology. As a result we had the largest oil spill in the world caused by an accident. It has disrupted the relationship between communities along the Gulf of Mexico and the natural resources they rely upon, such as fish, shrimp, oysters, and the beaches people use for recreation.

I started studying the *Exxon Valdez* disaster in 1989. Actually, I'm still studying that disaster because the litigation after that event drug on until 2008 when the Supreme Court heard the case and issued a ruling over the punitive damages that were assessed. My current study there is looking at how the litigation and the settlement have impacted communities in Alaska. We have a piece that's coming out in *Sociological Context* that basically looks at the BP oil spill as a recurrence of the *Exxon Valdez*.

Scientific research gets caught up in these disasters. BP is spending a great deal of money on scientific research. The government is also sponsoring scientific studies. Many scientists study impacts on the ecology, different species, and different parts of the Gulf in terms of deep water and shallow water marshes. What we found after *ExxonValdez* is that Exxon scientists were expected to get particular results, to use the science to make the best case for their position. The government, and their scientists, are, of course, making a case for the government's side. It's going to be litigated. There's a responsible party; that responsible party is responsible for paying out damages that's caused by the disaster. There is corporate science, government science, and citizen science. It's really difficult for individuals and communities to deal with this. Government-sponsored scientists in the Gulf of Mexico cannot release their research and findings because of the impending litigation. The same thing happened in Alaska after the *ExxonValdez*. I went to a conference, about a year after the spill, and scientist after scientist got up and talked about the theories they were working with, but they weren't allowed to talk about any of the findings because of the litigation. But the findings could have been used to prevent further damage and speed up restoration of the damaged ecosystem. Because their research was tied up in litigation, they weren't able to release their findings, and some would claim that this situation prolonged the ecological damages. Of course, Exxon kept their science to themselves because they were preparing for litigation. Now, BP is doing the same thing. These events lead us to question science and the scientific process. It's ultimately sad to see that we haven't really advanced more than we have 20 years ago. Communities are tied to these environments and the lack of credible scientific findings being out there for people prolongs the uncertainty. Prolonged uncertainty about recovery, and the extent of damages, drives social disruption and psychological stress on people.

How have you seen your field of study change over the years? You kind of spoke to that in ExxonValdez *to BP—*

In the broader field of disaster research, as I mentioned earlier, traditional disaster research is based in social organization and collective behavior, so it follows natural disaster models. With a hurricane, a tornado, earthquake, you look at how social organization responds to these events. What has happened in the last 25 years or so is more technologically based disasters have occurred.

Buffalo Creek, WV, is one of the first noticeable breaks in traditional disaster research. There was an attempt to frame that 1972 event as a natural disaster. Lots of rain came, the dam burst, 17 communities were wiped off the map, and over 110 people were killed. Kai Erikson interviewed people there and discovered that but the true cause was the coal company building an inadequate dam. They didn't maintain the dam, and it wasn't engineered properly. Someone didn't do what they were supposed to do or didn't do it right. So for most of the people at Buffalo Creek, it was a human-caused disaster. It did rain, but had the coal company engineered that dam properly, there would not have been a flood or disaster.

What kind of writing is usually done in your field?

There's a variety of writing. Most of my work is based on funded research. The funder wants some kind of final report—a description of what was studied, how the research was conducted, how data was collected and analyzed, what were the results, and usually a recommendation for what can we do to make things better, what can we do to prevent this kind of accident, this kind of disaster from happening, what can we do to diminish the impacts of disaster, or how can we make communities more resilient. So we are writing reports that make these sorts of policy recommendations. We also write articles for academic journals and chapters for books. There is not much writing for the popular press or media, although we're moving a little bit further in that direction, trying to get what we do out for the broader public. I'm trying to find a way to get the information on what sociologists do after a disaster to the public so that the public can understand what sociologists are studying and how they're helping. I don't think a lot of people understand or even know what a sociologist does when he or she studies a disaster. They may not even know sociologists study disasters.

What are some specific issues that undergraduate students might research or discuss related to your field?

In sociology in general, almost anything a student has contact with can be considered from a sociological perspective. There are some students who are enticed by the study of disaster because it seems exciting, although it can be emotionally challenging when you get out in the field and start talking to some of these people who have survived disasters, and they're struggling to put their lives back together, put their communities back together. I've had people break down and cry, talking about all the death and destruction out on the Gulf, the realization that his or her future might be up in the air or not as certain as it was. It can be very emotional. You have to be emotionally mature to listen to people's problems, their anger, their frustration, their sorrow. But, that being said, there are other things that students can do. One of the great things about sociology is that there are so many different sources of data. For example, I know a student who is looking at editorial cartoons depicting the deepwater horizon oil spill. The political cartoons and editorial cartoons hone in on relevant themes and highlight those through humor. It's not always funny but it's poignant. So you don't necessarily have to go to the community that's been impacted by a disaster to understand different aspects about the disaster. Content analysis is also something you can do with almost any social phenomenon. You can look at any social problem—poverty, housing, unemployment—and examine how the media frames it in different ways. There is clearly some political perspectives in the media, right, liberal, middle of the road. How do they frame the same event to reflect their particular political perspective?

With undergraduate work, what are some specific writing skills that you value?

You have to be able to write clearly and to be analytic. Sociology is a science. I think the social sciences are harder than the "hard sciences" because our subject matter responds to being studied. If you know you're being studied, you're going to act differently. Humans can go many different directions at the same time. How do you study that? Students must be able to write in a way that conveys the information but is less opinionated. There's a place for opinions, but it should be clear where that place is: the conclusion, the discussion, that's where a perspective or an opinion can be brought in, but it should be based on data that's independent of opinion. The data are what they are; analyze that and describe it, and then sociological perspectives should guide interpretation. Sociology is full of jargon, which needs to be used sparingly in sociological writing. Being able to convey information in a way that reduces the amount of jargon— words the general public does not understand—is crucial. If you're going to use a term that is part of sociology's jargon, explain it very clearly. The concept has a very specific meaning that needs to be clearly conveyed in the writing. That's difficult. I have to constantly check myself.

If you could choose any one book your students would have read before taking their first course with you, what would that book be?

I don't know that there's any single book that would prepare an individual for sociology. Any book that expands curiosity about the way humans construct their world, reconstruct their world, and live in that world would be good. There's a great deal of sociology in the Bible. If you're interested in disasters, I would recommend Kai Erikson's *Everything in its Path*. Erikson is a gifted writer. He writes in a jargon-free manner. As I like to say, he's a bright-shining light that illuminates rather than blinds you. So I think, in terms of trying to understand a writing style and adopting a writing style that conveys sociological information, knowledge, and findings, Erikson's book—any of his books—would be where I would send students if they're wondering, "How do I write sociologically?"

Dr. Bill Ryan, Professor and Director, Hotel and Restaurant Administration

Tell us a little about the field of study. What are some of the specific concerns?

We are a hospitality management program; we are not a culinary school. There is a big difference between the two programs. Our curriculum covers a broad spectrum. We prepare students to be managers in the hospitality and service industries. This means that they are going to be taking on the responsibility of supervising and directing the work of others on a larger scale. We prepare students to be successful in all aspects of the hospitality industry, whether that is restaurant or hotel, meeting, planning, all kinds of different segments. Our curriculum is set in such a way where we do the general education for the university. We have about a 58-hour core, which encompasses courses in food, lodging, and business primarily, not marketing, accounting, and those types of things. We allow our student to create an area of emphasis for themselves through professional electives where they can get more experience in hotel operations or restaurant management. They take twelve credit hours in their area of specialization.

Obviously, there are concerns of the field. It is a very unique and dynamic discipline. We focus in our program on major four areas. First, having a really good theoretical preparation, that is curriculum, classes. We just went through a major renovation of that. We went to our partners in education but also to our industry partners and looked at certifications, advanced education, and those types of things. We tried to update our curriculum to include those new skills. The second part is teaching laboratories, focused in real-life and business enterprises. Atherton Hotel, Rancher's Club, Taylor's Westside Café are places and venues open to the public. We operate these teaching labs using practices found mainly in business and immerse our students in that process. The third area we focus on is events, signature key-learning events. Doing these events—Chef Series and Wine Forum—gives students the ability to really gain some experiential components in addition to the labs, which takes the theory we present them and really gets it to work well in a situation. We just finished the Wine Forum of Oklahoma. They were involved across the board in planning: all of the meeting room spaces, planning budgeting, accounting, contacting of people, writing letters, plus the actual event itself. The fourth primary area is our student organizations. We tie these directly to national, professional associations: Meeting Professionals International, Club Managers Association of America. This is where students begin to make post-graduation contacts while they are in school. They work with professionals in the industry, visit sites, host meetings, have speakers, anything that a student organization might do. We are trying to prepare the student to be successful on an overall basis, not make them finely-trained in one particular area.

Tell us a little about your own specific areas of research.

My area of research has primarily been in organizational behavior and education. Being an administrator is an up and down battle to keep up with that research. There are not enough hours in the day to keep up with that. I work primarily with master and doctorial students. I have also done a few projects on my own.

How have you seen the field change over time?

I actually went through this program as an undergraduate. We are certainly more focused on being more responsive and meeting a greater range of needs. In the past, food was food. You bought it, cooked it, sold it, and went home. We are trying to create a new experience for our guests every moment they walk though our operations. It is a whole service world.

The other thing that has changed is this issue of communication, the social networking and the speed at which we communicate on a global basis. People use those media networks to find out about places to go and see and take their families. If I have a bad experience at a restaurant and post that on a website, then a million people may see that immediately just because my macaroni and cheese was cold. (That is one silly little example.) Also, the ability to have the world at your doorstep has changed. You can literally get on a plane and within fifteen hours be anywhere in the world. Businesses have to be much more responsive and much more international in nature.

What sorts of writing are involved for scholars in this field?

Hospitality education is a fairly young discipline. The doctoral programs have been around, in true hospitality education, for a short period of time compared to management marketing and law. We are actually an emerging field. We are just beginning at a PhD level to take a much more serious approach to scholarly works and writing. In the last five to ten years, the biggest theme of the scholarly writing has been on marketing issues, in other words, destination, tourism, getting the word out, service issues, customer service measuring, customer service satisfaction levels, choices people make. The focus is also more about employees, human resource issues, in other words, turnover, work/family conflict. We see that the research in the hospitality education is just as advanced and scholarly as in other disciplines. People are taking it very seriously.

The difference is that hotel/restaurant or hospitality education has a huge split. The folks in the business world are not interested in research and writing, in the formal sense of publishing in journals. They are interested in what works. The ability to translate what you discover through an empirical study into something a manager can put into place or a company can put into place on a daily basis is very important. The trade magazines use that information but they are not as formal as a journal process. I think we are seeing that in other academic disciplines as well. As we work with our graduate students, one of the hardest things is to get them to talk about the implications for practicality, what they can do with what they discover on a daily basis.

What are some specific issues that undergraduates might need to consider?

The biggest thing I would like to see an improvement in is the ability to work with critical thinking. In other words, identify the problem. It is a little like the strategic planning process. You environmentally scan, you identify alternatives, eliminate some, keep some, try and test them, and evaluate. Often times, hospitality students are somewhat intuitive. They see something and they just respond without analyzing the facts. When you get into management and the hospitality world, you are really talking about managing someone else's money and their time. If you have a series of investors or bankers that own your property, they are going to want to know that the decisions you are making are based in good process, good thoughtfulness and that you can critically think about all of the scenarios that may be there. We do some of these types of projects in our senior-level capstone where they are doing small business development or major case studies. That type of area would be helpful in terms of research.

Other than critical thinking, what are some writing skills that you evaluate in your students' work?

The ability to write a business letter. The ability to clearly communicate in writing is critically important. I am seeing a trend of text speak, where writing is mirroring texting and Twittering. People have difficulty writing a letter that is more than 140 characters long because that is not how the rest of the world is communicating. When writing, it is critical to understand that you are writing across generations and that you need to be able to write to your audience. If I write a letter to thank a donor for something, I try write that letter very specifically to them. If a student comes to me and says, "I would like you to write a reference for me," I say "Bring me a vitae and a job description of what you are applying for so that I can match that letter directly to what they are doing." The ability to match a letter, match communication, match correspondents to that target is really important.

If you could choose one book that all students should read before taking their first course in your department, what would it be?

I tend to be a little abstract sometimes. I have to think about what it would be like to be an undergraduate as opposed to where I am today. The book I would choose for me would be a little different. It might not be a book. It might just be a series or collection of *Dilbert*. *Dilbert*, along with the class work, really provides some insightful remarks into life. Also, a collection of *Calvin and Hobbes*. The perspective that *Calvin and Hobbes* have from the eyes and mind of a six year old is very insightful. I know that doesn't necessarily sound like the best answer from a college perspective, but if I am talking about a person who is really making a change in their life and really trying to understand some of the things that are going on, sometimes it is better to approach it from a slightly different angle to help someone understand the real meaning of something.... That's what I read.

Dr. Loren Smith, Regents Professor and Department Head, Zoology

Tell us a little about your field. What are your areas of research?

I work primarily in wetland ecology and wetland science. The things I work on primarily are called ecosystems services, those services that are provided by environments to society. For example, climate change issues—an ecosystem might help to ameliorate those challenges. If an ecosystem stores a lot of carbon, it has less carbon dioxide going into the atmosphere which is a greenhouse gas. Another service might be groundwater recharge. Wetlands recharge groundwater, which helps with drinking water and irrigation water for crops. I do a lot with biodiversity provisioning. In other words, all these ecosystems support biodiversity, which has value to humans.

For the field in general, what are some other specific concerns in zoology? How are those reflected at OSU?

There are numerous concerns in zoology. You could be talking about biodiversity concerns, conservation concerns, or you could be talking about the next drug that would be helping somebody beat a disease. That's how broad zoology is. We have people working on issues that relate to human health, and we have issues related to conservation and evolution. Because it is so broad, in the zoology department there are three majors: biology, physiology, and zoology. Its difficult to generalize, but each of those majors may attract a little different type of student, so you might have a more conservation job oriented student in the biology fields, whereas in physiology mainly pre-vet, pre-med, those types of individuals often want to go into healthcare fields, whether those are animals or humans. It's quite a diverse field, and we have just scratched the surface here.

How would you say your field has changed over the years?

In my field of interest, there's been much greater awareness of the environment and those types of concerns about how to conserve specific ecosystems to provide services. Years ago we might have talked about managing one thing, like ducks. Wetlands provide good habitats for ducks, and ducks are interesting to hunters and birdwatchers. Today however, we're talking about much more diverse services that these ecosystems provide, like pollinators: they're very important to people growing crops; they're important for honey production; you name it. So, this aspect of what's going on in the ecosystem is much broader than it used to be. Now the field is more integrated.

What kinds of writing are done in the field?

Generally, there are two kinds of writing, and the number one most common in our discipline is what I would call technical writing. We try to teach our students to write sound scientific papers. Generally it follows a format of "Here's why we're doing the study, this is how we did the study, these are the results, and these are why the results are important." It's very straightforward tech writing. Now even though it may be straightforward, good technical writing skills are rare, and whether we're talking about our undergraduates or our graduate students, it's a lot of work to teach people how to have good technical writing skills.

On the other hand, we have people who are what I'd call "science interpreters." They have to interpret the research and write it in a more popular format so the general public can understand it. I don't see that as much, but it's very difficult for most scientists to do since they have been trained in tech writing. I know a few people who do it well, but it's tricky. If you have a reporter coming to visit and you want to have them translate your research, your science into something the public can understand, it's real tricky, and most of the time there are mistakes. Not malicious ones. When a scientist is trying to explain this to a person who is not interested or not understanding that part of the field, there's a chance for errors.

Things get lost in translation.

Yeah, and it happens all the time. But a lot of times you'll run into particularly good writing, particularly in conservation and nature writing. There are some good popular-style writers out there in that field and in the medical field as well. They understand that.

You mentioned zoology is a very broad field. What interests draw students to zoology?

If they're interested in environment, evolution, behavior, toxicology, conservation, and/or ecology, this is a very good department to be in. If they're interested in medicine, this is where they should be because we do a really good job of training pre-health major students. Undergraduates get that basic training here in those foundational biological principles.

What are some opportunities available to undergraduates in zoology?

We have all sorts of different disciplines for our undergraduates to work in, and we try to get them all research experience, particularly in the zoology and physiology majors. We have students doing lab studies; we have students doing field studies; we have students doing internships. You name it in the biological disciplines and it can be accomplished here.

We've had students work for medical labs, for medical researchers; we've had students working in zoos; we've had them going to work in Alaska for the forest service, or down in Argentina to study something with an investigator here. There are a lot of different opportunities, all the way from environment to higher-level medicine. It's a diverse field, and we try to get them as much experience as possible.

What are some specific writing skills you value in student writing?

Technical writing skills. Once an individual knows how to communicate well the results of their research or the research projects they work on, they will go a long way in this field. That goes whether you're talking about medicine or pre-vet or wherever. It goes also to conservation and environmental type issues. If graduates have those skills and they can communicate that to whomever is funding that research, someone will support them. Research agencies require that expertise in written communication. Agencies, organizations, corporations all require reports, as do the advisors here. If a student is working on their project, the instructor is going to say, "Write a report on your research topic and experiment." It's all part of the learning process.

If you could choose any one book that every student would have read before taking their very first class in your department, what book would it be?

From the ecology standpoint, I'd say *Sand County Almanac* by Aldo Leopold. It's terrific. It's not only written very well, it really gets a good feeling of the conservation ethic across. However, there are numerous other books in this diverse field of Zoology that can help students focus.

Dr. Rick Wilson, Professor,
Management Information Systems

Can you tell us a little bit about your field of study?

Management Information Systems, or MIS, is a field that—from a business perspective—is relatively new. It represents the intersection of technology and business. We are a technical degree within a business school.

We are not computer science, we are not electrical engineering, but we still are technical enough that we are the most sought after undergraduate degree within the business community today. The November 2010 *Money Magazine* lists the top 50 jobs in the United States. Seventeen of those top 50 jobs relate to MIS. Jobs like systems analyst, network analyst, network security specialist, database administrator, and so on—these are the kinds of jobs that students can get with a MIS degree, and these jobs all rank high in such categories as "salary" and "security," as well as the more intangible areas of "interest" and "job satisfaction."

It almost goes without saying that the world is technology driven, and our field is all about integrating the business side of things with the technical. But when we talk about business, we're not just talking about profit. An MIS student, for example, might eventually take up the question of "How do we take new wind energy and get it in the grid to be both efficient and reduce our carbon footprint?" The MIS professional wouldn't do the engineering but would look more specifically at providing the technology solutions to support and manage its distribution.

Can you tell us about your specific area of research?

I've been a professor for twenty-one years, so there are quite a few. When I first got my PhD, I was involved with artificial intelligence. I wanted to know how to apply this concept to real world problems. At the time, a lot of people thought about AI as something negative, like HAL in *2001: A Space Odyssey*, something that could take over human intelligence. My research, though, was involved using neural networks—what we would now call data mining. We were learning to apply quantitative tools to find previously undiscovered patterns from data. My dissertation was interested in business applications of this process, something like what you now see in Amazon's "you might be interested in" feature.

Again, though, these applications are not always about making profits for giant corporations. I just watched a colleague give a presentation on the importance of data mining for the medical field—How can we use data mining to better diagnose different forms of cancer? How can we use analytics to better match organ donors with transplant recipients? Data mining also has applications in the world of sports. The publication I am most known for in my field is an article about using neural networks and quantitative models to rank college football teams. Because of my expertise, one of my models was considered to be a part of the BCS ranking system, but they eventually moved away from my model because I proposed a general model that would allow you to include different impacts of the strengths of opponents on rankings. My general model was not cut-and-dried enough for them, and they went with an inferior model, in my opinion of course. (Laughs)

As I hope you can see from these examples, faculty are involved with a lot of very practical cutting-edge, hands-on stuff that business immediately adopt and employ. And for that reason, it's an exciting field for students to get involved with at any level. A lot of impactful things can be done.

How has the field changed?

Technology evolves faster than a dinosaur like me would like, but if one wants to stay on that cutting edge, one really does have to be involved in life-long learning. This is especially true with technology. When I started at OSU, I was one of the first faculty members to have a PC. Think of what that world would be like if few people had personal computers. But today, your smartphone has more capacity than that first computer I got as a faculty member at OSU. As consumers of technology, we can easily become prisoners of that technology. In MIS, we hope to help people learn what to do with our rapidly increasing computational power. How do we apply that power to the data that we have—for good or for bad?

That thought gets us into one of the fastest and newest aspects of our field: security. It would be nice if everyone could play nice together, but the truth is that we are always at risk and so security is a very popular part of our program—everybody needs to be aware whether you are a technologist or not, but once you get into security you get into legal and ethical issues. How does the Miranda law relate to your smartphone? How do we balance the right to privacy with the right of law enforcement to track down criminal behavior? Those are the kinds of questions that the next generation of young people will have to address on the technological front. Our laws don't necessarily keep up with our technology.

What kind of writing do you have your students do?

MIS professionals have to communicate effectively. They have to take hard-to-understand concepts or a hard-to-understand technologies and translate that into something that anyone can understand. That's not always easy when we're talking about the functional specifications of a system because a student has to learn to be both concise and detailed. Students learn to do that in their project management courses, but I would like to see them continue to work more on those two skills—being concise and detailed—in all of their courses. I cannot emphasize this point enough: if you are going to be successful in your career you must be a good communicator.

If you could choose any one book all students would read before coming in your department, what would it be?

I thought about this question a great deal, and what I think all students should read is a book that shows them how exciting this field can be. The book is called *The Cuckoo's Egg*. It's one of the first books that address many of the ethical complexities of the Internet. It hits the highpoint of what I love about what I do. MIS people are problem solvers, and this guy was a problem solver. The book shows how, in our world of inter-related technology, the exploration of a small accounting error can lead to intrigue—Russian Agents, setting up stings, a true spy story. It's a book that shows how technology connects all of us. It's an interesting, fun story about a guy solving an interesting crime, and in a dramatic way shows what our students will be expected to do in their future. It might not be us trying to stop Russian spies anymore. It might be us trying to stop a 16-year-old kid trying to bring down a computer network just for fun, or it might even be us trying to stop a terrorist attack, but the book shows the kinds of problems that MIS students will eventually be called to solve. And we've seen that even here on OSU's campus. Just recently, a group of our students discovered and stopped a guy who had created a fake website that was stealing personal information from students. We are, to borrow the title of Huxley's book, in a *Brave New World*, and we are hoping that our students are going to be fighting the good fight.

Ray Murray, Assistant Professor, Journalism and Broadcasting

Can you tell us a little about your field of study?

I'm a journalism professor who was a longtime journalist before entering academia.

What are some specific concerns in your field?

I'm afraid the writing skills have eroded massively in the past decade. It seems spelling, punctuation, etc., are no longer taught, and students no longer feel the need to write well.

Can you tell us a little about your specific area(s) of research?

I have done extensive research on paparazzi in Los Angeles and New York. I also have conducted sports research regarding what newspaper editors would like new reporters to know in terms of multimedia skills and other basics. With other professors, I also have conducted research regarding news divisions being pitted against sports divisions in television. For example, does the news side take a story from sports if it is deemed important enough? I am also researching the usage of sports terms and how they have changed through the years.

How has your field of study changed over the years?

It has changed dramatically in the past decade because of convergence; reporters are expected to have much broader skills than only writing. Getting audio and video of events is crucial.

What kinds of writing are done in your field?

All kinds; from hard news to features to blogs. Writing is the lifeblood of journalism. You can't go anywhere without it.

What are some specific issues your undergraduate students might research or discuss related to your field?

How the industry has changed because of technology; here is a fun/impossible task: Research what journalism will look like in 10 years.

What are some specific writing skills you value in your students' work?

The ability to write a coherent declarative sentence with proper grammar and punctuation.

If you could choose one book that all your students would have read before taking their first course in your department, what would it be?

All the President's Men (I would say dictionary, but...)

Nancy Betts, Department Head and Jim and Lynne Williams Professor, Nutritional Science

Can you tell us a little about your field of study? What are some specific concerns in your field?

Nutritional Sciences deals with the processes involved with taking in food and water particularly for nourishment. It is a pretty broad field. At OSU, the department of nutritional sciences has a strong reputation for mineral nutrition, particularly with regard to bone health. We also have researchers who examine the role of iron and other trace minerals ("trace" = minerals found in very small amounts in the body) in preventing chronic disease development. Our researchers study bioactive food components such as antioxidants which reduce the kinds of inflammation that cause chronic disease. The main foods of focus are fruits and vegetables. We also have researchers who apply the laboratory research to everyday life, including nutrition education and behavior change to increase fruit and vegetable intake. A couple of our researchers work with sports nutrition; some work with international nutrition and some with reducing health disparities.

Can you tell us a little about your specific area(s) of research?

My specific area of research focuses on examining consumer food choice and exercise behavior. My work attempts to explain why people choose the foods that they eat and the amount of physical activity they decide to perform. The outcome of the research is in determining ways to help people change their dietary intake and exercise patterns in ways that will improve their health.

How has your field of study changed over the years?

Nutrition is a relatively young science and has changed dramatically over the years. Also, the food supply in the U.S. has changed dramatically and the opportunities for physical activity have decreased dramatically. Fifty years ago, the major nutrition problems were those of under nutrition resulting from vitamin and mineral deficiencies. Now the problems are over nutrition with obesity and chronic disease development. This is such an enormous change in such a short time that the nation simply has not been able to shift its thinking about nutrition. Much of the dialogue is still about not getting enough of something instead of about adjusting food intake in ways that balance it with physical activity.

What kinds of writing are done in your field?

Our writing is generally technical. I think that actually puts us at a disadvantage when trying to communicate with the general public. The people who are successful at "selling" a way of eating are people who can attract the general public by explaining in a down-to-earth (albeit scientifically incorrect and sometimes dangerous) manner.

What are some specific issues your undergraduate students might research or discuss related to your field?

Our undergraduate students have the entire range of research to choose from. We have scientists who conduct research with cells, animals, human blood and tissue samples, and human knowledge, attitudes and beliefs.

Besides what we've discussed here, what are some issues in your field that would be interesting to a first-year student?

We have a lot of interesting research: the effects of various types of berries on the development of diabetes, the effects of other fruits on development of heart disease and osteoporosis, the effects of iron on cognitive development in newborn infants, the question of what athletes eat and how can we help them eat to improve performance, ways we can help parents reduce the chances of obesity with their children, and more.

What are some specific writing skills you value in your students' work?

I would have to say "mastering the basics." The areas that they seem to need help with are punctuation, paragraph construction, spelling, grammar, and writing a little more technically (i.e., not using quite as much slang).

If you could choose one book that all your students would have read before taking their first course in your department, what would it be?

That's a difficult question to answer. I think the text used in NSCI 2114, *Principles of Nutrition,* is one of the best ones to begin with. There are so many so-called "nutrition" books that contain inaccurate and downright dangerous information/recommendations it makes my head spin! I guess my best response is if a student wants to read about nutrition before taking a nutrition course in college, he/she needs to try to make sure that the book is written by someone who has some credibility.

Acknowledgments (continued from p. ii)

Deborah Brandt, "Sponsors of Literacy," *College Composition and Communication*, 1998, Vol. 49, No. 2, pp. 165–185. Reprinted with permission from the National Council of Teachers of English.

S. L. Davis, "What Would the World Be Like Without Animals for Food, Fiber, and Labor? Are We Morally Obligated To Do without Them?" *Poultry Science*, 2008, Vol. 87, No. 2, pp. 392–394. Reprinted with permission obtained via The Copyright Clearance Center.

Davies, Stephen. "The Great Horse-Manure Crisis of 1894." *The Freeman*, September 54:7. 2004. Reprinted with permission from The Foundation for Economic Education.

Bryan E. Denham and Richelle N. Jones, "Survival of the Stereotypical: A Study of the Personal Characteristics and Order of Elimination on Reality Television," *Studies in Popular Culture*, 30.2 (2008): 79–99. Reprinted with permission.

Douglass, Frederick. *A Narrative of the Life of Frederick Douglass* (1855), Chapter 7.

Ferne Edwards and David Mercer, "Gleaning from Gluttony: An Australian Youth Subculture Confronts the Ethics of Waste," *Australian Geographer*, Vol. 38, No. 3, pp. 279–296.

Freire, Paulo. "The Importance of the Act of Reading." from *Literacy: Reading the Word and the World*. Bergin and Garvey Publishers, 1987, pp. 21–26. Copyright © 1987 by Bergin and Garvey Publishers. Reproduced with permission of ABC-CLIO, LLC.

Hirsch, E.D., Jr. "Cultural Literacy." Reprinted from *The American Scholar*, Volume 52, No. 2, Spring 1983. Copyright © 1983 by the author.

Harry Jackson and Niger Innis, "Going Broke by Going Green: Obama Administration Energy Policies are Impairing Our Jobs, Revenues, Economy and Health," *CFACT NEWS*, January 14, 2011. URL: http://www.cfact.org/a/1868/Going-broke-by-going-green. Reprinted with permission from the authors.

Christopher Kocela, "Cynics Encouraged to Apply: The Office as Reality Viewer Training," *Journal of Popular Film and Television*, 37.4 (2009): 161–68. Reprinted with permission obtained via RightsLink.

Kristof, Nicholas D. "Let Them Sweat." *The New York Times*. June 25, 2002. A25. Reprinted by permission of *The New York Times* via PARS International.

Marjaana Lindeman, Kateriina Stark, and Krista Latvala, "Vegetarianism and Eating-Disordered Thinking," *Eating Disorders*, 2000, Vol. 8, No. 2, pp. 157–165. Reprinted with permission obtained via RightsLink.

Jayson L. Lusk and F. Bailey Norwood, "The Locavore's Dilemma: Why Pineapples Shouldn't Be Grown in North Dakota," from *Library of Economics and Liberty*, January 3, 2011. Reprinted with permission from Liberty Fund, Inc., Jayson Lusk, and F. Bailey Norwood.

Copyright © 1989 by Peggy McIntosh. Reprinted from *Peace and Freedom*, July/August 1989, pp. 10–12. May not be reprinted without permission of the author. 781-283-2504.

Bill McKibben, "Waste Not, Want Not," *Mother Jones*, May/June 2009. URL: http://motherjones.com/environment/2009/05/waste-not-want-not. Copyright © 2009 Mother Jones. Reprinted with permission.

Lisa Miller, Ian Yarett, and Jesse Ellison, "Divided We Eat," *Newsweek*, November 29, 2010. Reprinted by permission of *Newsweek* via PARS International.

Mustafa, Nadia. "Fair-Trade Fashion." *Time* 169 (Spring 2007): 42–44. Copyright © Time, Inc., 2007. All rights reserved. No part of this material may be duplicated or re-disseminated without permission.

"Literature Study Groups: Literacy Learning 'With Legs,'" by Sue Christian Parsons, Kouider Mokhtari, David Yellin, & Ryan Orwig, *Middle School Journal*, Vol. 42, No. 5, May 2011, pages 22–30. Reprinted with permission from the Association for Middle Level Education, formerly NMSA.

Michael Pollan, "Introduction: Our National Eating Disorder" from *The Omnivore's Dilemma*, Penguin Press 2006, p. 1. Reprinted with permission from the author.

James Poniewozik, "What's Right with Reality TV," *Time*, 175.7 (22 Feb. 2010): 92–97. Reprinted with permission obtained via RightsLink.

From Rudell, Fredrica. "Shopping with a Social Conscience: Consumer Attitudes Toward Sweatshop Labor." *Clothing and Textiles Research Journal* 24.4 (2006): 282–287. Reprinted by permission of Sage Publications, Inc.

Jenny Rose Ryan, "A View to a Kill," *Bust*, April/May 2011 Vol. 68. Reprinted with permission from Bust Magazine.

Swinney, Jane and Rodney Runyan. "Native American Entrepreneurs and Strategic Choice." *Journal of Developmental Entrepreneurship* 12.3 (2007): 257–273. Reprinted with permission.

Stacy Takacs, "Jessica Lynch and the Regeneration of American Identity and Power Post-9/11," *Feminist Media Studies*, 2005, Vol. 5, No. 3, pp. 297–310. Reprinted with permission obtained via RightsLink.

Tam, Fiona. "Freed Child Slaves Refuse to Go Home." *South China Morning Post*. April 30, 2008: 6. Reprinted by permission of the South China Morning Post.

Henry David Thoreau, "Where I Lived, and What I Lived For," *Walden*, Boston: Houghton Mifflin, 1906, 100–103.

Mike Tidwell, "Snap Into Action for the Climate," *Orion*, May/June 2008. URL: http://www.orionmagazine.org/index.php/articles/article/2956/. Copyright © 2008 Orion Magazine. Reprinted with permission.

J.M. Tyree, "No Fun: Debunking the 1960s in Mad Men and A Serious Man," *Film Quarterly*, 63.4 (2010): 33–39. Reprinted with permission obtained via RightsLink.

"Gorgeously Green Lifestyle Checklist," from Sophie Uliano, *Gorgeously Green: 8 Simple Steps to an Earth-Friendly Life*, New York: HarperCollins, 2008, pp. 12–13. Copyright © 2008 by Sophie Uliano. Reprinted by permission of HarperCollins Publishers.

Wayne Visser, *The Age of Responsibility: CSR 2.0 and the New DNA of Business*, United Kingdom: John Wiley & Sons, 2011, pp. 191–197. Reprinted with permission of Wiley Publishers.